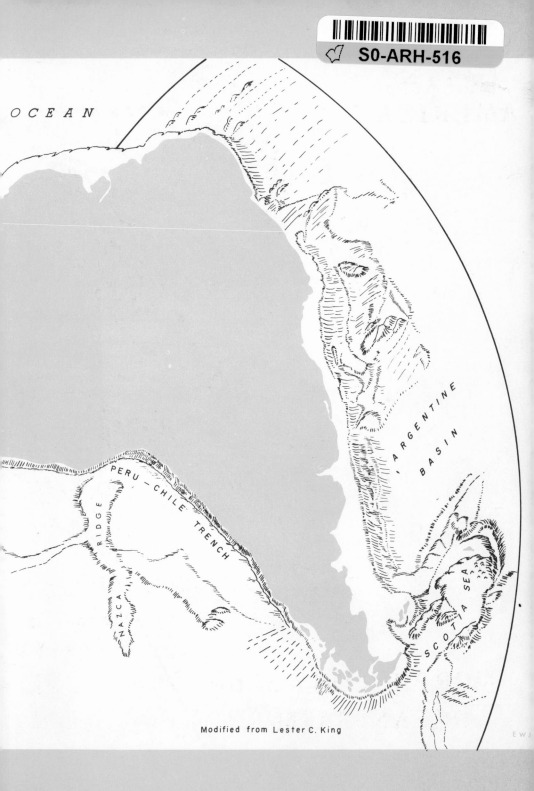

OCEAN

ARGENTINE

BASIN

PERU – CHILE TRENCH

RIDGE

NAZCA

SCOTIA SEA

Modified from Lester C. King

EWI

Introduction to Latin America

The Geographic Background of Economic and Political Problems

INTRODUCTION

MAPS BY EILEEN W. JAMES

THE ODYSSEY PRESS, INC. New York

TO LATIN AMERICA

The Geographic Background of Economic
and Political Problems

PRESTON E. JAMES

MAXWELL PROFESSOR OF GEOGRAPHY, SYRACUSE UNIVERSITY

Acknowledgments

We are indebted to the following sources for the illustrations in this book. Mexican Government Tourist Department, pages 52, 56, 58, 61, 74, 76, 78. United Fruit Company, pages 82, 86, 105, 106, 108 (both). Panama Canal Company, page 117. Creole Petroleum Corporation, page 122 (both). Colombia National Tourist Board, pages 137, 140, 144, 146, 147. Alliance for Progress, pages 150, 260, 308, 313. Panagra, pages 162, 165, 169, 177, 189. Pan American Airways, pages 192, 257, 270. International Telephone and Telegraph Corporation, page 227. Brazilian Government Trade Bureau, pages 234, 248, 266. Moore-McCormack Lines, pages 244, 251, 254, 272. Puerto Rico News Service, pages 290, 293, 296, 299. Central Office of Information, London, pages 301, 302. Wide World Photos, page 330.

Through the courtesy of the Pan American Union, pages 91, 94, 101 (both), 120, 125 (bottom), 220, 228, 263, 278, 289; and Hamilton Wright, page 62; International Roads Federation, page 65; Colonel Alba, page 96 (all); Braniff Airways, page 111; Asiatic Petroleum Corporation, page 126; Standard Oil of New Jersey, page 129; Venezuela Embassy, page 131; Victoriano de los Rios, page 134; Grace Line, pages 155, 158; Canadian Pacific Railway Company, page 157; International Labor Organization, page 171; International Cooperation Administration, page 173; Panagra, page 181; Anaconda Company (Andes Copper), page 187; General Motors Argentina, page 197; Pan American Airways, pages 205, 283; Pan-American Health Organization–World Health Organization, page 225; Coca-Cola Export Corporation, page 230; Brazilian National Steel, page 240.

Title page photographs are of Ecuador (left), Alliance for Progress, and of Caracas, Venezuela, Creole Petroleum Corporation. The Honduras photograph, page vi, is from the United Fruit Company, and the Bolivian scene, page xiv, is from Panagra.

Preface

No part of the world is changing more rapidly than Latin America. But there are many people in the United States who are not sure what is causing change south of the border and are bewildered by the apparently unfriendly attitude of people who not so long ago were described as the "sister democracies of the Good Neighborhood." For many North Americans whose judgment is clouded by obsessive fear of communist aggression the whole process of change in Latin America is only a manifestation of successful Soviet penetration of a once secure and peaceful community.

In the modern world such an oversimplification of the causes of change in any major part of the world is dangerous. It is dangerous because we may come to advocate policies which can only damage the position of the United States. If there ever was a time for wisdom and restraint, and for sympathetic understanding of the problems being faced by other nations, that time is now. It is the purpose of this book to apply the analytical insights of historical geography to the study of the states of Latin America so as to make clear some of the complex causes of the conflicts now sweeping over the other countries of the American Hemisphere.

A revolutionary change in the way people live and in the technology of making use of the earth's resources began around the shores of the North Sea in Europe during the second half of the eighteenth century. The Industrial Revolution was much more than the substitution of controlled inanimate power for human and animal muscles. There was an enormous increase in the capacity to produce useful things, and in the capacity to move things speedily and at low cost from place to place. For the first time in the history of mankind, more than a million people could be crowded together in the small area of a city and supplied with food, water, clothing, and shelter. The demand for raw materials from the earth increased beyond all precedent. A larger and larger proportion of the population of the so-called developed nations became urban people who were employed mostly in manufacturing industries or in a great variety of service occupations. The old masses of illiterate peasants, making a miserable living from farming worn-out land with obsolete methods, disappeared as the proportion of the working force employed in agriculture dropped from more than seventy per cent to less than twenty per cent. A major attack was delivered on the twin problems of illiteracy and hunger. And as death rates were lowered by modern medicine and hygiene, the total population of developing nations took a sudden jump upward.

Another revolution began at about the same time and also around the shores of the North Sea in Europe. This was the Democratic Revolution. For the first time in history all the people living in certain states of Western Europe demanded equality of treatment before the law, protection from the arbitrary acts of those in authority. The citizens of a country demanded the right to select their own form of government and to be spared the indignity of being included in someone else's empire. Majority rule and the secret ballot were adopted. The ordinary people established their right of access to knowledge through a free press, and their right to carry on a public discussion of issues of national policy. These ideas, distilled out of the general Western tradition, were for the first time put into operation in Great Britain, the Netherlands, and France; but they were first written down in the Declaration of Independence and the Constitution of the United States. In a very real sense the Democratic Revolution, as defined above, is our revolution.

Both revolutions began in Europe but have been in process of spreading over the world. Maps could be prepared decade by decade to outline the parts of the world reached by the two revolutions. Along the advancing fronts where an industrial society was replacing a preindustrial agrarian society, and where democracy was replacing autocracy, there was conflict, confusion, turmoil—and for those who lived well under the old system there was disaster. "Fascism" and "communism" describe systems in which the Industrial Revolution is eagerly adopted but in which all aspects of the Democratic Revolution are specifically denied. Both are reactions against the greatest revolution in the status of the individual that has hit mankind for thousands of years.

Today, the two revolutions are sweeping over Latin America. No other part of the world is feeling the impact of these fundamental changes more directly. Of course there is turmoil and confusion as old traditions and institutions are abandoned and people seek a new approach to the problems of living. Whether or not we approve is not relevant: revolutionary change of such magnitude is not to be resisted. No people can long refuse to adopt the new technology of production and transport. Those who would cling to the horse and buggy can survive only for a time, and then their whole way of living must undergo change, whether for better or for worse. And in spite of the challenge of communist autocracy there can be no doubt that when people have a free choice they will not willingly accept a system which denies the democratic principles of human dignity.

In Latin America there is a rising tide of demand for an end to systems of privilege and inequity, and for a fundamental revision of those economic and political institutions which have failed to provide a decent living for large numbers of the people. Furthermore, the programs of education and health are now increasing the proportion of people who are aware of the possibility of change and have the physical vigor to work for it. Some people are impatient with the delays and compromises inherent in democratic procedures, where public policy is adopted by persuasion, not by force, and these people may give their support to those political leaders who promise quick action. But the rising demand of the people in Latin America is simply for the right to develop their own ways of living, freely, without interference from outside. When Cuba came under the control of the Soviet Union, after struggling out from under one form of autocracy, popular support for communism dropped all over Latin America. Yet in those countries where the revolutionary changes are being resisted too strenuously, extremism may, for a time, take control.

It is important that each country in Latin America, even sections within countries, be examined for their peculiar and individual characteristics. The impact of revolution produces quite different results in the Indian communities of highland Peru than it does among the highly nationalistic people of recent European origin in Argentina. Portuguese Brazil, long noted for the adept practice of compromise, struggles to reconcile the often incompatible concepts of the national motto— "Order and Progress." Mexico, which went through its revolution between 1910 and 1915, has blazed a new trail to be followed by a people unprepared for democracy but with democratic goals. Venezuela, threatened with the use of force to topple its democratically oriented government, voted overwhelmingly in a free election to support democracy and to deny the communist autocracy.

The people of the United States need to understand what is going on in Latin America. They must avoid the tendency to interpret every disorder as a manifestation of communist intrigue instigated either in Moscow, or in Peking, or in Habana. Communist intrigue exists, and is an ever-present danger. It is a danger everywhere in the world when the first stage of the Democratic Revolution has been completed. At this point the trained communist agents are poised to take over—as they did under Lenin in the Soviet Union in 1917. But if the overwhelming demand of the people of Latin America for greater opportunity and for larger participation in the formation of public policy is resisted and is confused

with communist intrigue, the spread of autocratic communist governments, such as that of Fidel Castro, only becomes easier. Make no mistake,
we are in a world-wide conflict between democracy and autocracy, and
we do not win a conflict by defense. Americans must give positive support
to the Democratic Revolution—to the revolution whose ideals are a part
of the Constitution of the United States.

  This book is a shorter version of the author's *Latin America,* whose
first edition was published in 1942. Since the larger work includes detailed treatment of the different parts of the individual countries, the
student is referred to it for a more careful study of Latin America. The
Introduction to Latin America is intended purely as a quick survey of
current conditions in Latin America, with adequate attention to the complexity of individual differences from country to country. Generalizations
about Latin America as a whole may be dangerously misleading unless
they are placed in the context of the individual differences. The author
hopes in this way to make a contribution to the better understanding of
Latin-American realities.

P. .E. J.

Contents

An Overview

The Spanish Countries of Mainland Latin America

Portuguese Latin America

The Antilles and the Guianas

General Conclusion

Appendices

Maps

Illustrations

An
Overview

ORGANIZATIONAL CHART OF THE ORGANIZATION OF AMERICAN STATES

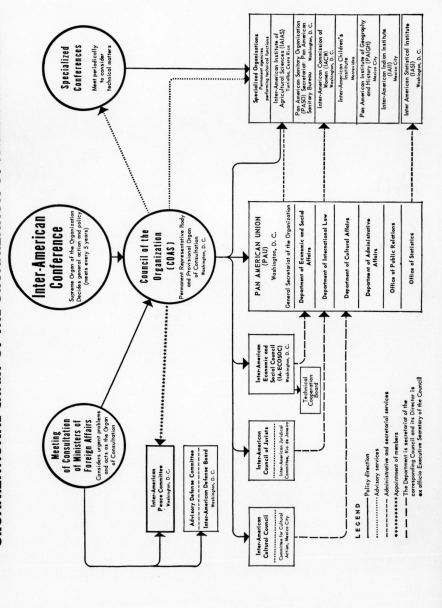

CHAPTER ONE

Principal Characteristics

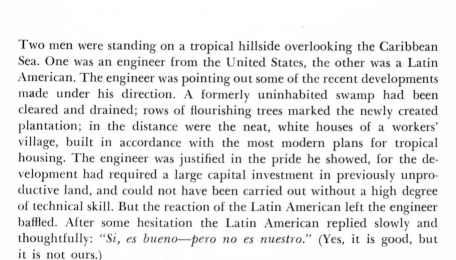

Two men were standing on a tropical hillside overlooking the Caribbean Sea. One was an engineer from the United States, the other was a Latin American. The engineer was pointing out some of the recent developments made under his direction. A formerly uninhabited swamp had been cleared and drained; rows of flourishing trees marked the newly created plantation; in the distance were the neat, white houses of a workers' village, built in accordance with the most modern plans for tropical housing. The engineer was justified in the pride he showed, for the development had required a large capital investment in previously unproductive land, and could not have been carried out without a high degree of technical skill. But the reaction of the Latin American left the engineer baffled. After some hesitation the Latin American replied slowly and thoughtfully: *"Sí, es bueno—pero no es nuestro."* (Yes, it is good, but it is not ours.)

This little event typifies one of the most difficult problems being faced today in Latin America. Of all the major parts of the world Latin America is in the process of the most rapid transformation. The traditional ways of living are being challenged as a result of the impact of two great revolutions—the Industrial Revolution and the Democratic Revolution. Millions of Latin Americans are joining in a demand for better conditions of life, and for an end to the inequities of the traditional Latin-American society. But these demands are not like those with which we are familiar in the United States. Equality in North America refers to equality of opportunity and the right of each individual, regardless of economic status, to be treated as an equal. In Latin America the idea of equality means the equal right of every individual to be different, and to be treated as a uniquely different person. When

3

business men and government officials from the United States attempt to establish what they consider to be a sound process of development, they are baffled by the reaction, even from educated Latin Americans. In Latin America the increase in the volume and efficiency of production is not the most important goal. The new technology and the new concentration of people in cities require certain basic revisions in the attitudes and objectives of traditional Latin America: the new society is no longer "theirs."

Another problem is the lack of confidence the average Latin American feels regarding people in power over him. This refers not only to army officers and other politically powerful people, but also the owners of capital and the managers of businesses. In Latin America those who have gained positions of power have all too frequently been accustomed to misuse that power for personal advantage. Dishonesty and corruption are often accepted as normal, and the exploitation of people with less power by those with more power is expected. This is nothing new. The Spanish conquerors started the system with respect to the Indians; the Portuguese were more direct in the introduction of Negro slavery. The Latin American who feels resentment against those in positions of political or economic power, even when the resentment is not justified, comes by this attitude as a result of long and bitter experience.

Both people and earth resources have long been exploited in Latin America. That this is not a new land is a fact that many North Americans find difficulty in understanding. Some of the lands that lie to the south of the United States had been exploited and abandoned by the Indians before the arrival of Columbus. In the centuries that followed Columbus the so-called "New World" was ransacked by Spaniards, Portuguese, British, French, Dutch, and other peoples of European origin. There are many parts of Latin America for which up-to-date information is lacking, for which there are not even reliable maps; but there are few parts which have not been explored and exploited first by one group and then by another. Actually Latin America is not a virgin land, awaiting the arrival of the pioneer—it is an old land, tramped over, many of its sources of accumulated treasure exploited and abandoned, many of its landscapes profoundly altered by the hand of man. Yet it is a land in which large areas remain comparatively empty of human inhabitants.

On the other hand, the population of Latin America is increasing at a rate faster than that of any other major part of the world. About 1956 the population of Latin America equalled the population of Anglo-America—a little more than 185,000,000 in each. It is estimated that by the year 2,000, when the population of Anglo-America will be about 250,000,000, the population of Latin America will have reached 500,000,000.

Latin America, which includes all the countries and colonies south of the continental United States, was occupied in 1962 by some 218,000,000 people, compared with 205,000,000 at that time in Anglo-America (United States and Canada). In Latin America there were 135,500,000 people in eighteen countries descended from Spain. There were 70,500,000 in Portuguese-speaking Brazil, 4,300,000 in French-speaking Haiti, and 2,500,000 in the two English-speaking commonwealth countries, Jamaica and Trinidad. There were also 2,500,000 people in the self-governing commonwealth of Puerto Rico, freely associated with the United States. In addition there were 1,486,000 in possessions of Great Britain, 608,000 in French possessions, 498,000 in possessions of the Netherlands, and 74,000 in territories of the United States and the Canal Zone.

International events have made it imperative that we, in Anglo-America, become acquainted with the conditions and problems faced by the other Americans. We need to understand why Latin America is in turmoil. We need to gain an appreciation of the problems of economic development in very poor countries. We need to have some idea what resources are available to support economic growth, and what capital requirements there are if these resources are to be put to use. We need to understand why North Americans are not everywhere popular. The common tendency to regard the changes in Latin America as a result of the communist conspiracy is a dangerous oversimplification. We need to know why Castro had such a following in Latin America until he proclaimed himself a Marxist-Leninist. We need to know which of the Latin-American states are unified and coherent and clearly viable; and which ones are composed of uncoordinated elements. We need to appreciate the states which have achieved a high degree of democracy, and to know the names and locations of those which are still under autocratic rule. These are the questions we wish to ask about these people who occupy the Western Hemisphere with us, and who have entered into cooperative agreements with us within the framework of the United Nations and of the Organization of American States.

People and land are the basic elements of the story. A human society is not understandable unless it is considered in relation to the land it occupies; nor is the significance of the land with respect to human settlement determined without reference to the varying kinds of human societies. In Latin America four principal characteristics may serve to summarize the conditions of the people and the land.

I. Relatively Small Population

One of the first facts to be observed in Latin America is that the population is relatively small. The eight million square miles of land in the part of the Western Hemisphere that lies south of continental

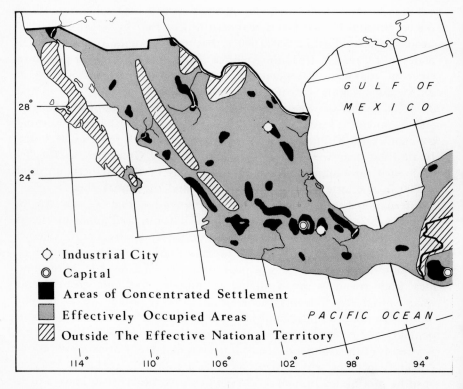

Map 1

United States represent about 15 percent of the total area of the world's inhabited continents: but the two hundred and eighteen million or more people make up only about 7 percent of the world's population. The largest political unit in Latin America, both in area and in population, is Brazil; yet Brazil's seventy million people—more than the number of people in Italy and Portugal combined—occupy a territory which is as large as all of Europe without the Scandinavian Peninsula, and larger than that of continental United States without Alaska.

The rate of population increase, however, is the highest of any major world region. Between 1920 and 1950, the population of Latin America as a whole increased more than 80 percent. During the same period the world population was increasing only 33 percent. Even the countries of Southeast Asia, in that period, increased only 63 percent.

II. Population Pattern One of Isolated Clusters

The people of Latin America are characteristically grouped together in clusters, in areas of concentrated settlement, and these clusters for the

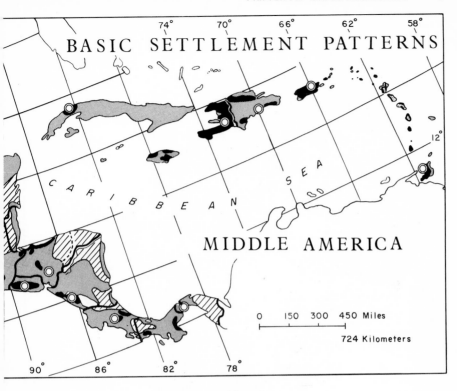

Map 1

most part remain distinct from each other, being separated by scantily occupied territory (Maps 1 and 2).

A population cluster is the most elementary arrangement of people on the land. Human beings generally prefer to live together in groups rather than to scatter at such intervals that contact with one another is difficult. The normal pattern of Occidental settlement in a pioneer land is one of scattered clusters, commonly strung together along a line of travel. A pattern of isolated clusters of people separated by thinly settled or unoccupied territory persisted in eastern North America until 1700. A population map of Europe in the early period of northward penetration from the Mediterranean would show a similar pattern. In the course of time the original areas of settlement of Europe and of eastern North America were enlarged until they grew together, little by little filling in the scantily occupied territory which once separated them; but in Latin America the clusters still remain generally distinct from one another in an elementary pattern which has never been filled in.

Even the areas of concentrated rural settlement in Latin America have a relatively low density of population. Some of the islands of the Antilles,

BASIC SETTLEMENT PATTERNS

ATLANTIC OCEAN

PACIFIC
OCEAN

SOUTH AMERICA

0   600 Miles
800 Kilometers

◇ Industrial City
◎ Capital
■ Areas of Concentrated Settlement
▨ Effectively Occupied Areas
▨ Outside The Effective
   National Territory

Map 2

to be sure, rank among the more crowded portions of the earth. Barbados, with more than a thousand people per square mile, and Puerto Rico, with nearly seven hundred, approach the densities more commonly associated with such places as Java and India. Outside of the Antilles, however, only a few of the regions of concentrated settlement of Latin America have rural densities of more than one hundred and twenty-five people per square mile. These few places are: the central area of Mexico, the highlands of Guatemala and El Salvador; the intermont basins of Costa Rica; the Antioquia region of Colombia; some of the high basins of the Peruvian Andes, and a part of the borders of Lake Titicaca; the Cochabamba Basin of Bolivia; parts of Middle Chile; the oasis of Tucumán in Argentina; and parts of the northeast coast of Brazil. But most of the population clusters of Latin America have a rural density of less than one hundred per square mile, and in many cases the density is less than twenty-five.

In the midst of each of the population clusters, even the smallest, there is an urban core or nucleus, and because the areas of concentrated settlement still remain distinct from one another, there is little overlap between the territory served by one city and that served by a neighboring one. In Europe and North America where the originally distinct areas of settlement have lost their obvious identity through expansion and the establishment of contact around the margins with other areas of settlement, the problem of separating the territory that is related to one center from the territory of another is very difficult. Commonly there is a wide zone of overlap between neighboring cities in retail trade, newspaper subscriptions, professional services, and the variety of other activities which are performed in an urban center for the people of the surrounding territory. But in Latin America this sort of overlap is rare: the economic, social, and political life of a region commonly focuses on only one large central city, and as a reflection of this the local lines of transportation and communication also converge on this one center.

Some of the cities appear to be surprisingly large when viewed in relation to the low density of the rural population in the surrounding area. Although there are many towns with a population of less than ten thousand, there are some which must be included among the world's great metropolises. Nine cities in Latin America have a million or more inhabitants: Buenos Aires, São Paulo, Rio de Janeiro, Mexico City, Lima, Santiago, Habana, Caracas, and Bogotá, There are seventy cities between one hundred thousand and one million, forty-two in South America and twenty-eight in Middle America. The number of such cities nearly doubled between 1948 and 1958. There can be no doubt of the importance of cities in Latin-American life.

Today the urban nucleus of a Latin-American area of settlement exerts such a strong attraction that the tendency is for people to move in toward that center rather than to expand the frontier into a new pioneer zone. There are many expanding frontiers in Latin America, but most of them are hollow ones, that is, they represent waves of exploitation moving across a country, followed by abandonment and population decline. These frontiers produce no net gain in the density of settlement. There are, however, in four parts of mainland Latin America—that is, excluding the Antilles—zones of concentrated settlement which are expanding, and their expansion is not accompanied by a decrease of the density of population in the original nuclei. These four places are: the highlands of Costa Rica, the highlands of Antioquia in Colombia, the Central Valley of Chile, and the three southern states of Brazil. Because expanding frontiers which are not hollow are so rare in Latin America, these four areas will merit our close attention.

The clustered pattern of population bears a simple relationship to the political units. In certain countries this characteristic is remarkably well developed: only one central cluster of people marks the core of such political units as Chile, Uruguay, Paraguay, and El Salvador. In most of the countries the population clusters form the cores of the major subdivisions—states, departments, or provinces. It is less common to find two clusters in one state, or one cluster divided between two states. Notable exceptions can be observed in the central area of Mexico, in Colombia, and in the highlands of Peru.

One result of this simple relation of the population pattern to the political areas is that the political boundaries generally pass through the scantily occupied territory between the clusters. There are few parts of Latin America where the boundaries cut through the midst of areas of concentrated settlement, and national boundaries do this even more rarely than state boundaries. The fact that areas of relatively dense population are cut by national boundaries in three places in Latin America is another exceptional condition which merits special attention. These places are on the border between Venezuela and Colombia, Colombia and Ecuador, and Peru and Bolivia.

A second result of the clustered pattern of population is the necessity for recognizing two kinds of political area. There is the *total national territory* over which a politically organized group claims jurisdiction— the whole area within the national boundaries. But only that part of the total territory which actually contributes to the economic support of the citizens of the country can be called the *effective national territory* (sometimes called the *ekumene*).

Finally, a third result of the clustered pattern of population is the nature of the transportation problems which Latin Americans have to face. Throughout most of South and Middle America the overland routes of travel lead from the interior to the nearest or most accessible ports; the land routes which connect one region of concentrated settlement with another, even within the same country, are developed only poorly. Transportation lines across the sparsely inhabited spaces between the clusters of population can, of course, be built and maintained at government expense as a military precaution or as a diplomatic gesture; but only where traffic originates in sufficient quantity along the line can it be supported on an economic basis. To be sure, automobiles and motor trucks are making these overland connections easier than before, since roads are less costly to build than railroads. But such a long inland route as the Inter-American Highway is all the more spectacular as a project and as a subject for diplomatic eloquence because such connections between the separate areas of concentrated settlements are still very rare.

The fact remains that the chief highways of approach to Latin America and the chief lines of connection between the isolated centers of population are the oceans. Even if airplanes are now changing the nature of the transportation problem for passengers and mail, the movement of commodities is still largely dependent on ships.

Whether the approach to Latin America from other parts of the world is by ship or by air the relative remoteness of the continent must be observed. South America is literally one of the ends of the habitable earth. Its closest neighbor is the commercially unresponsive shore of Africa. Furthermore, South America is equally remote from the centers of commercial activity in the modern world which are located on either side of the North Atlantic in eastern North America and Western Europe. The fact that South America is connected by land with North America does not in reality bring it any closer to this northern part of the Western Hemisphere than to Western Europe. The Isthmus of Panama, important as it may have been in providing a land bridge for the migration of the Indians, is of no importance today as a line of overland communications—in fact, it forms only a barrier to the sea routes. And South America lies almost wholly east of the easternmost part of the United States, so that the ports of such east-coast countries as Brazil and Argentina are actually closer to Europe than to New York.

III. Racial and Cultural Diversity of the Latin-American People

The population clusters appear in the map to be all alike; but actually they are composed of an extraordinary variety of racial and cultural elements, combined in many different proportions. This diversity of race and culture constitutes the third of the principal characteristics of Latin America. Race mixture has gone on with little restriction or taboo, and today more than half of the two hundred and eighteen million Latin Americans are of mixed ancestry. Furthermore, the ingredients are highly diverse. There are, to be sure, the three main elements—

Indian, Negro, and white or European (including people born in America of European ancestry); but each of these elements includes a wide variety of kinds of people.[1] The mestizo is the most common racial type, if he can be called a type, to be found in present-day Latin America. Let us consider the elements which have entered into this hybrid.

The Indians

Long before the arrival of the Spanish and the Portuguese explorers the Americas had been occupied by people from Asia. Because Columbus thought he had discovered India, the people he found were called Indians. These native Americans had come into the Western Hemisphere by way of Bering Strait. Although some tribes wandered off toward the east, the main current of repeated migration led southward, some groups even pushing across Central America into South America. There is little probability that any important numbers came by boat across the Pacific Ocean, and even less probability that any came from Africa across the Atlantic.

In spite of certain general similarities among all these native peoples of America there were wide differences both in physical character and in culture. To be sure, all the American Indians had certain common physical characteristics, such as a reddish brown or yellowish brown skin, and straight black hair. None of the American native cultures included knowledge of the Asian domestic animals other than the dog, and none of them included the use of the wheel. Beyond these general similarities, however, the cultures ranged from very primitive to advanced, from simple to complex. The tribes of the southern tip of South America, which subsisted largely on shellfish, are classed far back in the Stone Age. These were the most remote from Asia and presumably had started their migration very early, being pushed on by their more advanced successors until they had reached what is literally one of the ends of the earth. In contrast, certain of the native peoples of America were able to take a step which only a few groups in the whole history of mankind have been able to take—they had lifted themselves "from barbarism to civilization." These more elaborate cultures were developed by the *Mayas* of Guatemala and Yucatán, the *Aztecs* and certain other groups in central and northwestern Mexico, the *Chibchas* of highland Colombia, and the *Incas* of the highlands of Peru, Ecuador, Bolivia, and northern Chile.

The cultural advance these four Indian groups were able to make

[1] In Spanish America, the mixture of Indian and European is called a *mestizo;* the mixture of Negro and European is called a *mulatto;* and the mixture of Negro and Indian is called a *zambo.*

was reflected in a great increase in the numbers of people who could gain a living from the land; something like three quarters of all the native peoples in America at the time of the European conquest were located in the territories of these four advanced cultures. The obvious explanation is that a sedentary agricultural economy supports many more persons per square mile than does an economy based on shifting cultivation or on migratory hunting and fishing. Each of these cultures was based on that distinctively American food grain, maize.[2] In addition, the natives of America also made use of manioc,[3] beans, potatoes, squash, tomatoes, tobacco, and cacao. These other crops, however, were not so universally known throughout America as maize.

The Maya, the Aztec, and the Inca states had all reached and passed the zeniths of their development before the arrival of the Europeans. The Mayan civilization, which was the oldest of the three, was already decadent in 1492. The empires of the Aztecs and of the Incas had been formed by the conquest and assimilation of formerly separate and distinct Indian groups—a process similar to that which marked the growth of such European "nation states" as Britain, France, and Germany. The nucleus of the Aztec state was in the Basin of Mexico, and from there political control had been extended over a wide area. The Aztecs belong to the linguistic family known as *Nahua,* but their empire did not include all the Nahua-speaking tribes of Mexico. The Incas had extended their conquest from an original nucleus in the Basin of Cuzco, and had brought together in one great state the various tribes included in the two linguistic families, the *Quechuas* and the *Aymaras.* But at the time of the Spanish conquest the Inca state was already torn by civil strife.

The parts of America outside the territories of these four relatively advanced Indian cultures were only very thinly occupied. The greater part of the area of the Americas was occupied by a large number of separate Indian groups, only vaguely related in certain broad linguistic families. The tribes of tropical America ranged from semi-nomadic hunters, fishers, and primitive farmers, such as the Caribs and Arawaks of northern South America and the Antilles, to shifting cultivators whose basic food crop was manioc, such as the Tupi and the Guarani of Brazil and Paraguay. In southern South America, in addition to the very primitive peoples of

---

[2] *Maize* is the word which refers specifically to the grain which we, in the United States, commonly call Indian corn, or simply corn. According to general English usage, however, corn refers to any common grain. In England corn is used to refer to wheat, in Scotland to oats. In this book, therefore, we shall use the Indian word *maize* to designate Indian corn. It is now believed that maize was first domesticated somewhere in Central America.

[3] Manioc is also known as manihot, mandioca, cassava, and yuca. The latter is not to be confused with yucca, a genus of the family *Liliaceae.* Manioc is a plant with an edible root which furnishes a starchy food now widely used throughout the tropics, but formerly known only in the Americas. It is now produced commercially as the source of *tapioca.*

Southern Chile, there were semi-nomadic hunters and fishers who practiced some incidental farming, such as the Araucanians of Chile, and there were warlike nomadic hunters, such as the Abipones and the Puelche of the Argentine plains, whose chief food supply was derived from the wild guanaco. All these varied tribes together, however, made up only about a quarter of the inhabitants of the Western Hemisphere at the time of Columbus.

The Europeans

Diversity of race and culture in present-day Latin America is to be attributed not only to the native inhabitants but also to the European conquerors. There are many important contrasts to be noted between Spaniards and Portuguese; and both these groups, before they left the Old World, had already developed an extraordinary diversity of racial and cultural elements.

The Iberian Peninsula, the homeland of the Spaniards and the Portuguese, affords an easy passageway between Europe and Africa, and this was crossed repeatedly during the course of history by peoples of greatly contrasted origins. In the centuries between the struggle of Rome and Carthage and the discovery of America, the Celtic inhabitants of Iberia were mixed with other peoples from Europe and North Africa. First came the Carthaginians, then the Romans. The collapse of the Roman Empire permitted the invasion of Iberia by successive waves of "barbarians" from the north of Europe, the last of which waves consisted of the Goths. Then came the Moorish invasion from Africa which swept even across the Pyrenees into what is now southern France. Except for certain Christian Gothic states in the northwestern part of the Iberian Peninsula where the kingdoms of León and Castile were set up, and except for the border "march" maintained by the Franks in what is now Catalonia in the northeast, the Iberian Peninsula came under Moorish rule. Little by little, however, the Christians succeeded in pushing back the Moors, and in establishing estates ruled by feudal lords and protected by *caballeros,* or fighting men equipped with arms and horses. The Moors, forced to retreat step by step toward the south, were finally defeated (1492), and their long period of rule was ended; but for eight hundred years before the discovery of America the political and economic life of Andalucía in southern Spain had been dominated by these people of Muslim faith.

Because a majority of the people who migrated to the New World during the first century of the conquest came from southern Spain and southern Portugal the traits inherited from the Moors are of particular importance in a study of Latin America. One of the first effects of Moorish rule in Iberia was a change in agricultural practices: irrigation systems were built; fertilizer was applied to worn-out soils; and many agricultural techniques from Oriental lands were adopted. New crops were introduced, such as rice, sugar cane, and cotton. Skilled technicians from Damascus made Córdoba famous for its fine steel. From the East, also, Moors brought the manufacture of paper to Europe. Moorish and Semitic scholars made the University of Córdoba a cultural center which was perhaps unequalled in the whole world in that period, and in the libraries of this and other cities they stored the books which preserved Greek philosophy and science for the Western World. To Iberia came also Jews fleeing from persecution in Christian Europe, and Syrians, Egyptians, and many others, including black slaves from across the Sahara. All these varied racial and cultural ingredients were mixed and fused to form a new kind of people.

One can scarcely understand the Spanish or Portuguese conquest of the New World without a consideration of the centuries of conflict between Christians and Muslims which immediately preceded the discovery of America. Spanish society was grouped in small, semi-independent units, each unit under the control of a lord. In each group society was sharply divided: on the one hand were the aristocratic landowners and the *caballeros* who supported them; on the other hand were the serfs, bound to the land, dependent on the lords and the fighting men for protection. The ownership of an estate, or service in the army or in the church—these were the roads to prestige. Commerce and industry were left to the Jews and Muslims, and in the cities whole districts were set apart for these people. But Christian intolerance of the infidel was mounting, even when the infidels were providing the chief economic support for the whole system, and in 1391 the active persecution of the non-Christian elements began in earnest. Many Jews and Moors chose to become *cristianos nuevos,* or "new Christians"; many more were massacred. Among the Christian knights there developed a fanatical zeal for the spread of the Faith; but in the process the financial stability of the country was upset.

European Conquest of America

Two important events took place in 1492. The Moors were finally defeated in battle and forced to give up Granada to the Christians; and Columbus discovered America. It has been said that "Greed, Gold, and God" were the motivating forces which led the Spaniards into the New World. There can be no doubt that many of the conquerors were excessively greedy, especially those who, like Pizarro, conqueror of Peru, were not landowners at home, and who sought in America to achieve a coveted position in the aristocracy. There can be no doubt that there was need of gold, even among the people of highest social position, to repair the wrecked finances of Andalucía. There can be no doubt that many of the Spaniards who had been raised during the century of bitter conflict with the infidels came to the New World with a sincere, if fanatical, desire to kill infidels, or to convert them to the service of God. And there can be no doubt that both the Spaniards and the Portuguese, in common with most of the other European peoples, showed a marked reluctance to engage in that persistent hard labor which is required for the creation of a permanent society on an agricultural base.

For a people with these characteristics and attitudes the relatively dense populations of sedentary Indians in the areas dominated by the Aztecs,

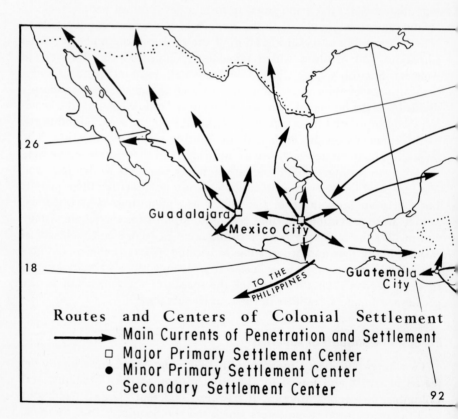

Guadalajara

Mexico City

Guatemala City

TO THE PHILIPPINES

Routes and Centers of Colonial Settlement
➤ Main Currents of Penetration and Settlement
□ Major Primary Settlement Center
● Minor Primary Settlement Center
○ Secondary Settlement Center

92

Map 3

the Mayas, the Chibchas, and the Incas exerted a special attraction. These peoples had already accumulated stores of what the Spaniards thought of as treasure. The Indians of these advanced states, moreover, were ready, after a brief struggle, to accept conversion to Christianity and to go to work for their new masters. To be sure, the Indians had no concept of private property in land, no concept of the commercial value of gold and silver, and these new ideas must have seemed as fantastic to them as men

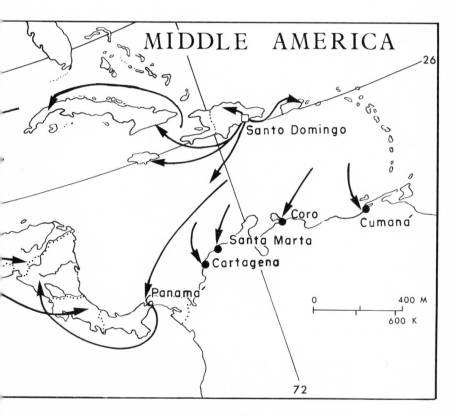

Map 3

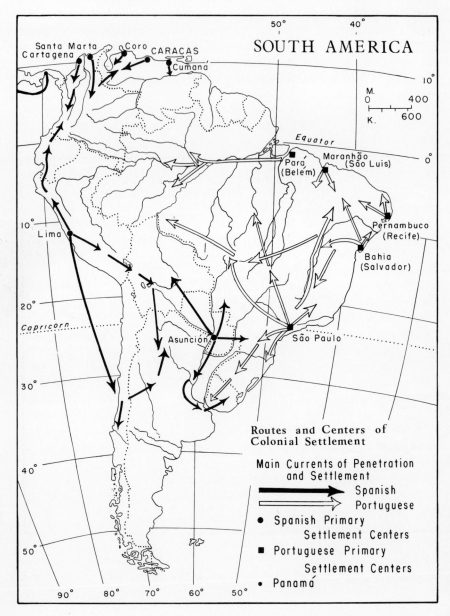

Map 4

on horseback. But the great majority of the Indians had long been accustomed to work for their rulers, and the conquest was at first no more than a change of rulers.

The distribution of Indians, therefore, was the most important single factor which determined the centers and lines of the Spanish conquest. The newcomers, after landing on the shores of the Gulf of Mexico and the Caribbean, explored far to the north and to the south (Maps 3 and 4). Within the first century most of the great sources of precious metals had been discovered and partly exploited. From the southern part of South America as far north as the present border between the United States and Canada, the Spaniards combed the new land for sources of wealth, motivated always by the hope of finding El Dorado. These Spaniards were not a soft people. They were not the kind of people to seek the easy way. It is quite beside the fact to insist that they sought to avoid the heat of the tropical lowlands, and that they ascended to the highlands to escape the discomforts of the lower altitudes. They were not stopped by heat, by cold, by steep slopes, by jungle swamps, or by warlike opponents. They were, however, attracted by the areas already well populated with infidels, where their form of society might be established with a laboring class already at hand. The distribution of Indians provides the clue to an understanding of the direction of the Spanish conquest.

Meanwhile, the Portuguese were settling Brazil. As a result of the Treaty of Tordesillas between Portugal and Spain (1494) the Portuguese had the right to all lands which might be discovered east of a line drawn north and south 370 leagues west of the Cape Verde Islands—approximately the present 50° west longitude. The Portuguese began slowly to colonize the eastern coast of South America. By the time of the discovery of America the Portuguese in Europe had achieved a much greater degree of national unity and coherence than had the Spaniards; their interest in the New World was less in the possible spread of Christianity and less in the opportunity it offered to implant their institutions than in the discovery of new and profitable sources of wealth with which to bolster the fortunes of the homeland. In eastern South America they did not at first discover any gold or silver, and they found an Indian population which was much too small to supply the necessary labor for the production of crops. Yet the Portuguese on the coast of northeastern Brazil set up the first plantation economy in the New World. They began the production of a single big commercial crop for sale in a distant market, with a system based on cheap land and cheap labor. The crop was sugar cane, and the labor was supplied by Negro slaves imported for the first time into America from Africa.

Thereafter sugar became so profitable that it attracted numerous competitors. The Spaniards planted cane in many places, and in most of these places they, too, imported Negro slaves. During the seventeenth century the Dutch attacked and occupied the prosperous sugar colonies of Brazil's northeast coast. They remained there for some thirty years before they were finally ejected by the Portuguese. During this time they learned how to grow the cane, extract the juice, and prepare and ship the sugar to the European market. Pushed out of Brazil they established colonies in the Antilles, where the sugar-cane technology was quickly passed on to the Spaniards, the French, and the British. The British seized Jamaica from the Spaniards, and the French established themselves on the western side of the island of Hispaniola. Soon British, French, Dutch, and Danish colonies appeared in the Lesser Antilles and elsewhere—wherever Spanish or Portuguese settlement had not been effective. At this same time the French and British began to colonize the forested eastern part of North America.

Recent Immigration

Still more recently, another element contributing to racial and cultural diversity has been added to the population of Latin America. During the nineteenth century and the present century new immigrants from a number of European countries and from Japan have come to the New World. Although an overwhelming majority of these immigrants have entered the United States, a considerable number have gone to certain parts of Latin America, and these parts are, therefore, quite different from the rest of the continent in their racial make-up (Maps 3 and 4). In most instances this new colonization has been directed to regions which previously were of little value and were little developed. From São Paulo in Brazil, southward across the southern states, across Uruguay, and over the Humid Pampa of Argentina to the dry lands of Patagonia, there was a stretch of territory which was almost entirely devoid of signs of gold, and which was thinly populated by native peoples. Most of it would not grow sugar cane. Except for its strategic importance to the rival colonial empires of Spain and Portugal this section of South America was of little use to the earlier conquerors. Because Spain had established a center of settlement in Paraguay, and had utilized the Plata River as a sort of "back door" to Peru, and because Portuguese colonists had threatened to establish themselves permanently on the shores of the Plata, the Spaniards paid some attention to this strategic route. But the land bordering the Plata was only a remote part of the colonial empire of Spain and was used only for the grazing of cattle and mules.

This stretch of territory, therefore, was still little developed when the new European immigration began. The considerable population of the region today is composed mostly of the descendants of people who have come to South America during the last hundred years—Italians, Spaniards, Portuguese, Germans, Poles, and lesser numbers of many other nationalities, including Japanese.

In Latin America[4] the racial composition of the population differs notably from one region to another. Six chief kinds of areas can be identified in terms of present-day racial character (Maps 5 and 6); (1) areas of predominantly European population, mostly of recent origin; (2) areas of predominantly Indian population belonging to the Quechuan and Aymaran linguistic groups (Andean Indians); (3) areas of predominantly Maya Indians; (4) areas of predominantly Indian population descended from other than the Quechuan and Aymaran groups or the Mayas; (5) areas with a mixed population with a large proportion of Negroes; and (6) areas with a mixed population in which the mestizo type is predominant (Indian and European).

IV. Diversity of the Physical Conditions of the Land

The fourth of the principal characteristics of Latin America is the fundamental physical diversity of the land[5] itself. The natural features of South and Middle America cannot be described without the use of superlatives. The Andes of western South America, which extend almost unbroken by low passes from the Caribbean to the Strait of Magellan, form the world's longest continuous mountain barrier. The Amazon, the third longest river of the world, is the one which is navigable for ocean-going steamers the farthest upstream. In the basin of the Amazon is the world's largest area of tropical forest. In Brazil, a little north of Rio de Janeiro, is one of the world's largest supplies of high-quality iron ore; in Northern Chile is the world's only natural source of nitrate. Returning again to Rio de Janeiro, we find this city located on the shores of what is commonly acclaimed as one of the world's finest natural harbors. The Humid Pampa of Argentina is probably the world's best endowed area— in terms of climate, water, soil, and surface—for the growing of grains and alfalfa, and the feeding of high-grade domestic animals. But when all these and many other superlative features and natural advantages are considered in the light of the needs of an Occidental commercial people, many of them seem to be poorly located, or to be combined poorly with other resources. The mountain barrier stifles the commerce which might develop between contrasted coasts. The great river sprawls across a con-

---

[4] Latin America, as the term is used in this book, refers to the geographical area which lies to the south of continental United States. A very considerable part of the population is not Latin in origin or even in culture.

[5] The word "land" is used throughout this book to refer in the broader sense to the natural surroundings or the habitat, including the surface features, the climates, the natural vegetation, the soils, the various natural resources—in short, the complex of natural features which forms the background of settlement.

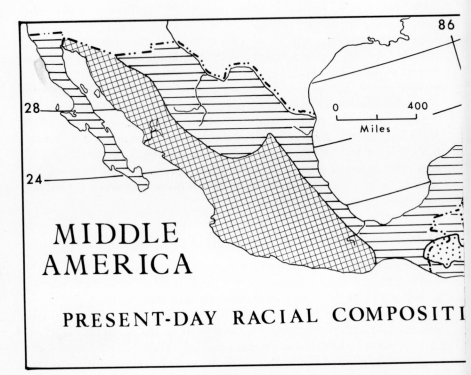

86

28

24

0   400
Miles

MIDDLE
AMERICA

PRESENT-DAY RACIAL COMPOSITI

Map 5

tinent through a vast forest filled with potential commodities of commerce, but neither the river nor the forest can be effectively utilized as long as the whole area remains one of very sparse population. The enormous body of rich iron ore is located in a continent notably lacking in coal. The nitrate deposits of Chile are separated from the seacoast by the steep slopes of an escarpment, and from the world's chief markets for nitrate by great distances of ocean. The magnificent harbor of Rio de Janeiro is hemmed in by the forbidding slopes of a highland which renders access to the interior difficult and costly. The ports which serve the productive Humid Pampa have been developed in spite of a complete lack of natural harbors; and the great city of Buenos Aires, which has arisen in response to the productivity of its hinterland, is one of the most poorly endowed metropolises in the world in terms of fuel and power resources.

It is a fact of very great significance in the modern period that whereas North America possesses more than half of all the world's coal resources, South America has such meager supplies of this fuel that it can turn out only about one per cent of the world's production.

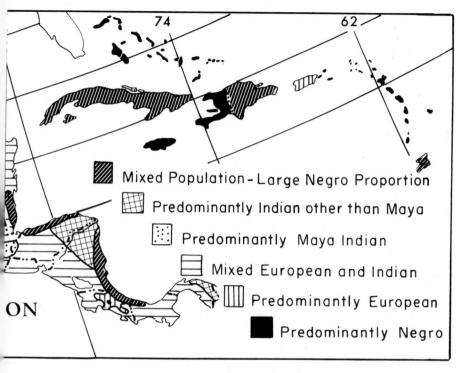

Map 5

Superlatives, yes—but superlatives that are poorly combined in terms of the needs of modern industrial society.

Surface Features

Middle America, which includes Mexico, Central America, the Antilles, and the Bahamas, forms a distinct break between North and South America. The geologic structures and surface forms of North America continue southward into Mexico to a little south of latitude 20° N. where they are abruptly terminated by a northwest-southeast chain of towering volcanoes. Southern Mexico, Guatemala, and Honduras belong to a structural region which extends under the Caribbean eastward to Jamaica, southeastern Cuba, Hispaniola, Puerto Rico, and the Virgin Islands—a region of folded and faulted rocks with a generally east-west trend. This "Central American–Antillean" region is connected to South America by two chains of volcanic ridges and peaks: the Lesser Antilles; and the highlands of Salvador, southwestern Nicaragua, Costa Rica, Panamá, and western Colombia (Map 7, page 25; Map 8, page 26).

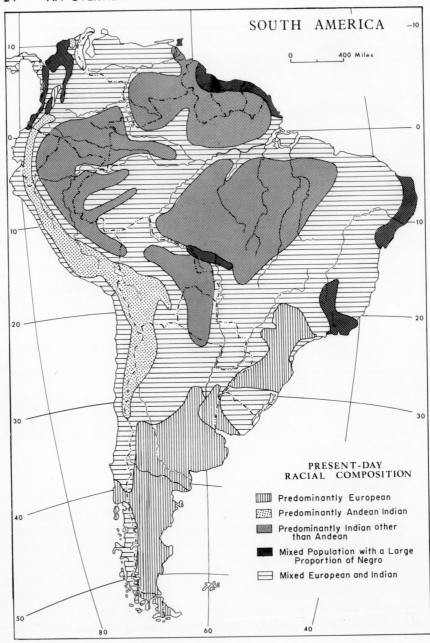

SOUTH AMERICA   —10

0   400 Miles

PRESENT-DAY
RACIAL COMPOSITION

Predominantly European

Predominantly Andean Indian

Predominantly Indian other
than Andean

Mixed Population with a Large
Proportion of Negro

Mixed European and Indian

Map 6

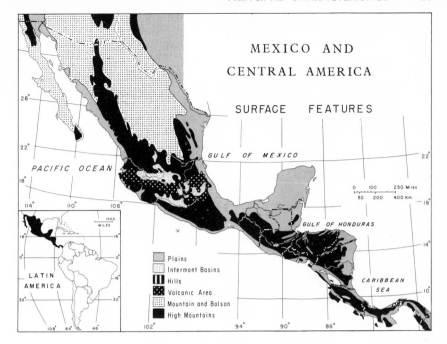

Map 7

Three chief surface divisions form the major lineaments of the strangely assorted continent of South America. These are similar to the divisions which, in happier relation to the climatic pattern and to the distribution of people, mark the surface of the continent of North America. On the west are the relatively young Andes; on the east are the Brazilian and Guiana highlands, geologically much older than the Andes, now partly covered by stratified rocks and lava flows, and in places surmounted by the massive stumps of ancient, worn-down mountains; and in the central portion of the continent lie the plains of the Orinoco, the Amazon, and the Paraguay-Paraná-Plata, filled with debris from the erosion of the highlands on either side.

For more than four thousand miles, from the shores of the Caribbean to the end of Tierra del Fuego, the Andes stand as a barrier between eastern and western South America. Compared with the western mountains of North America the Andes are narrower but considerably higher. Passes across the North American mountains can be found requiring a climb of only six or seven thousand feet; but most of the passes over the Andes, especially those which are located where there is need for a pass, are more than ten thousand feet above sea level. The Andes are scarcely two hundred miles wide, except in Bolivia where the width is doubled.

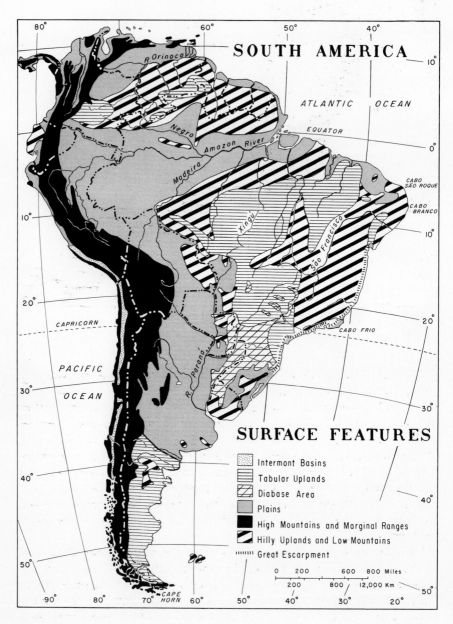

SOUTH AMERICA

ATLANTIC OCEAN

EQUATOR

R Orinoco

Negro

Amazon River

Madeira

CABO SÃO ROQUE

CABO BRANCO

Xingu

São Francisco

CAPRICORN

R. Parana

CABO FRIO

PACIFIC OCEAN

SURFACE FEATURES

Intermont Basins
Tabular Uplands
Diabase Area
Plains
High Mountains and Marginal Ranges
Hilly Uplands and Low Mountains
Great Escarpment

0   200   600   800 Miles
    200   800   12,000 Km

CAPE HORN

Map 8

The peaks reach altitudes from eighteen thousand to nearly twenty-three thousand feet. Mt. Aconcagua (22,835 ft.) is the highest mountain in the Western Hemisphere.

Geologic structures in the Andes, as in Middle America, are complex. To describe these mountains as a continuous chain is quite incorrect. Actually they are made up of several structural units more or less closely joined. In general, the mountains are formed by folded and faulted structures, but in three distinct areas there are groups of active volcanoes. These areas are in southern Colombia and Ecuador; in middle and southern Peru and along the border of Bolivia and Chile; and in the southern part of Middle Chile.

Since the Andes cross varied climatic zones, the processes of erosion and denudation which have sculptured the surface differ widely from place to place. The southern part of the Andes was heavily glaciated during the Ice Age, and even today the border between Argentina and Chile, just north of the Strait of Magellan, crosses an extensive mantle of permanent ice. Glaciers in this region still descend into the ocean at the heads of some of the fiords, or into the lakes on the eastern side of the range. North of latitude 39° S. the glaciers never emerged from the mountains and are now confined to higher and higher altitudes as one proceeds northward. Even on the equator, however, glaciation was once active, and small remnant glaciers still exist at the higher altitudes. In Bolivia and the northern parts of Chile and Argentina a dry belt crosses the cordilleras diagonally, and here the landforms typical of mountain deserts occur. From eastern Bolivia northward the rainfall increases in the mountain zone, and stream dissection becomes more and more active. Intermont basins at various altitudes are numerous in two chief sections: in Venezuela, Colombia, and Ecuador; and in Bolivia, Northern Chile, and Argentina. They are most common in areas of active volcanoes, or in the dry areas.

The pattern of surface features in South America east of the Andes, although bearing a broad similarity to the pattern of eastern North America, is quite different in its details. The greater part is made up of highlands, which extend with few interruptions from southern Colombia and Venezuela across Brazil to the northern bank of the Plata River, and which appear again in Patagonia. Throughout this vast extent of territory three chief surface elements are associated in varying patterns of arrangement. There is a base of ancient crystalline rocks, which forms a hilly upland; above this in a few places the stumps of old, worn-down mountains have produced massive, rounded forms similar to those of the Southern Appalachians in the United States; and covering the crystalline base, especially in the interior, is a mantle of stratified rocks, now forming tabular plateaus with steeply scarped margins. In dry Patagonia the granites and gneisses of the crystalline base are relatively resistant to the processes of erosion and stand out prominently as hills; but in the rainy tropics such rocks are speedily decomposed and mantled with soil, forming hills of a distinctively rounded outline. The stratified formations include chiefly sandstones, which, especially in the rainy lands, are so much more resistant than the crystalline rocks that they stand generally higher than the hilly upland throughout the Brazilian and Guiana highlands. Between the sandstone strata in southern Brazil, and in small patches throughout eastern South America, are sheets of dark-colored lava known as diabase. The diabase is especially resistant, and the edges of the lava sheets stand out prominently as cuestas. Some of the great waterfalls of South America occur where the rivers plunge over the edge of the diabase formations. The Paraná Plateau of southern Brazil is one of the world's largest accumulations built by successive flows of lava—similar in origin to the Columbia Plateau of Oregon and Washington, the Ethiopian Highlands of Africa, and the Deccan Plateau of India.

The arrangement of the plains of South America is very different from that of North America. In the first place they occupy a much smaller proportion of the continent. The Orinoco Plain is separated from the Amazon Plain by a belt of highlands. The Amazon Plain, which is wide along the eastern base of the Andes, narrows to only a ribbon of floodplain along the main stream east of Manaus. Southward along the Andes the plain of the Amazon is joined with the plain of the Paraguay-Paraná-Plata system, where the alluvium brought down by the rivers from both the Andes and the Brazilian highlands has covered all but a few of the more prominent features of the underlying rock surface. Unlike North America, there is no coastal plain along the Atlantic.

There is still another very significant difference between the patterns of the two continents. Because the highlands reach their greatest elevation in southeastern Brazil, back of Rio de Janeiro, where the highest summits are just under ten thousand feet above sea level, the larger rivers flow inland away from this region. The tributaries of the Paraná rise within a few miles of the coast in São Paulo, flowing thence northwest and then south; the tributaries of the São Francisco River, and those which eventually reach the Amazon, also flow toward the north, away from the southeastern coast. This divergence of the major streams deprives this part of the continent of any major natural focus of routes, such as the one which carries the traffic of the Middle West of the United States through the Mohawk and Hudson valleys to New York.

South America, on the whole, is not well provided with harbors, nor with navigable rivers placed where they can benefit the currents of commerce. The Paraná-Plata is navigable for ocean ships as far as Santa Fé, but to reach the artificial harbor at Buenos Aires dredges must work constantly to maintain a channel across the shallow mud banks of the Plata. On the West Coast, with only a few exceptions, ships lie at anchor in the open ocean a mile or more offshore, and load or unload by means of lighters.

Climates

Many different climates are to be found in Latin America. As in all the continents there is a general symmetry in the arrangement of the climatic types on either side of the equator and with reference to the continental east and west coasts. The higher middle latitudes of the southern hemisphere contain a much smaller area of land than the equivalent latitudes of the northern hemisphere. South America, south of latitude 40°, projects a relatively narrow finger into the wide expanse of the southern ocean. Therefore the types of middle- and high-latitude climates associated with places distant from the moderating effect of the oceans are not found in the southern hemisphere. Compared with North America the southern part of the hemisphere has moderate climates—they are neither so cold in winter nor so hot in summer. Nowhere, even in southern South America, are the winters comparable in severity to those of Canada or northern United States. Even in Tierra del Fuego, more than 50° south of the equator, the temperatures average above 32° in the coldest month although in the warmest month they average below 50°.[6]

Very high temperatures are also rare in Latin America. Map 9 shows how many days with temperatures above 110° can be expected in the average year. There are no parts of Latin America, except for a small bit of Mexico along the lower Colorado River, where more than fifteen such days are experienced, as they are in eastern California and Nevada. Very hot summer days occur in a belt extending from North Dakota to Texas, and to neighboring parts of northeastern Mexico. The only part of Latin America, outside of Mexico, where temperatures over 110° occur at any time of the year is in northern Argentina.

Along the western coast of both Americas the sequence of climatic types is similar on both sides of the equator. The cool, rainy climates of the higher middle latitudes on this coast are found in Southern Chile and in Southern Alaska and British Columbia. The similarity of the deeply fiorded coasts frequently swept by heavy storms which are found poleward of about latitude 45° on either continent is notable. The coast of Middle Chile, like coastal California, enjoys a Mediterranean type of climate, characterized by mild, rainy winters, and cool, dry summers; but because of the greater altitude of the Central Valley of Chile its summers are also cool, quite unlike the very hot summers of the much lower Central Valley of California. A little equatorward of 30° on both continents, the rainfall diminishes until only drought-resistant, or *xerophytic,* types of vegetation

[6] In this book the temperature is given in degrees Fahrenheit, the rainfall in inches.

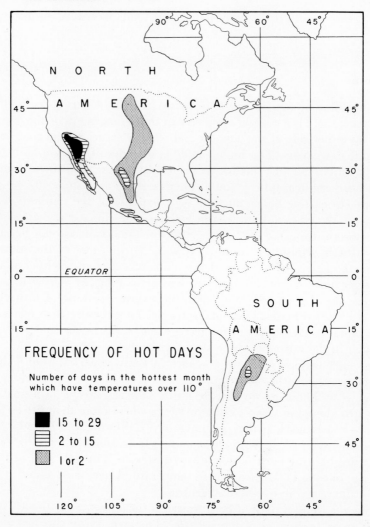

Map 9

can survive. Southern California and northwestern Mexico, like northern Chile, are deserts. The South American desert continues much farther toward the equator than does the dry west coast of Mexico. The former even reaches the northern side of the Gulf of Guayaquil in Ecuador, a few degrees from the equator, whereas the latter does not quite reach latitude 20° N. On the equatorward side of the dry lands, the west coast is moist, especially that part of the coast in Panamá, Colombia, and Ecuador which is bathed by the very warm waters of the Pacific Equatorial Counter Current.

The eastern part of South America, on the other hand, can be compared with the equivalent latitudes of North America as regards climatic conditions only as far south as the latitude of Buenos Aires. The east coast is generally warm and rainy—with the single exception of the northeast of Brazil, where there is a region of very irregular rainfall and frequent drought. Places in eastern South America as far south as Buenos Aires are comparable to places at similar latitudes in eastern North America as regards average temperature and rainfall, but the temperatures of the South American stations are not so high in summer nor so low in winter as those of the North American stations which they otherwise resemble. Because of the higher altitudes of the interior of Brazil, relatively cool climates extend northward to the regions inland from Rio de Janeiro and São Paulo. The highland climates of southern Brazil are similar to those of the southern Appalachians of southeastern United States.

South of the latitude of Buenos Aires temperature and rainfall conditions differ greatly from those of northeastern United States at equivalent latitudes. The temperatures are relatively mild, being much lower in summer and higher in winter than in the United States north of New York. Between Bahía Blanca in Argentina and the Strait of Magellan, the desert extends to the east coast—a rare characteristic in any part of the world. Although this southern part of South America is crossed by many storms, and is noted for its blustery, changeable weather, it receives very little moisture. The ranges of temperature in South America reach a maximum in the interior of Argentina a little north of the latitude of Buenos Aires—where the difference between the average of the warmest and of the coldest months is about 30°. In North America, ranges increase toward the north, because the increasing distance from the sea supplements the increasing distance from the equator; but in South America these two factors are opposed, and the ranges of temperature diminish again south of Buenos Aires.

To state that three quarters of South America as well as most of Middle America lie within the tropics is to present a fact, but perhaps a misleading one. It is misleading because of the common tendency to assume the bad effects of tropical climate, and also the tendency to think of all tropical climates as more or less alike. There is just as great a variety of climate within the tropical parts of the world as in the middle latitudes. An important distinction is to be made between the cool, cloudy desert of the Peruvian coast, for instance, and the hot, rainy conditions of Guiana or the hot, dry conditions along the Caribbean Coast of Venezuela. The highest temperatures in South America, as in other continents, are not observed near the equator, as is popularly supposed, but rather on the border between middle and low latitudes during the summer months. The parts of South America which have temperatures averaging above

80° in the warmest month are found along the Caribbean and Guiana coasts, throughout the vast tropical area of the Amazon Basin, and also over the plains of northern Argentina, most of which lie on the poleward side of the Tropic of Capricorn. The idea that the low latitudes are characterized by intense heat is based on the effect of the humidity encountered in certain parts of these lands, and also on the high *average* temperatures and the lack of any cool season. No such extremes of hot weather are found in the equatorial regions as occur during a summer heat wave in the North American Corn Belt.

Climatic diversity is especially great in the Andes. In any mountain region the variations of exposure to the sunlight and to rain-bearing winds have the effect of producing very intricate patterns of local climate; but there are also general altitude zones based chiefly on the decrease of temperature with increasing elevation. These high-altitude climates are in no way similar to the climates of the middle latitudes, for with increasing elevation above sea level the seasonal difference of temperature becomes less and less until it practically disappears (see the statistics for Quito in the Appendix).

In the low latitudes the greatest variety of vertical zones is to be found. The snow line rises to its highest altitude between 20° and 30° north and south of the equator, sagging slightly through the low latitudes. The snow line in Colombia is about 14,500 feet above sea level. On Mt. Orizaba in Mexico, 19° north, it is about 14,600 feet in altitude. On the dry west coast of Mexico and southern Peru or Northern Chile the snow line is considerably higher—in Northern Chile about 20,600 feet. In western Tierra del Fuego, on the other hand, permanent snow is encountered below 2,500 feet. The upper limit of trees and the upper limits of various crops all follow this general pattern. In general, snow lines and tree lines come closer together in wet areas, and have the widest spread where the rainfall is relatively low.

Vegetation

Closely reflecting the conditions of climate, water, and soil are the different associations of plants that distinguish one region from another. The vegetation, that is, the cover of non-cultivated plants, is broadly related to the character of the climate. Where water is abundant there is a cover of forest. Where water is less abundant there is a woodland composed of smaller and more widely spaced trees. Also in the transition zone between abundant and insufficient water there are areas of grassland, some pure grassland, some mixtures of grassland and scrubby woodland. Where water is deficient the plant cover fails to cover the ground completely. Rather there is bare ground between the plants. This is the distinguishing characteristic of dry land vegetation. Temperature, also, has

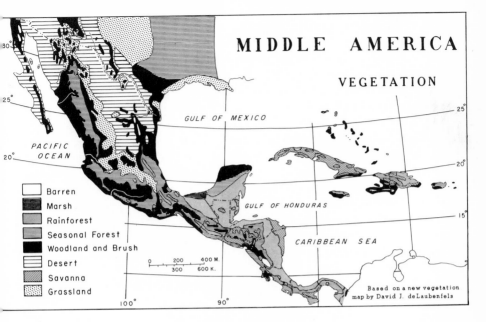

Map 10

its effect on the nature of the plant cover. Tropical plants are those that cannot survive frosts: mid-latitude plants exist in climates where frost comes often enough to eliminate those species that are not frost resistant.

Geographers and ecologists are in general agreement that man himself is a major agent of change in the nature of the plant cover. Wherever man has been during the thousands of years he has occupied the Americas he has profoundly altered the original character of the vegetation. The fires of prehistoric man, started for the purpose of aiding in the hunt, have had the effect of pushing back the woodlands and increasing the area of grassland, or of changing the nature of the forests. Nevertheless, the different types of vegetation that can be observed today have been in existence since prehistoric time—long enough to permit the development of distinctive soils and distinctive animal populations.

In a land where climatic data are insufficient and often unreliable, and where detailed soil mapping remains to be done, the cover of vegetation offers the best clue to the nature of the land and its potential productivity.

The vegetation is classified in four major groups. The *forests* consist of tall, straight-stemmed trees growing so close together that their branches interlace. The *woodlands* are made up of smaller trees, gnarled rather than straight-stemmed, and usually spaced far enough apart so that

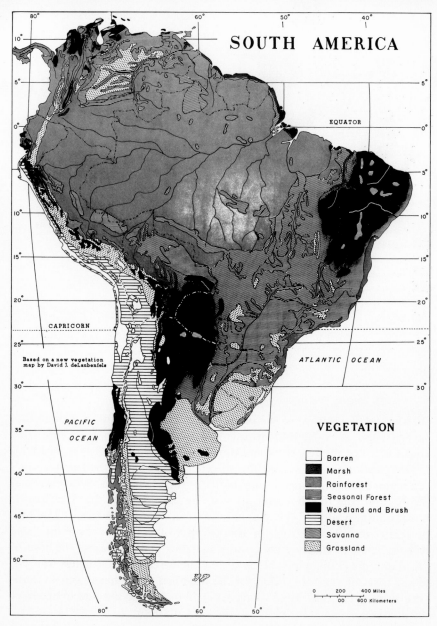

Map 11

branches may touch but are not interlaced. The *grasslands* include some that are entirely without trees, but many others that are a mixture of grass and woodland. The *deserts* include areas where there is bare ground between the plants, or where there are no plants at all.[7]

[7] Maps 10 and 11 are based on a new vegetation study of Latin America by Prof. David J. deLaubenfels.

CHAPTER TWO

The Appearance of Modern Latin America

These physical and biotic features of man's natural surroundings provide the stage setting on which modern Latin America has appeared. Here the traditional Spanish and Portuguese societies were established, in some cases embracing, if not digesting, a numerous population of native Indians. How did the modern states come into existence, and where are they with reference to the features of the habitat? And what are the problems of the modern period which are so deeply disturbing?

It is important to understand that the physical and biotic character of the habitat cannot control the action of the play. All too frequently we hear that people in the tropics can never work with energy and determination, or that countries not well endowed with natural resources can never be strong. Geographers have long insisted that the significance to man of the physical and biotic features of his habitat is a function of the attitudes, objectives, and technical skills of man himself. These are all elements of his traditional way of living—which we describe as his *culture*. Any change in technical skill or other element of a culture results in a change in the meaning of the habitat. What was a barrier to people with horses or on foot may cease to be a barrier to people with automobiles. Slopes that were not unsuited to cultivation by farmers with hoes, are quite useless for farmers with plows and tractors. Mineral resources that are of great value may, with some technical improvement in a distant place, become useless overnight. The significance of the habitat must always be interpreted in terms of the attitudes, objectives, and technical skills of the people.

There is one basic requirement. Any human society that is to remain permanently in any area must learn how to form workable connections with the land resources. If the agricultural practices result in soil erosion so that the land base is destroyed, land that was once habitable may cease to be so. The problems of economic development and of the viability of states must always be examined in relation to the features of the habitat.

In modern Latin America the existence of twenty-two sovereign states is of fundamental importance in any interpretation of economic or political problems. The states differ notably in wealth, in the development and use of resources, and in the nature of political attitudes. We need to understand how these states originated, what kinds of land they include, and what changes are sweeping over them in the modern period.

The Origin of States

One of the principle characteristics of this part of the world previously described is that the boundaries between states usually pass through empty, or thinly populated territory. An examination of the maps (Maps 1 and 2, 12 and 13) shows that some countries are built around just one central cluster of people, one area of concentrated settlement. Other

Map 12

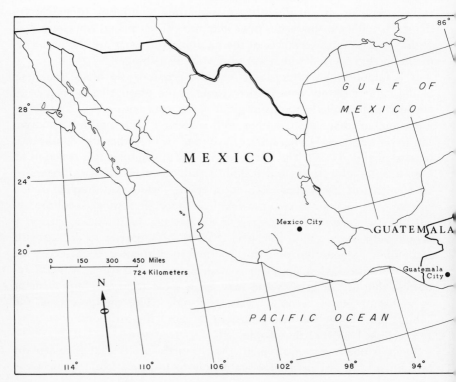

countries, however, include several separate areas of concentrated settlement. How did this come about? Or we might put the question this way: why did not every separate cluster of people form the core of a separate state?

After the American Revolution and the French Revolution of the late eighteenth century, new concepts of freedom and human liberty began to spread around the world. During the first half of the nineteenth century most of the present states of Latin America established themselves as independent countries, free from European control. Among the patriots who fought for freedom there were some who were genuinely devoted to the cause of individual liberty and of equality before the law. But most of the revolutionary leaders came from small circles of politically conscious people whose concept of freedom was made up chiefly of a desire to be free from outside interference. In each separate cluster of people there were political leaders who demanded, and in some cases were able to secure, the right to local self-government. The great majority of the people were not concerned.

Whether the resulting sovereign states included only one cluster of

Map 12

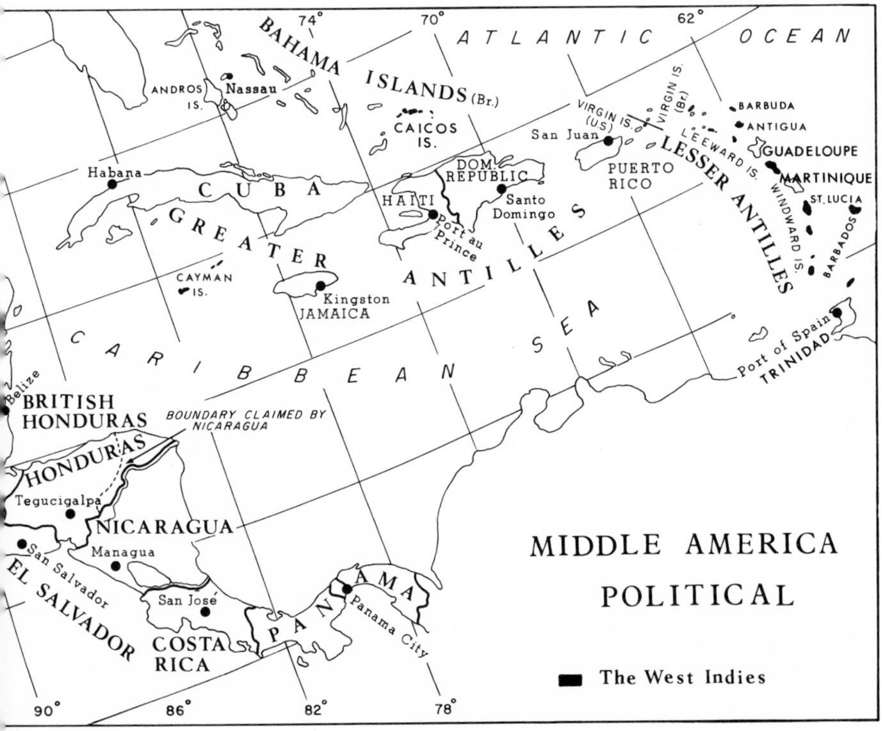

MIDDLE AMERICA

POLITICAL

The West Indies

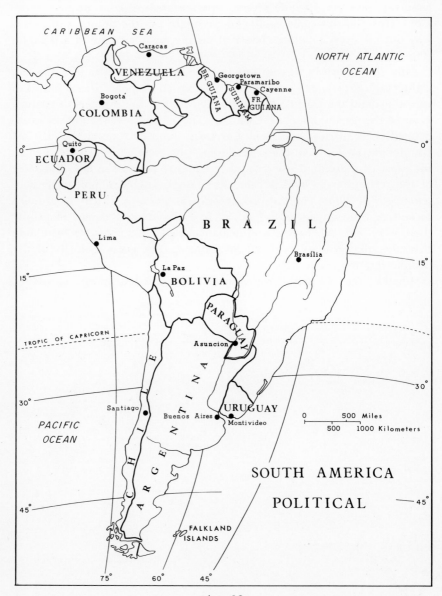

Map 13

people or several clusters depended on position with respect to the centers of colonial administration and on the strength of the local economy. At the end of the colonial period the Spanish colonies were grouped into four vice-royalties: the Viceroyalty of New Spain with its capital in Mexico City; the Viceroyalty of New Granada with its capital at Bogotá;

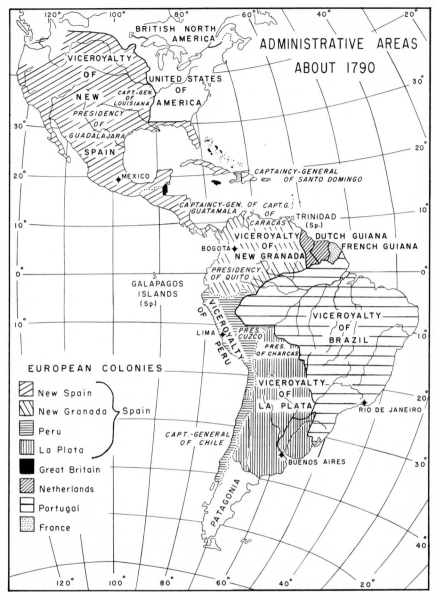

Map 14

the Viceroyalty of Peru with its capital at Lima; and the Viceroyalty of
La Plata with its capital at Buenos Aires (Map 14). Near the capital cities
the administrative lines were tightly held. But the difficulties of travel
were such that the lines slackened progressively with increasing distance
from the capital. In some places Captaincies-General, Presidencies, and

other administrative units were established as semi-autonomous subdivisions of the more remote parts of the Viceroyalties, as in the case of Guatemala and Chile. The northern part of the Viceroyalty of La Plata was included in the Presidency of Charcas. When the wars of independence succeeded in breaking the ties with Spain, the new governments located in the old capitals of the Viceroyalties were strong enough to maintain control of a number of separate clusters of people. But in more remote locations the clusters tended to break apart. Thus the separate clusters in Central America, from Guatemala southward, broke away from Mexico, and soon after broke into separate individual pieces. The clusters included in New Granada were at first held together by Bolívar, but later broke apart into three countries. Chile broke away from Peru. Bolivia and Paraguay made good their independece from Argentina.

In the case of the Portuguese colonies the situation was quite different. During the fourteen years before 1822, when Brazil became independent, the Emperor of Portugal had made his capital at Rio de Janeiro. This was the center of the whole Portuguese Empire. The declaration of independence by Dom Pedro I was supported by the political leaders of all the separate clusters of people. Only in the far south was there a separatist movement. Warfare between the Portuguese-Brazilians and the Spanish-Argentines over the border zone between them resulted in the creation of Uruguay as a buffer state.

In the Antilles, Spain succeeded in holding her colonies on Cuba and Puerto Rico until the war with the United States at the end of the century. However, the whole independence movement in Latin America was led, in 1804, by the revolt of the Negroes from their French masters in Haiti. The Haitians established control over the whole of the island of Hispaniola. Only in 1844 did the surviving Spanish groups in eastern Hispaniola gain their independence from Haiti.

The Struggle to Establish Order

A modern sovereign state is a politically organized area in which the people give their support to a government for the purpose of defending and fostering the development of a distinctive body of traditions and institutions. The traditions and institutions of a state are known as the *state-idea*. Unless a substantial majority of the people of a state give their support to this body of traditions and institutions, this state-idea, the state is a relatively weak one and could break apart under the pressure. If a state-idea is supported only by a minority, nothing but a strong central authority, maintained by force, can hold the state together. When independence was achieved in Latin America the state-idea with which most of the governments started was the negative one of freedom from outside interference.

During the past century or so the states of Latin America have been engaged in a struggle to establish order among the diverse and discordant elements which make them up. Order, as the word is used here, implies that a sufficient proportion of the people of a state subscribe to a common state-idea; or, lacking such a proportion of supporters, that a strong central authority enforces a state-idea which is held only by a minority. In most countries the establishment of order has proved very difficult. We find, in the same region of settlement, diverse groups of people mixed but not blended, whose traditional ways of living, whose technical abilities, whose fundamental attitudes are not only different but are so inharmonious that none can really prosper in the presence of the others. For example, there are certain nations which, since their independence, have been torn by the struggle for central control between two minorities: the large landowners, anxious only to be free from government interference; and the bureaucracy whose chief interest is in politics. There are other regions where the speculative exploitation of resources competes in the same area with a group of peasant proprietors seeking to establish themselves permanently on their own small farms. There are areas where one part of the population inherits a communal tradition of land tenure and another part inherits the tradition of the private estate. These and many other discordant elements produce such divergent attitudes toward the land and its use that harmony can be achieved only through the subjugation of one element by the other.

This struggle toward order among diverse elements is a process which can be observed in any community. Order is, of course, a relative term; it suggests that a substantial majority of the people are so harmonious in their basic traditions, skills, and objectives that one form of settlement or one coordinated group of connections between man and the land can be established and maintained. Methods of reaching such order are various. Some communities are brought together through service to an ideal, great enough and universal enough to command the allegiance of diverse individuals. Other communities achieve order through the struggle with a common problem, such as the conquest of a pioneer land, or defense against a foreign enemy. Still others are given an apparent order through the lulling effects of widespread prosperity. Different methods failing, many communities in past periods, and again in modern times, have enforced order through the operation of a strong central authority. In Latin America all these methods, and many others, have been tried with varying success; but in a number of regions of settlement and in many of the independent states built around them, the establishment of a coherent society has been retarded or thwarted.

Why should the Latin-American countries find so much difficulty in reaching a solution of this problem? We do not find among these people any scarcity of able leaders, any lack of outstanding political philosophers,

any dearth of poets or men of letters, or any absence of courage and resourcefulness and initiative. But we do find that Latin-American society
is troubled by perhaps a greater degree of original diversity than most
of the other Occidental peoples of the world; and we also find that these
basic racial and cultural diversities have been increased through the un-
balanced social and economic development of certain regions against a
background which remains economically medieval. The problems that
have to be faced in the establishment of order in Latin America are not
simple ones.

Impact of Diverse Racial and Cultural Elements

Whether the original racial and cultural diversity of the elements which
have entered into Latin-American society is to be described as an advantage or a disadvantage is a disputed question. The almost complete contrast in attitudes and objectives which exists between, for example, the
descendants of the Incas and those of the Spanish conquerors is so great
that even to this day the two have established only a minimum of coordination and harmony within the territory they occupy together. The
impacts of pagan and Catholic, of communal farmers who use the same
word for "duty to the state" as for "happiness" and the extremely in-
dividualistic Spaniards who have a strong sense of property rights—these
created internal conflicts which have yet to be resolved. Similarly in
Mexico, although an attack on these fundamental diversities has been
started, the lack of internal coherence is still far from solved. For these
states diversity cannot yet be accounted a benefit.

In no part of the world are studies of race mixture by impartial observers more needed than in Latin America, especially in the predominantly Indian and mestizo countries, and in Brazil. Many observers of
race mixture insist that the mestizos do not constitute a new race of
unified characteristics, but rather a mixture of ingredients so fundamentally different that they can never blend. On the other hand, there
are those who see in this mixture of Indian and European the basis of
a new race and a new civilization. There is a distinct movement in the
Indian countries looking toward a "rediscovery" of the artistic and technical skills of the Indians, a movement tending to discredit the Spanish
contribution. In Brazil the Negro mixture has produced every possible
shade of color from very black to pure white, with all sorts of intermediate
types including individuals, for instance, with blonde, kinky hair. Among
many of the pure white families of Brazil there is a considerable amount
of race prejudice; but not a few of the Brazilian writers extol the virtues
of race mixture in producing a new fusion of racial and cultural elements
—a new civilization. Among all these diversities, however, the struggle to
establish order, the struggle to assimilate, to create or maintain a coherent

nation, become problems of vital significance, and the changing character of these struggles conditions the relation of people to the land.

Social Diversities within the Preindustrial Society

Racial diversity, however, is not the only source of disharmony within Latin-American society. There are social and economic cleavages which divide communities into sharply contrasted classes. Some of these class distinctions are inherent in the society of traditional Latin America; but in the modern period the arrival of the urban industrial way of living has developed a new kind of difference separating the people of the larger cities from the people of the rural districts.

In traditional Latin America the economic and social life is dominated by the large estate. We shall describe this kind of society as *preindustrial*. Prestige and security in a preindustrial society are gained first through the ownership of a large tract of land. A very minor proportion of the total population forms the landed aristocracy, and is enabled to live in comfort and security and with a relatively high standard because of the large area from which income is derived and because of the relatively low cost of labor. When land is no longer available, prestige, if not security, can be gained by finding a position in the government service, or by winning a commission in the army, or by entering the priesthood. But these various forms of life are open only to the fortunate minority: the vast majority of the members of a preindustrial society are landless workers—peons, sharecroppers, tenants, or others. Usually they are permitted to make use of small areas for the production of their own food, and for the materials necessary for clothing and shelter; they repay the owner by providing him with wage laborers, or by paying him rent for the use of land for commercial crops. This is the Latin America of the semi-independent large landowner, who wishes above all to be left alone by all government authority; it is also the Latin America of political insecurity, in which first one group and then another plots to overthrow those who are in power, rarely because of genuine differences of ideology, usually because of the desire for the rich rewards of office-holding. This is the Latin America which verges on internal chaos to such an extent that it can be held together only by the successful operation of military dictatorship. This is the Latin America in which the army is the most powerful force in political life.

Impact of the Industrial Society

The history of the Occidental world during the last few centuries has been involved with the impact of the new *industrial society* and the older *preindustrial society*. This is what we call the industrial revolution.

Beginning in Western Europe, the new way of living, coupled with enormously increased productivity in all forms of economic activity through the use of controlled inanimate power, has gradually transformed whole sections of Europe and America. In some instances the transformation has taken place by gradual evolution; in not a few instances it has been accompanied by violence and warfare, both civil and international. The rapid increase in the need for raw materials of all kinds has produced the present intense rivalry for the control of the productive regions, especially of the sources of power. The English-speaking peoples, who were the first to adopt the new way of living, were able to gain control of about 75 percent of the developed power resources of the world; and the challenge to this control lies behind the present international turmoil. Latin America is now experiencing the impact of industrial society upon its traditional, preindustrial society. Where the industrial way of living has become established, a new and still more profound line of cleavage has been formed across all the previous diversities of Latin-American society.

The fundamental characteristics of the industrial society should be reviewed briefly. The use of controlled inanimate power changes the emphasis from production by cheap labor to production by machines—or, in terms of economics, capital investment assumes a position of preponderant importance, and the owners of capital rather than the owners of land assume places of the highest prestige and political power. Production is enormously increased, not only total production, but also per capita production. This leads to specialization and exchange, and hence to interdependence over wide areas. Trade is transformed from a small-scale exchange of luxury goods or specialties to a large-scale exchange of staples, and as a result communities are no longer supported by the products of the territories immediately surrounding them, but from a wide variety of producing areas, most of them beyond the control of the community which absorbs the products. With life organized on such a pattern society reaches a much higher standard of material comfort than any previous society has been able to reach; but this standard can be maintained only if a nation accepts the fact of wide geographical interdependence, turns away from provincial isolation, and cooperates with other nations in the maintenance of a stable financial structure of money and credits.

The industrial society brings profound changes in the details of human life. Prestige, we repeat, is to be gained through the ownership of capital which brings power, rather than through the ownership of land which brings security. Life becomes more speculative, less certain, but with rewards for the successful which are in a material way far beyond anything the world has offered before. There comes a notable change in the time concepts. With the increased tempo of life the vague concepts of preindustrial society, such as *por la mañana, por la tarde,* must be given up for more precise concepts, such as 9:45 A.M. or 3:10 P.M. Behavior of all sorts becomes more standardized. The picturesqueness of provincial costumes disappears under a uniform cover of blue denim overalls; people from Patagonia to Labrador watch the antics of Mickey Mouse; local differences in manners and customs are modified by the impact of the new patterns of life. In the big cosmopolitan centers of Latin America life follows the same routine as in North American or European cities— this uniformity is apparent in styles of architecture, styles of dress, forms of work and recreation—in short, the whole aspect of life is changed from its variegated preindustrial base to a uniformity repeated in all the Occidental urban centers.

These changes affect the distribution of people. As long as coal remains the chief source of power, manufacturing industry is carried on at the lowest cost in large concentrated units. People gather together in great cities—cities greater than any that the world ever knew before, cities of more than a million inhabitants. Although the use of electric power may have the effect of spreading manufacturing industry over a wider area, thus transforming the life in smaller towns and villages, the large concentrations of city people still perform more efficiently the urban functions of commerce and administration. These cities are still dependent on the productivity of the land for their support, but the land base has been greatly extended; and as a result the means of transportation which tie the cities together must be greatly elaborated.

The urban-industrial way of living has come to Latin America from outside, not by slow evolution from the earlier preindustrial base. In parts of Europe and in Anglo-America where the cities and the urban life developed out of the rural background there is a certain normal relationship between the size of the city and the productivity of its rural hinterland. When through the artificial erection of political boundaries and barriers a city like Vienna is deprived of the hinterland which it once served, the financial and economic life of the city is disrupted. When politically independent states attempt to return to isolation and self-sufficiency, the urban-industrial society falls into chaos. All these adjustments between cities and their territories and all these disruptions of the earlier adjustments can be witnessed in Europe today. In Latin America one finds cities which have become industrial and commercial centers with an industrial way of living, but which bear little relationship in size or in function to the rural districts back of them. The contrast between the cities and the rural districts is enormous: the average tourist who journeys by boat or airplane from one city to another scarcely catches a glimpse of the Latin America which is traditional, and which is still dominant in terms of area and numbers of people.

Urban-industrial growth has appeared at various places in Latin America. The largest developments of this cosmopolitan life center in Buenos

Aires, Rio de Janeiro, São Paulo, Santiago, Lima, Mexico City, Caracas, Bogotá, and Habana—all cities of a million or more people, all thoroughly modern metropolises, with a way of living entirely familiar to metropolitan dwellers throughout the Occidental world. Modern industrial development has appeared also in many smaller cities throughout Argentina, Chile, Brazil, Colombia, Venezuela, Mexico, and Cuba. Yet the industrial productivity of all Latin America is still very small compared with that of the United States or of Western Europe (Map 15).

The Democratic Revolution

Along with the industrial revolution, yet separate from it, another major change in the way of living of mankind is in process of sweeping over the world. This is the democratic revolution. Like the industrial revolution it made its start in Great Britain and in the countries around the North Sea in Europe. Although the roots of this movement go back to the Plymouth Compact of 1620 and before, it only became a major revolution in the eighteenth century. Since that time ideas of democracy have swept all the way around the world, setting up a variety of reactions and forms of resistance.

The democratic revolution includes at least five new concepts regarding the status of the individual. First is the right of the individual to equal treatment before the law. Second is the right of the individual to protection from the arbitrary acts of those in authority. Third is the right of the individual to select his own form of government and to be represented by a person of his own choosing where laws are made or taxes levied. Fourth is the right of the individual to discuss public issues freely and to express his choices in a secret ballot. And fifth is the right of the individual to knowledge and to the free use of it.

The democratic revolution is moving into Latin America. There are still a vast number of Latin Americans who are illiterate, who have never known such a thing as equality before the law, or protection from arbitrary police action, or the secret ballot, or even free access to news. But among the Latin Americans there have also been a few liberal-minded persons struggling toward the ideas of democracy. The French Revolution of the late eighteenth century had a profound effect on Latin America. Although the independence movement was quickly turned away from concepts of individual equality toward the principle of freedom from outside interference, nevertheless many of those who supported the independence movement were thinking of fundamental changes in the status of the individual. Such leaders as Domingo Sarmiento (1811-1888) of Argentina, or Benito Juárez (1806-1872) of Mexico, and many others, attempted to attack the system which gave special privilege be-

Map 15

cause of social or political position. Sarmiento devoted his life to the establishment of a system of public schools and to the problem of illiteracy. But a much larger number of political leaders in Latin America find ample reason for maintaining the traditional system in which power and prestige are granted on the basis of social status rather than individual achievement. In most parts of Latin America the democratic revolution has met resistances too strong to be easily overcome. The fact is that in some countries the great majority of the people, if they had a chance to express a choice, would support an honest, effective dictatorship in preference to a liberal regime. The desire to assume responsibility for decisions of policy has yet to be widely cultivated. On the other hand, there are some parts of Latin America where democratic ideals are widely held. There can be no doubt that in the years ahead the number of people who understand and support democratic ideals will increase at a faster and faster rate.

Meanwhile, the spread of the democratic revolution brings certain kinds of reaction—in Latin America as elsewhere in the world. One reaction is to strengthen central authority, supported by the force of the army and the police. The people are aroused by extravagant nationalism, demanding the exclusion of foreigners and foreign capital. Industrial technology is adopted, whether justified by economic facts or not, chiefly for the purpose of reaching for the mirage of economic self-sufficiency. Under such a fascist system, no vestiges of civil liberty remain. Another reaction against the revolutionary new ideas regarding the status of the individual is that of communism. Organized communist minorities take advantage of the underlying resentment against the power and privileges of the landowners, or of foreign business groups, and offer a rapid end to the traditional system. Programs of land confiscation and redistribution command widespread approval. Only later does it become apparent that the elimination of one system of privilege is followed by the establishment of a new system of privilege. Everywhere the democratic revolution has been felt. In some countries it has progressed amazingly well; in others the resistances are too strong, and democratic ideals of equality before the law and civil liberty simply do not exist. Here, then, is still another element of diversity that differentiates one part of Latin America from another.

*   *   *   *

A Geography of Man

The struggle to establish order among these diverse elements is a basic theme which endows the present-day arrangement of people in Latin America with meaning. In each independent state, in each separate cluster of people, this struggle takes a somewhat different form and has reached somewhat different stages. As a result, the significance of the elements of the land—the potential value of the natural resources—differs from place to place and from time to time. In extreme cases we find two or more diverse groups mixed but not blended in the same area of concentrated settlement, each group motivated by different attitudes and objectives and consequently each reacting differently to the variegated background of the land. In a few instances we are encouraged by what seems to be a real advance against the forces of disunity. When we examine the map of people in detail in the light of this theme we can no longer see it only as a pattern of apparently uniform dots irregularly clustered—we see each cluster as possessing a distinct individuality, as composed of people who have made a separate and distinctive contribution, even if only a negative one, to the struggle toward the development of a coherent society.

Such a study of the map of people also transforms it, in our minds, from a static thing to a stage in a process which moves forward out of the past and is projected into the future. The phases of the struggle, during the passage of four centuries, result in changing relations between the people and the land, and consequently in frequent shifts of the population. Many parts of Latin America, considered over the course of history, have notably shifting patterns of people; and in those areas which are stable—such as the predominantly Indian communities of Mexico, Guatemala, and the Andean highlands of southern Colombia, Ecuador, Peru, and Bolivia—the impact of the European has been relatively slight. On the other hand, some of the most important areas of Latin America, in terms of commercial productivity in the modern world, were, less than a century ago, only sparsely inhabited.

The destructive exploitation of resources takes on new meaning with the advent of the industrial society. Small-scale exploitation widely scattered over the continent characterized the preindustrial society: large-scale exploitation in concentrated areas is the mode of action of the industrial society. To be of value in the industrial world today, a resource must be large enough to support a large-scale development; otherwise the cost of production is too high. Yet the demand for raw materials is unequaled in all the previous history of the world. Those places where superlative resources are to be found become potential centers of rapid population increase and economic development. But permanence and stability, in a world itself undergoing a major transformation, are rare. Men still search frantically for the accumulated wealth of El Dorado, and, as it eludes them in one place, they move on to other places. Is the growth of the new industrial cities likely to bring stability and permanence, or only a new form of migration, a new and still more chaotic form of exploitation, to be followed by a new decline?

Jungle-covered ruins of Panamá Vieja, Spanish colonial city founded in 1519

The
Spanish Countries
of Mainland
Latin America

The National University Library, Mexico City

CHAPTER THREE

Mexico

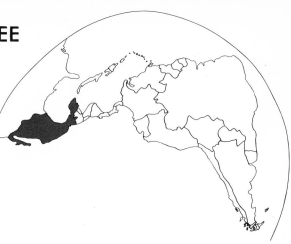

For a century and a half the Mexican leaders have been struggling to create a coherent national state out of diverse and discordant elements. In 1821, when the Spanish colony of New Spain made good its declaration of independence and became the Empire of Mexico, the leaders of the independence movement were seeking primarily to establish equal rights for those born in America and those born in Spain. The great majority of the people who lived in the new national territory were Indians or mestizos; almost all of them were illiterate farmers, for whom the question of equality with people born in Spain had no meaning. Mexico started its independent existence with a negative state-idea that was of concern to not more than five percent of the people. From 1821 to 1876 the country was poverty-stricken and turbulent. There were revolts and counterrevolts, as younger army officers who were not in profitable government positions sought to replace those who were in such positions. Now and then a sincere reformer made his appearance, like the Indian Benito Juárez, but reform movements aimed at improving the lot of the ordinary people were soon diverted into traditional channels. In 1876 Porfirio Díaz came into power by the usual process of army revolt.

Porfirio Díaz was one of Latin America's notably successful dictators. With a small group of trusted supporters, and with a powerful police force, he ran Mexico by decree. The government was carried on by a hierarchy of officials, all responsible to the dictator. He selected the state governors and gave them complete authority within their states. The power of the governors rested on the support of the small number of landowners. Local political bosses were picked by the governers. Any one who felt inclined to be uncooperative was openly assassinated, or just disappeared. There was complete stability and order. Only 15 percent of the

Maps 1, 3, 5, 7, 9, 10, 12, 14, 15, 16, 17, 18 are pertinent to this chapter.

total population could read or write. And not more than one or two percent were wealthy and enjoyed political power. In the central part of the
country some 95 percent of the heads of rural families owned no land.
The most striking contrast existed between the educated, gay, cosmopolitan, and very wealthy society surrounding the dictator and the great
majority of the Mexicans who were illiterate, sick, and hopeless in their
poverty. But under Díaz there was order and security, and foreign businessmen in the United States, Great Britain, and Germany thought of
Mexico as a safe place in which to do business.

Díaz was eighty years old when he was reelected president of Mexico
for the eighth time in October 1910. There was no outward sign of the
impending explosion, unless it was the appearance of Halley's comet
which presaged for the superstitious peasants the coming of disaster. But
by this time almost all of the wealth of Mexico was concentrated in the
hands of less than three percent of the people—the regime was under-
mined because not enough people had a stake in it. Suddenly violence,
disorder, and revolution appeared. Even the army and the police deserted
the dictator, who was forced to flee for his life.

The amazing thing is that the Mexican Revolution (1910-1915) was not
diverted into traditional channels. After 1915 it was captured by a succession of leaders, more or less honest, more or less able, but all devoted to
the social transformation of Mexico. *La Revolución* is a word that has
been used now by several generations of Mexicans and has become a
common part of the national tradition and the popular vocabulary. This
is a state-idea in the making, even if not every one agrees about what the
revolution has been doing.

But the struggle to establish a coherent society in Mexico has been
carried on in the midst of great difficulties. Diversity in the Mexican scene
is not solely a matter of racial and cultural differences. Diversity is also
produced by the physical land itself. Mexico has a little of everything.
In addition to the spectacular snow-capped volcanoes there are rugged
surfaces throughout the country where the slopes are so steep that the
people who live on them think in terms of "up and down" rather than
north, south, east, and west. Two-thirds of Mexico is like this. The other
third is classed as level, but it includes intermont basins, narrow valley
bottoms, coastal lowlands, and a wide limestone plain where solution has
produced underground rivers and sinks. There are parts of Mexico so
high that the air is cool, even in summer; there are also low-lying regions
where the temperature, especially in summer, is very high. About half of
Mexico, including the desert regions of the north and northwest, is deficient in moisture; but the other half receives an abundance of moisture.

The Mexican population is notably centralized. This is so whether we
regard Mexico as a whole or look more closely at any one of the Mexican
communities. The population as a whole is concentrated in one central

area in the central highlands, and the outlying districts are occupied by
a relatively scanty population scattered in small groups. When the distribution is examined more closely we find that even the central area is not
composed of one cluster of people, but of several separate clusters, each
with its own urban nucleus, each separated from neighboring clusters
by thinly populated territory. The national life focuses on Mexico City;
but in a similar way every smaller town and every little village is the focus
of life in the community of which it is the center. The dominance of the
center over the periphery appears again and again in all phases of Mexican life; and the contrast between the concentrated population of the
cities, towns, and villages and that of the thinly scattered rural settlements
is very great.

Is Mexico a rich land or a poor land? This question has been argued
by extremists on both sides since Cortés first reported to his king that he
had found a land of superlative resources. Mexico is a rich land for the
mining engineer who encounters little difficulty in locating the ores where
the rivers have done the work of excavation and where the coverage of
vegetation is scanty. Mexico is incomparable for the tourist who seeks
spectacular scenery and who can find something picturesque in poverty.
Mexico could be made into a very productive meat or dairy land, for it
possesses notable physical advantages for these forms of economy. But for
farming, Mexico is a poor land, since so much of its area is either too
steep or too dry to be classed as arable. And most of the Mexicans are
farmers.

Mexico was the first of the Latin-American countries to translate the
discontent of the overwhelming majority of its people into political action. In the background were many generations during which the economic rewards and the political power had been concentrated in the
hands of a smaller and smaller minority of the people. The Mexican
peasant, pictured in the cartoons sitting under a cactus with his hat pulled
down over his eyes, was sick, hungry, and hopeless. In a land repeatedly
described as containing incredible natural riches, most of the people were
living in poverty. Whether we in the United States approve or disapprove
of what the Mexicans have done is not the question: but it is important
that we understand what has been done and that we observe the results
in the establishment of a coherent state.

The Peoples and Cultures of Mexico

The varied assortment of peoples and cultures that comprise the population and the way of life in Mexico is largely the result of the mixture of
Indian and Spanish ingredients. Many millions of Indians were already
firmly intrenched on the land in central and southern Mexico at the time
of the Spanish conquest. These were the sedentary agricultural groups pre-

Deeply dissected mountain land in Chihuahua

viously described—the Indian communities whose distribution determined, if any one factor can be said to have determined, the course and pattern of Spanish settlement. The Spanish contribution to the racial make-up of the present-day population has been relatively small. The number of registered emigrants who left Spain during the colonial period destined to enter the territory administered from Mexico City, in New Spain, was only 300,000. Although each registration might include members of the family and servants, the total number of Spanish immigrants to New Spain must have been small compared with the numbers of Indians already in Mexico. Nevertheless the Spaniards possessed the advantage of technical knowledge which assured their political and economic conquest of the much more numerous native peoples. Today Mexico is a strange mixture of Indian and Spanish elements—a mixture which is not only biological, but also cultural.

Racial Composition of the Mexican People

Merely to state that in Mexico one major ingredient in the racial composition of the population is the Indian is to obscure the fact that the Indians themselves were diverse in origin and in culture. While today Spanish is the common language throughout Mexico, it is nevertheless significant that, in 1950, the taking of the census required the use of fifty different languages, and that 7 percent of the people neither speak nor understand Spanish. More than 80 percent of the people of Mexico are

Indians of one kind or another. Pure-blooded Indians, however, are estimated to make up only 29 percent, whereas Indians with some white ancestors make up at least 55 percent of the total. The people of unmixed European descent comprise about 15 percent.

These proportions have been changing gradually through the decrease in the number of the people of unmixed ancestry and the increases of the mestizo type. In 1805, the people of unmixed European descent were estimated to make up about 19 percent of the total. At that time the pure-blooded Indian group was estimated at 40 percent, and the mestizos at 41 percent. During the colonial period more than 30,000 Negroes were brought in to work on the sugar plantations and in other enterprises, but by 1805 the number of pure Negroes amounted to only about 21,000, or 0.2 percent of the total. The proportion of Negroes is now less than one percent.

The Indian contribution to the Mexican mestizo is a relatively large one. The mestizo of Mexico has more Indian ancestors than he has white ancestors. During the whole colonial period, as we have said, a relatively small number of Europeans were listed as departing from Spain for New Spain. Few reinforcements have come from outside since Mexico became independent. Díaz, to be sure, attempted to stimulate European immigration, and about 11,000 Italians actually came to Mexico shortly after 1878, but by 1890 not more than 5,000 were left. Since then, the number of Europeans who have come to Mexico has been negligible. From a racial point of view Mexico is overwhelmingly Indian rather than Latin.

Growth of the Mexican Population

Until recently the growth of the Mexican population has not been rapid. After the decimation of the Indians by diseases introduced as a result of the Spanish conquest, the number of people in the country began slowly to increase again. It is estimated that, in 1805, Mexico had a population of about 5,800,000—probably less than the Indian population of the same territory three centuries earlier. At the same time there were approximately the same number of people in the United States. After 1824 the Mexican population required eighty years to double itself, while the United States, during the same period of time, partly because of its flood of European immigrants, made one of the largest numerical increases that history records. The Mexican population in 1956 was estimated at over 30,500,000, while that of the United States was nearly 170,000,000. Since 1950, however, the Mexican population has been growing at a faster and faster rate—chiefly as a result of the widespread application of modern hygiene and medicine. Between 1950 and 1960 the Mexican population increased 35.4 percent—compared with a growth in the United States of 18.6 percent.

The Mexican birth rate is extraordinarily high. During the 1950's it was about 46 per thousand—almost twice as high as that of the United States. The birth rate has been very high as far back as the statistical data make such computations possible. Yet until the 1950's the areas of concentrated settlement in Mexico have changed little. There have been no frontiers of pioneer farming around stabilized cores of dense population. In fact the total population of the country grew only at a moderate rate.

Two chief facts account for the slow rate of population increase and for the lack of settlement expansion. First was the very high death rate which, until 1950, was among the highest in all Latin America. Before World War II it was over 22 per thousand (compared with death rates at that same time of about 22 per thousand in Guatemala, 20 in El Salvador, 20 in Chile, 18 in Colombia, and 10 in Argentina). About a quarter of all deaths were of children under one year of age: one child out of every eight born died within the first year. The diseases were those caused by malnutrition and bad hygiene—diarrhea, enteritis, and dysentery; but respiratory diseases, also, were widespread, especially on the high plateau around Mexico City. Now all these death rates, Mexico's included, have been considerably lowered. By the 1950's the Mexican death rate was down to 13 per thousand, and the others quoted above have been similarly lowered—which, of course, is the chief cause of the high net increase of population characteristic of Latin America as a whole.

The second reason for the slow rate of population increase in past years is that Mexico, during the whole four and a half centuries of

Medical School of the National University in Mexico City

European dominance, has been a country of emigration. During the colonial period Mexico supplied most of the people of pure Spanish descent and the people of mestizo blood who occupied the Philippine Islands. From the Pacific port of Acapulco many Mexicans set sail across the ocean to this still more distant colony of Spain. In the modern era large numbers of Mexicans have emigrated to the United States. Mexicans today form an important "minority" group in all the border states from Texas to California, and also in some of the large industrial cities of the north, such as Chicago and Detroit. Mexico, Chile, and El Salvador are alone among the countries of America in having experienced persistent movements of emigration.

Poor health and emigration both betray the existence of poverty— and poverty among the great majority of the Mexican people has been the normal condition of life. Perhaps we must blame the land for its low productivity of essential foods; or perhaps the blame should be placed on the manner in which the Mexicans made use of the land. We must remember the principle, already stated, that the significance of the land base changes with the attitudes, objectives, and technical abilities of the inhabitants. Before turning to a consideration of the characteristics of the Mexican land, therefore, we must attempt to form a picture of those elements of the Mexican way of living which have contributed to a chronic condition of poverty—a traditional land problem.

Attitude toward the Land

In the central area of dense population the traditional attitude toward land is based on a mixture of Spanish and Indian ideas. To a certain extent these ideas were in strong contrast, but in other respects they ran closely parallel. The difference between the communal system of tenure and the system of private property which separates the European and the native Indian groups in many countries of Latin America was less pronounced in Mexico owing to the existence of parallel institutions among the Aztecs and the Spaniards. In at least two ways the Aztecs had developed concepts of the private ownership of land, even though a primitive agricultural communism remained the predominant form of tenure. The lands held by the *calpulli,* or the clan, included certain tracts which were owned and operated by the whole group in common, but they also included other tracts which were partitioned among the heads of families and thereafter were regarded as essentially private property. Such lands could be passed on by inheritance. And the second form of private property in land formed an even closer parallel to the Spanish forms: certain of the Aztec nobles had assumed the role of feudal lords, having the right to the services of the inhabitants of specific communities. Long before the Spaniards came upon the scene a considerable proportion of the Mexican people were bending under the burden of a landed aristocracy.

Nor were the Spaniards unacquainted with the idea of communal land ownership. Although the large private property was the common form of land tenure among the Spaniards, the typical Spanish agricultural village held title in common to three kinds of land which were definitely excluded from private ownership. There were certain areas operated in common which were devoted to the support of the village government; there were common pastures and woodlands; and there was the open tract, located just outside the village gates, used in common for a variety of activities, but not for raising crops or for grazing animals. This tract was known in Spain as the *ejido,* literally the "way out," because of its location on the way out of the village.

Yet in spite of the existence of these parallel institutions the essential contrast between the Spanish and the Indian attitude toward the land remained enormous. For the Spaniard, the sure road to prestige and economic security was the private estate. Only the very small group of Aztec nobles thought of land ownership as bringing prestige. The majority of the Indian farmers who actually used the land, thought of their little plots of land as belonging to the community, and thought only of producing enough for their own needs. Commercial farming was unknown to the Indians. The few items taken to the local markets provided, then as now, more of an excuse for the producer to take part in the social pleasures of the market place than an element of economic support. If a few ears of maize or a piece of pottery offered for sale should actually be sold early in the day, the Mexican Indian would think of this transaction as a loss rather than as a gain. McBride estimates that the agricultural holdings were small, averaging only a few acres, hardly enough to provide even the bare necessities of food. Land was not held for profit; even among the nobles, the buying and selling of land was unknown.

The Spanish-Indian Impact

The Spanish system of the encomienda did not differ greatly from the Aztec system of tribute. The ruling Aztecs exploited the labor of the people they had conquered, and the Spaniards simply carried on where the Aztecs left off. In many instances the same units were taken over, a Spanish officer taking the place of an Aztec lord without further dislocation of the system. Cortés himself received from the Crown grants of encomiendas in various parts of Mexico, including 22 villages with a total population of about 23,000, occupying an area of roughly 25,000 square miles. By 1572 there were 827 encomiendas in Mexico, most of them located in the central area between Jalisco and Oaxaca, and in the Maya area of Yucatán.

Plumed serpent on the Temple of Quetzalcoatl in Teotihaucán

The system of the encomienda, however, did not survive the first century of the Spanish Conquest. In its place the grant of large tracts of land by the Spanish Crown gave the owner actual title to the land, not just the right to the collection of tribute. Gradually the encomienda system was given up, and in the course of time more and more of the land was put into private hands. Some of the grants were small ones of less than one hundred acres; but many of the grants were large ones, consisting of many thousands of acres.

The Spaniards also brought certain parts of Mexico under their control through the establishment of missions. Especially on the remote northern frontier, the Jesuit, Franciscan, and Dominican orders founded new centers of settlement, and around each center they brought together the Indians from many small scattered communities and reestablished them on the land as farmers, teaching new agricultural techniques and importing new crops, and, incidentally, exposing the Indians to the ravages of epidemics.

The impact of the Spaniards on the Indians produced a struggle which lasted for more than four hundred years. This was the struggle for the right to own land. It involved two contrasted forms of tenure: the *ejido,* or land-holding agrarian community occupied chiefly by persons of Indian descent; and the *hacienda,* or large privately-owned, feudal estate, usually in the hands of persons of unmixed or nearly unmixed Spanish descent. By 1823 there was scarcely any good land left that was not in private hands, yet there were only about 10,000 owners of land. The Church, at that time, was the largest single landowner. By the end of the Díaz regime in 1910, a program of encouraging the shift of vast

A National University classroom Mexico City

areas of public domain into private range lands had brought almost all of the country under private ownership. At this time in all but five states over 95 percent of the heads of rural families owned no land. Some eleven million rural people (out of a total population of over fifteen million) were living in small, isolated communities, raising their own subsistence crops on land they rented for that purpose, and gaining a miserable additional wage by working for the owners. The great majority of the Mexicans were living monotonously, in isolation, ignorance, and poverty, and plagued by bad diet and disease. Such was the dark picture which formed the background of the brilliant aristocratic society of the capital in the days of Porfirio Díaz. In no other Latin-American country had the concentration of land ownership in the hands of a few people gone so far.

The Mexican hacienda was more than a large land property—it was also a way of living. Ownership of a hacienda provided two things which every Mexican desired but few could hope to achieve: social prestige and economic security. Because the owner was relatively free from land and labor costs, he was able to sell his products profitably even when they were inefficiently produced and when transportation costs were high. In contrast to the almost complete self-sufficiency of the rural worker, the landowner was closely tied to the world of commerce. His standard of living was high, his diet varied and hearty; his children were educated in Europe, and the whole family had frequent opportunities to travel and develop a cosmopolitan familiarity with the outside world. Usually the hacienda owner left his estate in the hands of a manager while he and his family established their home in Mexico City or in Europe. On the occasions when the owner visited his hacienda each worker would stand, hat in hand, as this strange person from another world rode by.

Under these circumstances the establishment of an ordered society could only be accomplished through a strong central authority. Barely under the surface there was unrest and banditry. Even the revolt of 1810, which started Mexico on the road to independence, was at first an agrarian uprising. In 1857, Benito Juárez came to power with a similar movement; but like the others it was soon turned away from its basic objective— doing something about the land problem. To a considerable extent Mexican laborers who had been in the United States and had returned, were responsible for increasing the widespread discontent of the people with a system in which they participated so little. The Mexican Revolution (indicated by capital letters to distinguish it from minor revolts) which started with Madero in 1910 and ended with Carranza in 1915 was the conflict that set the stage for really fundamental reforms.

The famous Article 27 of the Constitution of 1917[1] attempts to formulate a new concept regarding private property in land. The concept is based on a functional theory of property—that the right to own property, including land, is dependent on socially harmonious use.

The Present Systems of Land Tenure

The program of land redistribution based on this article has transformed the rural life of Mexico. Between 1916 and 1934 some twenty-five million acres of hacienda lands were expropriated and assigned to peasant communities, in which a total of 939,000 farmers actually received land. During the presidency of Lázaro Cárdenas from 1934 to 1940, however, there was a great acceleration of the program, and in this period almost fifty million acres changed hands, and more, than 7,700,000 individuals received land. By 1950 about 90,000,000 acres had been taken from the haciendas and given to farmers in peasant communities. The hacienda as an economic unit and as a social institution was eliminated.

The word *ejido* refers to a farming community which has received land in accordance with the procedures set up under the constitution of 1917. The ejido is a rural, peasant community, a farm village. In Mexico as a

[1] Based on the decree issued by Carranza on January 6, 1915, and incorporated in the constitution of February 5, 1917; now somewhat reformed in the decree of December 30, 1933. See E. N. Simpson, *The Ejido, Mexico's Way Out.* Chapel Hill, 1937.

whole the average number of families in each ejido is less than a hundred. In two areas the ejidos are organized as collectives; everywhere else the lands belonging to the ejidos have been divided into private farms. Each family works its own farm, and in most ways treats it as private property. However, the land thus parceled out cannot be sold, and if the family moves away the title to the property remains with the ejido. The ejido is organized politically, with a general assembly, an executive committee, and a vigilance committee to watch the executives. Technical assistance, education, and credit are furnished by the federal government.

The amount of land granted to each *ejidatario* (head of an ejido family) was supposed to be varied according to the potential productivity of the land. If the land could be irrigated the maximum was first set at ten acres, later changed to fifteen, and then twenty-five acres. If the land could be cultivated but was dependent on local rainfall, the minimum area was set at 50 acres. If the land were too dry for anything but brush or agave, the minimum was 2,000 acres. Unfortunately, however, Mexico has never had much of its area surveyed on large-scale maps, adequate for the plotting of property lines; and there are few land classification studies, showing the distribution of soil, slope, and water supply. As a result some ejidos have found themselves with no land suited for the cultivation of crops at all; some have had no source of water available on the land given to them. Of the more than sixty million acres of ejido lands in 1940, only seventeen million could be used to raise crops, and of this only five million could be irrigated. Since 1940 the expropriation of land and its redistribution to ejidos has slowed down because there is no more land available in the areas of concentrated settlement.

Since 1947 another kind of rural holding has made its appearance. This is the small private farm. Land suitable for agriculture in the central area was already redistributed under the ejido system; but outside of the central area there was still much land in private holdings, used chiefly for cattle ranching. In 1947 a new colonization law was passed by the government, permitting the expropriation of range land and the establishment of farm colonies. To make this colonization program possible the government also undertook a major plan of irrigation and reclamation. One of the earliest, and best publicized, of these colonization schemes was in the valley of the Río Papaloapan which drains from the mountains of Oaxaca southeast of Mexico City, to the Gulf coast south of Veracruz. Flood control and hydroelectric development combined with the settlement of farmers on private farms created a whole new community in an area that was previously almost unoccupied. Where the land can be irrigated the farms can be as much as 25 acres in size. Where crops can be raised without irrigation farms can be as much as 500 acres in size.

Land cultivated under the ejido system still produces the greater part

Aqueduct at Querétaro, built by the Spaniards and still in use, stands beside the Inter-American Highway

of Mexico's crops. Ejidos produce well over half of the wheat, rice, sesame, henequen, cotton and tobacco. Yet the yields on ejido lands are between 20 and 25 percent lower than on private holdings, due in part to the lack of technical skills. The great cotton-producing area around Torreón, in the north of Mexico, has suffered seriously because lack of rainfall in the mountains to the west has left the great reservoir almost empty. The ejidos, more than the new colonies, suffer from lack of careful land surveys to determine in advance the availability of water and the distribution of soils.

These general statements concerning Mexico's revolutionary changes summarize conditions over a great variety of kinds of country. The land redistribution program cannot be properly evaluated without a consideration of the underlying qualities of the land itself, and of differences in land use that distinguish one part of Mexico from another. If it is true that the average Mexican farmer in an ejido is poorer today than he was before the Revolution, as some people insist, then we need to understand the causes.

The Land

To what extent is the prevailing poverty of the Mexican farmers the result of the physical quality of the land? Is the present concentration of the population in the central area due to the special agricultural productivity of that area compared with other parts of the country? When the Spaniards first arrived on the scene they were attracted by the areas which were already densely settled by sedentary agricultural Indians and the outlying regions with their sparse populations were much less attractive. Concentration in the central area was so great that during the Díaz regime an attempt was made to promote the colonization of other parts of the national territory, but with discouraging results. Is this concentration of people in the central area, then, an inevitable result of the physical quality of the land or an evitable result of the way of living? If we assume that the Indians concentrated in Anáhuac, as they called this region, because of its relatively great adaptability to the production of maize as compared with the arid north, should we also assume that Anáhuac is still, even with European techniques, the region of highest productivity in Mexico? Or is the present concentration of people in the central area out of harmony with the potential productivity of the land? These and other problems cannot be answered until we understand more clearly the nature of the physical background of surface and climate.

The Mexican land is one of extraordinary diversity. A large part of the national territory is mountainous, and the mountains include some which have been produced by the erosion of streams in areas of contorted rock structures and some which have been produced by the explosive outburst of volcanic ash and lava. Well over half of Mexico is more than 3,000 feet above the sea; and only about a third of the country can be classed as level. Over all these surface features one finds contrasted types of climate, partly controlled by differences of altitude and partly by relation to the sources of moisture.

Surface Features

The major element of the surface configuration of Mexico is the great highland area which extends from the border of the United States southward to the Isthmus of Tehuantepec and which occupies most of the width of the country (Map 7). Although the highland is exceedingly complex in its geologic structure and its surface form, it is convenient for our purposes to think of it as being composed of two chief parts: a *central plateau* and a *dissected border*. The surface of the central plateau is cut by few deep canyons, yet it is by no means flat, for above the moderate slopes of its bolsons and intermont basins stand block ranges and volcanoes. In the north the bolsons are mostly between 3,000 and 4,000 feet in elevation, and the block ranges rise about 3,000 feet above them. South of the Bolson de Mayrán the general level of the plateau rises: the intermont basins are mostly between 7,000 and 8,000 feet, although some are as low as 5,000 feet; and above these basins great volcanoes reach elevations between 12,000 and more than 18,000 feet. The dissected borders of the highland, unlike the central plateau, have been deeply cut by streams. Furthermore, the relief of the western and eastern dissected borders is made more rugged by deep accumulations of volcanic material, so that on these two sides the rim of the highlands is higher than the central part. On the southern dissected border, south of Mexico City, the general highland level between 6,000 and 8,000 feet is preserved, not in the basins, but on the ridge crests, and streams have cut deep valleys below what was a continuous surface.

Outside of the great highland region with its dissected borders, there are three other surface divisions of Mexico: the block mountains and basins of the northwest; the lowlands of the Gulf coast and Yucatán on the east; and the highlands of Chiapas on the border of Guatemala.

In the northwest, the surface features of southern California and Arizona continue into Mexico. The Peninsula of Lower California is made up of tablelands and terraces surmounted by a few isolated block ranges with structures similar to those of the mountains east of San Diego. The Sonora desert which lies between the Gulf of California and the Sierra Madre Occidental is a mountain and bolson country, similar to the Mohave of southeastern California. Even the structural depression which forms the Imperial Valley of California continues southward to form the Gulf of California. Throughout the Mexican northwest rocky surfaces predominate, cut at wide intervals by the steep-sided, flat-bottomed valleys typical of arid lands.

On the eastern side of the highlands, the Gulf Coastal Plain of Texas continues southward into Mexico as far as Tampico, where it is pinched out by the outliers of the Sierra Madre Oriental, and by isolated volcanic necks which stand abruptly above the general level of the plain. South of Tampico the coastal lowland is relatively narrow and in many places is broken by promontories where the highlands extend to the edge of the water. The lowlands bordering the gulf widen out again, however, at the northern end of the Isthmus of Tehuantepec, and the whole of the Yucatán Peninsula is a low-lying plain, interrupted by only a few groups of hills. Yucatán resembles Florida in that it is made up of horizontal limestone formations of relatively recent age. In the limestone, solution caverns have been opened up, and where the roofs of the caverns have collapsed there are shallow sinks, known in Mexico as *cenotes*. The drainage is underground, and there are numerous clear limestone springs.

The Isthmus of Tehuantepec separates the southern dissected border of the great highland region from the *Highlands of Chiapas*. This is the northwestern end of the mountainous region which extends through Central America to the lowland of Nicaragua. In Mexico it is composed of parallel ranges of block mountains, inclosing a high rift valley. Along the Pacific is the crystalline range known as the *Sierra Madre de Chiapas*. Inland from this, and parallel to the coast, is the rift *Valley of Chiapas*, drained by a tributary of the Río Grijalva. On the northeastern side of this valley, there are several other ranges of block mountains, composed of folded and faulted strata and capped with volcanic materials—flows of lava and falls of ash. These mountains are much dissected by streams.

Few indeed are the places in this mountainous land where surfaces of gentle gradient are to be found. And unfortunately, where such surfaces are extensive, the climatic conditions are in one way or another unsuited to the kind of agriculture the Mexicans have wished to practice.

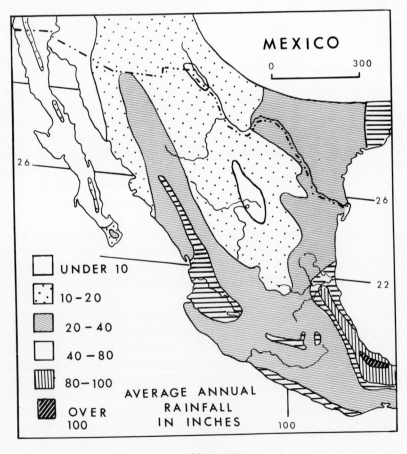

MEXICO

0   300

UNDER 10

10-20

20-40

40-80

80-100

OVER 100

AVERAGE ANNUAL
RAINFALL
IN INCHES

Map 16

Climates and Natural Vegetation

In a land of such rugged surfaces and of such contrasts of altitude within short distances the climatic conditions and the cover of natural vegetation have extremely spotty and irregular patterns. As in other mountainous countries, however, there is a general vertical zoning which becomes apparent when one disregards the many irregularities of detail.

The vertical zones of Mexico result from the general decrease of average temperatures with increasing altitude. The hot country, which the Mexican's call the *tierra caliente,* reaches to about 2,100 feet above sea level on the slopes of Mt. Orizaba near the east coast. Here there are tropical forests, and the land can be used to grow crops that cannot survive frosts, such as sugar cane. The land above this altitude is called the *tierra templada,* or temperate country. Here oaks are the common trees, and the major crop is coffee. This zone rises to about 6,000 feet. Above this is the zone known as *tierra fría,* or cold country. It includes the zone of conifers, above 11,400 feet as far as the upper limit of trees at about 13,100 feet. Between the tree line and the snow line there is a zone of mountain grasslands suited for the grazing of cattle. The snow line on Mt. Orizaba is about 14,600 feet.

Many writers emphasize the "temperate" nature of the climates of tropical countries at high altitudes. Altitude, they insist, compensates for the high temperatures of the low latitudes. They point out that places near the border of Mexico and the United States have approximately the same temperatures as places in the central plateau around Mexico City. The latter place, located south of latitude 20°n., has an average annual temperature of 60.1°, while El Paso, Texas, has an average of 63.0°. This comparison between average annual temperatures, however, only obscures the contrast in real temperatures between these two places. At Mexico City there is not only a much greater regularity in the daily changes of temperature, but the range between the average of the coldest and warmest months is very much less than the range at El Paso. A comparison follows:

COMPARISON OF TEMPERATURE CONDITIONS

	Mexico City	El Paso
Average of the year	60.1	63.0
Average of the warmest month	65.1 (May)	81.0 (July)
Average of the coldest month	54.3 (Jan.)	44.4 (Jan.)
Range between the monthly averages	10.8	36.6

Incidentally, El Paso, with a range between monthly averages of 36.6°, has a greater difference of temperature between summer and winter than any station in all of Latin America, including the similar latitudes of the southern hemisphere. The difference between a ten-degree range and a thirty-six-degree range spells the difference between a middle-latitude climate and the climate of a place at a high altitude in the tropics.

Most of the Mexican territory is deficient in moisture at least for part of the year.[2] The whole northern border of Mexico from the Pacific to the mouth of the Rio Grande passes through arid or semiarid climates. The very dry sections are in the northwest and in the northcentral part. A belt of arid country extends southward from western Texas almost to San Luis Potosí. Semiarid country includes all of the central plateau of the highlands except the southern and southwestern part—bounded by a line drawn roughly from Aguascalientes to Mexico City.

Climates with a rainy season which is not very rainy and a dry season which is really dry cover most of the rest of the country. The rainy season in Mexico generally comes in summer; but the northern part of the northwest shares with California the climatic regimen of winter rains and summer droughts. The central area receives most of its rain in summer, between June and September, during which period rain falls almost every day and the sky is generally filled with towering cumulus clouds. In fact so cloudy is the summer season in this part of Mexico that the maximum temperatures are experienced in May rather than July (see the climatic data for Mexico City in the Appendix).

Areas where the rainfall is adequate at all seasons of the year occur in only two sections of Mexico. There is one belt of dependable rainfall which extends southward from Tampico along the lower slopes of the Sierra Madre Oriental and crosses the Isthmus of Tehuantepec into the state of Tabasco. The other rainy section is along the Pacific coast of Chiapas, southeast of the Isthmus of Tehuantepec. These two areas together make up only about 12 percent of the Mexican territory.

Changes in the Mexican Economy

Considering all the handicaps to economic development Mexico has done quite well. The concentration of farmers raising maize in the central area where maize does poorly because of low temperatures and lack of rainfall posed a major problem, which is in process of being attacked by the establishment of farm colonies in places better suited to maize. Important new areas in the north and northwest have been irrigated. From

---

[2] An estimate of the relative areas of arid, semiarid, and rainy country in Mexico based on Thornthwaite's classification gives the following percentages of the total area (see E. N. Simpson, *op. cit.*):

Deficient in moisture throughout the year .... 49.9 percent
Deficient in moisture in the summer .... 1.4 percent
Deficient in moisture in the winter ....:.................... 35.9 percent
Deficient in moisture at no season .... 12.8 percent

the older irrigation districts of such places as Torreón, where the water supply has proved inadequate, people are now being transported for re-settlement in the wetter areas, such as the Highlands of Chipas near the Guatemala border. But agricultural improvement requires a reduction of the number of farmers. The proportion of people employed in farm-ing in relation to the total working force has dropped from 70 percent in 1930 to 58 percent in 1962. There has also been a marked decrease in the proportion of illiterates. Poverty has by no means been eliminated, but the national income is now more evenly spread among the people than it was even two decades ago.

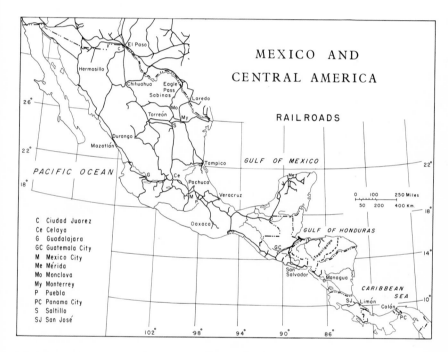

Map 17

The great problem of economic development is to increase the gross national product (the total value of goods and services) faster than the increase of population. This requires a balance between agricultural development and the development of manufacturing and service occupa-tions in the cities. After the initial decline in agricultural production resulting from the ejido program, there has been a steady increase. On the average, agricultural production in 1956 was 300 percent higher than in 1930. Between 1939 and 1956 the area under cultivation was increased some 33 percent to a total of nearly fifty million acres, including a 50 percent increase in the acreage under irrigation in the dry north and northwest. But the increase of production resulted not only from increase of area, but also from an increased production from each acre. This increase was brought about by the replacement of ox-drawn wooden plows or men with hoes by modern machinery, by the use of better seed, new breeding stock, and a variety of insecticides, fertilizers, and soil conditioners. All this increase of production could only be brought to the consumers as a result of improvements of the transporta-

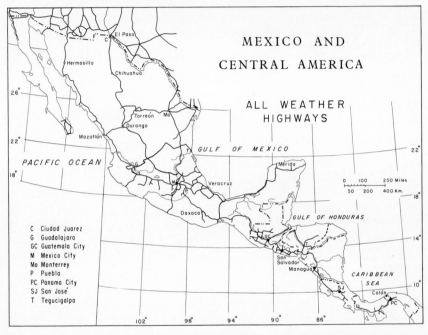

Map 18

tion system. Between 1945 and 1950 the railroads were all rebuilt on standard gauge (4 ft., 8½ in.). In 1939 Mexico had 5,660 miles of motor highways: in 1956 there were 21,130 miles of highways. The number of motor vehicles in the same period jumped from 139,000 to 622,000. Now more than half of the goods shipped within Mexico move by truck.

Since 1939 Mexican agriculture has been diversified. Maize still occupies more than half of Mexico's cultivated area and yields per acre of maize, long known as the lowest in the world, have been somewhat increased. But since 1939, the acreage of maize in the poorly-suited

Central Region has been decreased, and it has been increased in other regions. The acreage of wheat has been increased 300 percent since 1939, and that of rice 200 percent. Mexicans still eat three times as much maize as wheat, but since 1950 the per capita consumption of wheat has taken a sharp upward swing. Meanwhile crops grown for industrial use or for export have been changed. Mexico has now become the second country in the world in the export of cotton, and as a competitor of the United States in the world cotton markets, the Mexicans eye with great disfavor the use of North American cotton surpluses for sale at less than market prices in foreign countries. Mexico is now the third country in Latin America in the export of coffee, since 1950 passing the countries of Central America and Venezuela. Sugar-cane production is also greatly increased, and there are increased acreages devoted to fruit and vegetables.

The economic development has been balanced because along with the increase of agricultural production there also has been an increase of industrial production. Where modern agriculture is introduced, with a resulting decrease in the number of farm jobs, serious unemployment results unless new jobs are available in industry. Also if there is an increase in manufacturing industry and no accompanying increase in agricultural production, the new city workers find food scarce. The result is price inflation. In Mexico there has been a rapid rise of manufacturing to accompany the agricultural changes. Between 1940 and 1960, while the population was growing at a rate of about 3 percent per year the gross national product was increasing 6.5 percent per year. A large part of this increase was the result of a large investment in new capital formation, including expansion of the steel industry around Monterrey.

Manufacturing industry now accounts for a larger part of the gross national product than does agriculture. In 1940, agriculture, forestry and fishing contributed 20 percent to the national economy, and manufacturing industry contributed 16 percent. By 1960, when agriculture continued to contribute 20 percent, manufacturing industries contributed 26 percent. There was also a notable increase in the service occupations.

These rapid economic changes are reflected in the growth of the cities. Mexico City itself has grown faster than the others, expanding far beyond its political boundaries. There was also a rapid urban growth along the border of the United States, and in the irrigated areas of the North Pacific Region. But even the cities of the Central Region have grown, and in the Gulf Region entirely new cities have been founded. In 1962 about 44 percent of the Mexicans were living in cities.

Exports and Imports

The Revolution has had a considerable effect on the exports and imports of Mexico. Before 1910 the chief exports were minerals, and the chief imports were basic foods and railroad equipment. Even as late as the 1930's the chief exports were minerals (silver, gold, lead, zinc, copper, and antimony). Oil exports which started decreasing in the 1920's ceased altogether after 1938 when Mexico used all of its oil production for domestic purposes. Since 1939 the nature of the exports has changed rapidly. Agricultural exports (cotton, coffee, sugar, etc.), which made up 28 percent of the exports in 1939, made up 55 percent in 1955, but dropped to 36 percent in 1960. The leading exports are cotton, sugar, coffee, and frozen shrimp. The chief mineral exports include lead, zinc, and copper. Among the imports the basic foods have been decreasing and industrial goods and machinery have been increasing, making up half of the value of all imports in 1960. The leading customers for Mexico's products in 1961 were the United States (73 percent), Japan, West Germany, and Spain. The United States supplied 70 percent of the imports.

The port of Veracruz with the Plaza and Governor's Palace in the foreground

A very important part of Mexico's trade balance is derived from the increasing floods of tourists from the United States. The majority, of course, stop in the border cities, such as Tijuana or Nuevo Laredo, but increasing numbers now journey southward to Mexico City, Taxco, and Acapulco. Modern hotels in the cities and motels along the highways offer first-rate accommodations, and fine restaurants in the cities cater especially to the visitors. Since the 1950's the income from tourists has been the largest single source of national income.

The Mexican Economy Evaluated

The process of economic growth in Mexico offers an example of the importance of balanced development. The Mexican's use some 15 percent of the gross national product each year for new capital formation. This, together with a considerable investment from the United States, helps to support and modernize the economy at several different points simultaneously. This balanced approach to development is an often-overlooked essential, and Mexico demonstrates the results that can be expected when all aspects of the program are planned in advance. The purpose of decreasing the concentration of subsistence farmers in the Central Region has been served by increasing the agricultural area in the North Pacific, the North, and Gulf Regions. The reduction of the number of subsistence farmers everywhere has quickened the tempo of the economic life throughout the country. Notable has been the increase in small retail business in the villages and small towns. Before the ejido program went into effect the large landowners used to do a large part of their purchasing in Mexico City or in foreign countries. Now there is no part of the country where the retail stores have not felt an increase in business.

Foreign capital used to be invested in Mexico with little thought for the economic development of the country. A large part of the profits from the export of minerals or oil remained abroad. Foreign capital is still needed, and still welcomed; but only if it is invested on terms acceptable to the Mexicans. Between 1939 and 1950 $658,000,000 was taken out of Mexico in the form of profits and interest, but during the same period $300,000,000 was reinvested in Mexican enterprises. Since 1950 the trend is toward the reinvestment of a larger proportion of the profits.

There is still a great need for more capital, from both private and government sources. Large sums of money are needed for the kind of river-basin development and electric power development now being carried on in the valley of the Papaloapan, or for the construction of dams and irrigation works in the dry regions, or for the construction of all-weather motor highways. With political stability, Mexico would seem to offer an excellent opportunity for new investments.

The Political Situation

Since the Mexican Revolution of 1910 to 1915, Mexico has gone a long way toward the solution of the basic problem of establishing order and coherence within the state. Mexico is one of the countries of Latin America that has formulated a state-idea, sufficiently powerful to command the support of a great majority of the people. The system is not democratic, as we in the United States use this term; but it is distinctively Mexican.

Since the adoption of the constitution of 1917 and the election of General Carranza to the presidency, Mexico has been operated by only one political party. This was called the *Partido Revolucionario Nacional*. Since 1946, in order to indicate that the purposes of the Revolution were now accepted by every one, the party was renamed the *Partido Revolucionario Institucional*. Although other political parties (including those which are communist-inspired) are not prohibited, there has been no challenge to the authority of the P.R.I. When the president nears the end of his term of six years, and after consulting with other party leaders, he names his successor. The election, in which all citizens, men and women alike, express their opinions in a secret ballot, has only one slate of officers. The vote is an expression of support for the acts of the party leaders. The president has behind him the whole organization of the P.R.I. He names the governors of the states, and the members who may run for posts in the congress. He names the judges of the supreme court.

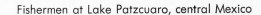

Fishermen at Lake Patzcuaro, **central Mexico**

Furthermore the party includes only civilians, and the Mexican army has become a strictly professional body.

Yet democracy of a kind is making its appearance in Mexico. The ejidos bring their members together in "town-meetings" for a discussion of local issues, and these issues are decided by vote of the majority. At the "grass-roots" level, democratic procedures are being nurtured.

The success of the Revolution and of the party in gaining the support of the overwhelming majority of the people of Mexico has cut the ground from under both fascists and communists. The extreme right is represented by the *Sinarquistas*, a group organized much like the famous "Black Shirts" of Mussolini's Italy. The communists have not failed for lack of effort, for certainly the position of Mexico on the border of the United States and the common fear of the United States entertained by many Mexicans would seem to offer the incentive and also the proper climate for communist infiltration. But the fact is that the Mexicans have a program of change, and it is one that is strictly their own. Foreign ideas, like communism, gain little support and the support has declined considerably since World War II.

The P.R.I. offers the only way into politics. But it embraces all shades of political opinion, from extreme right to extreme left. A person who seeks public office has only to prove his loyalty to the program of the Revolution. The other parties do not even trouble to organize slates of opposition candidates, so certain are the P.R.I. candidates of success. In Latin America any candidate for high political office uses a newspaper to give publicity to his views. But in Mexico even the newspapers are controlled by the P.R.I.—through the control of paper.

The Mexicans are a deeply religious people. This is one Latin-American country in which religion constitutes a real part of the state-idea. The Mexican Catholics focus their attention on the Virgin of Guadalupe, whose shrine is located near Mexico City. The Virgin is supposed to confer special favor on Mexicans; she is pictured as the ideal of Mexican motherhood. To a very real extent the Mexican state exists for the purpose of protecting and of supporting the ideals symbolized by the Virgin of Guadalupe.

The Mexicans are very close to the United States. Every school child studies history and in the history books he learns how the United States took the whole northern part of Mexico, and how the United States forces stormed the heights of Chapultepec and defeated the cadets of the Mexican military academy who were defending it. Along with the veneration of the Virgin of Guadalupe, the homage to the heroes of Chapultepec is also a part of the Mexican state-idea. Most of the Mexicans who can read hold an admiration for the economy of the United States; but there is also a widespread fear that the United States might again use its overwhelming power to force its weaker neighbors to adopt unwelcome polices. The Mexican is extremely conscious of his nationality, and proud of his government that can deal with other governments of the world as an equal. They are very sensitive to the suggestion of inferior status.

These attitudes are all a part of the state-idea that gives Mexico political cohesion and stability. Diverse racial groups, people of different social status, and of different income level, and people of all shades of political opinion, have become first of all Mexicans. Probably the poorest class is no better off than it was before the Revolution, and it has increased in absolute numbers. But meanwhile there has been a very great increase in the urban middle classes; and for these people the future offers hope. And all Mexicans look with pride at their writers, artists, and musicians who give expression to the deeper meanings of the changes that have swept over their country.

A street in Guanajuato reflecting the colonial atmosphere

CHAPTER FOUR

The Central American Countries

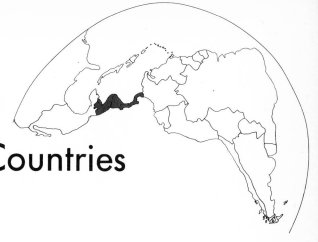

Central America is the long, narrow isthmus that extends eastward and southward from Mexico to the continent of South America. The traditional countries in this area are Guatemala, El Salvador, Honduras, Nicaragua, and Costa Rica. Panamá, which was formerly a part of Colombia, is sometimes included as a Central American country. British Honduras is still a colonial possession of Great Britain.

The isthmus is mostly mountainous. A backbone of highlands faces the Pacific coast with a steep escarpment as far southeastward as the Gulf of Fonseca. From this Gulf the Nicaraguan Lowland crosses the isthmus to the Caribbean. Southeast of the lowland a succession of curving mountain ranges, surmounted by volcanoes, bends through Panamá to the border of Colombia. There are narrow coastal lowlands on either side, and small basins set among the mountains in which population is concentrated.

The climatic conditions depend in part on altitude, and in part on position with reference to the winds. The Caribbean coast, with on-shore prevailing easterly winds is very rainy. It was once covered with a dense rain forest. The Pacific coast, on the other hand, has a rainy season in summer and a distinct dry season in winter. The vertical zones are similar to those of Mexico (Map 19).

Each of the countries has its own distinctive character. They are notable for the export of bananas and high-grade coffee, but none is really prosperous. Politically they range from a traditional dictatorship to a well-developed democracy. There are few generalizations that can be applied to the whole group, except that they share a similar habitat and that they are currently seeking to develop a degree of economic cooperation through the organization of a common market.

Maps 1, 3, 5, 7, 10, 12, 14, 17, 18, 19 are pertinent to this chapter.

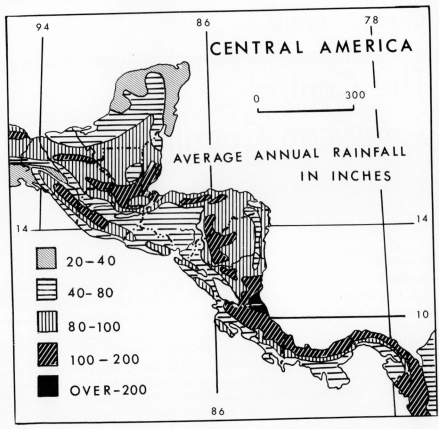

Map 19

GUATEMALA

Guatemala, even more than Mexico, is an Indian country. A larger proportion of the population lives in the Indian manner, speaks no Spanish, and raises only subsistence crops for local use. A minority of people of Spanish origin and of mixed Indian and Spanish, controls the national politics, carries on commercial agriculture with the help of the Indian workers, and forms the national character which people outside know as Guatemala. Between these two groups there is a vast gulf, and less has been done to bridge the gap than in any other Latin-American country where Indians form a majority of the population.

Guatemala's political troubles are intimately involved in the social and economic problems of the country. The Indian majority remains an economic burden, in spite of the fact that some Guatemalans think of the low price of Indian labor as one of the "natural resources" of the country. The Indian remains inert politically, scarcely even an interested spectator at the events that brought the communists to power behind a government willing to serve the wishes of Soviet foreign policy. The contrasts between Guatemala and Mexico are important to understand.

The People

Guatemala has the largest population of any country in Central America. In fact, something like 31 percent of the people who occupy the isthmus between the border of Mexico and the border of Colombia are in Guatemala. Yet only the southern third of the country is densely populated (Map 1, pages 6-7). In the high basins of the mountains bordering the Pacific coast there are densities comparable to those of the central area of Mexico. The whole northern third of the country, the part known as Petén, has almost no permanent inhabitants. This is the part which is in the tropical forests of the Yucátan Peninsula, on the border of Mexico and British Honduras. Here the national boundaries are drawn through country which lies outside of the effective national territory of either Mexico or Guatemala. The remainder of Guatemala is only thinly inhabited, and there is ample room for new settlement, or for the expansion of the older settled areas. Nearly half of the national territory has no permanent settlement.

Guatemala's population, like that of many of the Latin-American countries, increased slowly until recent years. During the first quarter of the nineteenth century, when Guatemala gained its independence, the population was estimated at about 500,000. By 1865 the number had grown to about 1,180,000. A census in 1921 counted just over 2,000,000; and another census in 1950 counted 2,788,000. From these figures the natural rate of increase (excess of births over deaths) was about 26 per thousand. Since 1950 the rate has gone up sharply to over 30 per thousand. The population in 1962 was estimated at nearly 4,000,000.

Guatemala's rate of increase was similar to that of Mexico, but the birth rates and death rates were quite different. Guatemala had the highest birth rate of all Latin America (51 per thousand, compared with 45 per thousand in Mexico), but the death rate was exceeded only by that of El Salvador (Guatemala 21 per thousand, compared with 15 per thousand in Mexico). These figures give some measure of the social effects of economic development.

The population of Guatemala remains overwhelmingly Indian. The proportion of people of unmixed Indian ancestry is about 60 percent. Another 35 percent is of mixed ancestry in which there is a large pro-

Maya Indian weavers

portion of Indian. Only 5 percent of the people are of unmixed Spanish ancestry. There are almost no Negroes. Estimates of the proportion of people of different racial inheritance, however, are complicated by the confusion of race with culture or way of living. Any one in Guatemala who does not live like an Indian, yet is not pure European, is called a *ladino*. How many ladinos are racially pure Indian cannot be determined from the census data. The Indians are the descendants of the Mayas, whose civilization once extended over most of Yucatán, and whose cities, overgrown with forest, are only now being rediscovered from air photographs.

The Pattern of Settlement

In Guatemala, as in Mexico, the distribution of Indians in the pre-conquest period has been reproduced in the modern patterns of population. The high basins of the southern highlands were occupied by a relatively dense group of sedentary agricultural people whose basic food crop was maize. The present town of Quezaltenango was the focus of this pre-Spanish settlement. Outside of the highland area, the rest of what is now Guatemala had a relatively small population of shifting cultivators or nomadic hunters and fishers.

The Spanish conquerors entered Guatemala from Mexico during the first decade after Cortés had founded Mexico City. The first expedition reached the southern highlands in 1523, and founded the first Spanish town on the site of the present Guatemala City in 1524. Antigua, founded in 1541, became the political center from which the whole Captaincy-General of Guatemala was administered (Map 14, page 39). In 1544, Father Bartolomé de Las Casas, who led the movement to prohibit the enslavement of the Indians, founded at Cobán the first of the Spanish missions in America.

Compared with Mexico, however, Guatemala yielded little in the way of quick wealth. To be sure there were silver mines near Huehuetenango, and these mines are still productive. But the ore bodies of this part of the Spanish domain proved disappointing. Many of the Spaniards moved on southeastward along the isthmus. The few who remained were granted large estates which they developed in the traditional Spanish manner. The greater part of each estate was used for the grazing of cattle or not used at all. On the better lands the owner tried to establish some kind of commercial agriculture that could pay the high cost of shipment.

In the course of time the highland area, which was the only part of Guatemala that was settled, was divided into two sharply contrasted regions. The line of division was roughly the 5,000 foot contour, the line which in this area marks the division between tierra templada below and tierra fría above. The tierra templada was the part preferred by the Spaniards; the tierra fría was left for the Indians. Guatemala City, just under 5,000 feet above sea level, on the divide between the rivers draining to the Caribbean and those draining to the Pacific, was near the boundary between these two contrasted regions of settlement. The country below 5,000 feet was mostly in the southeastern part of the highlands, in the drainage basin of the Río Motagua, and along the upper parts of the escarpment where the highlands drop down to the Pacific. The country above 5,000 feet was located mostly in the southwestern part of the highlands. The third part of the country, the lowlands of the tierra caliente below 1,600 feet, remained almost empty until the development of the banana plantations of the twentieth century. The vast area of the Department of Petén in northern Guatemala is covered with dense forest, crisscrossed by a maze of footpaths used by the chicle gatherers in going to and from the camps where the gum is prepared for shipment. This is the world's major source of chicle for chewing gum, yet this whole area, some 33 percent of the total national territory, is occupied by less than 1 percent of the total population.

The Economic Situation

There are three chief economic areas in Guatemala. The Indian country in the southwest is used for subsistence farming, with maize as the chief crop. The Indian communities hold their lands in common, and because they are crowded onto the narrow ridges that extend finger-like between the valleys, there is no room for expansion. The lower parts of the highlands below the 5,000-foot contour, are now used mostly for coffee plantations, owned by Guatemalans. And the coastal lowlands on either side of the isthmus, which were once almost unoccupied, have now been developed by the United Fruit Company for banana plantations.

Looking only at the commercial part of the economy, we find that since 1950 Guatemala has become almost a one-crop country. Coffee exports since 1950 have made up between 70 and 80 percent of the value of all exports. The wealthy people, the government officials, especially those who handle the finances of the country, are primarily concerned with coffee. No wonder the local newspapers use big headlines to describe the arrival of frosts in São Paulo, and list in detail the changes in the price of coffee in New York. No country whose economic life is so closely attached to just one product, and to one that fluctuates so unpredicably in price, can be described as free from foreign domination.

Before 1950 Guatemala was one of the "banana republics." The United Fruit Company began to develop banana plantations in the empty tierra caliente in 1906. The company built special banana docks and a railroad to handle shipments across the isthmus. Bananas made up more than 20 percent of the exports. But in this case, even more than in the case of coffee, the vital decisions affecting Guatemala were made by one foreign corporation. The one thing that could unite all political factions in the capital city was the dislike of the United Fruit Company. Conditions became so uncertain that the company preferred to increase its investments in other places rather than in Guatemala. By 1955, banana exports made up less than 10 percent of the total, and only some ten or eleven thousand workers were employed on company plantations. In 1957, however, conditions had improved so much that the company began a five-year program of replanting.

The government would like to diversify the commercial agriculture. It is pleased with the increased production along the Pacific lowland of such crops as sugar cane, abacá, cacao, and pineapples. Among the exports, also, are small amounts of chicle, honey, hides, and lumber. But all these crops and forest products taken together do not cover as large an acreage as the one basic subsistence crop—maize.

Guatemala's foreign trade is, from a Guatemalan point of view, too closely tied to the United States. Even as late as 1956 the United States took over 70 percent of the exports, and supplied from 60 to 70 percent of the imports. The government has been attempting to decrease the dependence on the United States. In 1961 dependence on the United States for purchase of the exports was reduced to a little over 50 percent, and new markets had been found in West Germany, Japan, and the Netherlands. Imports from the United States were cut below 50 percent.

The Political Situation

By 1954 the communists had almost consolidated their control of Guatemala. Why should they have been so successful in Guatemala? What were the distinctive conditions in this country that gave the communists such an opportunity?

The difficulty of establishing a coherent state out of the diverse social groups in Guatemala has been, and still is, very great. The cultural isolation of the Maya has yet to be broken down. Meanwhile there are increasing numbers of "white collar" workers in Guatemala City who are demanding that the Indians be included as first-class citizens of the country. These city people are idealistic, literate, and strongly nationalistic. They demand an end to the succession of military dictatorships, and to the traditional system of privilege for the politically powerful minorities. Here, as elsewhere in Latin America, there is a restless discontent with the old order of things, and this discontent has not gained political expression through normal channels.

Guatemala had an early history not unlike that of Mexico. In fact

Primitive wooden plow and deforested slopes in Guatemala

when Mexico declared independence from Spain in 1821, the whole of the Viceroyalty of New Spain was included. But in 1823, the more remote Central American part of Mexico broke away. Chiapas remained with Mexico. The break developed through the thinly inhabited country between the cluster of people in Chiapas and the almost exclusively Indian cluster around Quezaltenango. The Indians were not especially concerned about what country they were in. With this screen of indifference lying between Chiapas and Guatemala City, the people in the latter city were able to declare and make good their separate existence.

When Guatemala declared independence from Mexico, it included all the territory formerly included in the Captaincy-General of Guatemala except Chiapas (Map 25). Again, however, the difficulty of communications along the miserable roads connecting one cluster of people to another made administration difficult. The only purpose of the independence movement was freedom from outside interference. At the start this was directed against Spain; then it was directed against Mexico City; and in 1839 it was directed against Guatemala City. In 1839, El Salvador and Nicaragua broke away from Guatemala; and the still more remote Honduras and Costa Rica became independent more because of geographic position than because of any local feeling of nationality.

Guatemala started its own independent existence with no positive state-idea. The large landowners and the army officers had complete control of the new country, and no powerful voice suggested that the Indians should have any rights except to work. The political leaders tended to perpetuate their hold on the higher offices, and could not be shaken loose until the younger army officers, frustrated in their ambition to gain the financial rewards of high office, could develop the power to stage a revolution, a coup d'ètat. When discontent stirred too dangerously, the governments in power found that they could command a kind of coherence and order by pressing claims for the territory of British Honduras, which was then, and still is, claimed by Guatemala. The one thread tying all political groups together continued to be the resentment toward all foreign interference.

Matters were complicated when, in 1906, the United Fruit Company began operations in Guatemala. The company directed its attention to a part of the national territory until then almost unoccupied. It created economic values in areas previously outside of the effective national territory. And the revenue from taxes on banana exports provided a much-needed support for the treasury. But here was an obviously foreign enterprise, operated on entirely different principles from those common in Guatemala. Here was a part of the national territory in which even the laws were administered separately. In an economic sense it was good—but it definitely was not Guatemalan. When the company used its influence to gain advantages with the Guatemalan government, the resentment of the Guatemalans grew stronger and stronger. Nothing, not even a dispute with Great Britain over British Honduras, was as politically popular in Guatemala as an attack on the United Fruit Company. And since the company represented the United States, resentment of the United States was also strong.

Guatemala, like Mexico, was governed by a succession of military dictatorships. Like Mexico, too, some were liberal in policy, actually concerning themselves with the increasing poverty of the farm workers. All were strong when they started, and until overthrown, maintained the country in order and quiet. The last of the Guatemalan dictators was General Jorge Ubico who ran the country from 1931 to 1944.

Over the years an increasingly large and vocal group of students, professors, and government workers developed in Guatemala City. These people were greatly influenced by the Mexican Revolution, and many of them went to Mexico to study the changes taking place there. With the usual few interested in revolution for its own sake, there was a core of genuine liberals, concerned with establishing democracy, with ending the system of power and privilege—be it domestic or foreign. When General Ubico's dictatorship was overthrown in 1944, the liberals, who had been in exile, were able to take control of the government and demand an election. In this election the liberal-minded civilian Juan José Arévalo was named as president. A new constitution was adopted in 1945, in which numerous social reforms, patterned on the Mexican reforms, were presented. These reforms included measures to give the Indian all the rights of citizenship, to provide workers with social security, and with the right to form labor unions. Minimum wage laws were enacted. For obvious political reasons, all these measures were applied strictly to the United Fruit Company, but much less strictly on the plantations of the coffee-growers. Included also was a program of land redistribution, patterned on the Mexican law. Land not in use was to be expropriated and given to the landless peasants. Again, the law was applied vigorously to the property of the United Fruit Company (which owned a considerable area of tierra caliente still undeveloped, awaiting the expansion of the banana plantations), and much less vigorously to the property of the large landowners.

In 1951 Arévalo was succeeded by Jacobo Arbenz Guzmán. Arbenz has been described as an ambitious junior officer, long frustrated in his hope for advancement, and in his desire for wealth. He was one of the three who plotted the revolution of 1944. When he became president in 1951, Arbenz relied heavily on the support of the communists. A small, tightly organized group of communists had been successful in identifying communism with the social revolution started by Arévalo. They were aided by the unfortunate habit of the conservative landowners of labeling all social change as communist. The communists took the credit for the new social legislation and the land reform. Under Arbenz members of the party were the ones who supervised the land expropriation and redistribution; they were responsible for encouraging groups of peasants to seize land from the landowners. Meanwhile other party members gained control of the Guatemala radio station. The air was filled with Moscow-inspired descriptions of "Yankee imperialism," and with other propaganda directed against the United States. All this was highly popular because it took advantage of the strong sentiment of nationalism and the dislike of the United States, the most immediate focus of irritation. As Robert J. Alexander puts it, the communists "managed to divert a healthy movement for bringing democracy and social progress to Guatemala down the blind alley of international communist propaganda aimed at serving the ends of Soviet foreign policy."[1]

In 1954, a group of exiled Guatemalan army officers under Col. Carlos Castillo Armas organized a small force in neighboring Honduras. When this "army" marched across the border, the Guatemalan army refused to attack it. Soon the capital was occupied and Arbenz was forced to flee. Castillo Armas then assumed the presidency, which he held until his assassination in 1957.

The new government included many supporters who were opposed not only to the communists but also to the whole program of social reform. In many cases the land that had been expropriated was seized again by the landowners. Castillo Armas did, however, establish a new land-reform program, not under communist control. An effort was made to get the Indians to move onto government-owned land along the fertile Pacific Lowland. Idle land on the large estates was expropriated, but with proper compensation to the owners, and in these places also the landless peasants were settled. On the Mexican model, government technicians were attempting to turn the Indian subsistence farmers into producers of cash crops. Under the communists the title to the land remained with the government, but the new law gives the colonist possession of the land, and forbids resale for 25 years. A new tax was levied on idle land held by the large landowners in the effort to decrease the unproductive area. A part of the whole program was financed by a loan from the United States.

All this violence and turmoil gives evidence of a deep-seated unrest. It is not the Indian group that provides the unrest, but rather the new urban class in the capital and the smaller towns, and the organized workers on the coffee plantations and the banana plantations. The basic purposes—an end to the system of privilege, equality of treatment of the Indian, modern social legislation, opportunity to own land—are all changes in the traditional system that are being demanded throughout

[1] Robert J. Alexander, *Communism in Latin America*, New Brunswick (New Jersey), 1957; reference on page 350.

Latin America. Unfortunately the political leaders of Guatemala were unable to discern the hidden dangers in communist participation. The communists offered the most effective attack on the United States as well as on the persons occupying positions of prestige in Guatemala. That the communists, as always, were serving the interests of another foreign power, was not apparent at first, and when it did become apparent it was too late. But to eliminate the Communists by force is not enough. In the long run political expression must be given to the mounting pressure for social change. If the pressure remains pent-up for too long a time, the result can only be another explosion, and perhaps another opportunity for the communists to return to power.

BRITISH HONDURAS

The colony of British Honduras has been described as one of the world's tiny sore spots. But in a world with many sore spots, and many that are not tiny, a place in a remote location can easily be neglected. British Honduras, with its 94,000 inhabitants grouped around the town of Belize (50,000), is such a place. Its population is predominantly Negro, with a very small white group consisting of British civil servants, military people, and Anglican missionaries. Along the coast there are perhaps 6,000 native Indians and Negro-Indian mixtures who support themselves by fishing and raising manioc. In the wet forests of the backlands there are perhaps as many as 20,000 Maya Indians. They live in small villages and grow maize.

The products of British Honduras come mostly from the forests. One is chicle, the raw material from which chewing gum is manufactured; the other is mahogany. Both require only seasonal work, and a system of labor recruitment is followed which leaves the workers permanently in debt to the companies. Near Belize there are small areas devoted to the growing of citrus fruits and coconuts. A once-thriving cacao industry has now been entirely abandoned. The chief exports—mahogany and chicle— are marketed in the United States rather than in Great Britain.

British Honduras is claimed by Guatemala. This British possession is a remnant of the former British holdings on the Caribbean coast of Central America, which extended southward as far as the mouth of the San Juan River in Nicaragua. The Miskito Coast was occupied by the Nicaraguans after the British delayed their withdrawal. But the British have been unwilling to withdraw from their holding on the wet eastern side of the Peninsula of Yucatán. The British claim was recognized by the Spanish king in 1670. But the Guatemalans insist that the British have failed to carry out certain agreements, such as the construction of a road to provide eastern Guatemala with access to the Caribbean. There can be no doubt that the easiest outlet to the sea from the whole northern part of Guatemala is through Belize, and if important oil sources should be discovered in this area, the need for an outlet might become pressing. But the British are reluctant to hand over the English-speaking Negro populations of this colony to Guatemala. Guatemala, we may recall, is governed by people of mestizo or pure Spanish ancestry who have expressed a strong anti-Negro bias, and who have never accepted the importation of Negro workers into the banana plantations along the coast. The result is an impasse, in which the Guatemalans are denied the access to the coast which might permit the economic development of the empty northern part of their country, and in which at the same time the British taxpayers must continue to carry the burden of a dependent colony. The people of British Honduras suffer from poverty and illiteracy, and from a rate of increase that has already far outrun the local food supply.

EL SALVADOR

The problems of land and people, as we have seen, are quite different from country to country. But nowhere are the contrasts more sharply drawn than in Central America. Little El Salvador, the smallest of the twenty Latin American republics in terms of area, has an over-all popula-

Cattle on the way to market on a section of the Inter-American Highway near San Salvador

tion density exceeded only by that of Haiti. With a population of nearly three million living on a national territory of only 8,260 square miles the total density per square miles is 334. Such a comparison of total population and total land area is valid, as it is not in most other countries, because El Salvador shares with Uruguay, Cuba, Haiti, Jamaica, and Trinidad the distinction of occupying all of its national territory. The pressure of population on the land base is aggravated by the system of land tenure and results in widespread poverty, illiteracy, hunger, and disease.

The population of El Salvador is much less Indian than is that of either Guatemala or Mexico. Although 89 percent of the people have some Indian ancestors (11 percent pure Indian, 78 percent mestizo), very few of these people still speak Indian languages or continue to live in the manner of the Indians. To a much greater degree than among the Mayas, the Pipil tribes of El Salvador have adopted the culture of the Spaniards. The 11 percent that is of pure Spanish descent forms the land-owning aristocracy and the majority of politically powerful people.

The Economic Situation

The greater part of the area of El Salvador is owned by some fourteen very wealthy families. Coffee, the leading product of the country, is produced on their estates. The tenant farmers make use of the poorer soils and steeper slopes to grow subsistence crops of maize, rice, and beans. Maize occupies more acreage than all other crops combined. At lower altitudes the chief crops are cotton and sugar cane.

Efforts at economic development are focused chiefly on new sources of electric power, and on manufacturing industries. In 1957 the Rocke-fellers' International Basic Economic Corporation built a plant in San Salvador to manufacture soluble coffee. In 1961 this product made up 2 percent of the value of exports.

Nevertheless, the chief economic problem of El Salvador is the in-creasing pressure of population on the limited land base. With a high birth rate (well over 40 per thousand), any success in providing the people with modern medical care and better food results in an immediate and frightening net increase of the population. With a density already too great for the kind of agricultural economy that prevails, any in-crease results in more hunger and distress. El Salvador's net increase of population in the period 1950-1955 was only 23 per thousand. But the only reason why the net increase was not larger was that El Salvador had the dubious distinction of having the highest death rate in all Latin America, with the possible exception of Haiti—25 per thousand. Less than half of the people can read or write.

The foreign trade of El Salvador is tied to one product. In 1961 coffee made up 59 percent of the value of all exports. Cotton made up 18 percent. Smaller items included frozen shrimp, soluble coffee, and vegetable oil. Of all the exports, the United States took 35 percent, West Germany 9 percent, and the Netherlands 8 percent. Some 37 percent of the imports came from the United States, and lesser amounts came from West Germany, the Netherlands, and Japan. During World War II the share of the United States in El Salvador's trade was much higher, and even as late as 1953 was over 80 percent of the exports and over 60 percent of the imports. El Salvador, like all the Central American countries, prefers to trade with a variety of nations rather than to depend wholly on the United States.

The Political Situation

Every six years or so El Salvador goes through the motions of an election. Not uncommonly the president does not complete his term of office before he is removed by a revolt of his younger officers. In any case the army remains in control, and the army is strictly anticommunist. The political power in El Salvador, however, has rested fundamentally on the fourteen families who constitute the aristocracy of landowners. These families are, of course, entirely opposed to reforms of any kind.

El Salvador, on the other hand, is in the forefront of a new development in Latin-American politics, which is quite likely to become widespread. The officers of the army recognize the necessity of social and economic reform. They are liberals, in the Latin-American sense, meaning that they are opposed to autocracy of either the right or left, and recognize the pressing need for a change in the traditional system of privilege. In the Latin-American way these officers are promptly labeled as communists, or at least "pink." Yet they are vigorously opposed to the Communist Party. They are also in vigorous opposition to the rule of the fourteen families. The stage is set for a major political battle.

In 1961 an election brought into power a reform-minded, liberal group of army officers. This group of government leaders gave its wholehearted support to the program of the Alliance for Progress. With financial and technical assistance, the government has built a new hydroelectric plant on the Río Lempa, and has continued to support the expansion of manufacturing industries. The port of Acajutla has been modernized. It has breakwaters and new wharves with the newest loading and unloading equipment. The government has also made available for farm settlement certain areas hitherto used only for the pasture of cattle. By developing irrigation systems it has made some of these lands in the Lempa Valley and along the coast potentially more productive than ever before. Still, El Salvador has no unused land, and the pressure of people on the land base must be relieved chiefly by the development of urban industries. The properties of the fourteen families are still used in the traditional manner, and the owners have organized a vigorous campaign against land reform.

It is not for people outside of El Salvador to pass judgment on the issues of their domestic politics. But the issues must be understood. Naturally, the owners of land resist any effort to reduce the basis of their wealth. And naturally the landless peasants, many with new knowledge of reading and writing and with unaccustomed good health due to the new programs of sanitation and medicine, are demanding a larger share of the wealth and an end to the system of special privilege. Some observers insist that forcibly restricting this popular unrest will encourage a major explosion, and that liberal reforms constitute the only safe program. The industrial and democratic revolutions are in the process of changing unchangeable El Salvador—as they are elsewhere in Latin America.

New hydroelectric installation on the Río Lempa

HONDURAS

Honduras is second among the Central American states in terms of area; but its population of about 2,000,000 is less than that of its small neighbor, El Salvador. However, no valid comparison can be made between population densities in relation to total national territories in Honduras and El Salvador because a large part of northeastern Honduras lies outside the effective national territory. The population is grouped in several small clusters in the highlands of the southwest and in the valleys and coastal lowlands of the north. The problem of establishing national political and social unity has been aggravated by the rivalry of these separated clusters of people, notably by those of Tegucigalpa, Comayagua, and San Pedro Sula; but the revenue from banana exports provides a certain degree of stability because it gives the group in power a measure of strength with which to control internal rivalries.

The racial make-up of the population of Honduras differs in certain significant ways from that of any of its neighbors. The Lenca Indians differed from the Mayas in that their way of living was much less complex and their grip on the land much less firm; they differed from the Pipil Indians in that they were more warlike. Like the Pipil tribes, however, the Lencas have given up the Indian way of living, have learned Spanish, wear Spanish types of clothing, and have become indistinguishable from the mestizos as an element of the population. It should be noted, however, that Honduras includes, near the border of Guatemala, one important community that is Maya in origin. This is the cluster of people around Copán. Here the characteristic Mayan communal village forms a pattern of settlement unusual in Honduras. It is estimated that 96 percent of the people of Honduras have some Indian ancestors (10 percent pure Indian, 86 percent mestizo). People of unmixed Spanish descent make up only 2 percent of the total. The remaining 2 percent are Negroes who are concentrated in the banana lands along the Caribbean coast.

The Economic Situation

None of these diverse peoples, living in isolated clusters in the highlands, shared any sense of belonging together when Honduras became an independent country. In a sense a degree of unity has been produced by the pressure of more vigorous neighbors, especially by El Salvador. People in Honduras today are beginning to feel a sense of nationalism.

The economy, meanwhile, remains split between the banana-growers

Mayan statuary at Copán

Maya temple at Copán with insert of temple step which pivoted to throw enemies into dungeon beneath

of the Caribbean lowlands and the coffee-growers of the highlands. The coffee is produced on plantations that are operated by the owners. There are large land properties in Honduras, as in El Salvador, but they do not include so large a proportion of the total area. The large properties are used mostly for the pasture of cattle. The crop that occupies some 37 percent of all the cultivated land is maize. Maize and kaffir corn (*maicillo*), along with beans and rice, furnish the greater part of the diet of the Honduran workers. Wheat and meat are consumed chiefly in the cities by small groups of well-to-do people who are the more prosperous farmers or who make a living from politics and government service.

The coastal lowlands of Honduras, like the *tierra caliente* of Guatemala, were thinly occupied before the large fruit companies began operations. Two North American companies—the United Fruit Company and the Standard Fruit Company—cleared the forests, drained the swamps, built flood-control systems, fertilized the soil, wiped out mosquitoes, and turned the lowlands into highly productive banana plantations. In the 1950's Honduras was the leading exporter of bananas in the whole world. But then banana diseases, and the increasing competition of Ecuador began to reduce the share of Honduras in the world market. In 1961 Honduras exported only 13 percent of the world's bananas; but these exports provided 45 percent of the value of all Honduran exports. The planting of bananas in Honduras is likely to be reduced, and efforts are being made to increase the production of other export crops.

Two other elements of the economy come from the highlands. Honduras makes use of its pine forests, which grow in the *tierra fría,* to support a considerable lumber industry. Pine timber made up 10 percent of the Honduran exports in 1961, and a paper manufacturing plant has been built to process some of the pine locally. There is also some production of silver from mines near Tegucigalpa, the capital.

Honduras is closely tied to the markets of the United States in its exports and imports. In 1961 the United States purchased 54 percent of the exports, and supplied 53 percent of the imports.

The Political Situation

The people who live in the banana region along the Caribbean coast are worlds apart from those who live in the highlands of Honduras. To be sure, the banana region is reached easily from Tegucigalpa by air, and now a motor road and a railroad make land travel possible between coast and highland through San Pedro Sula. But for most of the people contacts are remote indeed.

According to Robert J. Alexander, "the country's whole north coast is dominated by two banana firms, . . . which command what are virtually states within a state, not only owning the land, but providing practically all the public and social services, and controlling the whole economic, social, and, until the 1950's, the political life of the region."[2] Here the foreign engineers and agronomists have created what they regard as a tropical paradise. The fever-ridden coastal swamps, which come closer to meriting the description "steaming jungle" than any other part of the tropics, have been transformed into a healthful, pleasant, and attractive landscape. In the modern homes and well-planned villages, workers live far better than they do in the traditional villages of the highlands. The company agricultural college, the company schools, the company recreation centers, and the company stores—all these things were developed for the purpose of bringing to Honduras the advantages of the North American way of living.

Why, then, should the workers want to strike? There are some North Americans who see in the greater political freedom experienced in the banana area since 1950 nothing but communist intrigue. Yet the communists never have achieved the importance that they did in Guatemala. When the banana workers did strike in 1954 many people blamed communist agitators from Guatemala; others, however, insisted that the strike represented certain grievances among the workers that had remained unexpressed before that time. Perhaps the greatest obstacle to an understanding of the situation is the difficulty of accepting the idea expressed by the words: *Es bueno, pero no es nuestro.* The fundamental urge to escape from foreign domination, which has characterized Latin American political thinking for more than a century, includes the desire to escape from the benefits of foreign ideas. The desire for freedom to make one's own mistakes is a very basic urge, not only in Latin America, but also throughout the underdeveloped world.

Honduras has, until recently, never experienced anything but a military dictatorship. Because the treasury was never very well filled, army discontent has not been uncommon. Revolutionary change was the only possible political process by which one administration could succeed another. From 1933 to 1948, General Tiburcio Carias Andino completely dominated the political life, maintaining order by military force, at least in the settled parts of the country. Since 1948 there has been some increase of political activity, marked by a rise of a liberal party with a program of social reform. Still, only a small proportion of the people of Honduras are involved in political decisions. In 1957 an honest election was held, in which a record 30 percent of the total population was eligible to vote. Actually only 18 percent of the total population voted, but the decision of this small politically conscious group was overwhelming support for the liberals. That such an election could be

---

[2] Robert J. Alexander, *Communism in Latin America,* New Brunswick (New Jersey), 1957; reference on pages 371-372.

held, even for a small proportion of the people, represents an important step forward toward democratic procedures. Not unexpectedly, the army put an end to this duly elected government in 1963 and reestablished a tight control of Honduran politics. Reform, it seemed, was coming too fast.

It is important also to note the position of Honduras with respect to its neighbors. In this part of Central America the countries that developed around the larger and more distinctive clusters of. people were Guatemala, El Salvador, and Nicaragua. These countries have developed a strong sense of nationalism, and compete aggressively with each other. Again and again Honduras has been subject to pressures from outside to throw its support to one or another of the others. Since the others were fairly evenly balanced, Honduras has often been in a position to play the decisive role. And on many occasions outside pressures have disturbed the internal affairs of Honduras.

NICARAGUA

Nicaragua is another country that is built around one central core of concentrated settlement. Largest in area of all the Central American countries, its population (estimated in 1962 as 1,552,000) is less than that of Honduras. Although the early history of Nicaragua was involved with the rivalry between two separate centers of settlement, León and Granada, the two have now grown together to form one single cluster of people. Large parts of Nicaragua are outside of the effective national territory.

The one nucleus of concentrated settlement occupies the Nicaraguan Lowland. It was in the lowland that the Spanish explorers found concentrations of Indians, whereas the highlands were even more thinly populated by native people than were those of Honduras. Spanish settlement, here as elsewhere, closely followed the pattern of Indian settlement.

The lowland Indians of Nicaragua, however, disappeared as a distinctive group early in the period of colonization by the Spaniards. To be sure, many mestizo children were produced, and today it is estimated that some 69 percent of the Nicaraguans are of mixed Indian and Spanish ancestry. Pure Indians make up only about 5 percent of the population, and these are found in the more remote parts of the country. The people of unmixed Spanish descent make up about 17 percent. Along the east coast the considerable concentrations of Negroes make up another 9 percent of the total.

The fact that Nicaragua is made up of one nucleus of concentrated settlement gives it a kind of unity it might not otherwise enjoy. The settlements of the Miskito Coast along the Caribbean, and the gold-mining communities inland from them, are remote indeed from the centers of Nicaraguan life. The government collects its tax on gold exports. If the banana planting had proved as profitable along the Miskito Coast as it did along the north coast of Honduras, a situation similar to that of Honduras would have been developed—an essentially foreign kind of settlement in a position isolated from the rest of the country, yet one of great importance to the national treasury. But the soils of the east coast of Nicaragua were too poor. When the banana diseases hit, the companies moved away.

The central nucleus of Nicaragua has yet to feel any large measure of impact from the ideas of the democratic revolution. A liberal military dictatorship has given Nicaragua order and at the same time a degree of personal freedom, except freedom to criticize the dictator. Nicaragua has long been of concern to distant powers, especially Great Britain and the United States, because of its potential canal route.

The Economic Situation

The 1,500,000 people in Nicaragua are faced with no problem of land hunger. Like Honduras, Nicaragua has plenty of public land for any one who wishes to colonize it. The people enjoy no very large degree of economic prosperity; but here again we find that poverty itself does not lead to discontent, but only poverty hemmed in by privilege and wealth. The income per capita ($158 in 1955) was certainly very unevenly distributed. As usual, in such a situation, the best-paying jobs are the top posts in the government. Nicaragua has a birth rate of 50 per thousand, which is exceeded in all Latin America only by the 51 per thousand in Guatemala. Like Guatemala, too, the death rate has been considerably lowered in the period since World War II, to 20 per thousand. As a result the population now shows a rapid net increase.

The condition of economic underdevelopment is reflected in the fact that the Nicaraguan population is still predominantly rural and agricultural. About 68 percent of the workers are engaged in agriculture, and only 40 percent of the total population live in cities and towns. The proportion of the people who can read and write is 40 percent—about the same as in El Salvador and Honduras.

In Nicaragua, as elsewhere in Latin America, the government has been attempting to change some of the subsistence farmers into cash-crop farmers. The most important crop in terms of acreage is still maize, which, along with rice and beans, provides the greater part of the Nicaraguan diet. The two most important commercial crops are cotton and coffee: cotton grown in the Nicaraguan Lowland, coffee grown in the highlands.

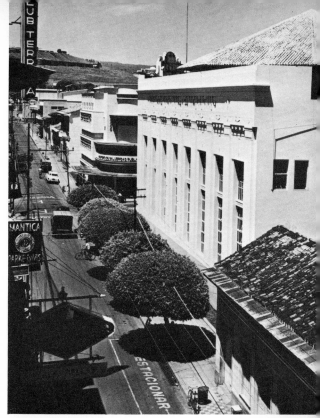

Street in Managua

Wharf at Corinto

Coffee has long been the leading export of Nicaragua but in 1955 for the first time cotton went into the lead. In 1961 cotton made up 30 percent of the exports and coffee made up 28 percent. Other commercial crops include sesame, from which vegetable oil is extracted and exported, and also some of the maize and rice. There is still a small production of bananas around Puerto Cabezas. Cattle are exported on the hoof to El Salvador. In 1961, in addition to cotton and coffee, the exports of Nicaragua included gold (13 percent). The imports were mostly machinery, chemicals, and pharmaceutical products. Nicaragua does a large part of its business with the United States. In 1960 the United States took 43 percent of the exports and supplied 53 percent of the imports. Exports also went to West Germany, (8 percent), the Netherlands, (6 percent), and Great Britain, (4 percent). Imports from countries other than the United States included machinery from West Germany and oil from the Netherlands Antilles.

The Political Situation

In spite of the unity of the chief nucleus of settlement in Nicaragua the country has yet to achieve coherence in its national life. It has been said that there are no Nicaraguans—only liberals and conservatives, costeños and españoles. When the people who lived around León and Granada asserted their independence from Guatemala in 1838 they were united in only one thing—the desire for freedom from outside control, the right to make their own mistakes. The struggle for supremacy between these two cities flared up immediately. León was the center of the liberal party: Granada was the center of the conservative party. When political parties occupy geographically distinct areas internal conflict is difficult to avoid.

The political situation in Nicaragua has long been complicated by the intervention of foreign interests. In 1841 Great Britain established a protectorate over the Miskito Indians on the Nicaraguan east coast, and in that same year they seized the port of San Juan del Norte. The United States started to turn its attention to the possible passageways across the isthmus only after the Mexican War had resulted in the expansion of the national territory all the way across North America to the Pacific Ocean. In 1850 the United States and Great Britain signed the Clayton-Bulwer Treaty in which both countries agreed not to occupy, fortify, colonize, or exercise dominion over any portion of Central America. Great Britain insisted that this did not include British Honduras, but it did involve the British settlements along the Miskito Coast. Nevertheless it was not until 1893 that the Nicaraguan army actually regained control of this eastern part of the country, although they had regained San Juan del Norte in 1852.

When Cornelius Vanderbilt became interested in developing the route across the isthmus for the people bound for California, he had to face constant difficulties with the warring political factions of Nicaragua. In 1855 he gave his backing to a North American adventurer named William Walker. Walker supported the forces of León, and with a band of 56 men that he brought with him he defeated the opposing troops. From 1855 to 1857 he was the president of Nicaragua, but eventually he was thrown out of office and fled the country. In 1860, involved in another bit of adventure in Honduras, he was captured and shot.

Foreign intervention continued. In 1874 the Germans blockaded the Nicaraguan coast in order to collect damages for an alleged insult to their consul. They collected $30,000 in damages. In 1893 the liberal, General José Santos Zelaya, became the dictator. But when, in 1909, he signed a treaty with Great Britain giving that country the exclusive right to build a canal, the United States withdrew recognition, and Zelaya was soon deposed. When conditions seemed thoroughly out of hand, in 1912, the United States landed a force of 2,600 Marines. When order had been imposed, the force was reduced to a legation guard of only about 100 men. In 1916 Nicaragua granted to the United States the exclusive rights to build a canal, for which the United States paid a sum of $3,000,000.

By 1925 the military occupation of another country had become unpopular in the United States. In that year the Marines were withdrawn from Nicaragua. But at once the civil war between liberals and conservatives burst out again, and in the spring of 1926 the Marines returned. Elections were carried out under the control of the United States and a liberal was elected. It was at this time that General Augusto César Sandino began his revolt against military intervention and against any government elected under foreign auspices. Sandino became the hero of all those persons throughout Latin America who resented the forceful interference of the "colossus of the north." When the Marines were finally withdrawn in 1933, Sandino promptly surrendered to the Nicaraguan government, after which, because of his large political following, he was shot.

The year 1932 marked the beginning of the period of Nicaraguan history during which the strong man was General Anastasio Somoza García. Somoza had been trained by the Marines and had been placed in command of the highly efficient National Guard. With his military backing he became the only real political power. In 1937 he seized the government, and thereafter he remained either as president or as the power behind the president until his assassination in 1956. During all this period he gave Nicaragua political order by prohibiting all opposition parties. He treated the country as if it were his own private estate. He took many steps to strengthen the economy of Nicaragua, usually to the advantage of the politically powerful people around him. After his death, his son, Luis Somoza Debayle, assumed the presidency, and in 1957 he was duly elected to that office.

In 1957 the long-quiet border dispute with Honduras again became active. Map 12, pages 36-37, shows the area in dispute between the two countries. It is a very thinly inhabited part of Central America, mostly outside of the effective national territory of either country. Honduras has actually administered the small towns as far as the mouth of the Río Coco, but since the area was mostly unoccupied and very remote from the centers of settlement in either country, the dispute remained quiet. In 1906 King Alphonso XIII of Spain had awarded the territory north of the Coco to Honduras, but Nicaragua never had accepted the award. In 1957 Honduras organized a new department within the disputed area, and began the construction of a road into it. Arrangements were made, also, with foreign oil companies to explore the area for oil. All this activity again aroused Nicaragua to reassert the claims, and both countries sent troops into that area. At this point the Organization of American States went into action, dispatching a five-man commission to the area. The commission secured a cease-fire order from both sides, and an agreement to ask the International Court of Justice at The Hague to rule on the validity of the award of 1906.

Nicaragua remains a country with little experience in the orderly processes of democratic government. It has been run by a dictator, supported by a well-drilled and loyal military force. The dictator has brought material benefits to the country, and has put a stop to the political disorders which, before 1912, caused endless destruction of life and property. But Nicaragua has no state-idea to command the support of a free people. In spite of its single core of settlement, Nicaragua has a long way to go in the development of a coherent political life, or in the acceptance of the basic concepts of democracy.

COSTA RICA

The contrast between Costa Rica and its neighbors is one of the striking facts of Caribbean geography. Of the twenty-two states of Latin America, only El Salvador, Haiti, the Dominican Republic, Jamaica and Trinidad have national territories that are smaller, and only Panamá has fewer inhabitants. But there are three distinctive features in Costa Rica. First, the farmers of the central area occupy the land with the greatest rural density of any part of Latin America—more than 1,500 people per square mile. Second, the central area of Costa Rica is one of the four parts of mainland Latin America where settlement expansion is taking place without a decrease of density in the core. And third, Costa Rica stands along with Uruguay as one of the two most democratic countries of Latin America.

The area of concentrated settlement which forms the central core of Costa Rica is located in the highlands where a small intermont basin with deep ash soils offers land of relatively gentle slopes in the midst of the tierra templada. The total area of this nucleus, including some of the mountain slopes which border the basin, is only about 150 square miles; but there are parts of this central area in which the density of the rural population is over 1,500 per square mile. Furthermore, the birth rate of about 45 per thousand is approximately the same as that of Mexico, and the death rate of about 11 per thousand is lower than that of Mexico: Costa Rica has the highest net rate of population increase of all the countries of Latin America for which statistics are available. Supported by rapid growth in the center, pioneer farmers have moved out from the intermont basin, developing frontiers of new settlement which are now well beyond the original nucleus.

There are many other ways in which the conditions of life in this central area are distinctive. Among all the countries of Latin America, Costa Rica, along with Argentina, Uruguay, and Chile, enjoys the prestige of having a population that is more than 80 percent literate. The great majority of the farmers in the central area own and operate their own farms, and small-farmer pioneers are found on the frontier of new settlement. The traditional large estate of Latin America is rare.

The crater of Irazú bordered by thick accumulation of volcanic ash before the eruption of 1964

Associated with this distinctive characteristic of land tenure and with the widespread literacy is the notable attitude of equality among the people; there is no small group of landed aristocracy which dominates the social life, manipulates the politics with the support of an army, and collects the larger share of the benefits of the economy. Furthermore, one does not find the signs of rural poverty so common in densely populated agricultural areas of Latin America. Costa Rica stands sixth in all Latin America in terms of per capita income. In the central area more than 90 percent of the people are of unmixed Spanish ancestry.

Yet Costa Rica, also, has its internal contrasts—its elements of diversity. In strong contrast to the homogeneous population of the central area, with its distinctive institutions and man-land relations, are the lowland areas on either side. On the Pacific side, especially in the Province of Guanacaste, nearly half of the people are mestizo in origin, racially indistinguishable from the people of Nicaragua. In this part of Costa Rica, moreover, there are many large land properties, a small landed aristocracy, and tenant workers who live in relative poverty. On the Caribbean side more than half of the people are Negro—mostly Negroes from Jamaica ·and Barbados who were brought in when the banana plantations back of Puerto Limón were first being developed.

The census of 1950 counted 800,875 people in Costa Rica. In 1956 the population reached one million and in 1962 was estimated at 1,251,000. For the country as a whole 80 percent are of unmixed Spanish descent, 17 percent are mestizo, 2 percent are Negro, and less than 1 percent are Indian.

Coffee on fertile volcanic ash in the highlands

The Economic Situation

Costa Rica, like the other Central American countries, has different kinds of economic development in the different parts of the country. The chief coffee-producing area is in the highlands, between about 2,000 and 3,200 feet. More than half of the planters own less than 1,000 trees each. With such small-scale operations it is difficult to introduce modern cost-saving machinery or farm practices. As a result Costa Rican coffee is high cost coffee, yet of a flavor superior enough to bring it premium prices.

The first banana plantations in the Caribbean area were laid out along the Caribbean coastal lowland of Costa Rica before 1910. And this was the first area to be invaded by banana diseases which, even as early as the 1920's ruined these plantations. The Negro workers in eastern Costa Rica were left stranded as the fruit company moved its operations elsewhere. In the 1940's, however, the fruit company redeveloped its agriculture in this part of Costa Rica, introducing cacao, abacá (for twine), oil palms, and other tropical crops. But by the 1940's a method had been invented for controlling banana disease through the use of spray. New plantations, equipped with overhead irrigation, were laid out in small lowland pockets along the Pacific coast of Costa Rica, near the new banana port of Golfito. This is now one of the leading areas of banana planting under the management of the United Fruit Company.

Costa Rica is one of the four areas of Latin America where frontiers of new pioneer settlement have appeared. The increase of population in the central area—34 per thousand—is the highest in Latin America. From the central area streams of pioneer settlers have moved out in several directions to clear and occupy previously empty lands. This outward movement has been going on for a long time—long before the government of Costa Rica and the United Fruit Company adopted the policy of developing the Pacific Coast region. There is still empty land suitable for colonization into which the pioneer movement can continue. It should be noted, however, that for the most part the pioneer settlers remain subsistence farmers, raising their own supplies of maize, rice, and beans, and adding little to the food supply of the crowded central area. To provide for an increase of the basic foods at decreased prices, large-scale projects utilizing the lowland areas are needed—and these require the service of a relatively small number of workers. The oil-palm plantations of the United Fruit Company, for example, can free the country from the necessity of importing vegetable oil for cooking. To provide more maize at less cost, the wet Caribbean lowlands offer potentially very productive lands—but not for small farmer settlement. It may be that, from an economic point of view, the small-farmer pioneer, raising his own foods and buying or selling little, is no longer justified.

Irrigated banana plantation in southeastern Costa Rica with close-up of overhead spray which supplies not only water but a chemical to control banana diseases

Costa Rica is outstanding, also, in that some 80 percent of its population is literate. Compared with other countries of Latin America, Costa Rica has the largest per capita circulation of newspapers and the largest investment in printing establishments. This high degree of literacy is reflected, of course, in the low death rate.

Yet Costa Rica does not stand high in its gross national product per capita. With an income per capita of $235 in 1955, it stood sixth in Latin America, but well below countries like Venezuela, Argentina, Uruguay, and Cuba. The level of living is much higher than that of its Central American neighbors except Panamá (which is a special case as we shall see).

It is significant that about 55 percent of the working force of the country is employed in agriculture. Manufacturing industry has made only a little start. The value of all manufactured products is still only about half the value of agricultural products. Yet the list of manufacturing enterprises is, itself, distinctive. To be sure the leading industry is that of food processing, making up about 27 percent of the total by value of product. But the second industry in Costa Rica is that of printing—23 percent. The textile industry comes third with 22 percent.

For a long time coffee has been Costa Rica's chief export. Before World War II the coffee exports were usually more than half of all exports by value, and in 1961 coffee made up 53 percent. Bananas before the war had dropped to only about 20 percent, but by 1961 they were up again to 25 percent. Cacao in 1961 made up 5 percent.

Costa Rica has long been closely tied to the United States in its foreign commerce. Before World War II, Germany and Great Britain used to take a considerable part of the coffee. For a time this European trade declined, but in recent years Germany has again become a major purchaser. Almost all the banana exports go to the United States. Of all the exports in 1961 the United States took 58 percent, West Germany 21 percent, and the Netherlands 4 percent. Of all the imports the United States supplied 46 percent, Germany 11 percent, and Great Britain 5 percent. They include wheat and wheat flour, textiles, machinery, chemicals, and fuels.

The Political Situation

Costa Rica is also distinctive among all the countries of Latin America in the relative progress of the democratic revolution. This little nation and Uruguay are the countries in which the processes of democracy are most firmly established. The Costa Ricans have been able to establish a notably coherent national life with a distinctive state-idea.

None of these accomplishments was reached without a struggle. To be sure Costa Rica, at least in its central area, has never been burdened with the Spanish agrarian tradition. The absence of sources of gold or of an Indian population meant that the country was not very attractive to the majority of the Spaniards in the early colonial period. Instead the people who settled in the Meseta Central were a selected group whose purpose was to create a permanent community, not simply to gain quick wealth and then return to Spain. Even seventeenth-century travelers to the Meseta Central remarked on the absence of an aristocracy and of a class that enjoyed prestige and privilege because of its status. Ideas of equality developed early, as did the tradition of the small independent farmer. To work for a living was never looked down on in Costa Rica.

Nevertheless experience in public administration was small in colonial Costa Rica. In this remote and isolated part of the Captaincy General of Guatemala, political problems generated little heat. When Guatemala broke away from Mexico, Costa Rica was included with the other countries farther to the north. Costa Rica was the end of the line, for no road reached the part of Colombia that was known as Panamá. In 1838 when the Central American countries separated, Costa Rica, without ever demanding its independence, found itself independent. And because of the lack of political interest, the new government came into the hands of a dictator. But the dictator had to earn his living like anyone else, for the national treasury contained no great store of wealth, and the idea of using the printing presses to create money made little sense to the hard-working Costa Ricans.

A succession of governments, some more totalitarian than others, were all more clearly guided by public opinion than in any of the other Central American states. Costa Rica developed a reputation for freedom of speech, for liberal concepts of government, and for the avoidance of force. In 1889 the first fully free election in all Latin America was held, and the ballots were honestly counted. In spite of the existence, by that time, of opposed political parties, the results of the election were respected and the majority party took control. Since 1889, with the exception of only two brief periods, in 1917-19 and in 1948, Costa Rica has operated as a democracy. There has been freedom of access to knowledge, freedom to criticize the government, freedom to discuss public issues. There have been opposition political parties. Elections have been conducted honestly and in secret. The tradition of democracy has become an important part of the Costa Rican state-idea. Attempts to seize power by force were met, in 1948, by a popular uprising. Since 1948, Costa Rica has had no army—only a national police force.

Partly as a result of the internal cohesion and the strength of the national tradition, Costa Rica feels less limited in its freedom of action by relations with other countries. It has worked out harmonious relations with the United Fruit Company, and the company has responded by investing considerable sums of money in production for the domestic economy—as in the development of the oil palm plantations. Costa Rica has felt little need to raise the specter of outside intervention in its dealings with the United States. In 1941, on December 7th, Costa Rica was the first American country to declare war on Japan, followed on December 11th by a declaration of war against Germany and Italy. In a world in conflict, there is no doubt which side Costa Rica supports.

PANAMÁ

The historical background of Panamá is different from that of any other Central American state. Until 1903 it was an outlying part of Colombia; its present status as an independent political unit under the protection of the United States was achieved principally as a result of the strategic importance of its position on one of the world's major pass routes. Since Balboa first revealed the geographical nature of the isthmus in 1513, the story of man in Panamá has been concerned with passage rather than with settlement. At one time or another all the great maritime nations of the world have coveted this little strip of territory, and

The Miraflores Locks on the Pacific side of the Canal

the forces which have shaped the larger communities on either side of the isthmus are international rather than local. Panamá, the present-day state, differs from all the other Latin-American states in that it possesses no central area of concentrated settlement focusing on an urban core. The nucleus of the state is the city of Panamá. But Panamá, the city, is not a product of Panamá, the country. It came into existence, and its importance has been maintained, because it controls a pass route. Meanwhile the three small clusters of people along the Pacific coast west of Panamá City are distinctly minor ones on the map of Middle America (Map 1, pages 6-7). The greater part of the territory of Panamá remains almost unoccupied.

The population of Panamá is smaller than that of any other independent state except Trinidad. It was estimated that the total number of people in Panamá in 1962 was 1,122,000, with another 41,500 in the Canal Zone. In the whole country some 41 percent of the people live in cities. The chief city, Panamá, had a population of 273,000 in 1960, while Colón, on the Caribbean side, had about 60,000 inhabitants. David, near the Costa Rican border, was a city of about 23,000.

As one might expect, the racial composition of the population is highly diverse, for people from all over the world are drawn together at the canal. It is estimated that 65 percent of the people are mestizo or mulatto, and 11 percent are European in origin. Some 13 percent are pure Negro, and 1 percent are Orientals, chiefly Chinese. Another 10 percent is made up of pure Indians, most of whom live in the isolated eastern parts of Panamá, outside the effective national territory.

Passage across the Isthmus

Although the Spaniards cruised along the Caribbean coast of the isthmus as early as 1501, the strategic importance of this place did not become apparent until Balboa crossed it to the shores of the Pacific in 1513. In 1519 an expedition founded the first town of Panamá (now Panamá Vieja, located some five miles to the east of modern Panamá). On the Caribbean coast several small ports in succession were used for the landing place. At first, Nombre de Dios was the chief Caribbean port; later Portobelo, which is a little to the west of Nombre de Dios, and which has a somewhat more commodious harbor. Much later, when the railroad and then the canal were built, these little places were all but abandoned in favor of Colón. On the Pacific side, however, the end of the pass remained more nearly fixed.

The importance of Panamá City to the Spaniards was very great. From this place the expeditions set out to the conquest of the Pacific side of Central America as far north as Nicaragua, and to the conquest of the whole west coast of South America as far as remote Chile. Although

Lima became the primary settlement center of western South America, all of the lines of connection between Lima and the mother country passed through Panamá. Here were gathered the ·goods sent out from Spain, and the treasure collected from the rich Americas to be sent back to Spain. Then, as now, Panamá City derived its importance from the convergence of oversea interests: in its vicinity no very large area of rural settlement became established, for people came to Panamá on the way to some other destination—few of them came to stay.

With the collapse of the Spanish Empire in the New World, Panamá for a time lost some of its importance. But it was not many decades before the interests of a new maritime power began to touch the isthmus. When, as a result of the War with Mexico, the United States extended its borders to the Pacific in 1848, and almost at once the world heard of the discovery of the gold fields of California, there ensued a wild rush to this new source of riches. By all sorts of routes the people not only from eastern United States but also from Europe made the long trip to California. All the pass routes across Middle America were tried: Veracruz to Acapulco, the Isthmus of Tehuantepec, the rift valley of Honduras, the lowland of Nicaragua, and Panamá. In 1850, great numbers of travelers arrived on the Caribbean side to cross to Panamá City. As a result, the old mule-and-cart road which had served for so many centuries was replaced by a railroad which made use of the low Culebra pass.

But the United States was not the only maritime power which looked covetously at Panamá. The idea of providing a passage for ocean ships across the isthmus had such obvious justification in terms of time saved on many different routes leading to Europe and eastern North America that several nations gave serious consideration to canal projects. Many of the British activities in the Caribbean during the nineteenth century were motivated by the idea of controlling the strategic approaches to a canal. The French, successful in the completion of the first of the world's great canals, the Suez, were the first actually to undertake the work in Panamá. In 1878 Ferdinand de Lesseps began operations for the construction of a sea-level canal, and continued until the collapse of his company in 1889. The French had failed to consider the serious effect of the diseases carried by the tropical insects on the health and energy of the workers.

The Spanish-American War, perhaps more than anything else, made it clear to the United States that as a matter of defense alone, the construction of a canal was vital. An agreement was reached with Great Britain by which that country gave up all rights to the Panamá route in exchange for a guarantee of equal treatment in the matter of tolls for British and United States shipping. Negotiations for the right to a canal zone were being carried on with the Colombian government, when the people of

Panamá, believing that the negotiations had fallen through and fearing that the Nicaraguan route would be selected instead, revolted and declared their independence from Colombia. The part played by the United States is not entirely clear, although it is certain that United States armed forces kept the Colombians from putting down the revolt, and that the United States government, with conspicuous haste, recognized and came to terms with the government of Panamá. The United States was granted "in perpetuity" the use, occupation, and control of a zone five miles on either side of the canal, except where the boundary was drawn closer to the canal in the cities at either end—Panamá and Colón.

Work on the canal started in 1904. A widespread attack on the problem of sanitation preceded and accompanied the actual digging. The conspicuous success of this attack has had a very great influence on the methods of combating tropical disease throughout the world. Workers on the canal were recruited not only in United States and in Europe, but also from the Negro populations of some of the islands of the Antilles, especially Jamaica and Barbados. A huge dam was constructed at Gatún, near Colón, impounding the water of the Río Chagres in a large lake. Access to the lake, which is 85 feet above the Caribbean, is gained through locks. The Gaillard Cut carries the impounded water of the lake across to the Pacific side, where two sets of locks permit descent to the Pacific. On August 3, 1914, the first ship passed through the completed canal.

A strip of land on either side of the canal was designated as the Canal Zone, over which the United States has "as complete authority as if it were under the sovereignty of the United States." Panamá City and Colón, which are within the ten-mile strip, are excluded from the Zone and remain under the control of Panamá; within the Zone are the new cities of Cristóbal and Silver City (adjoining Colón), and Balboa (adjoining Panamá City). With so much at stake in the maintenance and defense of the canal, obviously the government of Panamá must work in close cooperation with the United States. During World War II numerous military installations, including an important airfield, were placed outside of the ten-mile zone in Panamá territory. But with the conclusion of hostilities these installations were given up. The government of Panamá jealously guards against outside interference in matters which are considered purely domestic (Map 20).

The Economic Situation

The relatively small population of Panamá may be divided into five economic groups. At the top in terms of wealth is the relatively small number of well-to-do politicians, the handful of large landowners, the higher officers of the national guard. The country is run by these people

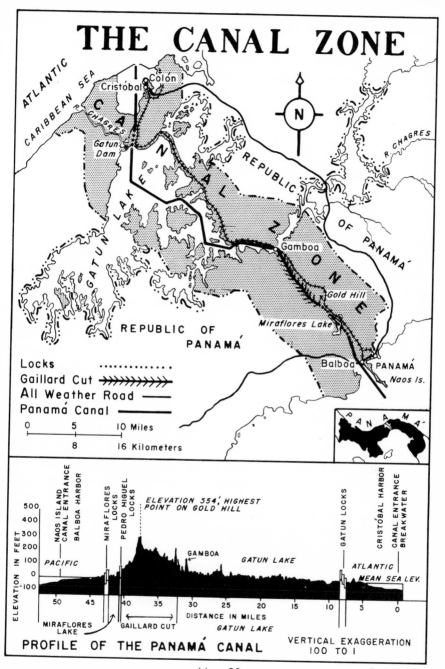

THE CANAL ZONE

Locks ·············
Gaillard Cut ≫≫≫≫≫
All Weather Road ——
Panamá Canal ——

0 5 10 Miles
8 16 Kilometers

PROFILE OF THE PANAMÁ CANAL

VERTICAL EXAGGERATION
100 TO 1

Map 20

for their own benefit. Next in order of income are a few foreign business-men, mostly small merchants and owners of hotels and recreation facili-ties. John Biesanz quotes Felipe Escobar as saying that "the Chinese had the retail groceries, Greeks the fruit trade, Spaniards, French, and North Americans the hotels, Hindus and Chinese the dry goods, Syrians, Turks, and Armenians the cheap clothing, and Jews some of everything."[3] That was in 1928. In 1941 the government of Panamá nationalized the com-mercial establishments, dispossessing most of the foreign operators, and turning their businesses over to Panamanians. But the Panamanians had neither the interest nor the tradition of working hard for a living. Most of them sold the businesses back to the foreigners. At any rate the foreign small traders are still operating, and still making a good living.

The third economic group is an increasing middle class of "white-collar" city workers. They are employed in the government offices, the retail stores, the banks, and in the Canal Zone. They do not make a good living, but if both husband and wife have jobs they can support a family. The fourth economic group are the workers in the cities and in the Canal Zone. Many of these have part-time employment in the cities of Panamá; some 12 to 15 percent are employed in operating the Canal, or in Canal construction and maintenance. When the Canal Zone has a lot of work to be done, these people are well paid; for most of the time they drift from job to job, working for very low wages that permit them a bare subsistence. Finally, the fifth economic group, some 53 percent of all those gainfully employed, are farmers who contribute little or nothing to the economy of the country. Obviously the average annual income per capita of $324 in 1955 was very unevenly spread among the people.

Most of the income of Panamá is derived either directly or indirectly from the Canal. If the Canal were to be shut down for any reason most of the people of Panamá would have no means of support. More than half of this income is paid in the form of wages and salaries. The wages and salaries paid for work in the Canal Zone to 12 to 15 percent of the labor force is about equal to the pay received by the other 85 to 88 percent for work outside of the Canal Zone. Most of the remainder of the direct income from the Canal Zone was paid to retail businesses outside of the Zone by people either living in the Canal Zone or passing through it in ships. The annual payment from the United States to the govern-ment of Panamá for the lease of the Canal Zone (formerly $430,000 a year; since 1955, $1,500,000) is a small fraction of the total income of Panamá. A very large part of the income is the indirect result of the presence of the Canal. The three chief sources of government revenue—the lottery, the horse races, and the taxes on liquor—are derived very largely from foreigners.

[3] John Biesanz, "The Economy of Panamá," *Inter-American Economic Affairs*, Vol. 6, 1952, pp. 3-28; reference on page 9.

The fact is that Panamá's economy is based on selling goods and services to those maintaining, defending, or passing through the Canal.

The exports that originate in Panamá included, in 1961, bananas (62 percent by value), fresh shrimp (27 percent), sugar (4 percent), and cacao (2 percent). Of all the exports 92 percent went to the United States, mostly in ships of the United Fruit Company. The imports are usually about four times as great as the exports. The balance is made up of tourist expenditures, sales to ships, and wages and salaries paid to people employed in the Canal Zone.

There has been little industrial development in Panamá. A few manufacturing establishments sell high-cost goods protected by high import tariffs. However, in 1958 two new oil refineries were being built by North American interests, both on the Caribbean side of the isthmus.

The Gaillard Cut through the backbone of the Isthmus

The Political Situation

A surprising number of political leaders in Panamá still believe that commerce cannot be the basis for a healthy economy. They are concerned at the degree of interdependence between Panamá and the United States. There are many who subscribe to the widespread idea that the only healthy economy is one based on self-sufficient argriculture and manufacturing industry. And there are many whose reaction to the Canal can best be summarized by the words *"Es bueno pero no es nuestro."*

But in Panamá there never has been any important development, economic or political, that was purely indigenous, purely derived from local sources. In 1739, when the Vice-Royalty of New Granada was established with its administrative center at Bogotá, Panamá was included in it. After the success of Bolívar's effort to secure independence from Spain, Panamá was included in the new state; but in 1841 when the new state was breaking apart, Panamá also declared its independence. Troops from Colombia, however, had little difficulty in recapturing this outlying province. Panamá again seceded in 1853, but rejoined Colombia again. During the period when the British, the French, and the government of the United States were all promoting the canal idea, Panamá was administered by officials appointed in Bogotá. The situation was ripe for graft and dishonesty. From 1898 to 1903 the area was in almost constant disorder and revolt. The declaration of independence in 1903 was different from previous movements only in the presence of armed forces of the United States and in the prompt recognition afforded the new state.

The government in Panamá is controlled by the people of the first of the economic groups previously described. These are the very few large landowners, a few business men, the higher officers of a national guard, and the professional politicians. There are political parties which appeal to the middle-class city people and to the students at the university for support. No party could remain in power which did not adopt a strongly nationalistic policy, and which did not follow the wishes of the politically powerful minority. In spite of the strategic importance of the Canal, the communists have played only a minor role in Panamanian politics.

It cannot be said that Panamá, since 1903, has developed any very considerable degree of national coherence. The state-idea which brings support to a government in power is often the idea of reducing dependence on the United States. The students, especially, called for the seizure of the Canal at the time of the Suez crisis. The formulation of a more sophisticated state-idea has yet to be accomplished. Meanwhile the economic and political dependence on the United States becomes closer and more irritating.

A CENTRAL-AMERICAN FEDERATION

There has been a persistent movement among the Central American states to form some kind of federation. When they were a part of the Captaincy-General of Guatemala, they were at least loosely administered from Guatemala City; but in the period when the Spanish colonial system was breaking up, the demands for independence, as we have seen, outweighed the desire for federation. In modern times it becomes more and more obvious that if a basis for union could be found all the states would be benefited. In 1951 at San Salvador, the representatives of the five states (Guatemala, El Salvador, Honduras, Nicaragua, and Costa Rica) took the first steps toward an economic union. The *Organización de los Estados Centroamericanos* (Odeca) actually started to negotiate for a common market in 1955. Since that time some encouraging progress has been made.

The reluctance of the separate states to give up their cherished sovereignty remains a basic fact. But by means of treaties and agreements, negotiated by the representatives of independent countries, they hope to eliminate tariff barriers, promote the free exchange of goods, liberalize the travel restrictions and permit the free movement of workers from country to country. Agreements have been reached to give certain manufacturing industries free access to the whole market. For example, paper manufactured in Honduras will not be excluded from Costa Rica, or tires manufactured in Guatemala forced to find a market within the confines of Guatemala. Already the signs of new economic opportunity are visible. Yet each step in the direction of cooperation runs directly against the individual traditions and distinctive characteristics of each of the countries. The problem is simple: can the leadership be found to formulate a single state-idea for Central America that will claim the support of a majority of those who today adhere to five separate state-ideas?

On the Llanos near San Fernando

CHAPTER FIVE

Venezuela and Colombia

Venezuela and Colombia are the two countries in the northwestern part of South America. The most densely populated parts of both of these countries are in rugged mountainous terrain, and because the chief ports which give access to the interior are on the Caribbean both countries have closer connections in that direction than with the other parts of continental South America. There is much diversity within both countries. The land itself is a mosaic of small areas, each offering the inhabitants a somewhat different kind of habitat and a different endowment of resources. There are, also, notable differences in the racial make-up of the population and in economic and political traditions. This basic geographic diversity is fundamental to an understanding of what is happening in this part of Latin America.

VENEZUELA

Venezuela is a spectacular example of the rapid economic development of a previously underdeveloped country as a result of the large-scale investment of foreign capital. Between 1880 and 1914 Argentina was the outstanding example in Latin America of the effect of foreign capital in the creation of wealth. Argentina was a product of British investments. Venezuela is a product of investment from the United States, chiefly in the production of oil. At the beginning of the twentieth century Venezuela was a poor tropical country, loosely controlled by warring factions of the army, and with the great majority of its people living in hopeless poverty. The rise of Venezuela in its economic production began after

Maps 2, 4, 6, 8, 11, 13, 14, 15, 21, 22, 25 are pertinent to this chapter.

Village in the Cordillera de Mérida south of Lake Maracaibo

Village on the shores of Lake Maracaibo

World War I, but by 1955 it had climbed to first place in all Latin America in gross national product per capita. Nevertheless, the process of transformation did not please everyone in Venezuela, perhaps not even a majority.

The Development of Venezuela

The independence movement among the Spanish colonies in America appeared early in Venezuela. Simón Bolívar, the leader in the liberation of northern South America, came from an aristocratic family in Caracas. His ideal was the freedom of American-born leaders to govern without interference from Spain. Freedom meant freedom from foreign authorities. Bolívar hoped to set up a "United States of South America" and for a few years he was able to hold together in Gran Colombia the territory now included in Venezuela, Colombia, and Ecuador.

Bolívar's dream of a united South America was shattered by revolt. The smaller political leaders in the several separate clusters of population, having been freed from Spanish authority, turned against authority from Bogotá where Bolívar had his capital. In 1830 Bolívar's own chief lieutenant in the wars against Spain declared Venezuela to be free from Gran Colombia. Bolívar, in despair, said: "Our America will fall into the hands of vulgar tyrants; only an able despotism can rule America." This was more than a hundred years ago; but the prophecy has been fulfilled quite literally during the succeeding years.

Between 1830 and 1935 Venezuela had more than a dozen rulers, but three "able despots" stand out above all the others. Páez was the first of these, the half-Indian, mestizo peon, who declared the independence of Venezuela in 1830. The second was Guzmán Blanco, who first came into office in 1870. From 1909 to 1935 it was Gómez. Under each of these despots Venezuela was run like a vast private estate for the benefit of the owner; but the result was the enforcement of order among the various factions and a consequent increase of material prosperity. In the intervals between, the country was ravaged by the conflict of warring elements no one of which was strong enough to beat the others to submission—these were periods of destruction and loss.

Juan Vicente Gómez was not descended from the aristocracy. He was the son of an Indian mother and a mestizo father who lived in poverty in the high Andean country along the Colombia-Venezuela border. He was a man of tremendous ambitions, a ruthless fighter, one who ruled his country with an iron hand. His opponents were killed or exiled. When the geologists found that Venezuela possessed important oil resources, Gómez, in the years immediately after World War I, made arrangements with the large oil corporations to undertake the expensive business of producing oil. The Venezuelan treasury was suddenly filled with money. In the depression years after 1929, Gómez brought his country through without any foreign debt. When he died in 1935 mobs tore his palace to bits.

Since the death of Gómez, Venezuela has been the scene of a mighty struggle between those who favor democratic procedures, including rule by law, and those who seek to continue the traditional system of personal power. Between 1945 and 1952 political parties were given freedom to organize and to discuss public policy—an unheard of thing in Venezuela. In 1947 elections were held in which the whole adult population, literate and illiterate, took part. Some 70 percent of the voters gave their support to a liberal, civilian government. In 1948, however, the army again seized power, and until 1958 Venezuela had another period of absolute dictatorship, backed by the action of a secret police operating outside the law. In 1958 a new revolt against the dictator took place. For the first time in Venezuelan history the military officers were fighting for civil liberty rather than for the spoils of office.

The Venezuelans

Bolívar and Gómez dramatize the contrasts which exist among the people of Venezuela and some of the difficulties involved in establishing order among such diverse elements. The ingredients which have entered into the human mixture in this country include Europeans, Indians, and Negroes. In the absence of reliable census data, we may use the estimates published in the United Nations Demographic Yearbooks. These estimates indicate that 20 percent of the Venezuelans are of unmixed European ancestry, and this includes many who, like Bolívar, had only one Indian ancestor a long time back. Probably not more than 7 percent are of unmixed Indian ancestry, and another 8 percent are pure Negro. Most of the Venezuelans are mestizos—persons of mixed European and Indian parentage in varying ratios.

Racial percentages are not uniform throughout Venezuela. Europeans are concentrated in the larger towns and cities—in Caracas, Maracaibo, or Valencia. Pure Indians, on the other hand, survive only in the more remote places—in the Guiana Highlands south of the Orinoco River or in the forests west of Lake Maracaibo. The Negro mixture is greatest along the Caribbean Coast, in such ports as La Guaira and Puerto Cabello. Even among the mestizos there is a notable difference between the people of the highlands and those of the lowlands. To understand these differences we must go back to the early days of the Spanish conquest.

The Indians and the European Conquest

In 1500 Venezuela was occupied by scattered tribes of Caribs and Arawaks. These people lived along the northern coast of South America

Cerro Bolívar, the mountain of almost pure iron ore, and in the valley, savanna and palms

Threshing wheat in the Cordillera de Mérida

and on some of the islands of the Caribbean. They were primarily hunters, fishers, and migratory cultivators.

Contact between the Spaniards and the Indians began along the coast of Venezuela during the first part of the sixteenth century. The first European settlement on the continent of South America which has survived to the present time was established at Cumaná in 1523. Four years later another colony was planted at the base of the Paraguaná Peninsula at Coro. From these two bases exploring parties pushed inland. West of Coro the Spaniards entered the Maracaibo Lowland and, coming upon Indian villages which were built on piles in the shallow waters of the lake, they named the country "Little Venice," or Venezuela (Map 4, page 18).

The territory these first Spanish explorers penetrated was less attractive than Mexico because of the sparseness of the Indian population and the absence of any accumulation of treasure. Nevertheless the Spaniards pressed inland searching for gold, and in the period after 1538 they did actually discover many places where the stream gravels yielded the precious metal. The placer mines of the valley in which Caracas was later founded, as well as those of many scattered localities throughout the highlands, were actively worked with gangs of Indian slaves, and for a time the Venezuelan mines seemed to promise great wealth. But none of

Bridge over mountain stream in the Venezuelan Andes

the sources of gold discovered at that time proved to be better than low-grade deposits, and the gold miners were forced to turn to agriculture.

More than twenty years elapsed after the settlements at Cumaná and Coro before the first permanent town was established on the highlands, although during that period the whole highland region had been tramped over and many of the valley bottoms had been dug up in the search for gold-bearing gravels. In 1555 the town of Valencia was founded in the intermont basin which has since become the leading agricultural district of the country. The good farming land was quickly partitioned into large estates which were divided among the Spanish officers; and on these estates the Indians, Christianized and enslaved, were set to work for their new masters. Barquisimeto was also established about this time in the midst of another farming district to the west of Valencia, and in 1567 Caracas was laid out. Spaniards who had invaded the country which is now Colombia and who had founded Bogotá turned again toward the north and established San Cristóbal and Mérida in the mountains south of Lake Maracaibo.

After these first highland settlements had been made, more than a century elapsed before the Spanish occupation of other parts of Venezuela began. To be sure, some of the savanna-covered plains of the Orinoco in the neighborhood of Valencia were utilized for the grazing of cattle and even for agriculture; but the penetration of the more remote parts of the country was delayed until late in the seventeenth century. Barcelona was not founded until 1671 and Calabozo till 1695. Maturín was founded in 1710 and Angostura, now called Ciudad Bolívar, in 1764.

Meanwhile, the mixture of races proceeded rapidly. The Spaniards did not generally bring their womenfolk with them to America, but took wives from among the Indians they conquered. While great numbers of the native peoples died from the epidemics of measles and smallpox the mestizo children showed a greater degree of immunity to these diseases than their Indian ancestors. Nevertheless, the landowners soon found themselves faced with a shortage of agricultural laborers. Where sugar cane was planted, Negro slaves were introduced to perform the hard work necessary for the harvesting and grinding of the cane. Since intermarriage was unrestricted either by law or by custom, the people of the districts where sugar cane was grown became considerably darker in complexion than are the inhabitants of the rest of the country.

Present Population

The population of Venezuela has been increasing only very slowly. At the beginning of the nineteenth century Alexander von Humboldt, the famous German geographer, estimated the number of Venezuelans to be about 1,000,000. In 1920 another estimate based on a wide knowledge of

the country but not on an actual census, placed the figure at 2,400,000—
not a very great increase in more than a century. Since 1950, however,
population has been increasing at a rate of about 4 percent per year. The
census in 1961 counted a population of 7,500,000.

Like all population data for large areas, these figures obscure important
differences in density and rate of growth or decline between one area and
another. There is a notable current of internal migration toward cities.
Caracas is now a city of nearly 1,500,000, Maracaibo is about 400,000, and
Valencia is a little more than 160,000. The population of Margarita Island
has been decreasing, but several parts of the highland area have been
increasing more than the average for the whole country.

The Regions of Venezuela

The territory which is now included in Venezuela is made up of four
major divisions, only one of which is densely populated. The backbone
of the country, not only in terms of its surface features but also in terms of
population, is formed by the Venezuelan Highlands, a branch of the
Andes. A chain of high mountains crosses the border from Colombia
south of Lake Maracaibo. Beyond the end of this towering range the
somewhat lower but still very steep Caribbean Ranges run eastward along
the coast, with a gap of about a hundred miles, to the eastern tip of the
Paria Peninsula.

The other three major divisions of Venezuela are not so densely populated as the highlands. Within the Y formed by the high Cordillera de
Mérida and the lower Sierra de Perijá on the Venezuelan-Columbian
border, lie the Maracaibo Lowlands, in the midst of which there is an
extensive lake of fresh water. This lowland constitutes the second of the
major divisions of the country. The third division is a vast plain, sloping
gently from the southern and southeastern base of the Andes toward the
Orinoco River—a region known as the Orinoco Llanos. The Orinoco
itself flows along the border between the Llanos and the Guiana Highlands, a hilly upland (the fourth major division) which makes up about
half of the total national territory.

Economic Development

Venezuela leads all the other countries of Latin America in economic
development. With a gross national product per capita in 1962 of $1,019
(compared with $2,538 in the United States) Venezuela's production per
capita is only a little less than twice that of the second country of Latin
America—Uruguay. But like all national averages these figures are misleading—for compared with either Uruguay or the United States, the
national income of Venezuela is less widely distributed among the people.

Great contrasts of wealth and poverty remain to aggravate the political problems of the government.

The Oil Industry

The initial stages of economic development in Venezuela were supported by revenues from the export of oil. The first productive oil well was drilled in the Lake Maracaibo region in 1917 by the Royal Dutch Shell Company, and in the decade thereafter most of the major oil companies were granted concessions and had started drilling. At present the largest producer is the Creole Petroleum Company (Standard Oil of New Jersey). The largest oilfield, and the one with the largest potential daily production of any field in the world, is Lagunillas, located on the eastern side of Lake Maracaibo. In the period since World War II several new oil fields have been brought into production outside of the Maracaibo Lowland, the largest of which are in the Orinoco Llanos. It is important that although Venezuela as a whole has only about 6 percent of the

Rock to build firm landing place on muddy shores, Lake Maracaibo

proved oil reserves of the world, it produces some 13 percent of total world production. Since 1930 Venezuela has stood second or third in annual production, exceeded only by the United States and the Soviet Union. As a result of successively more favorable contracts between the companies and the government, the revenue to the Venezuelan treasury has been substantial.

When the Shell Company began to produce oil in 1917, and when the enormous potential production of the Maracaibo Region became evident, the construction of an oil refinery was undertaken. The first refinery was built on the island of Curaçao, a part of the Netherlands Antilles that lies in the Caribbean about 40 miles off the Venezuelan coast. The oil was brought by shallow-draft tankers from Lake Maracaibo. The lake is deep and easily navigable, but the sand bar that separates the lake water from the Caribbean Sea is less than 10 feet from the surface (now dredged to provide access to deep-draft ships). Another refinery has been built on nearby Aruba. Since World War II, however, a large new refinery has been built by Creole on the Paraguana Peninsula on the Venezuelan coast, and oil is brought to this refinery in a pipe line.

Especially since World War II the Venezuelan government has followed the policy of investing the income from oil in new manufacturing industries. Caracas has become a major manufacturing center. A petro-chemical industrial complex is in process of construction near the Caribbean coast, and will be supplied with oil from Maracaibo through a pipe line. Investment is also being made in transportation facilities, electric power plants, and other elements of "social overhead."

The Steel Industry

Of major importance is the development of a great industrial complex near the junction of the Río Caroni with the Orinoco. During World War II, when the exhaustion of the rich iron ores of Minnesota approached, there was a vigorous search for new ore bodies. The existence of large deposits of high-grade ore in the Guiana Highlands of Venezuela, south of the Orinoco River, was announced, and both the United States Steel Corporation and the Bethlehem Steel Corporation began mining operation on a large scale. Venezuelan ore now comes regularly to the big steel centers at Sparrows Point in Maryland, and along the Delaware River. The Venezuelan government in 1955 took steps to stimulate the building of a steel industry of its own. A new steel plant was built at Puerto Ordaz on the Orinoco, and is supplied with electric power from a new hydroelectric plant being built on the Río Caroni nearby. Coal must be imported in returning ore boats to supplement Venezuelan coal. Limestone is available within the country. Only the hardeners of steel must be imported entirely from foreign sources (Map 15, page 47).

New steel plant at Puerto Ordaz on the Orinoco River

Agriculture

Venezuela is also trying to do something about agricultural production. Long an exporter of coffee and other tropical products, the chief problem of the modern period is to increase the supply of basic foods. But the agricultural sector of the economy has not kept pace with the increased productivity of manufacturing industry. Although some 41 percent of the workers were employed in agriculture in 1962, they produced less than 10 percent of the gross national product. Eighteen percent of the total national territory was used for agriculture, but most of this was located in the mountains where about 70 percent of the planted crops are on very steep slopes.

The government has undertaken to provide land for new settlement. Between 1959 and 1961 about 42,000 families were given land in 500 new farming communities, and in 1962 the number of families settled on the land was more than 52,000. As a result there was a 30 percent increase in farm production. But even this is not nearly enough to provide the factory workers with food. A United Nations study estimates that the average intake of calories per day per person is 2,200, but that the minimum number of calories needed to maintain a minimum standard of diet is 2,400. Poverty and hunger have not yet been eliminated.

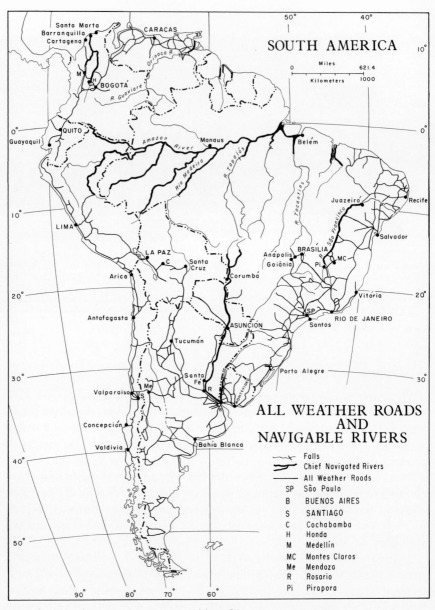

South America — All Weather Roads and Navigable Rivers

Map 21

132

The Growing Economy

Commercial production and commerce have resulted, nevertheless, in spectacular changes in Venezuela. The leading export of Latin America in terms of value is oil, and of the oil exports Venezuela sends out some 95 percent. Over 90 percent of the exports of Venezuela, too, is made up of oil and oil products. Of much less over-all importance to the country, but of much greater importance to the producing areas within the country, are the exports of coffee and cacao, and the new movement of iron ore. Because of the oil refineries on Curaçao and Aruba, the statistics show that nearly 40 percent of the oil exports of Venezuela go to the Netherlands Antilles. Actually, Venezuelan oil goes chiefly to the United States and Western Europe. Nearly 90 percent of the coffee, and almost all of the cacao and iron ore go to the United States.

The United States also furnishes more than two-thirds of the imports of Venezuela. The two chief kinds of imports are machinery and foods. Almost all the machines for mining and manufacturing, and for transporting the products and raw materials, come from the United States. The most important food imports are flour and preserved milk. Venezuela each year comes closer to meeting its own requirements for the basic foods—maize, rice, beans, and meat. But the rise of the standard of living is reflected in a notable increase in the variety of imported foodstuffs and also in the increased importation of consumer goods of all kinds. Clearly the more widely the total income is spread among the people the greater will be the volume and variety of the imports.

The fact is that no country in Latin America is going through so rapid a process of economic development as is Venezuela. The rate of urban growth reflects this. Caracas, before World War II, had a population of only little more than 200,000 within its city limits. At the time of the 1950 census it had reached 495,000. Three years later its population was estimated at more than 600,000. Caracas has expanded far beyond the city limits established by the boundary of the Federal District, and now sprawls into the neighboring parts of the state of Miranda. As a result statistics are of little value in measuring the real rate of growth. The population of Caracas taken as a geographic whole is well over a million. The government has used bulldozers to eliminate slum areas and turn them into parks, and has built beautiful wide avenues and ultramodern buildings to make Caracas one of the most spectacular cities of the world. Maracaibo has gained nearly one hundred thousand people in about three years. And places like Morón have started for the first time to appear on maps.

The rapidly expanding cities and the new urban centers all require attention to a long list of needs. Transportation must be modernized, and

Low-cost housing replacing slum dwellings, outskirts of Caracas

great advances have been made, since 1950, in the program of paved automobile highway construction. The cities must be given adequate water supply and sewage disposal systems. Caracas has recently been provided with a new aqueduct to bring abundant water from the Río Túy. Cities, too, must be provided with electric power. Venezuela is building numerous small diesel power stations to take care of immediate needs. Under construction are four large power plants, only one based on water power. Eventually the whole northern part of the country, at least, will be interconnected through one grid of power lines. Basic to all this economic development are the new manufacturing industries, mostly built with capital derived from the export of oil.

Venezuela, also, is making a strong bid for tourists. Some of the Latin-American countries, notably Mexico, derive an important part of the national income from tourists. Venezuela's bid is supported by the construction of a series of new, modern hotels.

The Democratic Revolution

The industrial revolution is producing these many spectacular changes in Venezuela. But economic development in many ways has the effect of retarding the rate of political change by making more complicated the problem of establishing order. Temporarily, at least, the formulation of a distinctive Venezuelan state-idea is made much more difficult by the rapid urban and industrial development.

After the death of Gómez in 1935, the army officers who succeeded him in office undertook to bring back to Venezuela a measure of political freedom and law. Political parties were permitted to organize. One result was the appearance of a strong liberal democratic movement dedicated to the promotion of those principles we associate with the democratic revolution elsewhere in the world. This movement captured the imagination and support of a great majority of the Venezuelans to such an extent that communism has remained weak and divided. In 1946 a new liberal constitution was adopted, and in 1947 an election was carried out under the provisions of the new constitution. To overcome the problem of illiteracy, ballots were printed on paper of different colors. The vote was secret and the count honest. The result was that the democratic candidate received some 70 percent of the votes.

It was in this period just following World War II that the democratic leaders of Venezuela worked out a new agreement with the oil companies. The principle of the 50-50 split in the profits from the export of oil was accepted. Since then the same principle has been used in many other parts of the world. The Venezuelan government used its half of the oil profits to pay for all the various aspects of economic development described above. The government adopted what is called "sow the oil policy." Long after the oil has been used up, the economy of Venezuela will remain strong because of the new capital investment in the tools of production.

In 1948 the army again seized control of the government. There were many people in positions of political power who regarded the compromises and delays inherent in the democratic process as intolerable. And there were others who supported the use of force to preserve the traditional system of privileges. For nine years Venezuela was ruled by a military dictatorship, under which civil liberty was entirely eliminated. Political opponents were exiled, or jailed and tortured by the secret police. The rights and dignity of the individual citizen were treated with cynical disregard, as they had been during the days of Gómez. The dictator said, "My country is not ready for the kind of democracy that brings abuses." In 1957 he had himself reelected for another term of office by a ballot on which no other candidates were offered.

In spite of the military and police force organized to support the government a bitter revolt broke out in 1958. The revolt would have been impossible without the support of units of the army, the air force, and the navy. Younger officers, for the first time in Venezuelan history, were fighting for civil liberty, not just to remove the older colonels and generals in order to make promotion more rapid. But the military units were also supported by a civilian group in which all political parties were represented. After a period of confusion the dictator was forced to flee, and a new military-civilian government was set up, purged of all those people who had supported the dictator. In 1958 Rómulo Betancourt was elected to the presidency on a platform dedicated to economic development and democratic reforms. The struggle to secure continued support for a democratic state-idea began again, but was challenged repeatedly by splits within Betancourt's party. There were many who felt that the Venezuelans were not ready for responsible citizenship, a feeling which was especially strong among those who had formerly enjoyed privileged status. Furthermore, the Venezuelans were the prime target for attacks by the Cubans under Fidel Castro. The Soviet Union could not fail to recognize prosperous Venezuela, with its supplies of oil and iron ore, as a most important objective of undercover sabotage. Although the number of communists in Venezuela was very small there were many who were antagonistic to the developing economy because of the fundamental changes this kind of development made necessary in the traditional ways of living. Betancourt, challenged by the traditional forces on the right and by the Fidelistas (followers of Fidel Castro) on the left, faced one crisis after another in the effort to lead his country into a new era.

In December 1963, Venezuela held another national election. For many months agents supported by Fidel Castro had been carrying out a series of raids, including the destruction of pipelines, the kidnapping of prominent people, and other acts calculated to call attention to their program of challenge to the democratic regime. The communists directed their followers to stay away from the polls. But on election day 90 percent of the people eligible to vote cast their ballots in as clear an expression of anticommunist sentiment as could have been arranged. Furthermore, there was a rising tide of popular dissatisfaction with some of the policies of Betencourt, and the President knew that he would not have the support given him in the previous election. Yet he ordered out the Venezuelan army to protect the access of the citizens to the ballot boxes, and the ballots were honestly counted. The parties supporting the liberal democratic policies of the government received 55 percent of the votes. For a country struggling to outgrow more than a century of autocracy, this demonstration of support for democratic procedures in the face of strong communist challenge directed from Cuba was a major accomplishment.

COLOMBIA

Colombia is the country which occupies the northwest corner of South America, where the great mountain system of the Andes as it approaches the Caribbean is frayed into parallel cordilleras separated by deep longitudinal depressions. Only the western third of the Colombian national territory lies within the region of mountains and valleys; but within this third there are more different kinds of land than are to be found in any comparable area in South America. There are giant peaks and ranges so high that their summits are permanently white with snow; there are high basins where the air is always chilly; there are forest-clad slopes where the tropical showers feed torrential rivers; and there are lowlands, alternately baked in the tropical sun and drenched with violent rains, where the air

The Cauca River in flood

is always warm and humid. This western third of Colombia is the part in which almost all the Colombians live. The eastern two thirds, which is mostly outside the effective national territory, is composed of a portion of the Guiana Highlands, a portion of the Orinoco Plains, and even a small bit of the Amazon Plain. Such is the variety of terrain, of cordilleras and intermont basins, of lowland plains, of towering heights and swampy lowlands, into which this country is divided.

The diversity of western highland Colombia is not solely a matter of mountainous terrain and varied climates. It is also a matter of diverse people. There are six distinct regions of concentrated settlement which differ from one another not only because of differences of the land, but also because of differences between the people and their forms of economy. There are districts occupied by a mestizo people, not unlike the inhabitants of the highlands of Venezuela; there is one district where most of the inhabitants are pure or nearly pure Indian, not unlike the people of highland Ecuador; and there are districts where Negroes predominate. The long course of Colombia's history of settlement provides many opportunities to illustrate the importance of people and culture in determining the habitability of different kinds of land.

The major features of western Colombia are boldly marked. Four great ranges of mountains, separated by deep longitudinal valleys, run north and south. Along the Pacific coast between Panamá and Buenaventura lies the Serranía de Baudó, a range which belongs geologically to Central America. On the east this range is bordered by a broad lowland extending from the Caribbean to the Pacific, drained in the north by the Río Atrato and in the south by the Río San Juan. East of this lowland, and bordering the Pacific south of Buenaventura, is the *Cordillera Occidental,* or western cordillera. Still farther to the east is the highest of the Colombian ranges, the *Cordillera Central,* also known as the *Cordillera del Quindío.* From the border of Ecuador as far as Cartago the Cordillera Occidental and the Cordillera Central are separated by a wide structural depression, a rift valley, drained in the south by the Río Patía, and in the north by the Río Cauca. From the northern end of this trench the Cauca makes its way toward the Caribbean through a series of profound gorges cut through the very rugged but not very high country where the Cordillera Central and the Cordillera Occidental are joined. The Cordillera Central is the easternmost of the Colombian ranges between the border of Ecuador and approximately latitude 2° north of the equator. Here the eastern cordillera, or *Cordillera Oriental,* has its beginning. This wide cordillera continues northward and northeastward into Venezuela. About latitude 7° N. it separates into two branches, one forming the western rim of the Maracaibo Lowland, the other the southern rim. Between the Cordillera Oriental and the Cordillera Central is the deep structural valley drained by the Río Magdalena—a lowland which merges at its northern end with the lowlands along the coast of the Caribbean. An-other individual mountain group, the Sierra Nevada de Santa Marta, stands prominently on the eastern edge of the Caribbean lowlands and towers above the Caribbean itself. This mountain group is separated from the end of the Cordillera Oriental by the structural depression drained by the Río César.

Vertical Arrangement of the Climates

In such a mountainous country as Highland Colombia the climatic con-ditions, and the natural vegetation which reflects these conditions, present a most intricate pattern. Variations in exposure to the sun, variations in hours of sunlight, and sharp differences in rainfall within small areas are characteristic. In general, however, all this intricacy of detail resolves itself into broad vertical zones, which are especially discernible when one of the mountain ranges is viewed from a distance.

Vertical zoning has more meaning in terms of human settlement in Colombia than in any other part of Latin America. Three principal facts account for this. In the first place, the Colombian Andes are near the equator and are high enough to reach the snow line. This permits the maximum possible amount of vertical differentiation, for as the snow line descends in higher latitudes so also do the other altitude limits. The sec-ond principal fact is that in Colombia, areas of relatively gentle slope are to be found at various elevations from sea level up to the snow line. Finally, the Colombian Andes are occupied by a European people whose many different ways of gaining a living make possible the use of·lands at all altitudes.

Four vertical zones were described by the geographer, Alexander von Humboldt. The tierra caliente has a general upper limit of about 3,000 feet. The tierra templada, or zone of coffee, lies between 3,000 and 6,500 feet. The tierra fría extends from 6,500 to a little over 10,000 feet. Above the tierra fría are the treeless páramos, which extend to the snow line at about 15,000 feet above the sea.

A very common and often-repeated error is to think of the high-altitude climates of the tropics as similar to the climates with the same average temperatures which are found at sea level in the middle latitudes. Many writers on Colombia have stated that by ascending to the tierra fría one reaches temperatures comparable to those of climates much farther from the equator. This is true if we consider average annual temperatures only; but it is far from true if we consider seasonal variation of temperature or variety of weather. In the tropical regions, even at sea level, the range of temperature between the average of the warmest month and the average of the coldest month is only about three or four degrees. As one ascends the mountains the ranges of temperature become less. At Bogotá, 8,660

Coffee picker
in Colombia

feet above sea level, the average annual temperature is 58.1°—exactly the
same as the average annual temperature of Knoxville, Tennessee; but in
Bogotá the difference between the averages of the warmest and the coldest
months is only 1.8°, while the difference at Knoxville is 38.1°. To describe
Bogotá as having a "perpetual spring climate," as is so frequently done,
is to create a very false impression, for there is none of the weather
variety characteristic of a mid-latitude spring.

The Colombian People

The people who occupy this exceptionally diverse terrain are of European, Indian, and Negro ancestry. Estimates of the proportions of these
ingredients are little more than informed guesses. Perhaps 20 percent of
the total population is of unmixed European ancestry. About 7 percent
of the Colombians are Indians who are nearly pure-blooded and who
continue to live much as did their ancestors. About 5 percent is Negro and
various Negro mixtures with both Europeans and Indians. Approximately
68 percent is mestizo. But these estimates can be quite misleading regarding the real mixture of people in Colombia, for within the three chief
racial groups there are many strongly contrasted varieties, and the racial
proportions differ widely from one part of the country to another.

The Native Indians

Before the European discovery of America the territory which is now Colombia was occupied by Indians of many different cultures. There were tribes whose way of living can be described as primitive, since it included very little choice in the manner of making a living and included little knowledge of the arts. But there was one group of tribes with a culture almost as advanced as that of the great Indian civilizations of Peru and Mexico. The Indians with the most advanced or complex way of living were the *Chibchas,* a sedentary agricultural people who occupied the high basins of the Cordillera Oriental. In this remote mountain region the Chibchas had been brought together politically under the leadership of two chiefs—the *Zipa* whose capital was near the present city of Bogotá, and the *Zaque* whose capital was on the site of the modern city of Tunja. The political ability of the Chibchas of this region of high basins was far superior to that of any of the other tribes in Colombia. The Chibchas of the highlands were superior to other Colombian tribes whose language was so closely related to theirs that anthropologists commonly group them together. Like most of the highland Indians of America, all the Chibcha tribes were dependent on the basic food staples, maize and potatoes. They also derived part of their food from the guinea pig which they had domesticated. Like the other highland Indians from Mexico to Chile, the Chibchas had no concept of private property in land. These Indians had established fixed settlements, and in places favorable to their form of agriculture the density of population was comparable to that of highland Mexico and Peru.

The Indians who occupied the Cordillera Central and the Cauca Valley are included in the general Chibcha group; yet in many ways they were distinct from the highland Chibchas of the Cordillera Oriental. Politically they were much less advanced: in the vicinity of Cartago, for example, the Spaniards found the Indians living under the rule of more than sixty petty chieftains. On the other hand, the Indians of this part of Colombia were more advanced than the highland Chibchas in their technique of pottery making and their knowledge of metallurgy. Since gold was plentiful in the territory they occupied, they were especially skilled in the use of this metal and of alloys of gold with silver and with copper. The tribes of the Cauca Region fed themselves chiefly by hunting and fishing, but they supplemented their diet with maize, manioc, and yams. They also planted cotton, and made cotton textiles.

As anthropological studies progress, a greater and greater variety of Indian cultures is described. Yet increased detail does not obscure two fundamental facts important in our attempt to understand the distribution of people. First is the fact that only the Chibchas of the eastern highlands had become sedentary farmers, cultivating the same land year after year. The other tribes were either migratory hunters and fishers, or shifting cultivators—that is, people whose villages were more or less fixed in position, but whose croplands were temporary. Densities of population comparable to those of Mexico and Peru were found only in the areas of sedentary settlement; the other parts of Colombia were very sparsely populated. Second is the fact that none of the peoples of Colombia possessed domestic animals, except the dog and the guinea pig. The result was that for these Indians many of the lands now utilized for pastoral activities were quite uninhabitable.

The European Conquest

A result of the Spanish conquest of Colombia was a great increase both in the area that could be used for human habitation, and in the variety of land use. The Spaniards brought with them cattle, horses, and sheep; they introduced wheat, barley, and sugar cane, and a number of farm practices previously unknown to the natives. These importations increased the agricultural productivity of the high basins because the European grains gave better yields at these altitudes than did the Indian maize, and domestic animals made possible the spread of settlement above the upper limit of the potato into the lands which had previously been considered uninhabitable.

The first Spanish settlements in Colombia were along the Caribbean Coast. Balboa founded a colony on the shores of the gulf of Darien which was perhaps the first European settlement on the continent, though the place was abandoned after a few years. The oldest surviving Spanish colonies are Santa Marta (founded in 1525), and Cartagena (founded in 1533). The first expeditions to enter the highland country to the south were organized to search for the mineral wealth which the stories of El Dorado had magnified. When the Spaniards discovered, in the eastern highlands, the relatively dense populations of sedentary peaceful Indians, they were surprised and delighted, for here, they soon realized, was the chief wealth of the country—Indians to work on the land or in the mines, Indians to be converted to Christianity.

Many writers assert that the Spaniards climbed into the mountains in order to escape from the heat of the lowlands, but the real incentives seem rather to have been gold and dense Indian populations. There is little to suggest that the Spaniards were the kind of people to place comfort or ease of living before the attainment of these objectives. Where gold was to be found, there the Spaniards settled; but such settlements were in many cases temporary, as all gold-mining settlements are apt to be. Where sedentary Indians were found, there also the Spaniards settled; and these settlements were likely to be permanent because they were based on the exploitation of a stable supply of Indian labor. Bogotá was founded in 1538. It was located in the Basin of Cundinamarca in the remote fastnesses of the Cordillera Oriental, accessible only with great difficulty from the coast, but easily accessible to the largest single area of densely concentrated native peoples. Bogotá, center of economic life in the colonial period, became, and still remains, the political center of Colombia.

The Spaniards entered from three directions. 1. From Santa Marta expeditions ascended to the high basins of the Cordillera Oriental, and after the founding of Bogotá, other expeditions went northward along the Cordillera Oriental, and even pushed into the Cordillera de Mérida in what is now Venezuela. 2. From Cartagena many Spaniards advanced southward into the Cauca Valley, where, between 1536 and 1540, they founded numerous small mining towns in localities where the stream gravels contained rich stores of gold. 3. Meanwhile a third group of Spaniards came northward from Peru by way of Quito, founding Pasto and Popayán in southern Colombia, and meeting the Spaniards from Cartagena in the latitude of Cali.

The Spanish conquest produced great changes in Colombia. The sedentary Chibchas soon learned to care for the European domestic animals and to cultivate the European grains. The Indians in the high basins became serfs attached to the large estates, owned by the officers of the conquering army; and new Indian communities were established in the páramos—the high country above the upper limit of agriculture, but below the limit of permanent snow. In these higher regions the Indians remained predominant in numbers, but the wealth in terms of the European economy was accumulated by the new land-owning aristocracy.

Meanwhile the more primitive Indians of other parts of Colombia were proving to be quite inadequate to meet the labor demands of the conquerors—whether in the placer mines or on the plantations where the new commercial crops, sugar cane and indigo, were cultivated. The native peoples were ravaged by imported diseases against which they had no immunity, and were unable easily to adapt themselves to the hard work demanded by the Spaniards. By the end of the first century after the conquest the more primitive tribes of Colombia had either been wiped out by epidemics or had withdrawn to the remote selvas of the Pacific slope. The Spaniards, therefore, resorted to Negro slaves, and Negroes came, in the course of time, greatly to outnumber the whites in certain parts of the lowlands.

Development of Colombia since the Conquest

By 1770 Colombia had a population of about 800,000. A century later the population had grown, chiefly by natural increase, to about 3,000,000.

In the vicinity of Popayán

Well into the nineteenth century gold remained the chief economic interest of the ruling group, and even today Colombia is one of the leading gold-producing countries of Latin America. In the twentieth century oil and platinum were added to the list of mineral products. Yet during all this time most of the people of Colombia were engaged in agriculture and not in mining. Maize was by far the leading crop, but commercial crops of sugar cane, tobacco, indigo, and cacao were also cultivated. During the second half of the nineteenth century, cinchona bark, the source of quinine, was gathered in the forests. These various economic activities suffered, before the Wars of Independence, from excessive taxation and trade restrictions imposed by the mother country, and, after independence, from the recurring internal conflicts which plagued the country.

The cultivation of coffee added an important factor to the economic life of Colombia. Not until after 1880 did the mild, high-grade coffee produced in the highlands begin to find a preferred place in the markets of Europe and North America. Little by little coffee came to be even more important than it was in Venezuela, and Colombia today is the world's second largest producer of this commodity. The spread of coffee planting in the tierra templada, on slopes too steep for most other forms of agricultural use, brought increased productivity and a rapid growth of new settlement to parts of Colombia which had previously been of little economic importance.

All these various economic activities served to mark off the Colombian territory into strongly contrasted regions. But during and since World War II even more striking diversification has been produced by the rapid development of manufacturing industries. Industrial development has been centered chiefly around Medellín in the Department of Antioquia, and the rapidly increased income of the people of this part of Colombia stands in sharp contrast with the poverty of other parts of the country. All this has made more difficult the establishment of order.

Economic Development

It was estimated in 1962 that the population of Colombia was nearly fifteen million. The annual rate of growth (3.4 percent) was second only to that of Venezuela in all Latin America. The population is supported chiefly by agriculture (54 percent), and the income per capita ($185 in 1962) was less than a fifth of that of Venezuela. Yet the proportion of people able to read and write (56 percent) was considerably higher than that of Venezuela.

Internal commerce between the different areas of concentrated settlement seems to have been developed earlier and to have gone on more persistently than in most other Latin-American countries. Even before the arrival of the Spaniards, the highland Chibchas used to exchange their salt for the gold prepared by the Indians of the Cauca Valley. The Spaniards increased and diversified this trade between highlands and lowlands, exchanging wheat and potatoes for sugar cane and cotton. Even during the period of chaos which followed the death of Bolívar the undercurrent of commerce continued to link the various parts of the country together.

Today the Magdalena Valley carries many articles of domestic commerce. Up the river go the cattle, sugar, and cotton of the Caribbean Coastal Lowlands consigned to the highland centers. The lowland cotton supplies part of the raw material for the textile factories of Medellín. Grain and potatoes from the high basins of Cundinamarca and Boyacá descend to help in feeding the lowland populations. Two important commercial crops in Colombia in terms of acreage are sugar cane and cacao; yet sugar and cacao enter scarcely at all into foreign commerce, for most of these products are consumed in the candy factories of Medellín and Bogotá. There are close commercial connections between the Cauca Valley and Antioquia. Even remote Pasto sends a trickle of commerce to the gold-mining communities of the coastal region. All of these currents of internal trade have been of great importance in overcoming the isolation of the separate areas of settlement.

The Basin of Cundinamarca on the outskirts of Bogotá, the University of the Andes in the middle distance

Foreign Trade

Coffee is the crop which has contributed most to the material prosperity of the Colombians, especially of the Antioqueños. Colombian coffee enjoys a favored position on the world markets because of its excellent flavor. Most of the coffees sold in the United States are given their distinctive tastes by the relatively small proportions of Colombian coffee which are blended with the much larger proportions of the Brazilian product. Colombian coffee on the New York market generally commands a much higher price than that of the Brazilian varieties. Since 1920 Colombia has been the world's leading source of mild, high-grade coffee, and has been second only to Brazil in total production. Even as early as 1910, coffee amounted to 53 percent of the value of Colombia's exports. In 1925 it amounted to 78 percent. Now it is over 75 percent. Colombia depends almost as much on coffee exports as Venezuela does on oil. Most of the coffee exports go to the United States.

The central business district of Bogotá

The export statistics, however, do not tell the whole story, for coffee is of even greater significance to the economy of Colombia than its proportion of the total value of exports would indicate. The production of oil, gold, and platinum is largely in the hands of North American corporations, and the export of these products brings a relatively small flow of dollars to Colombia. Furthermore, these mining enterprises require the services of only a small fraction of the Colombian workers—probably not more than 30,000 or 40,000 altogether. Oil, gold, and platinum, therefore, make only a small contribution to the national economy. But coffee is another matter. A large number of Colombians gain directly from the production of this commodity, and from its export Colombia derives most of its dollars needed to pay for imports.

This dependence on coffee is not entirely sound. In the first place coffee has been planted in many mountainous areas where slopes are steep and where soils are quickly eroded when the original forest cover is removed. Coffee planting on steep slopes has resulted in serious land destruction, especially in the Antioquia region. Around Manizales many deep gullies have appeared, and much land has been ruined. In the second place, so much attention has been paid to growing coffee that the production of basic foods has been neglected. Although maize occupies the largest acreage of any crop, not enough is produced to meet the needs of the Colombian people. There is a deficiency also of the other foods, especially rice, beans, wheat, sugar, and vegetables. It is hoped that the planned improvement of agriculture in the Cauca Valley will result in an important increase in the supply of basic foods.

Colombians also place great hopes on the success of the new Paz del Río steel plant at Belencito, 160 miles to the north of Bogotá in the *Cordillera Oriental*. Because of the availability of iron ore, coal, limestone, and water close to the plant it was estimated that the cost of production here could be the lowest in all Latin America. On the other hand, no other steel plant in Latin America faces such serious obstacles in the transportation of its product to market. In such places as Medellín and Cali, steel manufactured at Belencito would be more expensive than steel manufactured at Barranquilla from imported iron ore and coal. A high protective tariff permits the Paz del Río plant to sell its steel within Colombia in competition with imported steel. Colombia would seem to have gained a measure of economic self-sufficiency, but at a high cost to the domestic economy (Map 15, page 47).

The Political Situation

It would be difficult to conceive of a geographic pattern of internal arrangement that would appear to make the achievement of political unity and coherence more difficult than in Colombia. Yet the fact is that the ideas and ideals of liberal democracy have gained considerable support, and in spite of long-continued internal conflicts there is hope that the individual citizen may before long enjoy a greater measure of equality before the law and may participate in political decisions more effectively than he has in the recent past.

For a long time after Bolívar was forced to give up his efforts, Colombia was torn by civil war. The economy of the country suffered severely from the devastation. Only the Antioqueños around Medellín, in the *Cordillera Central* were spared from the most serious effects of the disorders because of the isolation of their settlements. Then for a time it seemed as if a political balance had been achieved and democratic procedures could be developed. This came about in part because the separate regions of settlement were more or less balanced, and no one of them was powerful enough to subdue all the others.

In the period following World War I the people of Antioquia (the Antioqueños) adopted coffee as an export product. Within a decade or so this one part of Colombia had gained a predominant position in the national economy. Since World War II industrial development in Medellín has further increased the contrast between the level of living and the economic outlook of the Antioqueños and the living conditions and outlooks of other parts of Colombia. Yet the Antioqueños continue to think of themselves as Antioqueños first, and Colombians second. A military dictatorship gained control of the country, civil liberties disappeared, newspapers were tightly controlled: in short, political order was imposed by force.

In 1957 a new effort to find a compromise between extremes of political opinion was made under the leadership of Alberto Lleres Camargo. The dictatorship was ended and steps were taken to return to democratic procedures. Under the dictatorship numerous projects for economic development were started, including the establishment of the Cauca Valley Corporation modeled on the North American Tennessee Valley Authority. In so far as poverty increases the danger of political conflict, economic development is seen by many people in Colombia as a pressing necessity. But there are also many who feel that the establishment of a free, democratic society is more important than economic development. Inside the country there is a struggle between these conflicting attitudes, and the struggle often breaks out into violence. The question is: Can a state-idea be formulated that will command the support of a great majority of the people, Antioqueños as well as the people of Pasto, or of Cali, or of the high basins of Cundinamarca and Boyacá? Some way must be found to bring cohesion to this diverse country, and to make diversity a source of strength rather than weakness.

Quito with the volcano Pichincha in the background and Indian farms on slopes

CHAPTER SIX

The Andean Countries

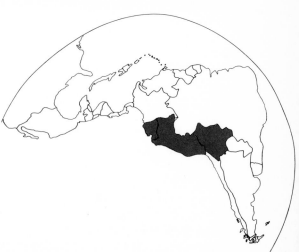

Ecuador, Peru, and Bolivia are the countries that occupy the rugged Andes and extend eastward to the plains beyond the mountains. About half of the total population of these three countries is of unmixed Indian ancestry. These are the Quechua and Aymara Indians that were under the rule of the Incas when the Spanish conquerors first reached South America. Even today, large numbers of Indians live much as their ancestors did, making a miserable living from the cultivation of potatoes and other hardy crops on the high and steep mountainous terrain. The three countries have these general conditions in common; yet each of them is distinctive, and the Spanish-speaking inhabitants, at least, are deeply conscious of their national individuality.

ECUADOR

In Ecuador the problem of establishing order and coherence in the national life stubbornly resists solution. The problem is vastly complicated in this country because of a simple geographic fact: the division of the country into two major contrasted groups of people, each occupying a separate area. One group is largely Indian, self-sufficient, unmoved by sentiments of nationality, and quite uninterested in foreign commerce; the other is largely mestizo, strongly conscious of nationality and commercially active. The first group occupies the high intermont basins of the Andes; the second group occupies the coastal region on the borders of

Maps 2, 4, 6, 8, 11, 13, 14, 15, 21, 22, 25 are pertinent to this chapter.

the Pacific. Between these two groups the establishment of harmony and coordination in the national political or economic life is extremely difficult. And because no great source of revenue for the public treasury, comparable to the oil of Venezuela, has ever been discovered in Ecuador, the country remains poor, and the central political authority remains relatively weak.

Compared with Colombia, Ecuador is much simpler in its geographic arrangement. The backbone of the country is formed by the high ranges of the Andes. There are two high cordilleras, surmounted by towering volcanoes and separated by a series of ten intermont basins, all of them lying within the tierra fría. To the west of the Andes is the coastal region, composed partly of swampy lowlands, partly of low hills. The coastal region is covered in the north by a dense rain forest, but toward the south as the rainfall becomes less, the vegetation changes from wet forest to dry scrub woodland and savanna. The third part of Ecuador lies east of the Andes. This is the *Oriente*, the rainy forested eastern slopes and piedmont of the Andes which descend toward the Amazon plains beyond.

The national territory of Ecuador is of uncertain area because of recent changes in the boundaries and the lack of precise surveys. It has been computed as 105,684 square miles. Not all of this area, however, is included in the effective national territory. Most of the Ecuadoreans live in the high basins of the Andes and in certain parts of the coastal lowlands, chiefly the Guayas Valley. Most of the Oriente is essentially unoccupied except by independent tribes of forest Indians. During the early 1940's the Peruvians invaded territory claimed but not effectively occupied by Ecuador. As a result, Ecuador was deprived of all contact with navigable water on the Amazon tributaries. Ecuador still claims the territory lost to Peru.

Population

Until 1950 there had never been a census of the population of Ecuador. In that year the official count registered a little over three million people; in 1962 the population was estimated at 4,600,000. At least 60 percent of the population is pure Indian, and perhaps another 22 percent is mestizo. The Ecuadoreans estimate that about 15 percent is of unmixed European ancestry. The remaining 3 percent is pure Negro and mulatto. However, these racial groups are not uniformly mixed throughout the country, for the Indians make up almost 100 percent of the rural people of the highlands. The pure Europeans are concentrated in Quito and Guayaquil. Indians, mestizos, and Negroes make up the population of the lowlands. There can be no doubt that Ecuador is an Indian country with a relatively small mixture of "Latin."

The Course of Settlement

The high basins of Ecuador were already occupied by a dense population of sedentary Indians before the Spanish conquest. Shortly before the Europeans arrived on the scene, the Incas had extended the boundaries of their Empire northward to include Quito. But the distance which separated this northernmost region from the capital at Cuzco was so great that communications were difficult to maintain and the power of the central authority was established only because the Inca himself spent much of his time in Quito. The Inca Empire was threatened with division and internal discord at the time when the Spaniards reached the shores of Peru.

Except for temporary landings along the coast made by Pizarro and his men as they worked their way southward, Ecuador was not entered by the Spaniards until after the conquest of Peru. In 1534 an expedition advanced northward from Peru and occupied the Indian town of Quito. From Quito the Spaniards continued northward into the Cauca Valley of Colombia, founding the towns of Pasto and Popayán.

The search for El Dorado, however, did not bring to light any great wealth in this part of South America. Restlessly the Spaniards pushed their explorations down the western slopes to the Pacific, and eastward to the headwaters of the Amazon. In 1542 the Spaniard, Orellana, sailed the length of the Amazon to its mouth, but without discovering what the Spaniards most desired—gold and large concentrations of Indians. Ecuador remained isolated and poor.

Isolation and poverty, rather than any strong sentiment of nationality, gave Ecuador its political independence. During the colonial period Quito had been administered first from Lima and later from Bogotá. When the Wars of Independence freed the colonies from Spain, Quito was included with Colombia and Venezuela in Gran Colombia which Bolívar attempted to form and administer from Bogotá. The collapse of Bolívar's state left the more remote parts, Venezuela and Ecuador, free to announce their independence.

Unfortunately for the establishment of order among such diverse elements as exist together in Ecuador, the political center of the country is located in the midst of the Indian communities of the Andes whereas the economic center of the country is located on the coast. Quito, the capital, a city of a little over 260,000 inhabitants, is situated where the problems of foreign commercial and political relations seem remote indeed. Guayaquil, the chief commercial city, with a population of more than 400,000, is located on a navigable river on the low plains west of the Andes. This geographical separation of the political and the commercial centers, and the fact that the contacts between the highland Indian communities and the lowland settlements are not intimate, are major factors in the interpretation of Ecuador's internal difficulties.

Ecuador as a Political Unit

The problem of establishing order and coherence in the national life of Ecuador still remains to be solved. The contrast between the stolid subsistence farmers of the Andes and the speculative planters of the lowlands makes almost impossible the formulation of a nationally acceptable state-idea. As a result governments are insecure and policies uncertain.

Ecuador remains a poor country. In 1962 with a population of more than four million, it had a per capita income of only $198. The small minority of wealthy landowners live quite well, and now an increasing number of small farmers are beginning to share in the economic rewards. The government has not accepted this lack of economic development as inevitable. A favorable tax policy is one of the factors leading to a spectacular increase of banana production in the Guayas Lowland. Since World War II, new highways have been built to connect Ecuador's mountain centers with the coastal region. A deep-water port in the estuary southwest of Guayaquil has been completed. A great effort has been made, also, to provide elementary schooling, with the result that 56 percent of the people can now read and write—the same proportion as that of Colombia.

The chief exports of Ecuador are all derived from plantations in the Guayas Valley. In 1961 bananas made up 52 percent of the value of all exports. Ecuador had by that time become the world's leading banana producer, accounting for 24 percent of world production. Other exports included cacao (16 percent), coffee (15 percent), and rice (3 percent). The United States purchased 61 percent of Ecuador's exports, but increasing amounts were also going to West Germany, Belgium, Colombia, and France. The chief imports include machinery, iron and steel products, foods, and tobacco, a large part of which is supplied by the United States.

Nevertheless, a large proportion of the people of Ecuador remain very poor. The country is still divided into two parts: the coastal region, and the high Andean basins, each with its own distinctive kind of population. Again and again since Ecuador became independent, the government has been too weak to establish and maintain control over the more remote parts of the country. The most recent loss has been in the Oriente. The Ecuadoreans still claim a large part of the eastern plains, even as far as Iquitos; but the Peruvians have established effective control over this area. During the 1940's a boundary was surveyed that in effect cut off Ecuador from navigable water on the Amazon tributaries. Ecuador still has a small Oriente where the spurs of the Andes run out toward the plains through a belt of foothills.

Stories of vast wealth continue to trickle back across the mountains. The search for El Dorado has been translated today into a search for oil. If oil should be discovered along this part of the eastern Andean piedmont, as is geologically possible, the overlapping territorial claims may well lead to open conflict.

Loading bananas by hand near Guayaquil

PERU

After more than four hundred years, Peru, like Ecuador, is still struggling with the unsolved problems arising from the contact of two incompatible cultures. In Peru the Indians had built one of the great pre-Columbian civilizations of America—the Empire of the Incas. To Peru was directed one of the main currents of Spanish colonial conquest. The Indians and the Spaniards met and mixed, but they never were amalgamated into a coherent society. The patterns developed by the Spaniards were superimposed upon those developed by the Indians, but with little real blending between the two.

Nor are these racial and cultural contrasts the only elements of diversity in Peru. The national territory is divided into a very dry west coast, mighty ranges of mountains, rainy and densely forested eastern slopes, and wet tropical plains. Furthermore, the significance of these contrasted parts in terms of human settlement has changed very greatly in the course of history. And additional diversity has come to Peru in modern times through the growth of an industrial society which contrasts strangely with the traditional Spanish society in the smaller towns and the rural districts.

Peru is still as much Indian as it is European. To understand the way of living of more than half of the people one must go far back to a study of the Inca civilization in the pre-Columbian period. For, always in the background of the growing industrial cities is the still unsolved discordance between Spaniards and Indians, a discordance which has marked the Peruvian landscape and colored Peruvian problems since the two civilizations first came into contact with each other.

The Empire of the Incas

The rise of the civilization of the Incas was, in itself, an extraordinary thing—an event overlooked by most North Americans because, unlike the history of the civilizations of Mesopotamia or Egypt, Inca history is not essential to an understanding of the main stream of Occidental culture. Only for some of the Andean peoples of South America—for the peoples of Ecuador, Peru, and Bolivia—is a knowledge of this Indian culture of compelling importance because of the numerous present conditions of life which can be traced back to Indian origins. The ancient civilizations of Mesopotamia, Egypt, India, and China all began in the highly productive valleys of great rivers, where closely knit and coherent societies originated partly through the necessity for the cooperative use of water. But the Incas built their civilization in a territory which would seem to be as unsuited to economic prosperity and political unity as any that could be imagined. From a center in a small intermont basin high in the Andes the lines of authority were extended far to the north and to the south over a land creased by profound canyons, and separated into compartments by gigantic, snow-capped ranges. In the land of the Incas, as one writer puts it, everything was inferior except man. The achievement, considered in this light, assumes all the greater importance.

Whatever may have been the earlier diversity of people and ways of living in the territory conquered by the Incas, the benevolent and paternalistic rule from Cuzco minimized the chief differences and set a uniform stamp over all but the most recently invaded communities. The whole empire was divided into four parts, each served by one of the great Inca roads which focused on the capital city: with reference to Cuzco these parts lay to the north, the northwest, the southeast, and the south.

Machu Picchu, ruin of Inca fortress in eastern Andes

Within each of these four parts the subjects of the Sapa Inca were systematically arranged in groups of standard sizes. Before the Inca conquest, the largest political unit was the *ayllu,* a village community of variable size which held its lands in common. The Inca recognized the family rather than the individual as the basic unit of the empire. Groups of families were administered as communities by appointed officials: groups of ten, fifty, one hundred, five hundred, one thousand, ten thousand, and forty thousand families. The groups were kept at these approximate sizes by the resettlement of families in new colonies. This whole logical and systematic organization was responsible to and derived its authority from the Sapa Inca, who held complete power over the lives of every one of his subjects and in whom was vested the ownership of land.

In the state organized by the Incas the individual existed only as a part of a household; and the household existed only for the service of the state. Inca administration had as its chief function the maintenance of production and the distribution of surplus commodities. The state had no important contacts with people beyond the borders of the empire— there were no problems of foreign relations, but only problems of domestic production and supply. The Inca engineers increased the arable area by control of the water supply and by the construction of terraces (or

The llama is Peru's domestic beast of burden

andenes) on the valley sides. Just as wheat, barley, and rice formed the food bases of the ancient civilizations of Asia and Africa, maize was the basic food of the Incas. But it was supplemented by other foods. At the higher altitudes the hardy grain quinoa and potatoes were important. The former, combined with peppers, was used in a kind of soup; potatoes were used to produce *chuñu,* a potato meal which is still one of the chief foods of the Andean Indians. The dried meat of llamas was also included in the diet of the ordinary people—fresh meat was generally restricted to the Inca and his family. In addition to these foods, the ordinary people had an alcoholic beverage made of maize—a kind of beer known as *chicha;* and they were addicted to the chewing of coca leaves mixed with clay. Both chicha and coca[1] are still consumed by the highland Indians from Ecuador to northern Chile.

The products of each community were divided, at the discretion of the Inca administrators, into three parts. One part went to the priests of the sun; one part was used for the support of the Inca and his family; and one part was left for the support of the community. There was usually a surplus above the immediate needs of the Inca. This surplus was stored in warehouses and was available for distribution in any part of the empire where crops had failed.

The lives of individuals were closely and benevolently regulated under this system. There was no need for imagination, no need for ambition and initiative, no need to depart from the standard routine, no need to worry about poverty and hunger. Work was assigned by age groups, beginning with coca picking and other light work for people between sixteen and twenty, culminating in a period of maximum labor between twenty-five and fifty, and decreasing beyond fifty. Marriages were arranged by the authorities, leaving the individual only a slight range of choice. The Incas carefully preserved certain recreations; they set aside three days in every month for fairs at which each family could exchange its products for the products of other families. At these fairs no set standards of value were imposed, but each transaction was the result of a specially arranged barter. As in the case of most of the Indian fairs of both South America and Middle America, going to market was fully as much a social function as a commercial one.

The problem of communications within the empire was a major one. The roads which led in four directions out of Cuzco were paved, or in places cut out of solid rock. Suspension bridges spanned some of the deep canyons. Since there were no wheeled vehicles and no domestic animals that men could ride, travel was entirely on foot, and the roads were designed accordingly. Communications were maintained by relays of runners—men specially trained from boyhood for this particular service.

[1] Not to be confused with cacao, the source of chocolate. Coca is a small shrub from which cocaine is extracted.

The domestication of some of the native Andean animals was also a major achievement. The Indians of the Inca Empire had no poultry, no horses, no cattle, no sheep, no hogs, and no cats; they used the dog only as a pet, or in some cases for hunting purposes. But they did domesticate two closely related animals: the llama and the alpaca.

The llama remains even now one of the most important beasts of burden in the highlands of Peru and Bolivia. As a carrier he is by no means as efficient as the mule. Although gentle and easily handled, the llama has a remarkably stubborn disposition, for when he is tired or feels overloaded he will promptly lie down and resist all efforts to move him, even resorting to the unpleasant habit of spitting, camel-like, at those who come within range. He can carry no more than about one hundred pounds; and he must be driven at a leisurely pace, in a train, grazing as he goes. A llama train can cover little more than ten miles a day.

The smaller and less sturdy alpaca, a relative of the llama, is still used for its wool. Fine alpaca wool was the basis of the Inca textiles.

The artistic and technical achievements of the Incas were of a high order. The designing and weaving of textiles from alpaca wool and from cotton was one of their most notable skills. Anthropologists point out that the natives of Peru discovered and made use of almost every known technique of weaving. Their pottery was colorful and finely modeled, yet it was made without the use of a wheel. Like all other native American cultures, the Inca culture included no practical application of the circle—a geometric figure of which, however, they were not ignorant. The Inca engineers never made use of wheels, they never built towers, or columns, or keystone arches. Yet they were able to build suspension bridges, to construct long irrigation ditches over rugged surfaces, to terrace the mountain slopes, and to build massive walls with stones so closely fitted together that, without mortar, they have resisted the forces of destruction to the present day. The Incas were skilled workers in metals, and although they had no knowledge of iron, they did know how to make bronze from copper and tin. They had no written language, but they kept accounts in the form of knotted strings, known as *quipus*. Their decimal system of figuring was much less cumbersome than the Roman system used by the Spaniards, or even than the money system now in use in Great Britain. And their peculiar plaintive music is only just now being "discovered."

The Inca state may be described as a benevolent paternalism. To make use of other terms, such as "socialist" or "communist," with meanings derived from modern European forms is only to obscure the truly indigenous quality of the Inca way of living. In one fundamental way the Inca concepts differed essentially from the concepts of the Spanish conquerors. The Incas had only an elementary understanding of the idea of private property. To be sure, the family dwelling and its contents, together with the land on which it stood, was regarded as belonging to its occupants as long as they, themselves, desired to use it. But the native Peruvians had no understanding of the ownership of land for prestige or profit. Land, as such, had no value—its value was only in terms of what it could produce; the ownership of land being vested in the Sapa Inca, and earlier in the ayllu as a community, such ownership did not constitute a means to prestige. Nor did the Incas understand the concept of the exploitation of natural resources for personal gain. In all these basic ideas they differed radically from the people who conquered them; and in the years since the conquest the descendants of both groups have yet to find a common ground of understanding on these questions.

The European Impact

The amazing story of the conquest of Peru by Francisco Pizarro and his little band of fewer than 200 men equipped with 27 horses is well known. Taking advantage of dissension among the rulers of the Empire, the Spaniards were able to complete the overthrow of the Incas in the comparatively brief period between January, 1531, and November, 1533, in which month the conquerors made their victorious entry into Cuzco. Once the leadership of the ruling group had been removed, the majority of the inhabitants, long accustomed to unquestioning obedience to central authority, easily accepted the new rulers.

Immediately after the conquest profound differences began to appear between the Spanish way of living and that of the Indians. These differences were reflected in the complete reorientation of the economic life which took place within a few years. The Spaniards were interested in their overseas connections, and as a result the coastal region was abruptly changed from a place remote from the center of political and economic activity to the place on which these activities focused. The longitudinal roads of the Incas were abandoned in favor of short transverse roads leading from various parts of the highlands to the nearest ports on the coast. Lima was founded in 1535, and, with its port Callao, assumed preeminence as the primary settlement center from which the Spanish culture was spread over almost all of western South America. Lima became the center of political power, the center of social life, the center of commerce—a city of fabulous wealth.

Contrasts in Land Tenure and Agricultural Systems

One of the first methods used by the Spaniards to collect wealth from the Indian communities was the system known as the *encomienda*. This system was based on the theory that conquered peoples should pay tribute

The headman in an Indian community carries a cane as his symbol of authority

to the conquerors. The Spanish crown delegated the right to receive this tribute from a specific group of Indian communities to certain of the officers of the army and to others who could establish their right to such a claim.

The encomienda, which carried with it no right to the ownership of the land, was scarcely enough for the conquerors of Peru. Few of the men under Pizarro, few even of the officers, were already members of the Spanish aristocracy: Pizarro himself had been a swineherd on one of the large feudal estates of Spain. Such adventurers passionately desired the opportunity to acquire land and so to gain a position of prestige. Grants of land by the Spanish crown, therefore, soon led to the creation of vast private estates, and to the formation of a new aristocracy. But the ownership of land which brought prestige did not also bring economic security to the owner unless that land included a supply of Indian workers, for under the Spanish system production of any sort, whether in the mines or on the fields, was dependent on the labor of the native peoples.

On estates, or *haciendas,* which measured thousands of square miles in area, the more remote districts could not be brought under the effective supervision of the owner or his managers. In the more accessible parts of the haciendas the owners made use of the Indian workers to raise commercial crops; but in the more distant places the Indian communities continued to use the land in the traditional way, only paying a kind of rent to the new owner. When properties changed hands the Indian communities were transferred as a part of the land; in fact, it was the presence of the Indians which gave the land its value. In this way the two contrasted systems of land tenure—the traditional communal system of the Indians and the system of private property introduced by the Spaniards—continued to exist together in the same area.

The European conquest also resulted in a serious decrease in the food supply. To be sure, the introduction of cattle made habitable large areas of high mountain grassland which had remained without permanent settlement in Inca times. But great numbers of Indians were removed from the coastal oases or from the highland agricultural centers for work in the mines, and since most of the latter were at very high altitudes this work proved very exhausting and many of the workers never returned to their homes. The irrigation systems which the Inca engineers had built, and the Indian communities had maintained, were permitted to break down through neglect. The increased habitability of the highlands through the introduction of cattle did not compensate for this loss of agricultural productivity at the lower altitudes, for the use of land for pasture does not produce as much food per square mile as does the cultivation of crops, especially with the intensive methods which the Incas had developed.

Population Changes

The decrease in the food supply was accompanied by an enormous decline in the Indian population. Great numbers of the Indians died from overwork in the mines and from epidemics of smallpox and measles. By 1580, about fifty years after the arrival of the Spaniards, the number of Indian inhabitants in the territory of the Inca Empire had been reduced by about a third.

The present Peruvian population is still predominantly Indian. Some 46 percent of the inhabitants are of unmixed Indian ancestry, and 38 percent is mestizo. Perhaps 15 percent is of pure European descent, and 1 percent is Oriental (Japanese and Chinese). It is significant that the proportion of pure Indian is being gradually reduced: in 1876 pure Indians made up 58 percent of the population. In terms of language, there is still a large proportion of people (35 percent) who speak no Spanish—only Quechua or Aymara, the two Indian languages. The number of people speaking only Spanish is also high (46 percent). Most of the Peruvians still live in the highlands (62 percent), where the clusters of people are predominantly Indian. About 25 percent occupy the coastal region, and 13 percent are in the forested eastern part of Peru.

The Peruvian Economy

In 1962 the population of Peru was estimated at 10,600,000. The rate of growth seems to be about 2.1 percent per year, which is less than the average for Latin America as a whole.

A very large proportion of these people are subsistence farmers. Essentially they are outside of the international system of buying and selling; the things they consume are mostly the things they have themselves produced. Some 58 percent cannot read or write. Many of them are tenants, or wage workers for part of the year on large private properties. Only about 16 percent are engaged in industry or mining. For this reason most of the discussion of the Peruvian economy based on statistics of exports and imports, and most calculations of the gross national production have to do with the ways of making a living of a minority of the inhabitants of the country. The estimate of $126 per capita income in 1962 obscures the fact that a few make a much larger income, and a great many make much less than this figure.

For the first three and a half centuries of European rule in Peru, the commercial part of the economy was focused of mineral exports. Silver and gold were the commodities for which the Spaniards prized their colony. It was not until late in the nineteenth century that sugar cane and cotton began to rival the mineral exports. In 1900, sugar cane made up 32 percent of the value of all exports. Since 1925, when the sugar plantations suffered much damage, cotton has usually been ahead of sugar as an export. During World War II, oil exports rose to first place in the list, and for a year or so cotton dropped far down. Generally, however, the agricultural exports have shown a steady gain, whereas the mineral exports have shown great fluctuations from year to year. Copper exports dropped after 1940, but with the development of the newly discovered ore body at Toquepala in southern Peru this commodity may again increase rapidly. Coal is a new item on the list of exports. Peru's imports are chiefly machinery, especially mining machinery, and foods, such as rice and wheat.

Each of the Peruvian exports originates in a different part of the country. The sugar cane is produced in a series of irrigated valleys along the northern part of the west coast, centering on the city of Trujillo. Cotton is grown around Piura, the northernmost of the Peruvian oases, and in the irrigated areas south of Trujillo as far as Lima. Oil also comes from the coastal region—from an oil field near the northern border of Peru. But the other minerals come from mines high in the Andes, notably the copper mines around Cerro de Pasco inland from Lima. Peru's coal comes from the valley of the Río Santa, inland from the port of Chimbote. The Río Santa has also been developed to produce an abundance

The weekly market is held on the streets of Pisac in the Peruvian highlands

of hydroelectric power, and a new steel plant has been built at Chimbote, using iron ore brought by ship from southern Peru.

Lima and Callao

The political, social, and economic focus of Peru is on Lima, and its port Callao. During the colonial period most of western South America came under the dominance of Lima, and the influence of this center was felt even as far as the mouth of the Plata in Argentina. Now Lima has been shorn of its control over this wide hinterland. Lima is a city of ancient traditions; but as the center of modern Peru it is becoming industrialized and is growing rapidly in population.

In 1535 Pizarro selected this site for the foundation of his capital because it combined two special advantages which were important to the Spaniards. In the first place they found here one of the larger irrigable areas of the coastal region, for the Río Rimac brings down an abundant supply of water to an alluvial plain of broad dimensions. The other advantage was the presence of an offshore island, and a long gravelly promontory which points toward the island from the mainland.

Island and promontory together provided a protection from the waves brought in from the open Pacific by the prevailing southwest winds. In Callao harbor it was possible to anchor in calm water. To be sure they could have found other large irrigable areas along the coast, and other places where small harbors offered protection to the small ships of the sixteenth century—for example, in the bay of Chimbote. It was the combination of a large irrigable area and nearby protected anchorage which was unique: for the first time this combination became significant when the seafaring Spaniards wrested the control of the country from the landlocked Indians.

The city of Lima, eight miles inland from Callao, was laid out in the characteristic Spanish manner on a strictly rectangular pattern around a central plaza. In most of the Spanish colonial cities the dimensions of the blocks, the width of the streets, and even the arrangement of the government buildings and the church around the plaza were all standardized. Lima incorporated all these features which characterize Spanish cities from California to the strait of Magellan—although this city was laid out before the plan had been prescribed by law.

Lima, now a city of nearly two million, performs a variety of functions. As the capital it has attracted and given support to an army of government workers, representative of all the different parts of Peru. As chief commercial center of Peru, it receives most of the country's imports, and most of the business enterprises of the country have offices there. As center of art and education Lima has drawn to itself many artists, literary people, and teachers; the University of San Marcos, the oldest university in South America, attracts students not only from Peru but also from beyond its borders. Because Lima is the capital of a Latin country it is also a social center, and in it are concentrated many of the aristocratic landowning families. Their high standard of living is possible for only a very small proportion of the whole population in a land where poverty is so widespread; this small group, through the exploitation of large areas of the Peruvian soil, has created in Lima the flower of the older Spanish civilization.

Disturbing changes began to appear in the urban scene during World War I. New political ideologies taken up by the relatively small but powerful student population are resulting in a more realistic study of the "Indian problem." But of even more profound significance is the new industrialization, and the changing attitudes engendered by it. In addition to the big mineral smelters in the Andes, the petroleum and sugar refineries of the coastal region, and the new steel plant at Chimbote, manufacturing industries have also now been built at Lima and Arequipa. Factories produce foodstuffs, cotton and woolen textiles, cigarettes, matches, beverages, leather, soap, and various items of clothing. In 1960 a factory in Lima started to process fish for meal and fertilizer.

The Pacific Ocean off the Peruvian coast is the feeding ground for enormous numbers of fish, yet the Peruvians made no serious use of this resource before 1961. In each year since 1961 fish preparations have made up some 15 percent of the value of all Peruvian exports.

Foreign Trade

For nearly a century Great Britain was Peru's best customer. British capital was invested in the oil fields, and in many other aspects of the economic life. In 1877 nearly two thirds of the exports went to Great Britain, and only 2 percent went to the United States. During World War I the United States moved ahead of Great Britain as the chief purchaser of Peruvian products. Great Britain gradually returned to first place in the 1930's only to lose that position again in World War II. Generally, the cotton goes to Great Britain, and the mineral exports go to the United States. The sugar cane, the oil, and the coal are exported to other Latin-American countries, especially Chile. Great Britain at one time supplied most of Peru's imports, but since World War I the United States has maintained the lead, providing more than 50 percent of the imports in the years after World War II.

The Political Situation

The formulation of a state-idea acceptable to a majority of the people who live together in Peru is complicated by a number of factors. It is complicated by the presence of the Indian group, whose basic attitudes are so different from those of the European group. It is complicated by the variety of economic interests within the country, and by the interests of foreign-owned corporations. It is complicated, too, by the difficulties of communication among the several separate clusters of people.

Under these circumstances democratic processes are difficult if not impossible. The politics have long been under the control of the land-owning and commercial aristocracy, supported by the officers of the army. A central authority based on military power keeps control, permitting only such opposition political activities as are deemed to be safe. To do less would be to invite revolutionary disorders; yet the continued curb of free political expression produces increasing irritation against those whose power and prestige come from social position or military status. Curiously, the communists in Peru are relatively weak.

There is a good reason for this weakness. In 1924 a political party known as the *Alianza Popular Revolutionaria Americana,* or APRA, was formed. Because its leaders were in exile from Peru, the party was actually formed in Mexico. The Apristas, or members of APRA, urge a land reform that will return the land to the Indian communities;

they urge a system of universal education to attack the illiteracy of the Indians; they urge the support of an economic program that will lift the Indian farmers out of a purely subsistence agriculture, providing for them new jobs in manufacturing industry; they urge a variety of advanced labor legislation to provide a greater measure of economic security. Essentially the Apristas are ready to stir up a revolution that would make the Indians truly a part of the Peruvian nation. Obviously they are resisted by the traditional political authorities. It is important to note, however, that the program of APRA has the support of a majority of the literate people of Peru, who, if they were permitted to express themselves freely, would vote the party into power. The existence of this strong, popular, liberal movement has the effect of "stealing the thunder" from the communists, who remain, therefore, relatively weak.

The establishment of order among all these diverse groups remains an unsolved problem. The modern urban life which has transformed ancient Lima; the spirit of technical efficiency which has vitalized some of the large cotton and sugar plantations; the essentially foreign character which sets off the mining communities from the region in which they are embedded—these things are representative of only a part of Peru. There is also the Peru of the pure Indians and the near-Indians: communal, self-sufficient, primitive, superstitious, so closely adjusted to the land as to defy the forces of change, indifferent to prospects of material progress, heedless of the currents of political controversy which sometimes reach revolutionary violence. Sooner or later the problem of the Indian will have to be faced, and facing it will inevitably involve profound social readjustments such as are going on today in Mexico. Yet at the moment these two incompatible ways of living, that of the Indian and that of the European, seem no nearer to mutual adjustment than at any time during the four centuries they have been locked together in the same land.

BOLIVIA

Bolivia is a weak state. Of all the countries in Latin America, Bolivia has the smallest proportion of agricultural land to total area (0.3 percent), and the largest proportion of the total national territory outside of the effective national territory. It has only 0.2 of an acre of crop land per person. A larger proportion of its population is illiterate (69 percent) than of any other Latin-American country except Haiti. Furthermore, the Bolivian population is arranged in scattered small units of settlement, isolated from one another and from the outside world by physical barriers. Before the War of the Pacific (1879-1883) Bolivian territory ex-

Indian fisherman on Lake Titicaca

tended to the Pacific around the port of Antofagasta. Bolivia lost its sea coast to Chile not only because the Chilean forces were stronger, but also because Chileans rather than Bolivians were carrying on the effective exploitation of the nitrate deposits of the Atacama. From 1932 to 1935 Bolivia was engaged in another war, this time with Paraguay. As a result it lost a large part of the Chaco which it had claimed but had not been able effectively to occupy. But since 1952 Bolivia has been undergoing a process of dynamic change.

The physical character of the habitat in which the Bolivians are struggling to establish a coherent state is marked by extremes of altitude and aridity. The Bolivian people are located mostly on the high Altiplano south of Lake Titicaca, and in the valleys of the Eastern Cordillera. Separating these clusters of people from the West Coast, there are high, bleak, wind-swept plateaus, towering ranges of volcanic peaks with passes above 13,000 feet, a desert which is one of the driest in the world, and an escarpment more than 2,000 feet in height which drops steeply to a harborless coast. In western and southern Bolivia the great dry belt of South America which extends from southern Ecuador almost to the Strait of Magellan crosses the Andes diagonally from northwest to southeast. Between latitudes 20°S. and 30°S., within that zone which is dry on the western sides of all the continents, South America is so very deficient in moisture that the land is almost entirely barren of vegetation. Even in the high Western Cordillera of the Andes there is so little rain that few streams emerge from the mountains. Only one river, the Río Loa, rises in the Andes and flows all the way across the desert of what is now Northern Chile to the Pacific Ocean. East of the Western Cordillera, over the whole southwestern part of the present Bolivian territory, the rainfall is so scanty and so uncertain that only a very few spots can be found where drinkable water is available.

The internal force by which a state might be enabled to expand across such physical barriers is lacking in Bolivia. Like Ecuador and Peru, this state is burdened by the problems arising from the presence of incompatible racial and cultural groups, the Spaniards and the Indians. But in Bolivia the problems of cultural diversity are further complicated by the arrangement of the population in small and more or less isolated clusters and ribbons of settlement. Furthermore, the Indians of the Titicaca Basin and of the Altiplano between Lake Titicaca and Lake Poopó are Aymaras. They are the descendants of a people whose civilization flourished in this region a century before the time of Christ. Conquered first by the Incas, then by the Spaniards, they have nevertheless maintained their language and their customs with little change and have been able to cling stubbornly to their ancestral lands. Among all these diverse elements the Bolivian state has never been able to develop any strong sense of political coherence.

An Aymara Indian child near Lake Titicaca

The weakness of the Bolivian state constitutes a threat to the peace and security of the hemisphere. Weakness in any state invites aggressive action, with or without force, by more powerful neighbors. Weakness in Ecuador invited armed invasion from Peru, as it did earlier from Colombia. But the danger of weakness in Bolivia is rendered much more serious than that of Ecuador for two chief reasons: first, the Bolivian territory contains important stores of tin and other metals, and of oil; and second, Bolivia's still undeveloped oil fields lie easily accessible to the two chief rival powers of South America, Brazil and Argentina.

The Bolivian People

Bolivia, like Peru, Ecuador, and the southern part of Colombia, is occupied by a population which is more than half pure Indian. Much of Bolivia was included within the limits of the Inca Empire, and Quechua is still a common language of many Bolivians. In the northern part of the Altiplano, around Lake Titicaca and Lake Poopó, are the descendants of the pre-Inca civilization whose language is Aymara. In Bolivia as a whole people of unmixed Indian ancestry make up about 53 percent; and mestizos form another 32 percent. People of unmixed European ancestry are only about 15 percent.

The various clusters of people in Bolivia, however, are quite diverse in their racial composition. In the highland regions the clusters located at the higher altitudes have the largest proportion of Indians. Around the shores of Lake Titicaca, where the density of population in certain areas exceeds 125 per square mile, the people are almost exclusively Indians. Even in the city of La Paz, the actual capital (although Sucre is the legal capital), the Indians form the majority of the inhabitants. In the Department of La Paz, Indians make up about 75 percent of the total. Lower down in the valleys and basins of the Eastern Cordillera there are more mestizos and Europeans: in the Basin of Cochabamba, for example, which has a density of population of over 325 people per square mile, 70 percent is made up of mestizos and Europeans. With such differences of racial composition added to the contrasted economic outlook found among the various groups, the formation of a strong national unity is extremely difficult.

The Aymaras form a distinct and important part of the Bolivian population. Walle reported that "while the Quechua is docile, submissive, and obedient, the Aymara is hard, vindictive, bellicose, rebellious, egotistical, cruel, and jealous of his liberty."[2] But if these people are hostile in their dealings with people of Spanish origin this attitude is not without cause. The Aymaras have been defending their lands and their way of living for centuries. Conquered first by the Incas, then by the Spaniards, they have been treated with cruelty and forced to accommodate themselves to the wishes of outsiders. Although the Aymaras, being mostly illiterate and unable to speak Spanish, have had little or nothing to say about the political and economic policies of Bolivia until recently, they nevertheless make up the overwhelming majority of the farmers, the herders, and the miners of the country. Again and again their traditional communal system of land tenure has been officially abolished, yet the Indian village, or *ayllu,* continues to operate on a communal basis as it has for thousands of years. The Aymara is fiercely attached to his land and nothing but force or absolute economic necessity can separate him from it. This is the solid core around which the 20 percent of the Bolivian people who are literate have attempted to form a state.

The Problem of Accessibility

A major problem in the formation of a viable state is to provide connections among the scattered communities of Bolivia, and with the outside world. The chief difficulties which stand in the way of transportation development are not only the rugged terrain and the steep grades necessary to reach the Altiplano, but also the geographical arrangement of the

[2] Quoted by Weston La Barre in *The Aymara Indians of the Lake Titicaca Plateau, Bolivia,* (from the *American Anthropologist,* Vol. 50, 1948: 1-250).

settlements themselves. The focus of economic and political power is not sharp, because the people of this core of the Bolivian state are scattered in numerous relatively small communities, each anxious for government support of local projects, but each ready to block the projects which bring advantages only to other communities. The largest cluster of people is in the Cochabamba Basin, and although the density is high in this basin the area is not great. The other communities are still smaller, many of them strung in narrow bands along the winding valley bottoms. The physical difficulty of providing these scattered communities with a common political and economic focus, of gathering enough of the products of the Eastern Cordillera together in one place to pay for the expensive construction of railroads or roads constitutes a problem that is not easily solved, even with financial aid from outside.

The story of the attempt to provide Cochabamba with a rail connection with the highland mining centers illustrates the difficulties involved. Between 1913 and 1917 work on a railroad was in progress. In anticipation of the final solution of the problem of access to a market, there was a land boom in the Cochabamba Basin. Despite the reluctance of landowners to

Clearing the scrub woodland by machinery in eastern Bolivia

sell even parts of their estates, certain pieces of land actually were sold, but for prices ranging as high as $2,000 an acre. But the railroad, which cost more than $154,000 per mile, had either to tap a large volume of traffic or charge very high rates. The area served could not provide enough traffic to make low rates economically possible, and high rates prevailed. Thus as a result of costly transportation, heavy mortgages, and high land valuations, only losses came to the landowners. The general depression which followed cast a gloom over the community from which it has scarcely even now recovered. Later when the railroad was extended eastward to Cliza, there was no land boom in that district.

The attempts to promote the movement of pioneer settlers from the highland communities to the lowland plains east of the mountains gained some success when a motor highway was built to connect Cochabamba with Santa Cruz. There are some who think the great hope of future development is the settlement of the empty lands in the lowlands. Yet so isolated were these new settlements in spite of the road that at one time the colonists threatened to secede from the rest of Bolivia and form a new state.

The lowlands that extend eastward and southward from Santa Cruz are also of interest to Bolivia's neighbors, especially Argentina and Brazil. This is the region known as the Chaco. Even as early as World War I, oil had been discovered along the Andean foothills. Argentina built a pipeline northward along the eastern edge of the Andes to tap the Bolivian oil. But since the war between Bolivia and Paraguay (1932-1935) the Bolivians have been determined to provide closer connections between the highland communities and the Chaco. The most productive Bolivian oilfield, located a little south of Santa Cruz, is now connected by pipeline to refineries in Cochabamba and Sucre.

The interest of Argentina and Brazil, however, continues. The Argentines are extending their pipelines and railroads northward. The Brazilians have completed a single-track, narrow-gauge railroad across the Chaco from Corumbá to Santa Cruz. Dreamers speak eloquently of a transcontinental railroad from Santos on the Atlantic Ocean to Arica on the Pacific Ocean. Of this, only the section between Santa Cruz and Cochabamba remains to be completed. The Brazilian railroad across the Chaco is to be paid for by a concession to explore for oil along the line, and by the oil exports to Brazil which might result if the exploration should prove successful.

The most remarkable thing about the Chaco problem is the fascination still exerted by the idea of a railroad. For a people long isolated and accustomed to the losing struggle with difficult accessibility, it may well seem that a railroad or a highway might offer the ultimate solution. But a thousand-mile long, single-track, narrow-gauge line cannot bring any inevitable flood of new settlers, or any new flow of exports. Nor would a transcontinental connection between Santos and Arica be anything more than a black line on a map. The volume of oil that might be shipped on such a line to São Paulo would scarcely help Brazil's oil problem. But if oil should be discovered along the Brazilian railroad, the railroad would prove most useful in shipping out the pipe for a pipe line. The least expensive form of transport for food products or cattle would be the motor truck. Furthermore, note should be made of the problems involved in exploring for oil. The best oil geologists in the world can do no more than point to places where oil might be found. A drilled well is very expensive, especially when it is located in a remote place where transportation is slow and uncertain. So far the governments of the Latin-American countries have been unable to carry on the work of oil exploration successfully, not because of lack of technical skill, but rather because of the high cost of such operations. Only the large oil corporations can command the necessary "risk capital." Yet if the Brazilians should prove unpredictably lucky and strike oil along their rail line soon, this would be a matter of major importance to the Brazilian economy, as we shall see later.

Bolivia has long struggled with the problem of providing access to the Pacific. Ever since the discovery of silver at Potosí during the early colonial period there have been three chief routes of travel to the Pacific and a fourth route that led southward to Argentina. The routes to the Pacific led to the ports of Mollendo (Matarani) in Peru, Arica, and Antofagasta in what is now Chile.

The flow of traffic between the settlements which form the center of the Bolivian state and the coast has shifted from time to time as the various railroads have been completed. The first railroad to be built, in 1874, was the line from Mollendo to the port of Puno on Lake Titicaca. Shortly after this, steamer service was inaugurated on the lake between Puno and Guaqui. By 1902, railroad and steamer provided a relatively fast connection between La Paz and the sea, and for a time the copper from Corocoro was sent out by this route instead of over the old mule and llama trail to Arica.

Meanwhile, in 1889, a railroad was built from Antofagasta to Uyuni, and was extended in 1892 to Oruro and in 1910 to La Paz. The opening of this line drained off all the mineral production of southern Bolivia, in spite of the fact that in 1884 Bolivia had lost to Chile its seaport, Antofagasta. The third railroad to reach the highlands was built from Arica to La Paz in 1913, with a short spur to Corocoro. This railroad, which makes use of a long section of rack and cog, is by far the shortest of the three routes to the Pacific. Arica is now constituted as an international port with a Bolivian custom house. In spite of the fact that it remains outside of the Bolivian national territory, this port is once again becoming the chief outlet on the Pacific, regaining a position it held during the colonial period when it was reached by mule trails not only from La Paz but also directly from Oruro.

The railroad which extends southeastward to Argentina, by way of La Quiaca, Jujuy, and Tucumán, was completed in 1925. This is now competing, but not with great success, for a share of the exports which originate south of Potosí.

In the modern period, highway construction is proving less costly. A truck road climbs to Puno from Arequipa, and continues along the southwestern shore of Lake Titicaca into Bolivia. This new highway now closely parallels the old colonial mule trail, running near La Paz, southward to Potosí, and thence on into Argentina. Now, also, a railroad is projected to complete the gap between Puno and the Bolivian railroads. When completed this might again permit the Peruvian route to compete with the line to Arica.

In 1963 the Bolivians proposed to Chile that the port of Mejillones, just north of Antafagasta, be given to them as an exclave of Bolivian territory. If the Chileans should agree to this, the old route through Calama to Antofagasta would again become Bolivia's chief connection with the outside world, and Bolivian sentiment would be appeased by giving them their own port on the Pacific.

The Bolivian Economy

The census of 1950 enumerates a little over three million people in Bolivia. More than two thirds of these people are engaged in farming, mostly subsistence farming from which a meager living is obtained in a harsh environment. Only 21 percent of the Bolivians are literate. The income per person in Bolivia was only $103 in 1955 but suffered a drop to only $60 in 1962. Only 0.3 percent of the total national territory is actually used for agriculture, which is the smallest ratio of cropland to total area in all Latin America. The concentration of people in the high and arid mountain regions aggravates the problem, and focuses on the potentially productive Chaco still another kind of attention—that is, attention to the Chaco as a zone of pioneer settlement.

Some 98 percent of the exports of Bolivia come from the mines. Of these exports tin makes up about 59 percent, followed by antimony, tungsten, lead, zinc, copper, silver, and gold. Yet the proportion of the total population actually employed in mining is only 4 percent.

Although Bolivia produces something like 95 percent of the tin of Latin America and 20 percent of the world production, it is a relatively high-cost producer. Most of the world's tin comes from Malaya and Indonesia, where the ore is dredged from stream gravels. In Bolivia the ore must be dug out of the solid rock in mines located at very high altitudes. But the strategic location of Bolivia in the "free world" makes it desirable to keep the mines in operation in spite of the cost. The United States took more than half of the tin exports, and Great Britain took a little less than half. Most of the other minerals go to the United States. The United States, also, furnishes most of the imports of wheat, mining machinery, and other manufactures.

Inside a tin and tungsten mine above 16,000 feet in Bolivia

The Political Situation

Government in Bolivia has long been based on military force. Three large tin-mining interests formerly held the real political power, and political decisions were made in Paris or New York, not in La Paz. The army kept order in Bolivia. But the War with Paraguay (1932-1935) made a very great impression on the people of Bolivia. Not only was there the shock of defeat, but also the Aymara men, who were recruited as soldiers, were given an opportunity to look beyond the limited horizons of their ancestral communities. After the war many drifted to the cities or to the mines where they ceased to be Indians and became second-class citizens.

In 1952 a revolutionary party seized control of the government. This party, the *Movimiento Nacionalista Revolucionario,* or MNR, has objectives similar to those of APRA in Peru. The MNR is supported by a large majority of the people—the intellectuals, the city workers, and the miners. The Aymara miners, still mostly illiterate, were nevertheless formed into unions and given a chance to express themselves politically. The movement is opposed by those who stand to lose by such a revolution, and perhaps also by many illiterate people who do not understand what is going on.

Expropriation and land reform are inevitably the first steps of such a revolutionary movement. And inevitably the first results are to decrease the total production of minerals and foods. Since the expropriation of the tin mines in 1952, costs of mining have risen and production is maintained at a loss. Since food production has not increased, food prices have gone up rapidly. The large private properties that were not effectively used were expropriated. Each tenant farmer was to be given between 25 and 2,000 acres of land, depending on the potential productivity. Unfortunately no basic survey of the land or of the quality of the soils has been made: there is not even a base map on which to plot the outlines of the farms. In the Titicaca Basin the Indian farmers have been permitted to remain on the lands they were cultivating. The program of land redistribution, as everywhere in the world where such a program has been undertaken, has run into the stubborn geographic fact that there is not enough productive land to go around. Unless the highland Indian farmer can be persuaded to emigrate to a wholly new and unfamiliar environment in the eastern plains he will be forced to leave farming and look for employment in some other occupation. Without a rapid development of industrial and service occupations to offer opportunities for the people thus torn loose from the land the whole undertaking may come to disaster. The Aymara Indians are not the kind to accept a continued frustration of what they are now led to see as their legitimate demands.

For the time, at least, Bolivia's strength as a nation has been reduced by revolution. The new political leaders face the same facts of underlying geography: that the population is scattered in small clusters, isolated one from another not only by physical barrier but also by language and traditions. The revolution aims to make the Aymara Indian a part of the Bolivian state, and opens for him new opportunities to better his conditions of life. But can the Aymara actually be incorporated in the Bolivian state? Other Indian countries will watch the developments in Bolivia with great interest. Meanwhile, political groups unsympathetic with the aims of the revolution could attempt counter-revolution, could even attempt to set up a separate political authority in outlying parts of the national territory. It would seem that the Bolivians are still beset by so many critical problems that the struggle to establish order and to create a coherent state have become more difficult than before.

CHAPTER SEVEN

Chile

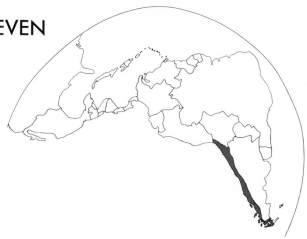

The population of Chile is clustered in one central region, and in a very real sense this one region is Chile. The national territory[1] of this remarkable country stretches for 2,630 miles from nearly 56° S., where Cape Horn points toward the Antarctic Continent, almost to 18°S., at Arica; yet at no place is the eastern border of Chile as much as 250 miles from the sea. Southern Chile is one of the rainiest parts of South America, where glaciers descend from snow-covered mountains to a deeply fiorded coast. Northern Chile is one of the driest places on earth; in it is one of the few weather stations where no rain has ever been recorded. Yet these two ends are Chilean only in the sense of possession. The real Chile is the beautiful land between: a land which forms a narrow strip between high mountains and the sea; a land covered with fields of growing crops and green pastures, bordered by graceful rows of Lombardy poplars, eucalyptus, or weeping willows; a land of dense population.

The geographical unity of Chile's one central cluster of people gave this country a distinct advantage in the development of a coherent society. This advantage, moreover, was supported by a racial homogeneity which is greater than that of any other west coast country. The usual social distinction appeared between the minority of landowning aristocrats and the majority of landless tenants, known as *inquilinos;* but this social gap was bridged in Chile by the strongly paternalistic character of the system. More than elsewhere on the west coast, the landowners lived on their estates and took a very definite part in the life of the rural communities. In this respect, the development of Chile has been notably different from

Maps 2, 4, 6, 8, 11, 13, 14, 15, 21, 22, 25 are pertinent to this chapter.
[1] In addition to the Chilean national territory on the continent of South America, Chile also owns several small islands far out in the Pacific Ocean: Rapa Nui (Easter Island), Sala y Gomez, San Felix, San Ambrosio, and Juan Fernandez.

that of the Andean countries where the landowners usually reside in the cities.

The rural population of densely populated Middle Chile has exhibited a marked capacity to expand. One salient fact about the population of Chile is that the present densities of rural settlement in the central region were reached before 1870; and since that time, while the total number of Chileans has more than doubled, the increase has been absorbed in a number of ways—partly by the pioneer colonization of the previously little-occupied lands which lie south of the Río Bío-Bío in Southern Chile.

The established order of society in rural Chile has now been challenged. None of the countries we have already described has experienced so strong a penetration of the industrial way of living as Chile. Rural Chile is still a land of large estates, of landed aristocrats and landless tenants. But now an urban Chile has appeared—industrial cities with wageworkers and owners of capital. Today Chile makes use of more energy per capita—as supplied by water power, coal, and oil—than any other Latin-American country. Against a background of large estates, on which the farm practices are still for the most part primitive and on which life is lived as in an earlier century, there are rapidly growing industrial cities, such as Santiago, Valparaiso, Concepción, and Valdivia. Industrial society brings new diversity into the Chilean scene; people who work for wages and people whose prestige is based on financial success have developed attitudes and objectives which are utterly foreign to those of the people in the rural communities around them. But the traveler who has seen only the cities, and who has passed through the country only on a modern electric train, does not really know Chile.

The Chilean People

Chile is a mestizo country. Its population includes none of the profound racial diversities found in the lands farther north. Only about 5 percent are pure-blooded Indians. The number of people of Spanish descent whose ancestry remains unmixed is approximately 30 percent. The remainder, 65 percent, are mixtures of Indian and Spanish in various degrees. This mestizo group is nearer the Spanish side of the mixture than are the mestizo groups of Peru, Bolivia, and Ecuador. It is said that in the more prominent families of Chile there have been no Indian ancestors for seven or eight generations.

The Indians of Chile

The Chilean Indians were not at all like the Quechua and the Aymara groups which had been dominated by Inca rule. It has been estimated

On the outskirts of Valparaiso high above the port

that at the time of the Spanish conquest there were some 500,000 natives in the middle part of Chile, roughly between the modern Valparaiso and Puerto Montt. In the forests south of the Río Bío-Bío, the warlike Araucanians had held the Incas at bay, using the woods to good advantage in fighting armies whose previous experience had been in open country. The Araucanians had achieved a culture level not unlike that of the Iroquois of North America: they were hunters and fishers, but they derived a large part of their food supply from a shifting cultivation of maize.

The Araucanian tribes inhabiting the more open country north of the Río Bío-Bío were brought under the influence of the Incas. The latter succeeded in pushing their conquest south to the Río Maule, but since the road to Cuzco was long and difficult, the hold on this remote frontier was weak. Just inland from Valparaiso lies a basin, watered by the Río Aconcagua, to which the Incas gave the name "Vale of Chile," and in which they established their southernmost settlement. South of the Vale of Chile, in the vicinity of the present city of Santiago, the Araucanian tribes had been taught, or had, themselves, learned, how to build simple irrigation ditches and how to raise crops year after year on the same land. Thus fixed in position, they formed a kind of "march" to protect the Inca settlements farther north from the attacks of the still warlike and semi-nomadic tribes from the southern forests. These sedentary Araucanians, rather than the more primitive tribes farther south, made the largest contribution to the racial composition of the Chilean mestizo. But Inca rule, even in the Vale of Chile, was not able to wipe out the strong sense of independence and individual initiative which still distinguishes the descendants of the Araucanian tribes from the Quechuas of the Andean countries.

The Spanish Conquest and Race Mixture

The first Spanish explorers to penetrate the really formidable barriers that isolated Middle Chile were moved by the same desires as those which led Pizarro to his conquest of Peru. But Chile had little to offer. Its stream gravels contained little gold; and its Indians were much less docile than those of Peru. When Pedro de Valdivia tried to organize an expedition he found few volunteers ready to face the hardships of the overland march to a land of reported poverty. Nevertheless, with a small army he reached Middle Chile and founded the city of Santiago in 1541, and the city of Concepción in 1550. Almost at once the newcomers were involved in war with the Araucanians—a war which continued with few interruptions until the second half of the nineteenth century. In spite of the absence of precious metals and the warlike character of the Indians, the Spaniards were drawn to Middle Chile because of the productivity of its soils and because of the similarity of its climate to that of Spain. The surface of Middle Chile was soon marked off in big agricultural or pastoral estates the ownership of which created a new aristocracy. Those who desired wealth in the form of gold went elsewhere.

The Spaniards who first came to Chile seem, like the Indians, to have been different from those who established themselves in other parts of Spanish America. During the first two centuries most of the invaders came from the south of Spain, from those provinces in which the Moorish influence had been present longest and was most penetrating. After the beginning of the eighteenth century, however, Chile began to attract more and more people from the northern part of Spain, and these, according to the Chilean writer Luis Thayer Ojeda, were a very different type from the restless, adventure-loving southerners.

Race mixture was as free and as little accompanied by prejudice in Middle Chile as in other parts of Latin America. There were few white women in Chile during the early years of the Spanish conquest, and each soldier was soon attended by several native women. It is said that there were four women to every man in the frontier posts established to protect the settlements against Araucanian raids; in one week during the year 1580 sixty children were born at a post where 160 men were stationed. The territory was soon swarming with mestizo children produced by the mating of two exceedingly virile and warlike racial types—the best of the Spanish soldiers, selected for bravery and endurance because of the difficulty of reaching Chile, and the women they had captured from the indomitable natives.

Social differences soon began to appear in this new society. The contrast between the owners of land and those who did not own land was becoming greater and greater, in spite of the fact that no racial differences separated these two classes. Among the mestizo children, the girls had the better chance to marry well; the boys usually were less fortunate. Indian and Spanish blood, however, mixed freely whether among the landowning aristocracy or among the tenants who were becoming more and more closely attached to the big estates.

Out of this mixture has come a new racial type, the Chilean mestizo, who is a far more virile and energetic person than the mestizo produced by the mating of Spanish and Quechua. The Chilean laborer, whether in the city or the country, is noted for physical strength, endurance, bravery, loyalty, and a spirit of independence. To what extent these qualities are the result of a more invigorating climate, or of a better diet, or of superior racial inheritance contributed both by the Indian and Spanish elements, cannot be estimated. It is more than likely that all these things have contributed to the peculiar qualities of the Chilean people.

Middle Chile

The result of four centuries of Spanish control in Chile has been the notable concentration of people of this type in the region which may be termed the "cradle of Chilean nationality." In the original Vale of Chile, and in the Central Valley between Santiago and Concepción, a relatively dense population has been built up. In the rural areas around Santiago the density is between 150 and 250 people per square mile. Santiago itself is a city of nearly 2,000,000, and both Valparaiso and Concepción are over 100,000.

The Chilean nation is formed around just one nucleus of concentrated settlement. About 73 percent of the total population is in Middle Chile, the area between Coquimbo and the Río Bío-Bío near Concepción. If to this core area is added the northernmost part of Southern Chile, between the Río Bío-Bío and Puerto Montt, this includes 90 percent of all the people in Chile. In Middle Chile are concentrated all the activities of Chilean life; the political, economic, social, and artistic center of the nation is Santiago. As far as politics are concerned there is no subdivision of the national territory into provinces or departments: there are no provincial legislatures, no state governors, no separate police forces. The provinces of Chile are used chiefly for census purposes.

Middle Chile, roughly from Valparaiso at the outlet of the Vale of Chile, to Concepción, near the mouth of the Río Bío-Bío, is a land of mild, rainy winters and cool, dry summers. This is like the climate of California, except that in the Southern Hemisphere mid-winter is in July rather than January. This is the climate that reminded the early Spanish colonists of Spain. With the snow-capped Andes to the east, the central valley offers scenery of great beauty. South of the Bío-Bío, where rainfall comes in every month, the climate reminds one of Washington and Oregon—a similarity that is reenforced by the presence of a string of majestic, cone-shaped volcanoes. This is Chile's famous "lake district" which is rapidly becoming a recreation area for fishing in summer and skiing in winter that attracts visitors from all over the world.

Middle Chile is still a land of large private estates. But the concentration of land in the hands of a few families is decreasing. The redistribution of land in Chile, however, is not being done by government decree, but by the operation of economic laws. The Chilean aristocracy has never hesitated to sell land and use the money to invest in manufacturing industry or in other kinds of business. Each year some of the estates are divided into small properties and put up for sale. Whereas the large landowners are accustomed to use much of their properties to grow alfalfa for the feeding of cattle, the small owners are more apt to plant fruit orchards and vineyards.

As the total population of Middle Chile continued to increase (although the rural density remains about what it was in 1870) the extra numbers of people have been absorbed in four ways. First, many of the former tenants were employed in mining activities—in nitrate and copper mines, or in coal mining. Second, at the conclusion of Chile's war with Peru and Bolivia, many of the returning soldiers were granted small properties on the southern frontier south of the Bío-Bío. In the forests, German colonists who came to Chile after 1850, had developed the methods of clearing land and planting crops. The pioneers copied them. Today this northern part of Southern Chile is a major area of wheat production. Third, there has been a steady movement of emigration from Chile into the Argentine communities on the eastern side of the Andes. And fourth, there is an increasingly rapid movement of people from the rural areas into the cities.

Northern Chile

Northern Chile is the very dry Atacama Desert. This at one time belonged to Bolivia and Peru, although it was never effectively occupied by these countries. With the enormous development of the nitrate fields which was well under way by 1860, Chile's interest in this previously worthless country to the north was greatly increased. Much Chilean capital was invested in nitrate mining and refining equipment, and friction developed between the Chilean owners and the governments of Bolivia and Peru. War broke out in 1879, and by 1883 the Chilean forces were victorious. Chile at that time established its hold on the Atacama, and excluded Bolivia from the Pacific. Although nitrate has declined in importance since the development of the atmospheric nitrate process which can be carried on wherever there is an abundance of electric power, there has been a great increase in copper mining. Copper is now Chile's most valuable export (70 percent in 1961).

Southern Chile

The northern part of Southern Chile, which was for a long time left to the Araucanians, was first successfully occupied by a farming people when the Germans arrived in 1850. After the war with Peru and Bolivia, the movement of pioneer small farmers into the forests began, and continued until almost all the arable land was occupied. In addition to farming, coal mines were developed on the Lebu Peninsula, just south of Concepción.

South of Puerto Montt the coast of Chile is deeply embayed, reminding one of the coast of British Columbia and southern Alaska. This is one of the stormiest parts of the world. High winds, low, scurrying clouds, rain or sleet, and along the outermost islands the surf where the world's stormiest ocean dashes against a continent—such is the nature of Southern Chile. Except for some sheep pastures to the east of the Andes, and some new oilfields opened up in Tierra del Fuego, this part of Chile remains scantily populated.

The Growth of the Industrial Cities

The transformation of Chilean life, which has been going on at a faster and faster rate since 1920, is reflected in the growth of industrial cities. When the inquilino is jarred loose from the estate on which his ancestors worked, he becomes a *roto*, one who is unattached. Many of the rotos take jobs in the mining communities. Now that land for pioneer settlement in the south is no longer abundant, the cities offer the chief opportunities for employment. In the cities there is a growing middle class of shopkeepers, small-business men, government workers, and workers in an increasing number of service occupations. And in the cities there is an increasing number of jobs for wage workers in manufacturing industries. Chile has almost caught up with Argentina in the percentage of people living in cities—60 percent compared with 62 percent in Argentina. Argentina and Chile are considerably ahead of the third Latin American country, Venezuela, which has 54 percent of its population in cities.

Although Chile has many small cities and towns, only four can be classed at present as centers of urban industrial development. The most important of these is Santiago, the capital. Santiago was laid out in 1541 on the typical rectangular plan which the Spaniards used almost everywhere in that period. As the focus of the political life of the thriving new colony, Santiago soon established its position as the largest and most beautiful of the Chilean cities. By 1865 the national capital had a population of 115,000. The rate of growth turned up sharply during World War I, and by 1920 Santiago had passed 500,000. The census of 1952 counted 1,750,000 in the metropolitan area. The original rectangular nucleus is now the hub or center of a wide zone of industrial suburbs and slums where the growing city has invaded the surrounding countryside. The population of the metropolitan area is well over two million.

Chile's second city is the port of Valparaiso, located near the mouth of the Río Aconcagua at the outlet of the productive Vale of Chile. A railroad descends to the coast through a narrow valley cut through the coastal plateau, and reaches the sea at the beautiful residential and resort town of Viña del Mar, only a short distance north of the port. Valparaiso itself is built on a north-facing bay which provides shelter from the southerly winds. The steepness of the slopes at the water's edge made the use of a rectangular pattern impossible: the streets at successively higher levels follow the semicircular contours of the bay; so steep are the connections between different levels that elevators have been installed to carry passengers from one level to another. The business district is built on a narrow terrace near the edge of the water; above it are residential areas; and, higher up, hilltop slums overlook the whole scene. A breakwater now gives the bay protection from the storm winds from the north, and makes it possible for ships to tie up at docks. In 1960 Valparaiso and Viña del Mar had a combined population of over 260,000.

The two other industrial cities of Chile are Concepción and Valdivia. Both of these cities are built along the banks of rivers where a lowering of the coast has created small estuaries. Concepción, on the Bío-Bío, is served by its port, Talcahuano, placed where the water is deep enough for modern steamers. Valdivia has also built an outport, Corral, located on the deeper water near the mouth of the river. Concepción now has a population of nearly 150,000 and Valdivia has a population of more than 50,000.

Truck road to a copper mine near Potrerillos with the Atacama Desert in the background

Rise of the Urban Industries

These four cities—Santiago, Valparaiso, Concepción, and Valdivia—contain the majority of Chile's new manufacturing industries. Many of the plants were built during World War I, at a time when Chile was cut off from its accustomed sources of manufactured articles. In 1900 only forty-four million Chilean pesos were invested in industries, including mining industries; but by 1928 the amount had been increased to two billion, two hundred million pesos. A considerable proportion of this investment has come from foreign sources, chiefly North American, but there is also a new capitalist class in Chile which began its rise on the wealth acquired in the nitrate business. In the south almost all the industrial establishments are owned by Chileans of German descent, whose activity and economic background are responsible for bringing the urban way of living to Concepción and Valdivia.

The Chilean industries are based chiefly on local sources of raw materials and on hydroelectric power. There are flour mills, breweries, bodegas (wineries), sugar refineries (refining Peruvian raw sugar), textile factories (mostly wool), furniture factories (chiefly in Valdivia, using local supplies of wood), leather tanneries and shoe factories (mostly in Santiago, Concepción, and Valdivia). There are also plants which produce cement, glassware, soap, paper, matches, tobacco products, and many other items. A new steel plant has been built at Huachipata, a suburb of Concepción. It is supplied with iron from a high-grade deposit of iron ore in Northern Chile, and with limestone from an island off Southern Chile. Some of the coal from local coal mines can be used when mixed with imported coal. It is expected that the Huachipata plant will become the nucleus of a considerable development of manufacturing based on the available supply of steel (Map 15, page 47).

The Economy

The census of 1960 enumerated a total population of 7,900,000 in Chile. Some 30 percent of the working force is employed in agriculture, but this proportion is decreasing. Some 20 percent is employed in manufacturing industry, and perhaps 5 percent in mining.

Chile has been the world's second largest exporter of copper for a long time. The ore body at Chuquicamata, in the Andes to the east of the Atacama Desert, is one of the largest in the world. Copper mines are also located at Potrerillos in Northern Chile, and El Teniente, in the Andes east of Santiago. But copper as a basic source of revenue for the Chilean economy is dangerous. The value of the exports varies considerably from year to year. Since 1950 the ratio of the value of copper exports to the value of all exports has ranged from 29 percent in 1950 to 72 percent in 1956.

Other major Chilean exports include iron ore (9 percent in 1961), and nitrate (6 percent). In 1961 iron and steel, and other manufactured products made up 2 percent of the exports, and wool made up another 2 percent.

For several reasons, however, this dominance of commerce in minerals is one which the Chileans deplore. In the first place, the instability of the population dependent on the mining industries for support is notable, especially in the Atacama where there is no other way of making a living when the income from the production of nitrate diminishes. In the second place, the dominance of the foreign trade by nitrate and copper leaves Chile almost powerless to control its own commercial destinies, for the nitrate business is owned mostly in London, and the copper business almost exclusively in New York. In the third place, since most of the government revenues have come from export taxes on copper and nitrate, the whole political structure of the country rests on the unstable conditions of the world mineral market.

For a long time Chile had to import wheat. This and other foodstuffs used to make up from 15 to 25 percent of the value of all imports each year. But since 1960 Chile has been able to produce enough food for its own needs. The leading imports are now machinery (including motor trucks), petroleum products, cattle, and chemical products.

The United States is Chile's best customer. The United States takes between 30 and 40 percent of the exports and furnishes a similar proportion of the imports.

The Political Situation

Chile was long considered one of the most stable countries of Latin America. Its political life had been disturbed by few troubles, and the successive governments had all been dependable in meeting foreign obligations. It was stable, as many countries in Latin America still are, because its essentially preindustrial society was undisturbed by change. The army and the landlords were in full control. Since 1920, however, Chilean politics have ceased to be calm. The movement of the inquilinos into the cities and the rise of the urban-industrial group have brought new pressures on the preindustrial political institutions that have in-

Mount Osorno in the Chilean Lake District, old-fashioned transportation in the foreground

evitably led to unsettled conditions. There has been a series of military coups, dictatorships, and a popular revolution. In 1931 and 1932 Chile faced financial disaster because of the very large decrease of its exports during the depression years. Its exports dropped to less than a sixth of their 1929 value, and government revenues dropped to less than a third. Political instability, then, is the reflection of deep-seated changes in Chile's way of life. A struggle is now going on between the new urban workers and the conservative landowners, the traditional rulers of Chile. Underneath this struggle is population pressure—land hunger and the resultant demand for a more equitable distribution of the arable lands, a demand which is not adequately satisfied as yet by the gradual breakup of the large estates through sale.

There is a large volume of popular discontent. The wages of the mine workers and the factory workers are still low. For a time the rotos were contented because they seemed to be better off than they were as inquilinos. But as more city people began to buy food at the markets, in the face of inadequate supply, prices have risen dangerously, so that now wages are not enough to provide for the needs of a family. There is strong popular support for a government program of land redistribution. Taking advantage of this discontent, a small but well-organized communist minority has exerted an influence on the government all out of proportion to its numbers.

Recent Chilean governments have been attempting to avoid the development of revolutionary pressures. But there is always the danger that people who are impatient with the slow tempo of change will attempt violent solutions. The only possible answer is more production at lower cost per unit, not only of manufactured items but also of the basic foods. Inevitably this must mean many readjustments in Chilean institutions.

So within the geographic unity of the compact nucleus of Chile we find once again that the population is actually composed of diverse and uncoordinated elements. Social complexity underlies the apparently simple clustering of people in the center and underlies also the apparent unity that comes from strong central authority focusing on this one area all the political and economic interests of the distant territories. In this central region the density of rural population reached a static condition nearly a century ago; and continued population increase has been absorbed in various other ways, notably on the frontier and, more recently, in the cities. But frontier and city have both introduced additional elements of diversity into the Chilean scene. Since the pioneer zone is now largely occupied, and no new frontier is available, the problems which arise from increasing population pressure within a restricted area can no longer be escaped. Political and social changes are inevitable if these diversities are to be reconciled, whether such changes are effected by the processes of orderly evolution or by popular revolt.

CHAPTER EIGHT

Argentina and the Falkland Islands

Argentina is a country with a split personality. Among the Argentines there are many who subscribe to the ideas of a free democracy. The internationally famous newspaper, *La Prensa,* has long stood for equality before the law, for widespread public education, for free access to knowledge, and for the public discussion of political issues. But there are also many Argentines who subscribe to the most violent forms of nationalism, including hatred of everything foreign, and who favor a strong dictatorship backed by police authority to keep order at home, to lead toward the goal of economic self-sufficiency, and to establish Argentina in a position of equality among the world's leading powers. A resolution of these divergent state-ideas is not easy to find.

Among the independent countries of Latin America, Argentina has occupied a position of preeminence for a century. Until recently it has been first in income per person; it has the lowest percentage of illiteracy, and the largest percentage of people living in cities; it has the largest area of farm land per person, and the smallest percentage of its labor force employed in agriculture. In 1949 it was the only Latin American country not classified as economically underdeveloped. Much as Venezuela owes its spectacular rise to first place in income per person to the investment of capital from the United States, Argentina owed its economic development in the nineteenth and early twentieth centuries to the investment of capital from Great Britain.

Argentina is composed of highly contrasted regions, yet its national life is strongly concentrated in the one great region which lies behind Buenos Aires, the Humid Pampa. There are important differences which distinguish the part played in the national life by each of the outlying

Maps 2, 4, 6, 8, 11, 13, 14, 15, 21, 22, 25 are pertinent to this chapter.

Lake on the margin of the Andes in northern Patagonia

regions. But all of them face toward Buenos Aires. In Buenos Aires, and
the Humid Pampa which forms its immediate hinterland, are located
most of Argentina's productive capacity and most of its capital. In this
central area are most of the factories, most of the farms, most of the railroads and roads, and most of the people.

Argentina is also composed of contrasted economic and social groups.
There are wealthy landowners and tenant farmers; there are the owners of
industry, and industrial wage workers. All these groups tell the story of
the development of a modern urban-industrial society against a traditional agrarian background. And, in Latin-American style, all these
economic and social forces tend to burst apart the frail political forms
devised to give them expression.

Argentines are possessed of a strong nationalist sentiment. They are
violently pro-Argentine, and sensitive to any suggestion of subservience

to foreign interests of any kind. Few Britons understand clearly why the Argentines are not more grateful for the capital which supported their economic growth; and few North Americans can weigh impartially the motives which lead Argentina again and again to disrupt the assumed unity of the Western Hemisphere nations. Few people in the United States realize the extent to which the politically powerful groups in Argentina resent economic domination by British or North American interests, or the extent to which these groups are concerned about what they think of as the threat of Brazilian rivalry, or the extent to which they fear the spread either of communism or democracy.

Major Physical Divisions of Argentina

The Argentine national territory includes a wide variety of country. Argentine geographers recognize four major physical divisions, each with numerous subdivisions. Except in the far south, the western border of the country is in the Andes. The first major division of the country, the *Andes* and the eastern *Andean Piedmont,* includes the cordilleras from the dry north to the heavily glaciated and ice-covered mountains of Patagonia. It includes also the very dry southern part of the Bolivian Altiplano, and the lower, but also very dry mountain-and-bolsom desert west of Córdoba and south of Tucumán. The eastern piedmont of the Andes with its succession of oasis settlements may be included with this first major division of the country.

The second major division is known as the North. There is the vast alluvial plain of the *Chaco,* with its tropical scrub-woodland cover. On the east and south of the Río Paraná there is Argentine *Mesopotamia,* the land between the rivers (the Paraná and the Uruguay), composed partly of floodplain, partly of gently rolling and well-drained interfluves. In the far northeast there is an arm of Argentine territory which extends onto the *Paraná Plateau.*

The third major division of the country is the *Pampas*—the great plains which lie south of the Chaco and east of the Andean piedmont. Most of these plains were originally covered with a growth of low scrubby trees and grasses, a vegetation type known as *monte;* but toward the southeast of the Pampas, where the rainfall is heavier and the summers remain cool, tall prairie grasses were once probably more important than the monte. It is customary to divide the Pampas into a wetter eastern part and a drier western part—designated respectively as the Humid Pampa and the Dry Pampa. When the Argentines refer to *La Pampa,* they are referring to the territory of that name which lies mostly within the Dry Pampa.

Finally, the fourth major physical division of Argentina is *Patagonia,* the region south of the Río Colorado. This is a land of arid, wind-swept plateaus, crossed at wide intervals by strips of green vegetation along the valley bottoms. In the far south of Patagonia, Argentina shares with Chile the land of continuously cool and stormy weather, where winters are never severe, but where there is never any real summer.

The People of Argentina

Against this diverse background the Argentine people have distributed themselves in a very uneven pattern. Large parts of the national territory are almost empty. Two chief areas of concentrated settlements can be seen: one is the string of irrigated oases along the eastern Andean Piedmont, including those around Jujuy, Tucumán, Mendoza, and Córdoba; the other is the Humid Pampa focusing on Buenos Aires.

The degree to which the Argentine national life is concentrated in the immediate hinterland of Buenos Aires is extraordinary, especially when we understand that this concentration is a product of the last century. Buenos Aires itself is not only the largest city of Argentina and the largest city in Latin America, but also it is the largest urban center of the Southern Hemisphere, and second only to Paris among the Latin cities of the world. The Humid Pampa makes up about 22 percent of the total area of Argentina; yet in this one region there are some twelve million people, about 65 percent of all the Argentines. In this region are nearly 70 percent of all the railroads, 84 percent of all the automobiles, 86 percent of all the territory used for the production of cereal and flax, 63 percent of all the cattle, and 85 percent of all the industrial production. Argentine economists figure that in this one region is concentrated 82 percent of the productive capacity of Argentina.

In proportion to the concentration of economic activity in this region the density of the rural population is surprisingly low. There are only a few spots near Buenos Aires where the population exceeds 100 per square mile. The zone with densities between 25 and 60 per square mile extends westward from the capital city for only about 200 miles. Most of the Humid Pampa has a rural density of between 10 and 25 people per square mile. On the other hand, more than 70 percent of the people in this region live in towns and cities. In the metropolitan area of Buenos Aires there were nearly five million people in 1962. Outside of Buenos Aires, but within the area of the Humid Pampa, there were eight cities of more than 100,000 population.

The other clusters of people in Argentina are quite different from the great cluster around Buenos Aires: the oasis settlements of the Andean piedmont represent a much older colonization, and a colonization which came from the north and west, from across the mountains, rather than from the east across the plains.

Outside of the piedmont oases, and certain smaller concentrations in the North, the rest of Argentina is very sparsely settled. Nearly half of the national territory, in fact, is occupied by less than 8 percent of the people: over vast areas there is a population density of scarcely two people per square mile.

Racial Character and Origin of the Argentine People

The Argentine people are different from any Latin Americans we have discussed hitherto. The overwhelming majority are of unmixed European descent. In 1930 it was estimated that 74 percent were Argentine-born of European parents, and 24 percent were recent immigrants born in Europe. Since 1930 the current of immigration has greatly decreased, so that the proportion of European-born Argentines is now less than 24 percent. The official Argentine estimates place the proportion of people of unmixed European ancestry at 97 percent; but this figure certainly conceals the presence of considerable numbers of mestizos in the outlying parts of the country on the borders of Chile, Bolivia, and Paraguay. In the Humid Pampa the population is exclusively European, and made up mostly of families that have arrived in Argentina since 1853. Only about 3 percent of the whole population is pure Indian; and the proportion of Negroes is negligible.

The Argentine territory was originally settled by people who came from Peru, Paraguay, or Chile. The first attempt to establish a settlement on the Plata shore in 1536 ended in failure. Asunción became the primary settlement center from which the Spaniards spread over much of the surrounding territory. Corrientes, Santa Fé, and Buenos Aires (1580) were established by people from Asunción.

Meanwhile, however, the Northwest of Argentina was being occupied by people who came either directly or indirectly from the other great Spanish culture center, Lima. The chief route of settlement followed the old Inca road to the southeastern outpost of the Inca Empire, near Tucumán. Since the early route to Chile avoided the Atacama and the high Puna country by making a long circuit to the east and then crossing the single range of the Andes south of latitude 28° S., this eastern piedmont of the highlands was intimately connected with the settlement of Chile during the sixteenth century. A strong current of immigrants from Chile in more recent times has supplemented the population of the Argentine oases from Mendoza to Neuquén, and people of Chilean origin are the chief settlers of the eastern Andean border in southern Patagonia. The reasons for this outward movement of Chileans during the latter part of the nineteenth century have already been discussed: its result was the development in this part of Argentina of a population of mestizo character, with a background of tradition quite different from that of the inhabitants of modern Buenos Aires.

The people of all the early settlements had trouble with the nomadic

Indians of the Argentine plains. The Abipones, the Puelche, and other tribes of the Pampas and Patagonia, although not numerous, were independent and warlike. They resisted the invasion of the Spaniards as they had that of the Incas. These migratory hunters of the guanaco and the rhea never could be tamed for agricultural labor as the Guarani Indians of Paraguay were tamed. If they lacked the shelter of the forests that their brothers, the Araucanians, enjoyed, they nevertheless were more than a match for the Spaniards on the arid or semiarid plains and plateaus where knowledge of the water sources was of primary importance. The adoption of horses and firearms by these Indians had much the same effect as on the Indians of the Great Plains of North America. Greatly increased mobility and capacity to kill the wild game was a temporary advantage; but the exhaustion of the wild animals made the Indians even more warlike in their struggle for wider hunting grounds. Until the last quarter of the nineteenth century a line of forts across the Humid Pampa provided an inadequate protection for the settlements along the Paraná-Plata shores and the route to Córdoba. As late as 1876 it was estimated that 40,000 head of cattle were stolen every year in Indian raids—many of them being sold in Chile. With the campaign of 1879–1883, however, the Indians were pushed back and the line of forts was extended to include more and more of the grassy plains. Not until the year 1880 was the settlement of Bahía Blanca, at the southern margin of the Humid Pampa, connected by land with the towns to the north and west. But the Indian days are now gone, and only on reservations in the more remote and unattractive regions can pure-native peoples be seen today.

During the colonial period the piedmont settlements of the northwest and west belonged to a different world. They were connected economically with the west coast. At Salta a fair was held each year at which mules and cattle from the grassy plains were sold to the mining peoples of the Andes. But the seminomadic *gauchos* of the plains or the inhabitants of the small Plata ports had little real contact with the inhabitants of the piedmont oases.

The Settlement of the Humid Pampa

Argentina started its phenomenal growth as a modern state in 1853. When the country gained its independence the chief focus of settlement was along the Andean piedmont, especially on the city of Tucumán. A long period of civil conflict followed between those who wanted a federal structure with a large measure of autonomy for the several states and those in favor of a highly centralized structure, focusing on Buenos Aires. Under General Rosas the centralists were victorious, and the country was reoriented both politically and economically away from the Andean piedmont toward Buenos Aires. Rosas was overthrown in 1852, and the following year Argentina adopted a new liberal constitution. Argentina advanced toward the modern period with four fundamental characteristics: first, a scanty population—only about 900,000 people in 1800, and 1,200,000 in 1852; second, a people almost exclusively interested in horses, cattle, and sheep, and not at all in agriculture; third, an abundance of free land of first-rate quality for grazing and grain farming; and fourth, the tradition of the large private estate.

There was no precedent for the transformation which followed. The Argentine grasslands, together with the other mid-latitude grasslands

Firewood from the delta of the Paraná

of the world, passed through a spectacular and unique period of development. The advance of the frontier of settlement across first-class agricultural lands, accompanied by the widespread prosperity brought by expanding markets and increasing land values, was a phenomenon characteristic of one period of economic history, and chiefly, too, of one kind of place. Most of the world's humid grasslands were scantily occupied and little used except for pasture before the middle of the nineteenth century. The various techniques developed during the last century not only made possible the agricultural use of the grasslands, but also the connection of these remote places with the city markets by much cheaper forms of transportation than had hitherto been available. Agricultural machinery for the first time in history made possible the cultivation of large areas from which the yield per acre was small; on the open grasslands barbed-wire fences (invented in Illinois in 1873) made possible the separation of agricultural land from pastures, and also one pasture from another so that the breeding of animals could be controlled; well-drilling machines and cheap windmills made it possible to get water where water was difficult to find at the surface; and railroads and steamboats made it possible to ship the products of the farms to the expanding city markets.

A fundamental characteristic of this period of human history was the rapid increase in the rate of population growth in the world as a whole. This population increase formed the basic support for the expanding markets, which, in turn, made possible the system of credits and investments. And credits and investments led to continuously expanding production, which provided support for more and more people. It is difficult, sometimes, to realize how unprecedented were the changes introduced during this period of human history, and how unprepared mankind was to adjust human institutions to an economy of plenty.

The New Means of Transportation

The transformation of the Argentine Humid Pampa began with the development of the means of transportation, with the construction of roads and railroads. Roads were remarkably difficult to maintain. As long as travel was free in any direction—as it was in the period before fences were built—the problem was not serious; for when the ruts were worn too deep into the loose soil the carts or horses could follow a new route to one side of the old one. But when fences were placed along the property lines and the roads could not be shifted, wagon wheels soon cut through the grass cover and exposed the fine Pampa soil. During and after each rain the fine material was turned into a quagmire, and when the mud dried out, the wind picked up the powdery dust and whirled it away, with the result that, in time, the roads were several feet below

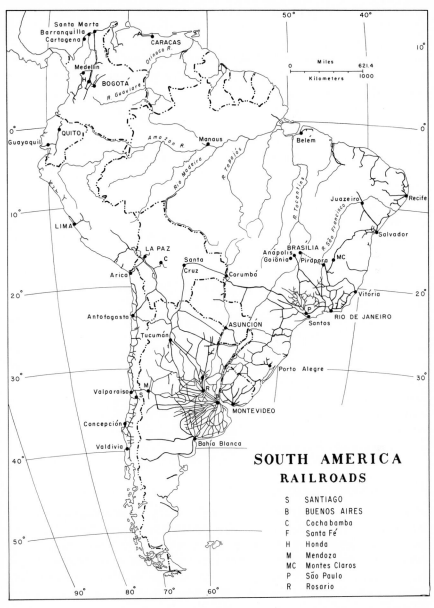

Map 22

SOUTH AMERICA

RAILROADS

S   SANTIAGO
B   BUENOS AIRES
C   Cochabamba
F   Santa Fé
H   Honda
M   Mendoza
MC Montes Claros
P   São Paulo
R   Rosario

199

the general level of the plain. Even now the rural roads are impassable for motor vehicles except in dry weather; in a country so free from stones, even gravel for road surfacing must be imported from a distance.

The constuction of railroads, on the other hand, has been very simple. On the nearly level surface there is no need for cuts, fills, bridges, tunnels, or even for curves. In few parts of the world are construction costs lower.

The first railroad started operations in 1857. It ran for six miles in a straight line southwestward from Buenos Aires. Shortly thereafter a railroad was built along the old colonial mule route from Rosario to Córdoba and Tucumán. During the next few decades railroads were built out of all the leading ports of the Humid Pampa, usually running in straight lines toward indefinite—or impossibly distant—objectives. A few of these lines have actually been extended beyond the borders of the Humid Pampa, but most of them have not. By 1910 Argentina's central region was crisscrossed by a series of overlapping fans, converging on Buenos Aires, Rosario, Santa Fé, and Bahía Blanca.[1]

The Argentines generally think of the Humid Pampa as being divided into four major zones, each zone served by the main line and branches of one of the large railroads. The whole southeastern part of the region constitutes the zone of the Ferrocarril del Sud, the main line of which runs southward from Buenos Aires, and which connects with La Plata, Mar del Plata, and Bahía Blanca. A second zone is formed by the main line and branches of the Ferrocarril Oeste, which runs southwestward from Buenos Aires. The third zone is a narrow one, served by the main line of the Ferrocarril de Buenos Aires al Pacífico, which runs westward from the capital through Junín to Mendoza. The fourth zone is that served by the Ferrocarril Central Argentino, which runs from Buenos Aires northwestward to Rosario, Córdoba, and Santa Fé.

These various railroad lines were not financed by the Argentines. Wealth among the *estancieros* was in the form of herds and land, not money or bank credits. After 1853, when foreign capital felt secure in Argentina, many investors in Europe saw opportunity for profit in this rapidly expanding region. Between 1880 and 1886 the flow of British capital into Argentina was especially strong; most of the railroads were built by British companies, made use of British rolling stock, and burned British coal. The meter-gauge line to Tucumán and the Northwest, however, was built by a French company.

---

[1] The first railroad and many of those which followed were built on a broad gauge (5 ft. 6 in.)—a gauge adopted originally to fit rolling stock which the British had built for use in India but had sent to Russia for use in the Crimean War. There is no uniformity of gauge, however. Some of the lines are built on the so-called standard gauge (4 ft. 8½ in.), and some are built on narrow gauge. The line which runs from Buenos Aires through Córdoba and Tucumán northward to Bolivia was built on a one-meter gauge.

The New Estancias

The railroads paid good dividends to their stockholders; and to the people of Argentina they brought unheard-of prosperity in the form of booming land values. But the whole process of land settlement and of property division was fundamentally different from the process of settlement in the grasslands of the United States which was going on at the same time. In North America the small homesteader after 1862 was able to get a farm of one hundred and sixty acres practically free of cost. In Argentina, the land, even before the coming of the railroads, was already partitioned in large units and given to a favored few in government grants.

The spread of the large estates over the Pampa was rapid after 1853. The first advance southward from the Paraná shore was made in the east. As early as 1875 the line of forts protecting the occupied part of the Pampa from the Indians had been pushed forward to the southern coast, east of the Sierra de la Ventana. The next year, in 1876, the line of forts had been pushed still farther to the west, and by 1879 the forts were along the Río Negro. The Indians were finally eliminated as a menace to the settled parts of the country in a military campaign from 1879 to 1883. The previously unoccupied parts of the Pampa were divided into vast private estates, 100,000 acres or so in area. Some 300 families gained possession of most of the area of the Humid Pampa.

The Pastoral Base

Life of the new estancias was still not agricultural. The owners were mostly Argentine creoles, men raised in the pastoral tradition, men whose chief occupation was the handling of herds of cattle, sheep, and horses, men for whom the surest road to prestige rested in the ownership of land. Foreign markets, as far as the landowners were concerned, meant markets for cattle. At first the herds were made up of the Argentine cattle, descendants of the scrub animals of the colonial period. They were permitted to run at will on the vast, unfenced range, and to breed without care and without thought of quality. Such animals were good for the production of such things as hides, tallow, and salt beef; but the meat was lean and had a strong taste. In 1877 the first refrigerator ship made it possible to send frozen meat to Great Britain, but British taste would not accept Argentine meat. The result was the importation of high-grade beef cattle from Britain, and the careful breeding of these animals on fenced-in pastures. This important shift from scrub cattle to carefully selected animals took place between 1880 and 1900.

The change in the pastoral technique created many other changes in the relation of people to the land, in the productivity of the land. The scrub cattle could get along well enough on the poor native grasses. They could endure the insect pests of the Chaco, or the long overland marches with little feed and water. But not so the big clumsy beef animals bred from British stock. Because the new cattle could not survive the ravages of Texas fever, the southern limit of the country, infested with ticks, or *garrapatas*, became for the first time, a significant boundary. But in addition to requiring tick-free pastures, the new animals required a better source of feed than the uncultivated pastures could supply. Rapidly, after 1890, the estancieros came to realize the necessity of shifting from a grazing industry based on uncultivated pastures to one based on a cultivated crop. Alfalfa was the feed crop they adopted, and on the Humid Pampa alfalfa did exceptionally well. But alfalfa had to be planted on plowed land, and then cut and fed to the animals. These practices required the services of many more workers than had ever been needed to care for the wild scrub animals of the earlier period. At last the estancieros wanted immigrants.

Immigrants

Other people in Argentina had felt the need for more settlers long before the estancieros did. Juan Bautista Alberdi (1810–1884), one of the foremost political philosophers of Latin America, was engaged in writing his famous treatise on a proposed basis of political organization for the Argentine Republic while the country itself was in the grip of the tyrant Rosas. "The enemy of union," wrote Alberdi, "is not Rosas, but distance." He was one of the first to recognize that to govern a land it is necessary to populate it. Alberdi and many of the other important men of his time never ceased to emphasize the necessity for stimulating the immigration of Europeans. That Europeans actually came in large numbers to the Argentine Humid Pampa distinguishes this region as well as the nation of which it is the economic center from the other nations and regions we have discussed up to this point.

In 1856 the first group of agricultural immigrants was brought from Europe. This group consisted of 208 families of German- and French-speaking Swiss. Since the land in the more accessible parts of the Humid Pampa was already in private hands, this colony was established on land granted by the Province of Santa Fé, and located a short distance northwest of the city of that name. The first colony, known as Esperanza, and developed largely through the initiative of a private citizen, Aaron Castellanos, was soon bordered by a number of other similar colonies of European immigrants. After 1882 the district around Santa Fé became one of the first important sources of wheat.

The tide of immigration began to rise more and more rapidly. The total population of the country, which had been 1,200,000 in 1852, increased to 2,500,000 in 1880, and of these 173,000 were people born in Europe. The first peak year of immigration was reached in 1889, when 218,744 second- and third-class passengers came to Buenos Aires. In every year, however, there was a considerable return current of emigrants who were either discouraged and homesick, or successful and ready to return to the homeland to settle down in higher social positions. The immigration figures for 1889 must be balanced against 40,649 emigrants. The depression and panic of 1890–91 resulted in a net loss of population in Argentina, but thereafter the tide swelled rapidly again, to advance with few setbacks to the peak year of 1913, when 302,047 entered and 156,829 left. Between 1857 and 1900 approximately 2,000,000 immigrants arrived in Buenos Aires and 800,000 departed—giving a net increase of 1,200,000. After World War I immigration set in again, reaching another peak in 1929, when there were 427,455 arrivals and 348,234 departures. During the 73 years between 1858 and 1930 the total immigration amounted to 6,300,000 people. Since 1930 immigration has been small.

Meanwhile the racial character of the Argentine population was being profoundly altered by this stream of new Europeans. The composition of the population in 1914 and again in 1935 is presented in the following table:

RACIAL CHARACTER OF THE POPULATION OF ARGENTINA*

	1914	1935
Born in Argentina of pure European stock	5,185,000	9,480,000
Born in Argentina with traces of Indian or Negro stock	400,000	300,000
Born in Europe	2,300,000	2,500,000
Total population	7,885,000	12,280,000

* From A. E. Bunge, "Present Economic Situation of the Argentine," *Revista de Economía Argentina,* 34:286.

The European immigrants whose arrival so radically changed the character of the Argentine people were largely of Italian and Spanish nationality. These two groups together made up almost 80 percent of the newcomers. Between 1857 and 1924, of those who remained in the country, 1,300,000 were Italians and 1,025,000 were Spaniards. Represented also in the stream of immigration by substantial numbers were French, Germans, Austrians, Russians, British, and Swiss. Since 1930 most of the immigrants have come from eastern Europe, especially Poland.

Tenants and the Rise of Agriculture

The immigrants were desired by the landowners, we have said, because they were needed to plant and cut alfalfa for the high-grade beef animals. The native Argentines themselves were still interested, primarily, in breeding fine cattle and horses, and in providing these animals with adequate feed. The immigrants brought agriculture to Argentina, and agriculture was encouraged by the landlords as a by-product of the expansion and improvement of the grazing facilities. The most effective way to prepare the land for the planting of alfalfa was to rent it for a period of four or five years to tenants and to permit them, for a share of the crop, to raise wheat. The estancieros and their hired hands were neither willing nor numerous enough to undertake this work of cultivation. They were, however, anxious to secure tenants for their estates, and soon found that in addition to increasing their alfalfa acreage they could derive considerable profit from a share of the crops. The contracts obliged the tenants to plant the land with alfalfa and to move away after a specified number of years. The alfalfa fields then yielded well, giving as many as three cuttings a year, for five or ten years, after which new tenants would be secured, and the cycle repeated. Naturally the tenant homes were rude, temporary shelters, and the attachment of the agricultural workers to the land was loose and easily broken. Yet it was the tenant group that made the Humid Pampa one of the world's leading surplus grain and meat regions.

With the rise of wheat farming to a place of major importance, the demand for more workers to take care of the peak load of the harvest season began to exceed even the supply of tenants. In November and December there was an insistent demand for field hands to work for wages on a temporary basis. In response there developed a regular seasonal migration of laborers who would come from Italy to Argentina in the spring and early summer of the Southern Hemisphere, and who would return to Italy during the months from March to June to harvest the Italian wheat crop. Many of these *golondrinas,* or swallows, as they were called, made the trip between Italy and Argentina again and again. After 1914, this form of seasonal migration practically ceased.

Only with the development of commercial agriculture, between 1880 and 1900, did the present outlines of the Humid Pampa come sharply into focus. As the new beef animals, fed on alfalfa on fenced pastures, replaced the half-wild animals, and as cultivated grains and alfalfa replaced the pasto duro and the monte, a new regional boundary began to appear. Grain-farming and alfalfa pushed westward as long as yields were sufficient to make this system profitable. Yields of wheat and alfalfa were high enough within what we now call the Humid Pampa; farther to the west there was not enough moisture to support adequate crop yields. Wheat and alfalfa were cultivated approximately as far as the 16-inch rainfall line west of Bahía Blanca, and as far as the 23-inch rainfall line west of Santa Fé. Less rainfall is needed to produce adequate crop yields in the south where temperatures are lower and evaporation is less. These particular values of rainfall became significant natural features because of

Calle Florida, one of the major commercial streets of Buenos Aires

the farm technology and the balance of costs and prices during this part of the nineteenth century. The Humid Pampa, as distinct from the Dry Pampa, made its appearance. The development of the Humid Pampa is reflected in the statistics of exports: in 1894 the three chief pastoral products together (wool, meat, and hides) made up 63 percent of the total value of exports; but in 1903, for the first time, the value of the combined agricultural products (maize, wheat, and linseed) exceeded the value of the animal products. The immigrant farmers supplied the necessary man power to reshape the economic destiny of the region and to redraw its geographic bounds; but the Argentine landowners were the ones who profited most from the spectacular increase of land values.

Buenos Aires

The development of the agricultural possibilities of the Humid Pampa was accompanied by the spectacular growth of the urban nucleus on which

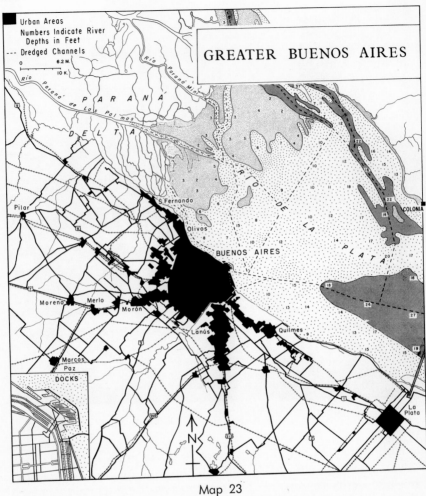

Map 23

all these developments focused. In 1778, when Buenos Aires was opened as a port, the population was only 24,203. In 1855, at the beginning of the modern period, the new Argentine capital had only 90,000 inhabitants. By 1870, however, it had increased to 270,000; and by 1890, it had reached 668,000. Buenos Aires passed the million mark in 1909, and at the time of the census of 1914, it had 1,500,000 people. After World War I the growth of the city continued, reaching 2,197,000 in 1932. At present its population is estimated at well over 4,000,000. Associated with this rapid growth have come all those social and economic phenomena which are characteristic of modern Occidental cities: the rapid rise of land values in the center; the development of "blighted areas" in the old residence zone near the center, and in the suburbs; the rapid expansion of the city along the lines of travel, including the establishment of detached suburbs and satellite towns; and the over-rapid subdivision of land into small residence lots in the scramble for profits by land speculators. Like so many great cities of the modern world, Buenos Aires has spread far beyond the original political area.

Modern Argentina

The whole metropolitan area of Buenos Aires, with a population approaching five million, includes about a quarter of the population of Argentina. The long struggle for domination between the traditional centers of Argentine life along the Andean piedmont of the Northwest and the upstart port has now come to an end. The leadership of Buenos Aires is not only political. Like Paris, or London, or New York, the Argentine capital draws to it the men of outstanding ability born elsewhere in the country.

Now new threats to the coherence of the Argentine state have appeared. Two major conflicts are being fought out. One is between those who favor a continuation of the system of overseas trade which made some people in Argentina wealthy and prosperous and those who favor economic self-sufficiency in the largest possible measure. And the second conflict is between those who support the principles of liberal democracy and those who favor a tightly organized dictatorship. The lines between these two sets of conflicting ideas are not sharply drawn, and even the major political parties are divided within themselves on these issues.

The Economic Situation

The almost twenty million people in Argentina have been accustomed to living well. From shortly after 1880 until 1955 the income per person in Argentina was higher than that of any other Latin American country. There was a time when almost half of all the foreign commerce of Latin America was Argentine. Argentina has the largest proportion of people living in cities (62 percent), and is the only country in which fewer people are employed in agriculture than in manufacturing industry (agriculture 25 percent; industry 29 percent). Argentina leads all Latin America in literacy (87 percent); and it is the only country in Latin America in which the food consumption of the people is greater than the estimated caloric requirements. The Argentines have been accustomed to eating steak every day. It came as a great shock during the dictatorship of Perón when one day in each week had to be designated as meatless because of a shortage of beef. In 1955 the gross national product per capita in Argentina had dropped to $496, and by 1962 it was down to only $185.

This drop in the gross national product was a direct result of the economic policies of Perón. For the first time since the 1880's the system of prosperity based on trade with Britain and on investments of British capital was being effectively challenged. This represents a very fundamental change in the traditional economic policy.

The Argentines have long been accustomed to selling their products in foreign markets. In the colonial period, as we have seen, the mules and the leather produced in the northern part of the Humid Pampa were sent through Tucumán and Salta to the prosperous mining communities of the Andes. Manufactured goods from Spain and silver came back in return. Argentina took its place among the chief commercial nations of the world during the latter part of the nineteenth century. The North American Civil War following soon after the fall of Rosas offered Argentina an unexpected opportunity to gain a foothold in the European markets, especially those of Great Britain. Argentina supplied meat and wheat; and in exchange, Great Britain supplied coal and manufactured articles of all kinds. British investments in railroads and packing plants, British purchases of Argentine foods, British sales of manufactured products in the expanding Argentine market, British coal shipments which formed the bulk cargoes to support the British steamship lines—these were the links which connected Argentina with Great Britian. The prosperity of the one was closely reflected in the prosperity of the other. Argentina could supply food at relatively low cost to the urban people of Great Britain, and the urban people of Great Britain were kept busy manufacturing the many things which the Argentines needed to buy. For the owners of capital and the owners of land, the system was a highly satisfactory one. Even the tenants who were doing most of the work were, for a time, satisfied with the arrangements since they were living much better than in Spain or Italy. But the system contained the seeds of its own destruction, for there was a very great inequality in the distribution of the income. The landowners in Argentina were, as a group, among the world's wealthiest people.

Even before the outbreak of World War I, however, small but significant changes in these relationships were appearing in Argentina. In 1880, Argentina imported some two and a half million pounds of flour and produced almost none. But in 1913, newly constructed flour mills in Buenos Aires were producing two million pounds a year, and were being expanded. It was, however, the dislocations of 1914 that brought the first important challenge to the theory that such remote countries as Argentina should produce only raw materials and that the industrial centers of Europe and North America should supply the necessary manufactured articles to these places.

When Argentina was cut off from the usual sources of manufactured goods, she turned to the development of domestic manufacturing industries. Machinery was imported. Factories were built, and tariffs were set up to protect the infant enterprises. By 1920, shoes made from the local supplies of leather and cut for the Argentine trade could compete, for the ordinary market, with expensive imported shoes. Similarly, the woolen textiles made in Buenos Aires could meet the competition of all but the high-grade textiles from Great Britain. Before World War II Argentine manufacturing industries, protected by high tariffs, came to dominate the domestic market.

The Problems of Industrial Development

Many years ago the French geographer, Pierre Denis, pointed out that in many ways Argentina was like the prairie states of the United States, but with the land abruptly cut off at Chicago. The thriving domestic economy of the United States was based not only on the food production of its prairies, but also on the markets and industries of the east. Argentina, because of its proximity to the ocean, could reach foreign markets easily. But no great country in the world seems to be so thoroughly lacking in the mineral and power resources on which manufacturing industry must be supported. In Argentina there is an abundance of raw materials from the farm and ranch, and even some sources of industrial minerals; but there is a notable lack of power resources.

Until the 1950's Argentina was dependent on imported British coal to run the railroads and the factories. British coal was high in quality and low in cost. Because it formed a bulk cargo on ships sailing out from Britain destined to bring wheat back, the shipping costs were low. But when World War I suddenly reduced the coal shipments, Argentina faced a serious crisis in its fuel supply. In World War II this happened again. To keep the railroads running, wood was used as a fuel, and even maize and other grains soaked in linseed oil. By the end of World War II British coal was more expensive, partly because the British mines were nearing exhaustion, partly for other reasons.

Argentina began to search frantically for domestic sources of coal. Small coal seams of poor quality were found along the Andean piedmont between San Juan, Mendoza, and San Rafael. The largest domestic source, however, was found at Río Turbio, near the Chilean border in southern Patagonia. The coal has a high sulphur content and cannot be made into coke. On the other hand modern technology is providing a way to use such low-grade coal in industry. Río Turbio coal can be used near the mines more cheaply than imported coal.

Argentina has also been searching for oil. In 1907, petroleum of fair quality was discovered at Comodoro Rivadavia in Chubut, and production from that field has been increased until it now furnishes a major part of the domestic production. New fields have also been brought into production along the Andean piedmont from Salta to Neuquén, and an Argentine pipe line has been extended northward along the piedmont into Bolivia.

The successful search for oil and the development of oil fields, all over the free world, have been carried on by the large oil companies. Oil exploration requires a large supply of risk capital as well as technical skill. When an oil field is successfully developed it seems to many nationalist-minded people that the resources of a country are being drained away by a foreign corporation, not used for the benefit of the country itself. The kind of foreign investment that underlies oil production is the kind that is most disliked by those who support the policy of national economic independence. As early as 1936 the Argentine government placed its oil development under the exclusive control of a government agency: *Yacimientos Petrolíferos Fiscales,* or Y.P.F.

The Economic Policies of Perón

In 1946 the dictator Juan Domingo Perón was elected president of Argentina. We shall discuss the political aspects of the Perón period later; the economic policies of Perón included the establishment of a strict government control of the national economy. The central bank was nationalized, thus assuring the government of a supply of credit to finance its undertakings. All foreign trade was placed under the control of a government agency. The producers of meat and grain sold their products to this agency, and the agency sold the products abroad at the best possible prices. The income derived in this way was not returned to the agricultural interests. The government paid off its foreign debt by purchasing such foreign-owned utilities as gas, electricity, and telephones. The British railroads passed out of British ownership largely to pay for essential imports of beef in the immediate post-war years.

In 1947 the Perón government announced its first "Five-Year Plan" (1947–1951). The plan included large public works and industrialization aimed at making Argentina economically independent of the rest of the world. As a result slums were cleared, roads were built, irrigation systems were improved, and cities were given a modern look. The number of factories jumped from about 40,000 in 1935 to more than twice that number in 1950; and the number of workers employed in manufacturing industry increased from 577,000 in 1935 to 1,108,000 in 1950. In addition to the food industries already in existence, there was a considerable increase in leather goods and textiles, in metal and machinery, and in petrochemicals, paper, and plastics. Foreign capital was welcomed, but only under strict government control. Argentina remained dependent on imported coal, but to reduce this dependence a pipe line was built to carry gas to Buenos Aires from Comodoro Rivadavia.

The Argentine government wanted to have its own steel plant to reduce dependence on imported steel. A United Nations study, published in 1954, estimated that steel could be produced in Argentina at about the same cost per ton as the price of imported steel. The site for the plant was at San Nícolas on the Paraná River downstream from Rosario. Iron ore was brought by rail from a small ore body in the Sierra de Córdoba. Coal was imported from Peru. Limestone and the hardeners of steel were available in Argentina and were assembled at San Nícolas by rail. The San Nícolas steel plant has a capacity of 600,000 tons of steel per year. This domestic supply, it was estimated, would save Argentina more than half of its annual foreign exchange needs. The plant was financed in part by a loan from the Export-Import Bank.

A new petrochemical industrial complex was built in 1961 at San Lorenzo, another port on the Paraná River near Paraná opposite Santa Fé. The plant was financed in part from Argentine capital, and in part from private capital supplied by five North American corporations. Oil was brought by pipeline from the oil fields along the Andes near the Bolivian border. The plant was to produce enough synthetic rubber, benzine, and other chemicals to supply the Argentine market.

The need for a large increase in domestic oil production became clear; and at the same time even Perón was convinced that such an increase could not be accomplished without foreign capital and skill. In 1955 Perón announced the signing of a contract with the Standard Oil Company of California for oil exploration. But this act finally brought together enough opposition in the armed services so that Perón was forced to give up his office and flee from the country.

But the need for a larger supply of oil continued, and the government administered Y.P.F. could produce scarcely 35 percent of the domestic needs. Between 1958 and 1960 the government signed contracts for oil exploration with thirteen private companies in the United States and Europe. As an immediate result Argentine oil production increased 30 percent between 1958 and 1959, and by 1961 Argentina had more oil in sight than it could use. Meanwhile the political opposition to the contracts with foreign oil companies increased. One of President Arturo Ilia's first acts when he became president in 1963 was to cancel them.

By 1963 Argentina was in deep economic trouble. Once a major exporter of wheat, the Argentine production in 1962 was only a little more than domestic needs. In 1963 the wheat crop was 18 percent below the average of the decade 1952–1962. The rapid expansion of the manufacturing industries resulted in a production of consumer goods far greater than the domestic market could absorb. As a result, factories began to cut back. The San Nícolas steel plant in 1962 operated at less than half capacity. In a labor force of some six million there were nearly 600,000 unemployed.

Argentine Foreign Trade

Before World War II Argentina was the leading commercial country of Latin America. This country produced 98 percent of all the wheat exported from Latin America; 80 percent of all the meat; 50 percent of all the hides and skins; 95 percent of all the linseed; 95 percent of all the maize; 59 percent of all the cereals other than wheat and maize; 57 percent of all the wood and wood products, including quebracho extract; and 52 percent of all the wool.

Great Britain and the United States are the two chief markets for Argentine products. Since World War II, however, Argentina has sought to broaden its foreign markets and so to reduce dependence on Great Britain and the United States. The government made a trade agreement with the Soviet Union, expecting to receive Soviet machinery in return for food products; but the Soviet government did not carry out its part of the deal. The table below shows the percentage of Argentine exports going to various countries in 1938, 1945, and 1954.

EXPORTS OF ARGENTINA GOING TO CERTAIN COUNTRIES*

Percentage of total exports

Country	1938	1945	1954	1962
United Kingdom	33	25	18	17
Netherlands	7	1	6	14
Italy	3	—	3	12
West Germany	12	—	9	10
United States	9	22	14	7

* For 1938 and 1945 data: The Pan American Union.
  For 1954 data: The Committee on Latin American Studies, University of California at Los Angeles.
  For 1962 data: the Britannica Book of the Year, 1964.

The imports of Argentina are mostly manufactured goods that require skills and capital investment not available in Argentina. In 1962 some 43 percent of the imports were machinery, motor vehicles, and motor vehicle parts. Fuels and chemicals, and iron and steel manufactures continued to make up about 30 percent. About 29 percent of the imports came from the United States; other suppliers were West Germany, the United Kingdom, Italy, and France.

The Political Situation

The split personality of Argentina is reflected in the two great conflicts now being waged. The most prosperous country in Latin America, the one most favorably endowed by nature for the low cost production of meat and grain, now turns aside from international interdependence to develop national self-sufficiency at whatever cost. And the country which, in the second half of the nineteenth century, seemed to offer great promise of developing along democratic lines, now faces a major struggle between the incompatible ideologies of democracy and totalitarianism.

Domingo Faustino Sarmiento was born in San Juan in 1811. He came from poor parents, for his father was a mule driver. At the age of sixteen he came upon a biography of Benjamin Franklin. From Franklin he learned that a democracy could thrive only if it gave every child an equal chance to become an informed, literate citizen. During the period of General Rosas, Sarmiento was exiled to Chile, where he became well-known as a liberal writer. In 1845 he visited the United States and Europe, and became a disciple of Horace Mann. Returning to Chile he established the first teacher-training school in Latin America; Chile's school system became the best in all the Latin American countries. After the fall of Rosas, Sarmiento returned to Buenos Aires where he helped to set up the new government. He was Argentina's second president, and during his presidency (1868–1874) he established schools, museums, libraries, and art collections. Democracy in Argentina was well launched. After the death of Sarmiento in 1888, the liberal tradition was carried on by the universities, and by the great newspapers of Buenos Aires.

What happened to democracy in Argentina? In the first place it is clear that Sarmiento's educational reforms were only preliminary. Politics after 1853 remained under the tight control of the small minority of land-owners. To be sure, the governments were progressive and stable, but they were not democratically selected, nor were policies opened to public discussion. No government could be elected, and no policy be adopted without the approval of the landowners.

By the early decades of the twentieth century political conditions began to change in Argentina. The flood of immigrants had changed the traditions of the people. And as more and more immigrants left their tenant farms in the rural areas to become city wage workers they escaped from the political control of the ruling groups. Especially when World War I made industrial development in Buenos Aires necessary, a new class of urban workers and a new middle class of shopkeepers and government employees began to appear. The long rule of the Conservative Party was broken in 1916 with the election of Hipólito Irigoyen, the candidate of the *Union Civica Radical*. The Radical Party was firmly based on the city voters.

The Radical Party was tumbled from power in 1930 by a military coup. The fact is that the democratically elected governments had become seriously corrupt and inefficient. When the world-wide depression hit Argentina the government collapsed. From 1930 to 1946 a series of minority governments came to power, maintaining themselves for a time partly by military force, partly by graft and corrupt practices. Democracy was sadly discredited. From 1930 to 1958 the government of Argentina remained in the hands of army officers.

In order to understand Argentina it is necessary to understand what the army officers want, and what they fear. First, the officers are strongly nationalistic. The fact that the Argentine economy was built on the basis of close connections with Great Britain and with the United States limited the freedom of action of the political leaders. Argentina, instead of subscribing to the ideas of political unity in the hemisphere, as first set forth by Sarmiento, proposed instead to make the country a third force in the world, leading the Latin-American nations away from the dominance of the United States. During World War II the government was strongly in favor of Germany and Italy—countries in which most of the officers had been educated and with whose policies they were heartily in accord. When it seemed that the government was about to yield to pressure to break relations with Germany and Italy in 1943, another army coup kept Argentina neutral.

Meanwhile a very important shift of the population was taking place. When the acreages of grain were reduced, the tenants planted their farms with alfalfa and moved away. Having no places to go in the rural areas they moved in large numbers into the cities, especially Buenos Aires. But there was no unemployment problem, for Argentina was rapidly building new industries, and was undertaking programs of slum clearance in the city itself. To a much greater degree than in 1916, here was a worker group free from political control in the cities. Moreover the workers were not at all indoctrinated with the traditional ideas of democracy, for their background was Italian and Spanish. It was at this point that Juan Domingo Perón, an obscure army colonel with tremendous personal ambitions, made his appearance as Secretary of Labor in the military government. He promoted a whole series of social and economic benefits for the workers, among whom he became a popular hero. He called the workers his *descamisados,* his shirtless ones. For the first time in Argentine history there was a political leader working for the poor people. He brought them together as a class, opposed to the rule of the landowners and to the "Yankee imperialists." Aided by his glamorous wife, Eva Duarte Perón, he rose quickly in power, until in 1945 he assumed the presidency. By that time the army was concerned about the rise of this new political leader, and they tried to remove him from office and place him in confinement. But so great was the popular uprising in Buenos Aires that the army had to give in.

In 1946 Perón held an election. It was probably Argentina's first uncontrolled and entirely honest election. Perón, the hero of the descamisados, received 1,478,372 votes, compared with 1,211,666 received by his rival.

Perón's policies were calculated to gain and keep the support of the workers. In addition to his economic policies, which we have discussed above, he decreed a variety of social changes, including higher minimum wages, paid vacations, various social security and health measures. He aroused the workers against the traditional rulers of Argentina, leading even to the burning of the famous Jockey Club, center of the social life of the aristocracy. He took a stand at meetings of the American states in favor of isolationism, and opposed everything that looked like "Yankee imperialism." He drew Argentina closer to the Soviet Union, while strictly controlling communist activity in Argentina. He painted a picture to his devoted followers that showed Argentina assuming a new position of dignity in the world, midway between the Soviets and the nations of the free world.

Perón led his country into bankruptcy. After the death of Eva Perón he took desperate measures to keep his followers in line, for many were already disillusioned when his economic promises were not fulfilled. He even went so far as to arrest certain priests of the Catholic Church who were charged with efforts to undermine his government. But finally, when he planned to permit the entrance of a North American oil company (Standard Oil of California) to undertake the development of Argentina's presumed oil reserves, the army officers felt the time had come to revolt. After a short period of bitter fighting, Perón was forced to flee, and a military government assumed control.

The army has wanted to return the country to constitutional rule, but on one policy they were unyielding—there could be no return of ex-President Perón, even if the people voted for him. An election that went strongly in favor of Perón was annulled. Then when an elected president showed too much of a tendency to form economic ties overseas he was ousted by another army revolt. As we have said, one of the first acts of President Arturo Illia when he took office in 1963 was one that was very popular with the army—canceling the oil contracts. The election of Dr. Illia was notable because of the marked decline in Perón's political support. However, the country remains seriously divided on basic issues, and a solution of the problem of establishing order seems still to be uncertain.

THE FALKLAND ISLANDS

The Falkland Islands are located about 250 miles off the coast of Patagonia in the South Atlantic Ocean at latitude 52° South. They are a colony of Great Britain and have, for a long time, also been claimed by Argentina. The main islands are two—East Falkland and West Falkland

—but there are some 200 smaller islands administered as a part of the same colony. The total area is 4,618 square miles, and the population counted in the census of 1962 was 2,172, a decrease from the 2,230 counted in the census of 1953. The people are almost entirely of British descent. The capital is Stanley (1,135 in 1953; 1,074 in 1962).

The islands are mostly a rolling, hilly, and treeless moorland, with a climate which is too cool for crops, yet with winters which are not excessively cold. The land is used for the pasture of sheep, and wool is one of the regular products of the islands. But the islands have been more important as a whaling station, visited by the whaling ships that operate in the Antarctic. Since the invention of the large floating factories in which whales are processed at sea, the need for a land base has decreased, but whale meat and whale oil are still the leading exports of the Falkland Islands.

The story of the dispute over the ownership of these islands between the British and the Argentines is a long one. The Argentines call them the Islas Malvinas, and on the maps in Argentine school books the islands are described as "occupied by Great Britain." The fact is that during the colonial period both Spain and Great Britain planted colonies, but occupied them only temporarily. From 1811 for a period of ten years they were entirely uninhabited. Independent Argentina, asserting its claim inherited from the Spanish claim, made attempts to establish a colony on them after 1820. In 1831 a whaling ship from the United States was detained by the Argentines, whereupon the United States sent a warship to the islands and dispersed the Argentine settlers. In January 1833 the British government sent an expedition to occupy the Falkland Islands, and since that date they have been continuously a possession of Great Britain. The British hold that, according to international law, the actual use and occupation of a territory prevails over theoretical claims. Meanwhile, any Argentine government which presses vigorous claims against the British achieves additional popularity at home.

CHAPTER NINE

Paraguay and Uruguay

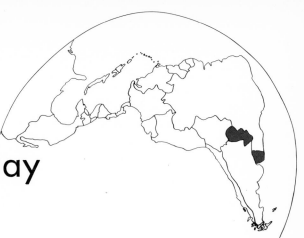

Paraguay and Uruguay are two small states that border Argentina. Except for their position and small size they are in every respect different. Paraguay was still in 1964 under control of a military dictatorship, and had yet to feel the impact of the Industrial Revolution and the Democratic Revolution. It was among the poorer countries of Latin America. Uruguay, on the other hand, is in many ways a model of democracy. Its productive economy was, however, scarcely productive enough to pay the high costs of welfare voted by the people.

PARAGUAY

Paraguay is a small subtropical country located in the interior of South America to the north of Argentina. Its capital, Asunción, is located on the right bank of the Paraguay River, 625 miles north of Buenos Aires. With a climate which is mild but not too mild, and rainy but not too rainy, and with a soil which might yield abundant harvests of such subtropical crops as maize or rice, the central district in which the Paraguayans are concentrated possesses the physical qualities to permit an agricultural people to live in comfort if not in luxury. But it takes more than a comfortable climate or a satisfactory soil to lift people out of poverty.

The Paraguayan state is geographically simple. It is composed of one nucleus of clustered population, and its boundaries are drawn through the scantily occupied territory which surrounds this single nucleus. The

Maps 2, 4, 6, 8, 11, 13, 14, 15, 21, 22, 25 are pertinent to this chapter.

one cluster of people, moreover, is racially homogenous. Yet Paraguay, like the other states we have discussed, does not fail to illustrate in its own peculiar way the dominant theme of diversity. Not only are the Paraguayan people quite different in physical appearance and in racial composition from all the other population groups of the continent, but also, within the country, there are major contrasts of class and caste. There are profound differences between the minority of landowners, army officers, and government officials on the one hand, and the great majority of landless workers on the other. The Paraguayans are a gentle people who seem anything but warlike and belligerent; nevertheless the destiny of this inland state has been warped by two disastrous wars within a century. What Paraguay might have been is no longer important.

The People

The Paraguayans are mostly mestizo. Some 97 percent of them have at least one Spanish ancestor; but the predominant racial strain is Guarani Indian. Perhaps 3 percent are pure Indian, but the number of people of pure European ancestry is very small. Some of those who are unmixed with Indian are the descendants of Germans and other Europeans who settled in Paraguay after 1870. There are almost no Negroes and very few Orientals.

The Indians of Paraguay belong to the linguistic family known as Tupi-Guarani. This linguistic family is thought to have originated in the Basin of the Río Paraguay, and to have spread from that center over a large part of South America east of the Andes. The Guarani had even invaded the Quechua country in the Front Ranges of eastern Bolivia and established themselves there before the arrival of the Spaniards. They make up most of the coastal people of Brazil, and even far in the interior of the Amazon, tribes which speak this same language are found. Before the arrival of the white men the Tupi-Guarani tribes practiced a shifting cultivation of maize and manioc, supplementing their diet with fish and game. Generally they were a friendly people, quite in contrast to their pugnacious brothers, the Abipones and the Puelche of Argentina or the Araucanians of Chile, or even the various other Indian groups of the Brazilian interior.

The Spanish Conquest

The establishment of a Spanish primary settlement center on the eastern side of South America had very different results from those which followed the founding of Lima. In Peru the Spaniards thought for a time that they had discovered El Dorado; but no such wealth awaited the colonists who came to South America from the east. In 1536 an expedition under Pedro de Mendoza landed on the shore of the Plata and established a settlement which was called Buenos Aires. But the boundless grassy plains contained no wealth of gold and silver, and the nomadic warlike Indians were not disposed to be friendly. Nor could the Spaniards practice the kind of agriculture which, in the modern era, has turned this region into one of the world's leading sources of food. To the sixteenth-century Spaniards the Argentine grassy plains were low in potential productivity. In spite of its strategic location near the mouth of the Plata, Buenos Aires lacked the qualifications in terms of mines or large native populations which might have permitted it to become a primary settlement center. Shortly after its foundation, the colony was abandoned.

Meanwhile the Spaniards had pushed on up the Paraná, hoping to find a short route to Peru. In 1537 they had advanced far enough upstream to get beyond the savage Pampa tribes; and on the first bit of high ground which bordered the river within Guarani country, they founded the town of Asunción. As a route to Peru, however, the Paraguay-Paraná-Plata proved to be anything but satisfactory. Even to reach Asunción was such a difficult task through the maze of shifting and shallow channels that a later Spanish expedition was brought overland directly from the east coast of what is now Brazil. Asunción was isolated; but in the territory which has since become the nucleus of Paraguay, the productivity of the land and the numerous native population of friendly and adjustable Guarani offered the conditions necessary for the establishment of a Spanish feudal society.

Asunción became a primary settlement center. Lacking any source of wealth comparable with that which made Lima one of the wonders of the sixteenth-century world, this inland town of Asunción nevertheless played the part of a nucleus of Spanish settlement from which the Spanish occupation of southeastern South America radiated. Colonists advanced northwestward across the Chaco to found the town of Santa Cruz not far from the eastern base of the Andes. Settlements were spread also toward the east; and the final successful establishment of Spanish colonies on the margins of the Argentine grassy plains was accomplished by people who descended the Paraguay-Paraná-Plata from Asunción. Santa Fé was one of these colonies, founded in 1573; in 1580 the site of Buenos Aires was reoccupied.

Present Population

Few Spanish reenforcements came to Paraguay after the early expeditions of the sixteenth century. As a result, the Guarani contribution to the Paraguayan mixture is a relatively large one—not only of blood, but also of language and ways of living. To the European eye, however, the Paraguayan mestizo is by no means displeasing; for his complexion is

Farm home in rural Paraguay

lighter than that of the mestizo produced by the mating of Spaniards and the highland Indians of the Andes, and his features are not so harsh. The Guarani language is still the popular language of Paraguay, and many of the place names throughout this part of South America, including the southern part of Brazil, are Tupi or Guarani words.

A third element of the Paraguayan population of today is made up of European immigrants who entered the country after 1870. The number is small, for most of the Europeans who came to South America during this period settled in Argentina or Brazil. But a few families of Italians, French, Spaniards, English, and Germans found their way to Asunción and settled there, intermarrying with the Paraguayans. At the present time the influence of this group in the economic, political, and social life of the country is of much greater importance than their numbers would suggest.

The Course of Settlement

At first it looked as if the settlers of Paraguay might succeed in creating a paradise. After the establishment of the nucleus of Spanish colonization around Asunción the first penetration of the southern and eastern part of the country began in 1608 with the arrival of the Jesuit missionaries. The scattered and shifting tribes of Guarani Indians were gathered together around the missions and were taught to adopt a sedentary way of living. Thirty-two Jesuit missions were established in Paraguay east of the Río Paraguay. For the Indians the new way of living based on farming, cattle raising, and the collection of forest products meant a more adequate and varied diet and greater security from famine. Unfortunately, however, the Jesuits could not maintain their isolation. Little by little they began to produce goods for sale outside of their small communities, eventually even trading their wines and tobaccos in the distant settlements along the eastern front of the Andes. This economic expansion brought the Jesuits into conflict with the large landowners who wanted both the profits of commercial enterprise and the assistance of the Indian workers. In 1767 the Jesuits were expelled and, for the Indians, paradise was lost. The mission communities fell apart. Those in the outlying sections of the country were entirely abandoned as the Indians drifted toward the central area around Asunción. The natives, unwilling to return to their former way of living, were speedily attached to the large estates through a system of debt bondage—in other words they were reduced to a state of peonage. The result was the depopulation of the outlying districts and the increase of population in the center.

Independence and War

When the first independent Argentine government was set up in Buenos Aires in 1810, a claim was made for jurisdiction over the whole area then included in the Viceroyalty of La Plata. The Paraguayans, however, had no desire to be ruled from Buenos Aires. The political leaders at Asunción were successful in resisting Argentine efforts to expel the Spanish authorities, but since the only connection with Spain was downstream by way of Buenos Aires, the Paraguayans soon had to set up their own independent government. Without conflict, Spanish authority was passed to the dictator, J. G. R. Francia. In 1840 Francia was succeeded by Carlos Antonio López, and he was succeeded by his son Francisco Solano López in 1862. During all this time the country was ruled by a powerful clique of army officers with the support of the few landowners. Always afraid of being forced to become a part of Argentina, the dictators built a strong army.

A major concern of the rulers of Paraguay was to gain an outlet to the sea that would free them from Argentine control. They were negotiating with Uruguay for such an outlet in 1864 when Brazil intervened to protect its southern boundary. The Paraguayans then resorted to force. Crossing the arm of Argentine territory east and south of the Río Paraná, they attempted to invade southern Brazil. This brought Brazil, Uruguay, and Argentina into an alliance against them, and started a war that lasted from 1865 to 1870. It took five years for the armies of the triple alliance to defeat the Paraguayans, but at the end of the war Paraguay was devastated. Before the war Paraguay had a population of about 1,300,000: at the conclusion of the war the population had been reduced, according to some estimates, to less than 250,000, of whom only 28,746 were males.

From this crushing disaster Paraguay struggled slowly back, aided not a little by the European immigrants who brought new hope to a tired people. By 1912 the population was estimated to be about a million, and the ratio between the sexes was nearly normal again. But the economic development of Paraguay progressed slowly in the face of high transportation costs. In 1913 a railroad was completed all the way from Buenos Aires to Asunción, using ferries across the Paraná near Buenos Aires, and again near Posadas. But the volume of traffic was so low that high freight rates had to be charged. A recent report states that the cost of shipping a cargo to Asunción from Buenos Aires is about the same as the cost of shipping the same cargo to Yokohama from Buenos Aires.

The river has never offered an easy solution to the problem. Its braided channel is subject to frequent shifts of position, and winds about to such a degree that many miles of sailing are required to cover only a short direct distance. Settlements located on the banks of the main channel are left with no access to the river when the channel shifts to another part of the floodplain; or sand bars are formed which make the river too shallow for navigation at the landing places. The main channel touches the base of higher ground not subject to flood at only a very few spots—notably at Santa Fé in Argentina and at Asunción. Modern, ocean-going steamers can ascend the river only as far as Santa Fé, and encounter much difficulty above Rosario. Yet in spite of the fact that the Paraguay-Paraná-Plata is such a poor river for navigation, it provided, until the present century, the only connection between Asunción and the outside world.

The Chaco

Most of the Paraguayan people are concentrated on the eastern side of the Paraguay-Paraná-Plata. The Chaco, which lies west of the river, is a world apart. As far as physical conditions are concerned, this great alluvial plain between the river and the base of the Andes bears a striking resemblance to the Ganges Valley of northern India. The climate of the two

regions is similar; the scrub forest of both can be placed in the same
general category of natural vegetation; and the similarity is increased by
the presence in both regions of great sprawling rivers, subject to annual
floods and frequent shifts of channel. Only in detail do the two pictures
differ. But the one is densely populated—more than a thousand rice- and
wheat-growing farmers per square mile; and the other is one of the larger
areas of very sparse population in Latin America. The Chaco is divided
among four states—Argentina, Paraguay, Bolivia, and Brazil; yet only a
small proportion of it can be included in the effective national territory
of any of them.

This is the wilderness over which the Paraguayans and the Bolivians
fought a war starting in 1932. Bolivia and Paraguay have each set forth
abundantly documented legal arguments to support their claims to the
territory north of the Argentine border and west of the Brazilian border.
Between 1926 and 1931 the Paraguayans established about 35 villages of
Canadian Mennonites some 125 miles west of the Río Paraguay on land
which the Bolivians also claimed. Meanwhile the Bolivians placed army
detachments far to the east in territory which the Paraguayans claimed.
Although the whole area remained largely a wilderness, with few trails
and few places where boundaries were clearly marked, the Paraguayans
and Bolivians both pushed forward their outposts. The Bolivians were
being led to believe, incredible as it may seem, that the extension of
political territory to the banks of the Paraguay would in some miraculous
fashion solve the problem of isolation. The Paraguayans were no doubt
motivated to a certain degree by the strong hope that oil would prove
to be available not only along the Andean front, but also in the plains
east of the mountains. From 1932 to 1935 the two countries were locked
in a death struggle: each of them, already burdened with debt, con-
tracted new debts to pay the huge cost of armaments. In the United States
much comment was aroused at the time by the fact that so little difficulty
was experienced in financing these armaments, even in the case of two
countries so obviously bankrupt. In our complicated international system
of commerce it is not always clear who will eventually stand the losses
which inevitably follow from such loans. The war was concluded in 1935
only because both sides were literally exhausted. A new boundary was
drawn approximately along the battle front as it was at the time of the
armistice—it represented a considerable gain for Paraguay, but left the
known oil fields in the hands of Bolivia.

The tragedy of this conflict resides in no small part in its futility. That
Bolivia would find access to the outside world an easier matter if its
boundaries extended to the Paraguay is an error; not only because of the
essentially inland position of Bolivia's nucleus of settlement, but also because of the nature of the river. It is futile to hope that the speculative development of an oil field would relieve the burdens of debt and

poverty. Nor can either Bolivia or Paraguay provide the man power necessary for the agricultural or pastoral settlement of the Chaco. Neither of these countries has centers of expanding population, and neither of them has gained significantly in population through immigration. When and if settlement of the Chaco is made, it is far more likely to be made either by Argentina or Brazil. The present uncertainty enveloping the question of control of the Chaco, and the rival expectations for profit from the wealth of oil which is undoubtedly there waiting to be exploited, must be recognized as a danger to the peace and international harmony of the South American countries, especially Argentina and Brazil.

The Paraguayan Economy

Paraguay remains one of the poorest countries in Latin America. Except for a handful of wealthy people, living standards are very low. Within the one central nucleus of concentrated settlement the political life is dominated by a small group of landowners and army officers; the great majority of the people have no share in the making of political decisions. Isolated from neighbors by lack of communications across national borders, Paraguay's destiny is closely tied to conditions in Argentina, which controls its overland access to the outside world.

According to the census of 1950 Paraguay's population was 1,341,000, and is estimated to be increasing at a rate of 2.1 percent per year. More than 65 percent of the people are rural, and 70 percent are employed in agriculture. Yet only 4 percent of the national territory is actually used for agriculture. All these data reflect a severe case of economic underdevelopment in a country in which most of the people are subsistence farmers, raising foods and fibers for their own use on land they do not own. The chief crops are maize, manioc, sweet potatoes, beans, rice, sugar cane, cotton, and tobacco.

There is no direct highway connection between Asunción and any of the other countries that border Paraguay. To be sure a motor highway runs south from Asunción five miles to a place on the Río Paraguay where there is a ferry connection with an Argentine road on the west bank. This road is passable all the way to Buenos Aires. Highways within Paraguay connect the capital with Encarnación and Villarica, mostly duplicating the service offered by the railroad. A road is planned to run from Villarica to the Iguazú Falls, where it will connect with a Brazilian road to the port of Paranaguá; and another road is planned to run from Asunción northeastward to Capitán Bado and there also to connect with a Brazilian road. In 1957 Santos was declared to be a free port for Paraguayan goods. When and if these roads are completed, Paraguay will for the first time have an outlet which does not pass through Argentina—

Providing a source of safe drinking water in rural Paraguay

then the struggle for the domination of Paraguay by the two great rivals will begin in earnest. At present the only overland connections are by river steamer and railroad downstream to Buenos Aires. Asunción, however, has become a major center of international air travel and now enjoys air connections with all the neighboring countries (Buenos Aires four hours; Rio de Janeiro six hours).

The chief Paraguayan exports are cotton, quebracho, timber, hides, and petitgrain oil. Cotton is the most widely grown commercial crop. The quebracho extract (tannin) comes from five tannin factories located at Puerto Cooper, Puerto Pinasco, and Puerto Casado, to which the logs of the quebracho tree are brought for processing from the woodlands along the river. Four of these factories are owned by Argentines, one by a North American company. The timber comes mostly from the semideciduous forests of eastern Paraguay. The hides come from cattle pastured chiefly in the central area and in bordering parts of the country. If the hides were of better quality they could be tanned from local sources of tannin and thereby give rise to a leather manufacturing industry. The petitgrain oil is distilled from the unripe fruit of bitter orange trees, and is used in the manufacture of perfume. Paraguay supplies some 70 percent of the world market for this product.

The statistics of trade show that some 45 percent of the Paraguayan exports and 38 percent of the imports are credited to Argentina. Actually some of this represents trans-shipments. Other countries with which Paraguay trades are the United States, Italy, and the United Kingdom.

The Political Situation

Neither the Industrial Revolution nor the Democratic Revolution has yet reached Paraguay. But Paraguay has developed more of a sense of national unity than most of its neighbors. Perhaps this can be explained in part by Paraguay's inland position and by the geographic unity of its one nucleus of concentrated settlement. Ever since 1810 Paraguay has sought freedom from outside interference but the search had been largely frustrated. Although Paraguay emerged from the Chaco War as the victor over Bolivia, the military effort left the country even more impoverished than before. Also the returning soldiers were less ready to accept economic misery and the lack of opportunity for political expression than they had been before the war.

No government today can neglect the problems of economic development. The Paraguayan authorities are attempting to expand the agriculture, partly through the efforts of a North American land company operating near the border of Brazil where new farms are offered for those who can pay for them. The great majority, however, cannot buy land. Most of the farmers are squatters on large private estates, using plots of land temporarily for a few years of subsistence crops and then moving elsewhere. There are a few extractive industries where opportunities for employment exist outside of agriculture, and a few textile factories in Asunción.

Yet while the Paraguayan people are burdened with poverty, the Paraguayan land goes on offering bounteous crops and a rich store of forest products. If the funds spent on armaments could have been spent on more productive ends, real economic values might have been created which would have brought prosperity to Paraguay, even if this country never was able to sink one productive oil well. The Paraguayan landscape, with its rolling hills, its rich green pastures, its waving palms, is still a pleasant one: except for the ambitions of some of its rulers Paraguay could have been a paradise.

A herd of cattle in rural Uruguay

URUGUAY

Uruguay is the most coherent and the most democratic state in Latin America. Yet these conditions were not achieved without a struggle. For a long time the territory along the northern shore of the Plata River—which the settlers in Buenos Aires called the *Banda Oriental,* or eastern shore (of the Uruguay River)—was a no-man's land between the Portuguese and the Spaniards. It was invaded again and again from both sides, as each sought to occupy and hold the strategic position at the mouth of the Plata. Uruguay gained its independence because of the intervention of Great Britain, and the agreement between Argentina and Brazil to recognize the existence of an independent buffer state between them. Uruguay, like Argentina, has been largely populated by immigrants from Europe who came after the middle of the nineteenth century. Much more than Argentina, Uruguay has a population that is largely rural. Yet Uruguay in 1962 stood second in Latin America in income per person, and is second only to Argentina in the rate of literacy (85 percent). Since the beginning of the twentieth century the Uruguayans have been able to establish order and coherence through democratic procedures, and have made a distinguished record of peaceful progress.

A government-operated packing plant in Uruguay

The Uruguayan People

Uruguay, like Paraguay and Chile, is composed of only one area of concentrated settlement; but unlike either Paraguay or Chile, this one area includes the whole of the national territory. Uruguay is the smallest of the South American republics, and it has the distinction of being the only one in which the total national territory and the effective national territory are identical. The one cluster of people is centered around Montevideo, a city of about 940,000 in a country with a total population of about three million. No other city in Uruguay has passed sixty thousand; the industrial towns along the Río Uruguay—Paysandú, Salto, and Mercedes—are just under sixty thousand. In the southern part of the country between Montevideo and Colonia, there are between 60 and 125 rural people per square mile; but toward the north the density drops rapidly to fewer than 25 people per square mile. In the northwest there are fewer than 10 per square mile, but no part of the country is unoccupied.

The composition of the Uruguayan population is similar to that of Argentina. In and around Montevideo most of the inhabitants are of pure European descent. They came in large proportion from Italy and Spain, but many other European nationalities are represented by small numbers. In the outlying parts of the country there are enough people who have some Indian ancestors to give the mestizo class in the total population a proportion of something like 8 percent. Negroes constitute about 2 percent of the population and there are almost no pure Indians.

The Uruguayan Economy

Strangely enough for so progressive a state, the population of Uruguay can only be estimated. Uruguay and Peru were only independent countries in Latin America which failed to take a census of population about 1950. Data were gathered with great care concerning the animal population, and concerning all aspects of the economy except man power. The last time Uruguay counted its population was in 1908, at which time there were a little over a million people. In 1962 the Uruguayan population was estimated at about 3,000,000. If this figure is approximately correct, the rate of growth is one of the lowest in Latin America.

Even when allowance is made for the uncertainties of the population estimates, it is clear that the Uruguayans have achieved a relatively high level of economic well-being. In the proportion of people who can read or write Uruguay stands almost equal to Argentina, and a little ahead of Chile and Costa Rica—all of which have populations more than 80 percent literate. In spite of the fact that about 50 per cent of all persons gainfully employed in Uruguay work as pastoralists or farmers, and only 11 percent are employed in manufacturing industries, the gross national product per person was estimated in 1962 to be $559, a figure exceeded only by Venezuela. The Uruguayans enjoy an excellent diet, in which meat is a prominent item.

The Uruguayan economy is closely controlled by the government. Nationalized industries and utilities are not operated for the purpose of producing revenue for the government or personal income for the operators; instead they are operated for the purpose of producing consumer goods and services to sell at low prices. Gas, electricity, telephone service, transportation, as well as foods and gasoline, are priced low enough so that the great majority of the people can share in using them. Government-owned banks and insurance companies provide loans and insurance at low rates. Uruguayans receive old-age pensions, health and liability insurance, free medical service, and numerous other benefits. Work is strictly limited to an eight-hour day, and child labor is carefully regulated. Workers have annual vacations with pay. As long as wool exports are high, this whole expensive operation is covered by income. But in 1958, with costs running higher than income, serious doubts were raised about the continued feasibility of the program. By 1962, however, exports of wool and beef were high again. It remains to be seen whether the "welfare state" can be supported by a largely pastoral economy.

The waterfront in Montevideo

Foreign Trade

The exports of Uruguay come chiefly from the animals. Wool has made up more than 50 percent of the value of all exports each year since 1950. Other exports include meat, meat products, and hides.

Uruguay, like Argentina, has long been tied in its foreign commerce to Great Britain. Like Argentina, also, the Uruguayans supplied meat to Britain during the war at a time when Britain could send little or nothing back in exchange. Uruguay took advantage of the credits thus accumulated to buy out the British interests in railroads and industries. Britain used to take a large part of Uruguay's exports, but during World War II and until 1950, the United States was Uruguay's best customer. In 1955, for the first time, the Netherlands became the leading consumer of Uruguayan products, and exports to Brazil equalled those to Great Britain, while the United States slipped back to its pre-war position (8 percent in 1938). The following table shows the proportion of Uruguayan exports going to selected countries:

PROPORTION OF URUGUAYAN EXPORTS
TO SELECTED COUNTRIES

	1945	1950	1955	1956	1961
The Netherlands	1.7	2.5	23.3	24.4	11
Brazil	2.4	1.0	14.2	19.1	—
United Kingdom	23.7	14.7	14.1	10.0	24
United States	45.7	50.9	8.7	11.6	14

In 1961, Uruguay's imports came from the United States (23 percent), West Germany (13 percent), Brazil (8 percent), Venezuela (6 percent), and Argentina (6 percent).

The Political Situation

Uruguay owes its political progress to the fortunate coincidence of two things: an outstanding liberal political leader, and a small, compact community. There are other examples in Latin America of political leaders with democratic ideals, but they have been found in countries with complex political geography, such as Colombia or Argentina; and there are other examples of small, compact communities where nations are built around just one central cluster of people, but in these countries the leaders have often been chiefly interested in their own personal advancement and in the creation of powerful armies, as in Paraguay. Uruguay had one compact area of concentrated settlement with the one urban core, and after 1903 it had the leader. His name was José Batlle y Ordoñez (1856–1929).

Batlle became president for the first time in 1903. According to the constitution then in force the presidential term was four years, after which the president could not be a candidate for reelection. But in most of Latin America, leaders who have once tasted political power are loath to relinquish it. With a constitution or against a constitution a leader who can command sufficient military power not infrequently establishes a dictatorship and denies the citizens their right to vote, or even to discuss political questions. But in 1907 Batlle refused to continue in office, in spite of the fact that he had by that time gained a very large public following. Uruguay has long had two major political parties—the *colorados* and the *blancos*. Batlle was a colorado, a progressive, a man who was vigorously opposed to dictatorships. After his term in office he went to Switzerland to study first-hand the methods of democratic government.

In his second term as president (1911–1915) Batlle introduced the reforms for which he is famous. He made an accurate diagnosis of the causes for the chronic disorders of his country and he set himself to find a political solution. He recognized that one major cause of disorder was the gap, so common throughout Latin America, between the wealthy landowners and the workers. "It is not necessary," said Batlle, "that the rich should be made poorer, but only that the poor should be made less poor." In his effort to find legislation that would make the poor less poor, he was aided by the fact that the gap between rich and poor was by no means so great in Uruguay as it was in Argentina. Furthermore, the large landowners were much less opposed to entering into business than were the landowners across the Plata. The reforms proposed by

Batlle gained many supporters not only among the members of his own party, but also among the blancos, the traditional conservatives.

The constitution under which Uruguay was governed had been adopted in 1830, modeled on that of the United States. In it the president assumed broad powers. This was a situation which worried Batlle. He recognized that the traditional Spanish-American demand for freedom consisted in reality of the demand by political leaders to govern their own communities without interference from outside. The tradition of the strong man, the *caudillo,* the political boss, was deeply implanted. Batlle thought that a remedy for this tendency would be to reduce the power of the president by making him simply the presiding officer over a governing council. The idea was derided by the blancos, and even many of the colorados were not ready to support it wholeheartedly. A new constitution adopted in 1917, which went into force in 1919, represented a compromise in which the president still had large powers.

But the influence of Batlle did not come to an end with his death in 1929. Many of the Uruguayan leaders since that date have been determined adherents to his ideas. Pressure to change the presidency became especially strong after an attempt to seize the power by force in the 1930's. Finally in 1951 the blancos agreed to the reform originally set forth by Batlle, and in 1952 Uruguay ceased to have a president. The executive branch of the government is in the hands of a governing council.

Democratic procedures have become traditional. There is complete freedom of news and knowledge, and freedom to discuss political questions. All adults have the right to vote, women as well as men; and the vote is by secret ballot, honestly counted. Corruption and graft in public office have to an amazing degree been eliminated. Public support for the economic reforms previously discussed remains strong, yet criticism of these reforms has been unrestricted.

In 1958, with the costs of the reform program rapidly mounting, the voters began to shift toward the opposition. To be sure, a minority wing of the blanco party favors an extreme form of economic nationalism and a totalitarian form of government, but there are many members of this party who would not support a return to the traditional governmental forms. An election held late in 1958 swept the blancos into office with a substantial majority, and the possibility of a revision of Batlle's constitution was raised.

The election of 1958, however, again demonstrated the strength of Uruguay's democratic traditions. Although the colorados had held office throughout the present century, the party respected the wishes of the voters and turned the government over to the victorious blancos. The great majority of the people, colorados and blancos alike, subscribe to the basic purposes for which Uruguay has come to stand.

Portuguese
Latin America

The huge statue of Christ looks down on the city of Rio de Janeiro and the entrance to Guanabara Bay from the top of the Corcovado

CHAPTER TEN

Brazil

The United States of Brazil is the Portuguese-speaking country that occupies nearly half of the continent of South America. Its area of 3,287,195 square miles places Brazil fourth among the countries of the world in continuous land area—exceeded only by the Soviet Union, China, and Canada. Brazil's area is greater than that of continental United States without Alaska, and about the same as that of Europe without the Scandinavian Peninsula and Finland. Yet this vast area is occupied by only a little more than 75,000,000 people—about a third of the population of all Latin America, and a little more than a third of the population of the United States. Furthermore, the Brazilian people are grouped in a series of clusters near the eastern coast, while large parts of the backlands remain very thinly occupied.

At first glance it would seem that Brazil offers great possibilities for population expansion and for a rapid westward movement of the frontier of settlement. Although the United Nations Food and Agriculture Organization estimates that only about 2 percent of the total national territory is at present actually used for crops, the estimates of the potential crop land are usually highly optimistic. But not always. There are some students of Brazil who insist that the limits of better quality agricultural lands have already been reached, and that the empty backlands are not actually of much potential value. The major problem of Brazilian geography—and a problem of the utmost practical importance—is how the resource base of this vast territory should be evaluated. Unfortunately the detailed field surveys on which such an evaluation must eventually be based have not yet been made.

A part of the answer can be found by viewing the Brazilian land in the perspective of historical geography. What has been the experience

Maps 2, 4, 6, 8, 11, 13, 14, 15, 21, 22, 24, 25 are pertinent to this chapter.

Map 24

of people who have tried to make use of the backlands? And what has been the story of settlement in the areas already densely populated? What factors have led to the growth of two great cities, only a little more than two hundred miles apart, each more than three million in size?

The reader who has followed the story of settlement in Latin America thus far will appreciate that there are no simple answers to these questions. The study of the interplay of forces which has produced the present distribution of people in Brazil requires an understanding of the changes that have taken place through time, and also of the differences from place to place. It involves an analysis of the changing significance of the physical features of the land as the attitudes, objectives, and technical skills of the people have changed. All too often efforts to interpret the course of events in Brazil and to project meaningful forecasts into the future have failed through too much reliance on over-all averages and generalizations regarding the country as a whole. The fact is that Brazil is highly diverse, not only in the characteristics of the land, but also in the characteristics of the people.

The Brazilian Habitat

What can be said of the Brazilian land? Is it, or is it not, endowed with superlative resources? Many writers on Brazil have pointed out that only a very small part of the vast national territory is too wet, or too dry, or too steep to permit some kind of economic use. If slopes up to 35° are considered useful for agriculture, as they are today in Brazil, then not more than 20 percent of the national territory can be considered beyond the limits of potential use. A much larger proportion of the Soviet Union and Canada are unproductive because of cold, and a much larger proportion of China is unproductive because it is too dry. Furthermore, Brazil is known to contain a vast store of iron ore and manganese. But there is another side to the picture. Perhaps more than any other large country in the world, and certainly much more than the United States, Brazil faces problems resulting from the unfavorable geographic arrangement of its features. Resources are not combined in area in a way to favor low-cost development. Along the greater part of the eastern coast the land faces the sea with a steep escarpment through which there are few easy routes of travel. The passage to the interior is especially difficult back of the superlative natural harbor on which Rio de Janeiro is situated. Meanwhile the world's longest navigable river winds endlessly through empty forests. Very little of the Brazilian territory is mountainous: yet the mountains are all located in Brazil's core area back of Rio de Janeiro and São Paulo. From the mountains the rivers radiate inland, running thousands of miles southward to the Plata or northward to the Amazon to find a way out to the sea. The absence of a clear natural focus of routes scatters and isolates the clusters of people.

The greater part of the Brazilian national territory is included in the Brazilian Highlands. This is an area made up of hills and plateaus, surmounted in a few places (notably just north of Rio de Janeiro) by low mountains—none of which reaches 10,000 feet in elevation. The eastern edge of the highlands consists of a sharp drop to the Atlantic coast, a feature known as the Great Escarpment. This extends, with only three breaks, all the way from Salvador in the state of Bahia to Porto Alegre in the state of Rio Grande do Sul. There is very little flat lowland in Brazil. There is no Atlantic coastal plain, but only a few delta plains of small size. A large area of swampy lowland extends along the Paraguay River on the border of Bolivia. The largest lowland areas is the upper Amazon Basin where Brazil borders Bolivia, Peru, and Colombia. Where plains do occur they are remote from the areas of concentrated settlement.

The whole northern part of Brazil is covered with tropical rain forest, or *selva*. This is a luxuriant growth of trees supported by an abundance of moisture and an absence of cold. But the nature of such a forest and

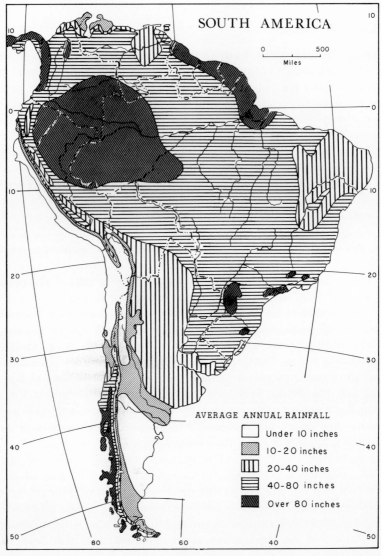

SOUTH AMERICA

0   500
Miles

AVERAGE ANNUAL RAINFALL

☐ Under 10 inches
▨ 10-20 inches
⫼ 20-40 inches
☰ 40-80 inches
⦀ Over 80 inches

Map 25

the land under it is often misunderstood. The soil under a rain forest is deeply leached of its soluble materials and is essentially infertile for shallow-rooted crops. Except for the narrow Amazon floodplain, where soils are replenished by each flood, most of the Amazon Basin has very poor soils which soon dry out and erode when the protective cover of trees is removed. The one great natural resource of this area is the huge volume of water carried in the Amazon itself.

Along the eastern side of the highlands from Natal to Porto Alegre the surface was originally covered with a semideciduous forest—composed of smaller trees than the selva, and with soils not so heavily leached. The Brazilians divide this kind of forest into a *mata da primeira classe* (first-class forest) which is considered to be the best for agricultural use; and a *mata seca* (dry forest) which is of marginal utility. The first-class forest was widest in eastern Minas Gerais, Espírito Santo, Rio de Janeiro, and São Paulo states.

In the Northeast of Brazil, inland from the fringe of dry forest along the coast south of Natal, and east of the selva which extends as far as São Luiz de Maranhão, there is a semiarid country, originally covered with a scrub woodland. The bushy trees are protected by thorns. This dry woodland is known to the Brazilians as *caatinga*. This is a region of great poverty, where the inhabitants struggle to maintain themselves on a land frequently devastated by either flood or drought.

A large part of the interior of the highlands is covered by a woodland savanna—a mixture of scattered small, deciduous trees, or thickets of scrubby trees, interspersed with areas of coarse savanna grasses. The Brazilians call it *campo cerrado* (literally a closed grassland, because the horizon is hidden by the scattered trees). This is a land of marked seasonal rainfall—with an abundance of rain during the summer (October to April) but with very dry winters (May to September). Geologists believe that this part of Brazil has been exposed above the sea to the leaching action of rainfall for a very long period of geologic time. As a result the soils are perhaps even less naturally productive than the soils of the selva. This is the great thinly-populated backland, or *sertão,* that the Brazilians want to populate with a wave of pioneer farmers from the concentrated settlements near the east coast.

Mineral Resources

Brazil possesses superlative but poorly matched mineral resources. When the French geologist Gorceix, in a poetic moment, exclaimed that Brazil's state of Minas Gerais had a "breast of iron and a heart of gold," he neglected to point out that there was in that state a deficiency of fuels which could be used to produce the high temperatures necessary for smelting. The gold and diamonds of this region did form the basis of the prosperity of Brazil during the eighteenth century—in fact, during that period Brazil produced 44 percent of all the gold of the world. But the iron and manganese, and the many other industrial metals available in Brazil, have only recently been mined on more than a small scale. Manganese has been exported for many years, but not on a scale which would be justified by the size and quality of the ores. Iron smelting with charcoal has been going on for a long time—until the problem of providing a steady supply of charcoal has become acute because of the almost complete destruction of the nearby forests. A very good grade of steel is produced. During World War II a new steel plant was built at Volta Redonda in the Paraíba Valley—the largest steel plant now in operation in all Latin America. Ore comes from Minas Gerais, and some of the coal from the South of Brazil. But Brazil's coal contains such a high proportion of ash and sulphur that it must be processed before it can be used to make coke. At Volta Redonda it is mixed with coal imported from West Virginia. Brazil also possesses important quantities of copper, lead, zinc, nickel, chromium, quartz crystals (for use in radios), industrial diamonds and gem stones. Its chief zone of minerals is the prominent range of mountains running roughly north and south through central Minas Gerais, known as the Serra do Espinhaço. Important manganese deposits also occur on the Bolivian border, near Corumbá and in the Territory of Amapá, just north of the mouth of the Amazon.

The Gilherme Guinle steel plant in the Paraíba valley, formerly Volta Redonda

The lack of fuels and the difficulties of developing water power are major handicaps in Brazil. The coal of Rio Grande do Sul and Santa Catarina is low grade and expensive to use. No large oil pools have been discovered, although certain oil technicians estimate that Brazil actually possesses within its borders something like six percent of the total oil reserves of the world. Brazil is still struggling with the problem of how to attract foreign capital for the necessary exploratory work without permitting any one large corporation to monopolize any fields which are discovered. Brazil now produces only about two percent of its needs.

Brazil has a hydroelectric potential which is estimated at nearly twenty million horsepower. Again it is unfortunate that the largest potential sites for hydroelectric development are in places remote from the centers of settlement. The Iguaçu Falls, on the border of Brazil and Argentina, are so far away from the industrial centers of either country that until recently the power could not be transmitted to them. About half of the power resources of Brazil are in the drainage basin of the Paraná, most of which was too far away to be used until the new long-distance transmission techniques had been worked out in the Soviet Union and Sweden. The largest hydroelectric installation in Latin America was built near São Paulo, where water is dropped over the Great Escarpment from the head of one of the tributaries of the Paraná. The greater part of Brazil's electric capacity is developed in the Southeast, near São Paulo and at the Paulo Afonso Falls on the Rio São Francisco.

The People

None of the many advantages and disadvantages inherent in the physical make-up of Brazil have real significance for us in terms of human settlement until we know about the people and their way of living. Perhaps nowhere on the earth is there a greater mixture of different kinds of people than in Brazil. The primary ingredients are Portuguese, Indian, and Negro, but during the past century the population has been much altered by the arrival of millions of immigrants from Europe and Asia. All these elements have mixed freely, for one of the important traits brought by the Portuguese was the absence of any taboo against race mixture, except among the aristocracy. Each ingredient, therefore, has given certain easily observable physical characteristics to the new race of Brazilians, and has contributed numerous culture traits to the Brazilian civilization.

Early Racial Ingredients

The Indians who inhabited Brazil in 1500 were chiefly of Tupi-Guarani stock—a linguistic group to which the Indians of Paraguay also belong.

In almost every respect these Indians of eastern South America were a contrast to the Quechuas of the Andes. The Tupi-Guarani tribes were hunters, fishers, collectors, and shifting cultivators. They lived in small, scattered groups with no form of intertribal political organization. Their basic food crop was manioc rather than maize. It is estimated that the Indian population of 1500 in all of Brazil was only about 800,000.

As a source of labor, the Tupi-Guarani proved quite inadequate. In the first place, great numbers of them died of European diseases in the early years of the conquest. Those who survived were handicapped by the traditional Indian attitude toward work. Agriculture was left to the women; the men devoted themselves to hunting, fishing, and fighting. The men could not adjust themselves to the agricultural work demanded by the Europeans. Free intermarriage, however, between the Portuguese men and the Indian women introduced many of the physical and psychological traits of the Indians into the resulting population.

Negroes, also, made an important contribution to the composition and character of the Brazilian people. Beginning in 1538, Negro slaves from Africa were brought across the ocean, especially to the Brazilian Northeast, where there was a demand for field hands in the new sugar industry. The Negro was not only a good worker, but he also possessed a knowledge of technological processes which has often been overlooked. The Negroes of the Sudan, it should be remembered, were the inventors of the process of iron smelting. This technological ability they brought with them to Brazil, along with their rhythmic music and their superstitions. The Negro foremen on the plantations, or later in the gold mines, knew more about the technological processes than did many of the Portuguese owners. From the seventeenth to the nineteenth century, agricultural and mining enterprise in Brazil owed a large debt to the Negro laborers and technicians.

From the Portuguese, however, came the main characteristics of the Brazilians. Even before their departure from Europe, the Portuguese were already made up of a most remarkable variety of racial and cultural elements, inherited from the various peoples who had successively conquered the Iberian Peninsula. Like the Spaniards, they included ingredients of Celtic, Nordic, and Mediterranean origin; and especially in the south of Portugal, around Lisbon, there was a large mixture of Moorish blood and of Moorish and Semitic culture traits. Moreover, the Portuguese from Lisbon were familiar with the use of Negro labor, for slaves had been brought to this part of Portugal in considerable numbers during the fifteenth century when Prince Henry's ships were exploring the west coast of Africa seeking the way to India. Like the Spaniards, too, the Portuguese had the traditions of feudalism and of large private estates—traditions which profoundly influenced the relations of people to the land throughout Latin America.

The Portuguese had long been accustomed to commerce and to adventuring in distant places when they came to America in search of quick wealth. Like most of the Europeans who came to the New World—including the English—the foremost objective was to loot the rich resources of a virgin land. The Portuguese were much less interested than the Spaniards in implanting their institutions in America; they had little of the fanatical zeal for the spread of Christianity that their Spanish brothers possessed. They were attracted less by the prospects of earning a living by persistent toil than by the opportunities for speculative profit. As one Brazilian writer puts it, the ideal was "to collect the fruit without planting the tree." Whereas some of the peoples of America have been led by force of circumstances to be content with less spectacular returns from more intensive forms of economy, the Brazilians, with their huge land area, and their small numbers, are still seeking new ways for the speculative exploitation of the treasures stored up in nature. This is the Brazilian variation of the theme of El Dorado.

Course of Settlement

History and geography have both contributed to the settlement of Brazil and to the development of the present patterns of population. In the history of settlement in the four hundred years since the Portuguese first planted successful colonies on the coast of South America, three products, in turn, have dominated a period. Each period has been characterized by the spectacular rise of a commercial product, by the sale of this product in an expanding market and the collection of promoter's profits, and by the eventual decline of prosperity owing to increasing competition from areas of production outside Brazil, where people were willing to invest in "the planting of the trees." Each of Brazil's great products has led to the development of one specific region, and has given rise to an area of concentrated settlement around an urban nucleus. As one product after another has passed its zenith and begun its decline, the population has moved on to new frontiers, or remained decadent. The chief products which have thus punctuated Brazilian history and have colored the Brazilian map are sugar, gold, and coffee. In addition there have been minor interludes neatly set off in time and space—dominated by rubber, cacao, oranges, and other products.

The early decades of the colonization of Brazil by the Portuguese, however, were not associated with any of these commercial developments. The first settlement was established in 1502 at Salvador in the state of Bahia. But the Portuguese found no sources of gold and gems comparable to those of India, and no rich native civilizations which invited pillage. Brazil was neglected, because at the beginning of the sixteenth century Portugal was a poor country with a population which probably did not number more than a million; and for many decades she had all she could handle in the development of her connections with India and the other parts of the East. Brazil was neglected until the encroachments of the French and the Spaniards made it imperative for Portugal to establish colonies on the American coast, or to relinquish her claims. The division of the coast of Brazil into *capitanias*, each under the direction of a person selected by the Portuguese crown, led to a very uneven distribution of settlements, for those capitanias which came under the direction of capable organizers and administrators flourished, while others which came under the direction of men of lesser ability were often not settled at all. A successful colony was founded at São Vicente, near the site of Santos, in 1532, and another at Olinda, near the site of Recife in the state of Pernambuco, in 1537; Recife itself was not founded until 1561. Meanwhile a mission was established on the site of the present city of São Paulo in 1554—the first of the Brazilian settlements on the highlands.

On the docks at Salvador to which farmers all around the shores of the Reconcavo bring their produce by sailboat

The three chief primary settlement centers from which the Portuguese carried forward their conquest of Brazil were São Paulo, Salvador, and Recife. These are the places which correspond to Mexico City, Cartagena, Lima, and Asunción in Spanish America. Rio de Janeiro, founded on its present site in 1567, was at first only a fortress and naval base for the protection of the coast, and not at all a primary settlement center.

Sugar Colonies

The rapid rise of the commercial production of sugar in Brazil took place late in the sixteenth century. Sugar cane was introduced in 1532 and planted around São Vicente; but not until the second half of the sixteenth century did the spectacular rise of this new product begin and then it was the Northeast, centering upon Salvador, which prospered. A considerable difference appeared early between the colonists who came to São Vicente and São Paulo, and those who came to Salvador and Recife. According to Freyre the Portuguese who settled in the Northeast included a considerable proportion of wealthy people, many of whom came from the north of Portugal and had long been accustomed to the direction of large estates. The people who settled at São Vicente and São Paulo were mainly from the south of Portugal—mostly poorer people who did not possess enough capital to go to the aristocratic colonies of Bahia and Pernambuco. The Northeast was also much closer to Europe and to Africa than was São Vicente. Distance in the days of small sailing vessels was of greater significance in human affairs than it is today. At any rate, it was the people of the Northeast who were able to buy Negro slaves, to build sugar refineries, to clear the land, and to plant sugar cane; the people of São Vicente, with their Indian slaves, were unable to share in any important way in the prosperity of the sugar period. The plantation owners of the Northeast soon found themselves selling on a rapidly expanding market, and producing at costs which, after the initial investment, were very low. During most of the seventeenth century, the Northeast of Brazil was the world's chief source of the new and increasingly popular food product, sugar from cane.

So profitable did the sugar-producing area of the Northeast become that it invited conquest by other European powers. In 1624 the city of Salvador was occupied by the Dutch. Although they were soon forced to withdraw from Salvador, the Dutch succeeded in occupying Recife and in spreading their control of the Brazilian coast all the way from the Rio São Francisco to the Amazon. The Portuguese colonists, however, returned the attack and, without help from Portugal, pushed the invaders back step by step until, in 1654, they recaptured the city of Recife. This was a very important event for Brazil. The cooperative effort necessary to retake Salvador and Recife built certain loyalties and traditions which explain in part the present solidarity of the Northeast as a region.

Gold

While sugar production was bringing wealth to the people of the Northeast, especially in the states of Bahia, Pernambuco, and Paraíba, the settlers in the south were enjoying no such prosperity. The people of São Paulo were poor; they had discovered no source of wealth within their means to exploit; yet they were not at all content to accept this situation. From São Paulo a series of semimilitary expeditions went forth into the interior of the country. These expeditions were called *bandeiras* and the members of the expeditions were called *bandeirantes*. The first objective was to find gold—which had already been discovered in many of the stream gravels of the country south of São Paulo. But gold in the South proved to exist only in small quantities, and the bandeirantes had to seek other forms of wealth to exploit. They found Indians; large numbers of the native peoples, having first been brought together around the mission stations, were carried into slavery. Intermarriage with the Indian women became common, and the area occupied by the explorers from São Paulo soon had a considerable proportion of half-breeds—a racial type which in Spanish America is called mestizo, but which in Brazil is called *mameluco*[1] The bandeirantes traveled slowly over the vast interior of the continent, pushing the borders of Brazil far to the west and to the south, as far as they could go without entering dense forests. Searching restlessly for slaves, gold, or any other sources of wealth, they grazed their animals on the savannas and even stopped to plant and harvest crops on the way. These hardy adventurers established the colony of Colonia on the shores of the Plata opposite Buenos Aires in 1680; they pushed westward to the Paraguay north of Asunción; they even roamed into the Northeast, into the scrub woodland country inland from the sugar colonies. Finally, in 1698, they discovered rich gold-bearing gravels in the central part of Minas Gerais, on the headwaters of the Rio São Francisco. Shortly thereafter, other gold discoveries were made: at Cuiabá in Mato Grosso in 1719; and near the former capital of Goiás in 1725. In Minas Gerais, in the country a little to the north of the gold fields, diamonds were discovered in 1729.

The discovery of gold and gems, especially the discoveries in central Minas Gerais, came at a time when the prosperity of the sugar-cane planters of the Northeast had passed its zenith. Declining yields on soils which had been cultivated for many years, and increasing competition from other areas were decreasing profits in the Brazilian region. It is

[1] The word *mestiço* in Portuguese refers to any person of mixed blood, often mixed white and Negro.

not in the Brazilian tradition, under such circumstances, to aim at reducing the costs of production through the use of better agricultural
practices. Income in the Northeast was spent to raise the standard of
living of the aristocracy, not for investments which might lower the cost
of production per unit. That would be "planting the trees." Brazil suffered, moreover, from the curse of great area; virtually limitless area
meant the ever-present possibility of moving on to new lands and of
exploiting new resources; it meant the lack of any compelling reason
for the intensification and stablization of economic life in any one region.
When gold was announced in Minas Gerais, the result was a gold rush, in
which not only Paulistas and Portuguese from the home country participated, but also many former sugar-cane planters of the Northeast
who came bringing their slaves.

The gold period started early in the eighteenth century, reached its
peak of development between 1752 and 1787, and was definitely over by
the beginning of the nineteenth century. During this time southern and
central Minas Gerais was transformed from a wilderness into a well-
populated agricultural, pastoral, and mining region, dotted with many
small towns, and with its rural districts partitioned among a relatively
small number of landlords. The settlement of this part of Brazil led to
the development of Rio de Janeiro as a port, for this place came to be
the chief outlet for the gold, and the chief urban nucleus of the new
region of settlement. Great quantities of gold were sent back to Portugal,
greatly to the profit of the king and of the mine owners in Brazil. But
little of this prosperity was shared by the workers of Minas Gerais. By
the beginning of the nineteenth century the best sources of gold and
diamonds had been exhausted, and Brazil was ready for a new form of
speculative development.

Coffee

Brazilian history in the nineteenth and early twentieth centuries was
dominated by the commercial production of coffee, and this activity was
concentrated in the state of São Paulo, inland from the city of that name.
Like the sugar-cane planters, the people of São Paulo found themselves
providing a very large proportion of the world's supply of a new commodity which was rising rapidly in popular favor. Coffee planting started
around Rio de Janeiro and at other places on the coast from Santos to
the Amazon; but by the end of the first quarter of the nineteenth century
there was a definite concentration of coffee in the Paraíba Valley, inland from Rio de Janeiro. From this district, coffee planting spread westward into São Paulo State—a movement which was increasingly rapid
after 1850. Most of the European immigrants who came to Brazil after
1850 went to the new coffee lands of São Paulo, with the result that the

The Iguaçu Falls

new region of concentrated settlement was occupied by a very different kind of people from those of the older sections of Brazil. Coffee supported the rise of the great city of São Paulo. Now, in the modern era, São Paulo has become the leading center of manufacturing industries in all of Latin America. The coffee era came to an end in about 1930.

Other Commercial Products

Meanwhile, other agricultural or forest products were leading to the rapid development, followed by the equally rapid decline, of other parts

of Brazil. Rubber created havoc in the Amazon Valley. The rubber-pro-
ducers of this area reached a mighty crescendo of speculation and wild
spending in 1910; but thereafter rubber ceased to be one of the exports
of Brazil. Cotton, cacao, various wild fruits, nuts, dyes, and other sub-
stances led to minor and local flurries of speculation at various times and
places. The collection of maté leaves in the Araucaria forests of Southern
Brazil is one of these. In each case Brazil, after a period of feverish
growth, was forced to yield to other sources of supply, where more intensive methods of production were applied. The result, in Brazil, has
been a lack of stability of settlement.

Subsistence Agriculture

But during the four and a half centuries of Brazilian settlement, commercial agriculture has been less important in terms of area than subsistence farming and the grazing of cattle. While contrasted regions
were being developed by commercial agriculture, the basic use of the
land has been remarkably uniform throughout the history of Brazil and
throughout the settled area.

The system is one of land rotation carried on in a seemingly limitless
area. First a landowner comes into possession of a large tract of forest,
perhaps on the margins of one of the areas of speculative development.
With few exceptions the large landowners, like those of Argentina, have
been more interested in raising cattle than in agriculture; but to create
pastures in lands covered with semideciduous forest it is first necessary to
clear the forest. For this hard work the landowner makes a contract with
a tenant. The latter stakes out an area of some ten acres and starts clearing it. He cuts down all but the largest trees, and at the end of the dry
season (September in many parts of the country) he sets fire to the debris.
After the burn he plants crops in whatever space he can find among the
charred logs and stumps. On soil enriched by wood ash he secures good
yields of maize, rice, beans, and manioc. After sharing some of the crop
with the landowner, the tenant has a small surplus above the needs of
his own family with which he can buy *xarque* (salt beef) or *rapadura* (a
sugar candy) or *caxaça* (a brandy made from sugar), or perhaps some
cotton cloth for his wife. But after a few years, usually not more than
three, the poverty of the soil begins to show up in decreased yields. The
tenant then plants pasture grass and moves to a new part of the forest.
The landowner has some new pasture for his cattle, but he takes no
care of the pasture and little by little a second growth of trees chokes
out the grass. After a few years he moves his cattle to another pasture,
leaving the old clearing to the forest. In the course of four centuries
vast areas of Brazil have been cleared and abandoned, not once but
again and again.

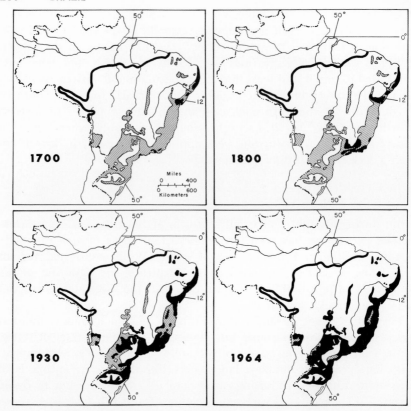

Clearing of the Brazilian Forest: 1700-1964

██ Cleared Area
▨ Forested Area
⟩ Southern Border of the Selva

Map 26

The Destruction of the Forest

The kind of agriculture we have described has been applied very largely to one kind of country—the land covered by the semideciduous forest. For more than four centuries the relatively small area of this forest type has supported Brazil's commercial agriculture and also the production of food for the Brazilian people. Agriculture has not been successful in the grasslands because the soils are so poor that harvests do not repay the effort of planting. Nor has agriculture been successful in the rain forests, for in these regions also the soil yields too little. In 1700 only the forests of the Northeast and a few spots around São Vicente and Rio de Janeiro had been cleared. Between 1700 and 1800 large areas in the vicinity of Rio de Janeiro, in the Paraíba Valley, and in southern Minas Gerais were cleared to provide food for the gold and diamond miners. By 1930 the clearing of the forest had swept over São Paulo and southward into the southern states. It had also progressed in the Northeast. By 1964 only a very little of the virgin forest remained. Near Rio de Janeiro and São Paulo, and in the Paraíba Valley the second growth had been cleared so often, and at such brief intervals that now even second growth brush will not come back on the bare land. On steep slopes soil erosion goes on at a terrifying rate. Before most Brazilians were aware of the situation, Brazil had destroyed the resource base on which the country had depended. Instead of unlimited area, now there was land hunger as pioneers hacked away at the last remnants of forest a thousand miles inland.

Charcoal and firewood for cooking in the outskirts of Salvador. The hills in the background were once covered with forest.

Immigration

Not until the nineteenth century did the population of Brazil increase rapidly. Birth rates were relatively low, and infant mortality was very high because of bad hygiene and the lack of nourishing foods. The immigration of Negroes in the Northeast built up there the densest population of any part of Brazil. In fact, as late as 1870 half of all the Brazilians lived in this region. Early in the nineteenth century the German geographer Alexander von Humboldt estimated that the population of Brazil was composed of about 920,000 whites, about 1,960,000 Negroes, and about 1,120,000 Indians and mixed Indians and whites—a total of only 4,000,000 near the end of three centuries of settlement!

A rapid increase in the population of Brazil took place during the period of new European immigration after 1850. Since 1822, when Brazil became an independent country, about five million immigrants have arrived, most of them since 1900. But not all of Brazil was equally affected by this stream of new arrivals: over half of them went to São Paulo State, where coffee was demanding the services of an army of workers.

This stream of immigrants was made up mostly of Europeans. About 34 percent were Italians, 30 percent were Portuguese, 12 percent were Spaniards, 3 percent were Germans, and the remaining 21 percent included many different nationalities. There are today a little under two hundred thousand Japanese in Brazil—also mostly in São Paulo State. After 1918 the number of Italian immigrants dropped to almost nothing, while Poles, other eastern Europeans, and Japanese have increased rapidly.

Colonies of the South

The first people to penetrate the southern part of Brazil, the part south of the São Paulo Coffee Region, were the bandeirantes who made use of the prairies for the grazing of cattle and mules. Later, in 1824 in Rio Grande do Sul, and in 1850 in Santa Catarina, colonies of German farmers were established. In these states, however, the immigrants were not tenants or wage workers on large estates, but small landowners, occupying and cultivating their own properties. In the course of time, these colonies were added to by new groups of Italians and Poles.

The outstanding fact regarding the settlements of southern Brazil is that they have started to expand. The clusters of people in the three southern states of Brazil are all growing rapidly, and, with little new immigration to support them, frontiers of pioneer settlement have appeared around the margins of the original nucleuses and new colonies have budded off from the older ones, but without any decrease in the density of population in the original centers. This is a condition which is discovered in only four parts of mainland Latin America. At first the pioneers followed the example of the first settlers by creating a permanent and stable form of land use. But in recent decades continued expansion has resulted in the appearance of the traditional system of land rotation, and in the rapid destruction of large areas of virgin forests in the southern states.

The Cities and the Sertão

Does Brazil have a great capacity for further population expansion? Is it true that a new, vigorous movement into the thinly peopled backlands might be developed, creating the kind of wealth that supported the economy of the United States during the decades following the Civil War? Brazil's population has been growing at a faster and faster rate. In 1872 there were about ten million Brazilians; in 1920 there were well over thirty million; by 1960 there were more than seventy million; and the latest estimate (1962) is more than seventy-five million. The rate of growth is among the highest in Latin America. Meanwhile the strongest movement of people inside Brazil has been from the rural areas into the cities, and from the thinly peopled backlands into the areas already well populated. Brazil's cities have been growing in spectacular fashion, and the more they grow the more they appear to be out of harmony with the development of their hinterlands.

Brazilian cities are rapidly becoming ultramodern. Brazilian architects lead the world in creating new forms. The people who live in these cities are learning rapidly to abandon some of Brazil's traditional ways of living. Some Brazilian writers now insist that the "real Brazil" is not to be found in the cities at all. The real Brazil, they say, is only to be found in the back country—in the thinly peopled wilderness beyond the frontiers of concentrated settlement; in the land which the Brazilians call the sertão.[2]

The sertão is not a wilderness in the sense that it is made up of unexplored territory. Actually it has been tramped over, lived in, its resources exploited, and its landscapes modified in many ways over the course of more than four centuries. The sertão forms a sort of penumbra around the margins of the effective national territory: a transition zone of shifting population, but one in which a way of living has become established which has withstood the forces of change over hundreds of years. Aside from groups of people temporarily engaged in seeking for gold, the economy of the sertão is essentially pastoral—the grazing of herds of cattle on the open range. Scattered throughout the vast area of the sertões

[2] Pronounced sair-tong'. The plural is sertões, pronounced sair-tó-aish.

there are small groups of people clustered more or less permanently around ranch headquarters or in small towns. Contact with the regions of concentrated agricultural settlement is made through annual fairs held in border towns: beyond the frontier of close settlement the pastoral sertão extends indefinitely inland; its area can be roughly, but not exactly, delimited as the zone with a population density between two and ten per square mile.

The pastoral inhabitants of the sertão are not like the Brazilians in the cities or even those in the agricultural areas. They are almost pure

Vegetable farmers near Salvador

Portuguese with a mixture of Indian. They are essentially democratic, knowing no rigid class distinctions, for the ranch owners look, act, dress, and live like their workers. They are a fiercely independent people, courageous, resourceful, and superstitious; but they are so widely scattered or gathered in such small groups that they cannot support the cost of those numerous things which bring a society forward from a pioneer life to one which can be described as civilized. Here it is likely that the pioneer way of life is permanently established.

To the Brazilian who lives in or around the cities, the sertão is a land of mystery. Its influence on Brazilian economic, political, and artistic thought is profound. The clusters of people along the coast are isolated from each other by this great thinly populated territory. For hundreds of years people have believed that a vast wealth of resources was lying dormant in the interior, and groups of settlers have gone out to seek this Brazilian form of El Dorado; yet the only permanent settlers in the sertão, the only people who have been able to establish a permanent workable connection with the land, are the widely scattered herders. These settlers are not to be thought of as a fringe of pioneers engaged in the first rapid occupation of new lands in advance of a moving frontier: they are, rather, the fragments of population left from the many groups which have attempted to exploit the interior; they represent a very old, stabilized society in a land long occupied.

Brasília

The idea that the capital of Brazil should be located near the geographic center of the national territory, and near the headwaters of Brazil's system of rivers, was expressed even during the colonial period. When independence from Portugal was announced, the arguments in favor of establishing a new capital in the backlands were eloquently presented. Still later, in every constitution that Brazil has adopted since the end of the Empire in 1889, there has been a section authorizing the establishment of a new federal district and a new capital city in the interior. Still, the magnitude of the costs involved, and the problem even of reaching the backlands kept delaying the project. It was the determination of President Juscelino Kubitschek to do something about moving the capital that translated words into action. In 1957 the Brazilian Congress approved the actual construction of the new capital. The government moved to Brasília on 21 April, 1960, although the construction of the city was by no means complete.

The site selected for the new capital is in the midst of campo cerrado some 80 miles northeast of Anápolis and nearly 600 miles by air from Rio de Janeiro. The headwaters of one of the tributaries of the Paraná has here excavated a dale—a broad, gently sloping amphitheater—slightly below the general level of the Planalto. The elevation is about 4,000 feet above the sea. Only a short distance to the north are the headwater tributaries of the Tocantins; and only a little to the east is the head of a tributary to the São Francisco.

The whole idea of designing a new city to rise in spectacular fashion above the campo cerrado appeals to the genius of the Brazilian people. Here is a chance for the use of imagination, unfettered by structures inherited from the past. A contest was held for the design of the new city, and the winner was an engineer named Lúcio Costa. The city has the outline of an airplane. The Residential Axis (the wing) extends for some seven and a half miles, running at right angles to the Monumental Axis (the fuselage). The latter is about five miles long, leading to the group of government buildings around the Plaza of the Three Powers (executive, legislative, and judicial) at the eastern end. The two parts of the Chamber of Deputies are housed in two 28-story structures, designed by Brazil's famous architect Oscar Niemeyer, one of the designers of the United Nations Building in New York. The little streams in the area have been dammed to form a huge lake which borders the city on the northeast and the southeast. The lake is about two miles wide and some 20 miles long. On a promontory, where the two arms of the lake join, the presidential palace is located—also with a striking new design drawn by Sr. Niemeyer. In modern form are the cathedral and the other public buildings.

Brasília is restricted to the function of federal capital. It has no industries, and its commercial and recreational facilities are for the service of the government employees. The city is planned for a population of 500,000. With scant attention to the costs involved, the city has been built as a living monument; it will be connected with the occupied parts of Brazil chiefly by air, but also, according to present plans, by all-weather highways. It is already connected with Anápolis by a gravel road; and from Anápolis motor highways extend to Rio de Janeiro and São Paulo. New roads are proposed to connect with Salvador in Bahia, and with Belém at the mouth of the Amazon.

Brasília is almost certain to become one of the great artistic achievements of mankind. The approach to it by air over the vast empty stretches of the sertão will make its modernistic buildings and its imaginative layout seem all the more extraordinary. It does not seem at all probable that the establishment of this new city will lead to a great movement of pioneer settlers into the central part of Brazil. The fact that the building of Brasília is enormously expensive, and may not seem economically justified, does not alter the fact that the whole project is strictly within the Brazilian tradition.

We return, then, to our problem: why are there so few people in Brazil? The answer is not to be found only in those areas where concentrated

The two houses of the Brazilian congress at Brasília looking east with the artificial lake in the background

settlement scallops the eastern border of the country. The answer must also be sought in the regions beyond. Perhaps the persistence of the tradition of collecting the fruit without planting the tree is, itself, a reflection of large area, of which so great a part is sertão. For more than four centuries the Brazilians have been struggling to break that sequence of cause and effect—a sparse population, the resulting predominance of destructive exploitation, and the resulting failure of the system to support more people. For more than four centuries the sertão has absorbed almost every effort to intensify the economic life; after all this time the greater part of the area of Brazil remains almost empty. And now, for the first time, the Brazilians are face to face with the fact that no more uncut virgin semideciduous forests remain. Instead of unlimited area, perhaps they have already reached the limits of settlement. The great question mark lies beyond: what can be done with the campo cerrado, the sertão of today?

The Brazilian Economy

By the end of 1963 Brazil was in deep economic trouble. The cost of living index rose 52 percent between 1961 and 1962; and the cruzeiro which was pegged at 18 to the dollar as recently as 1957, dropped to over 1,000 to the dollar. In 1962 the gross national product per capita was only $202, which was lower than the gross national products per capita of such states as Nicaragua, Honduras, and the Dominican Republic. The fact is that Brazil is feeling the direct impact of economic change, and by no means all of Brazil's leaders are in agreement regard-ing the desirable direction of change or even whether change itself is a good thing. The motto on the Brazilian flag reads *Ordem e Progresso,* which means "Order and Progress." But perhaps this ideal is impossible to realize—perhaps it must be either one or the other, and there are many who would prefer to see the old order survive.

Most serious among Brazil's troubles is the lack of balance in economic development. There is a lack of balance among the parts of the popula-tion; there is a lack of balance among the sectors of the economy; and there is a lack of balance among the geographic areas of the country.

Social Imbalance

Brazil's economic troubles are revealed by the fact that the wealthy people are becoming richer while the poor are becoming poorer. Specula-tive gain is still possible for those with money to invest—most recently in urban apartment buildings in Rio de Janeiro and São Paulo. It is possible to realize a 40 or 50 percent return on money spent for such buildings. The poor people can also speculate—by buying lottery tickets in obedience to the slogan of the federal lotteries *Fique rico* or "Get rich."

The lack of balance among social groups is revealed from another perspective. In 1940 when the population of Brazil was 41,114,000, some 27,230,000 (or 66 percent) of the people were subsistence farmers who had next to no purchasing power and who contributed almost nothing to the gross national product. These people produced most of what they consumed, and consumed almost all they produced. They were essen-tially outside the economic system of buying and selling, a dead weight of hopeless poverty around the neck of struggling Brazil. But in 1960, when the total population had reached 70,528,000, the proportion of people outside the economic system was still almost 66 percent (46,527,-000). And it is estimated that by 1980 measures of economic develop-ment currently being applied will only have reduced the economically unproductive people to 60 percent of the total. As long as so large a proportion of the Brazilian people remain economically unproductive, the Brazilian economy must remain speculative and uncertain. This situation can only be remedied when a sufficient amount of domestic capital is invested in productive enterprises (not apartment buildings) so that the number of jobs increases faster than the number of people.

Sectors of the Economy

Especially in São Paulo state, there has been a spectacular increase in manufacturing industries. The Brazilian gross national product between 1950 and 1961 grew at an annual rate of 5.7 percent. This growth was in a varied list of new industries. The old textile industries no longer completely dominate the industrial picture. In addition to the new steel plants and oil refineries, a great variety of consumer goods are produced. Brazil by 1963 had become the eighth largest manufacturer of automobiles in the world. Some 95 percent of the component parts of automobiles are manufactured in Brazil. The country produces all it needs of wheels, axles, clutches, pistons, batteries, tires, and bodies. It is now rapidly increasing its manufacture of tractors. All of this represents a major change, even in the years since World War II. In the decade between 1950 and 1960 the number of workers employed in urban industries increased 70 percent. And during this same period, the number of rural workers increased 17.5 percent.

For the first time there were thousands of urban industrial workers with money to spend. And the first desire was to buy more food—more rice and beans and dried beef. But rice and beans and dried beef soon were in short supply. Agricultural production was increased, but not rapidly enough to keep up with the demand. As a result food prices have soared. The first contact of many Brazilian workers with the operation of a money economy has been one of frustration and bewilderment. The lack of food in the markets was partly a result of insufficient production, partly the result of a cumbersome system of middlemen and a lack of rural storage facilities that would permit the farmers to hold their crops for more favorable prices.

There is no complete agreement on how to increase the production of food. There are many Brazilian political leaders who are still thinking in terms of the preindustrial world. At the time of Malthus, in the late eighteenth century, an increase of food had to be gained by placing more farmers on the land, clearing a pioneer zone of its wild vegetation and creating new farm acreage. But this is no longer the way to increase the food supply without increasing prices. The pioneer farmer is a high-cost producer. Food is produced in larger quantities at lower cost by using modern farm methods (machinery, fertilizer, soil conditioners, insecticides, plant and animal selection), and by decreasing the number of farmers. The spectacular increases of food production in the United

Rural University of Minas Gerais at Viçosa

States since 1950 have been achieved with fewer and fewer farmers, on less and less farm acreage. It would be no solution of Brazil's food shortage to move large numbers of pioneer small farmers onto the campo cerrado beyond Brasília.

Some of the landowners in São Paulo state have demonstrated how modern technology can be applied even to Brazil's worn-out soils. They have shown how the new methods, with the necessary capital investment, can be applied profitably in the increased production of rice, beans, maize, and meat. In São Paulo and Paraná the federal government has adopted a program of reducing the acreage of coffee trees in favor of food crops and cotton. In 1962 Brazil had 4.3 billion coffee trees in production. By August 1963 some 450,000,000 trees had been destroyed, and the plan was to cut back as soon as possible to a total of 2.3 billion trees. Modern farm technology applied to these lands, freed from the speculative production of coffee, would do much to increase the low-cost foods available in the cities.

Lack of Balance among Geographical Areas

There is also a notable lack of balance among the different parts of Brazil. One hears the quip that Brazil is like a locomotive pulling twenty empty freight cars. The locomotive is São Paulo, and the other states are the empty freight cars (twenty-two in 1964). More than 40 percent of Brazil's gross national production originates in São Paulo, and São Paulo has by far the largest concentration of manufacturing industries. In Rio de Janeiro and São Paulo and in the hinterlands of these cities, one finds something like 75 percent of the domestic market for consumer goods in Brazil. The people, especially of São Paulo city, are fired with the desire for an improvement of the level of living through productive work. Even in this basic attitude toward economic development the people of São Paulo are in sharp contrast to the people of many other parts of the country.

The federal government is conscious of this lack of balance among the parts of Brazil. An effort is being made to increase the industrialization of the densely populated Northeast—for example by developing a large petrochemical complex near Recife. In part this spread of industry to outlying areas will be supported by new hydroelectric developments. In 1957 a huge new power plant was opened at Paulo Afonso Falls on the São Francisco River in the Northeast. Power is transmitted from this source to all the cities from Salvador to João Pessoa in the state of Paraíba.

Power is part of what the economists call "social overhead," which is an essential part of economic development. Since 1949 the federal government has given its support to an ambitious plan to improve the health conditions, the food supply, the facilities for transportation, and electric power. Important steps have been taken, but much remains to be done. The construction of new all-weather roads seems to be proceeding only slowly until one remembers that this vast country had almost no all-weather roads even as late as the 1930's.

Exports

Since the last days of the Empire, coffee has been Brazil's leading export; and during this period Brazil has maintained her position as the world's leading coffee producer. Before World War I Brazil was producing over 75 percent of the world's coffee. In the period before World War II Brazil's share of the world production was about 60 percent; but since World War II Brazil has accounted for less than 50 percent of the total. This drop in Brazil's proportion is due in part to the increase in world production, especially in production from Colombia and Central America. Total world production was about twenty-eight million bags in 1935–39 as compared with thirty-four million bags in 1954–55, and sixty-six million bags in 1962–63.

Meanwhile coffee has remained the leading commodity among Brazil's exports. Coffee accounted for the largest proportion of the value of all exports in the decade before 1930, when it reached nearly 70 percent. Although it has dropped from this high figure, it still remains between 50 and 60 percent of the total. The volume of production, too, has dropped from the peak year of 1936, when twenty-six million bags were produced, to less than twelve million bags. From this low, production recovered in 1953–54 to almost twenty million. Production in 1961 was thirty-six million bags, but it has since dropped below twenty million bags due to the program of coffee-tree destruction.

EXPORTS OF BRAZIL—VALUE OF COFFEE, COTTON, AND CACAO*

as percentage of the value of all exports in selected years

Years	Coffee	Cotton	Cacao
1901–10	51.3	2.1	2.8
1921–30	69.6	2.4	3.2
1931–40	50.0	14.2	4.2
1947	36.6	14.4	4.9
1949	55.5	9.9	4.7
1953	66.0	7.1	4.9
1960	56.0	4.0	5.0

* *Annuário Estatístico do Brasil.*

Cotton, which is the second or third export product of Brazil in terms of value, has never been one of the country's economic "rulers." Cotton, unlike sugar, coffee, and rubber, did not enter the world market as a new product of which Brazil held a virtual monopoly. Cotton-growing in Brazil has brought prosperity only in those years when other sources of supply in the world have failed. Brazil has played the role of a marginal producer, whose participation in the world market becomes possible only when areas of cheaper production cannot meet the demand. During the last half of the eighteenth century, Brazilian cotton, coming almost entirely from the Northeast, held a place of importance on the European market, but a decline of cotton prices during the early part of the nineteenth century, resulting from the increasing shipments from regions where the costs of production were lower, forced the Northeast out of the market. Brazilian cotton was again in demand when the Civil War in the United States curtailed production from the "Cotton Belt." The peak of production at this time came in 1871–72, when 362,130 bales were exported from Brazil, with the Northeast accounting for over 350,000 bales, or about 96 percent. This figure was not reached again until 1934. During World War I high prices resulted once more in an increase of cotton growing in Brazil, this time in São Paulo state. In one of the war years São Paulo's share of the Brazilian production was over 50 percent. Since 1930 the share of the total accounted for by São Paulo has varied from about 30 percent to over 80 percent. In the period when Brazil's cotton could not penetrate the international markets, it did find an increasing market in the textile factories of São Paulo. In recent years this has been the chief use of Brazilian cotton. During the 1930's, when the United States had adopted a policy of restricting production to maintain prices, Brazil again entered the world markets; in 1938 cotton made up 18 percent of all exports, and in that year Brazil accounted for 70 percent of the cotton exports of Latin America. During World War II, when shipping space was greatly restricted, there was a large drop in cotton exports, but after the war the exports increased again.

Cacao is the third of Brazil's leading export products. Between World War I and the beginning of World War II, the cacao district in southern Bahía was rapidly developed out of previously unused selva. Brazil pushed ahead of Ecuador and Venezuela in the exports of cacao. By 1938 Brazil was producing more than 50 percent of the cacao exported from all of Latin America. During the war, cacao shipments were greatly reduced, but exports picked up again after the war. Brazil in the 1950's was producing some 16 percent of the world's supply.

The other exports of Brazil which have maintained or increased their importance since World War II include a variety of agricultural, pastoral, and forest products. Lumber is coming in increasing quantities from Paraná and São Paulo. Fruit exports include chiefly oranges and bananas. Brazilian hides and skins, including such unusual items as alligator skin and snake skin, maintain their place on world markets. Oilseeds, Car-

Soaking jute on the Amazon floodplain

naúba Wax, and vegetable oils, such as castor oil, oiticica oil, and babaçú oil, are exported from the Northeast. Some maté is sent from Paraná.

During World War II, Brazil's maufactured products were able for the first time to reach a place of prominence on the list of exports. Immediately after the war, manufactured goods were second only to coffee, making up 20 percent of the total. About 11 percent of the total exports were cotton textiles. Brazilian cotton goods were sent in large quantities to South Africa and Argentina, and even appeared in the retail stores in the United States. Cotton textiles were still third on the export list in 1947, in which year they brought in the largest value to the manufacturers. But since 1947, the reconstruction of the more normal currents of trade practically cut off this export market. The result was the first major financial crisis in the speculative development of one of Brazil's major manufacturing industries.

In the purchase of Brazilian products the United States has long been in the lead. About half of Brazil's coffee finds its market there (55 percent in 1938; 42 percent in 1955). During World War II the United States purchased nearly 50 percent of Brazil exports, but this proportion has now dropped again with the reopening of the European markets. In this same period, Argentina's share of the Brazilian exports rose to nearly 12 percent, chiefly textiles and timber. In the future Argentina may offer a foreign market for Brazil's steel and steel products. Before the war there was an important current of exports to Japan, in which cotton was a major item. Since the war this trade has been redeveloped.

In 1963 the Brazilian government started a program to increase the export of iron ore. Private North American and European capital had long been interested in developing the Brazilian ores, which are located about 200 miles inland from the port of Vitória in Espírito Santo a little east of Belo Horizonte. Here the experts figure that Brazil has one of the world's largest concentrations of high-grade ore, still largely untouched. Some of this ore is brought to Rio de Janeiro for shipment, but in 1964 a new modern ore-shipping port was completed near Vitória to handle the largest ore carriers. In 1963 West Germany was buying some 40 percent of Brazil's ore exports, the United States about 17 percent. Arrangements had been made, however, to increase the ore shipments to Japan and, through Yugoslavia, to the countries of Eastern Europe. The Brazilians hoped to increase iron ore exports to replace the declining exports of coffee and cotton.

Imports

Before World War I Brazil's imports consisted of coal and a great variety of manufactured articles. The great expansion of the industries of Brazil during the last two decades has resulted, however, in certain major changes in the list of imports. Machinery now stands first on the list, making up 27 percent of the total in 1961. Most of the equipment for the Brazilian factories must be imported, and since much of the textile machinery is now obsolete, a rise in machinery imports is to be expected. Oil is second on the list of imports, making up 18 percent. Before World War II iron and steel products were high on the list of Brazil's imports, and most of them came from the United States. There were rods, bars, sheets, tubes, and rails. With the development of Brazil's steel industry this trade has decreased, but in 1961 motor vehicles still made up 8 percent of the value of all imports.

The period just before the outbreak of World War II witnessed competition between Germany and the United States for first place among the countries sending these commodities to Brazil. While exchange difficulties were handicapping the payments for goods from North America, Germany was ready to barter locomotives for cotton. Brazil found that the industrial equipment manufactured in Germany was of good quality and could be imported by Brazil because of these special arrangements at less cost than machinery from the United States or Great Britain. World War II put an end to this trade, and left Brazil closely dependent on Britain and the United States, chiefly the latter, for its machinery. The share of the United States in Brazil's imports after the war reached more than 50 percent. This situation was not entirely to the liking of the Brazilians.

Relation of Exports and Imports to Population Centers

Brazil's foreign trade is to a large extent concentrated in a few regions. Of all the exports, nearly half (48 percent) are shipped out from Santos. From 11 to 16 percent are sent from Rio de Janeiro, and about 7 percent are from Salvador (mostly cacao). The import trade, also, is concentrated in Rio de Janeiro (44 percent) and Santos (41 percent). The third port, Porto Alegre, receives less than 5 percent of the total. The significance of the two leading ports with respect to the volume of imports is tending to increase.

There are two main reasons for this concentration of the imports at Rio de Janeiro and Santos. In the first place, the majority of the Brazilians who can buy things from abroad live in the hinterlands of São Paulo and Rio de Janeiro. Here are the chief markets for locomotives, for industrial machinery, and for automobiles; in these cities are most of the people who eat white bread; in Rio de Janeiro and São Paulo are most of the new buildings which require such construction materials as reenforcing rods and beams—though some are also found in Porto Alegre. In the second place, Rio de Janeiro has become the chief distributing point from which imported goods are shipped by coasting steamer to the other parts of the country, from Rio Grande do Sul to Manaus.

Threshing rice in the Jacuí Valley of Rio Grande do Sul

Domestic Trade

Rio de Janeiro is the hub of internal trade. Of the goods exported by coasting steamers for Brazilian destinations before World War II, Rio de Janeiro accounted for 30 percent; and of the goods imported from other Brazilian ports, Rio de Janeiro received 19 percent. As long as Brazil's areas of concentrated settlement remain near the coast, the continued supremacy of Rio de Janeiro in terms of domestic trade would seem to be assured.

No other Latin-American country can look forward to such a continued development of domestic commerce as Brazil. This estimate is justified not only because of the relatively large number of people within the limits of one political unit, but also because of the great variety of resources and products which exist within Brazil's vast area. Potential products range from those of the tropics to those of the middle latitudes; and from those of the farm and ranch to those of the mine and the factory. The adoption of protective tariffs has increased the internal exchange of goods, and the abolition of state export duties in 1930 has still further aided the free flow of commodities from one part of the country to another. Nearly half of the domestic commerce of Brazil consists of manufactured articles; about a third is made up of foodstuffs; and the remainder comprises various raw materials and livestock. Any movement leading to an increase of the purchasing power of the rural Brazilians would have enormous repercussions on the growth of domestic trade and domestic industries.

The Political Situation

In 1822, when Brazil became independent from Portugal, it was the son of the Portuguese king who made the declaration. He became Pedro I of Brazil. In 1831, however, Dom Pedro I abdicated in favor of his five-year-old son, and for nine years Brazil was administered in the name of the emperor by a regency. From 1840 until the end of the Empire in 1889, Dom Pedro II was the monarch. During the period when most of the other Latin-American countries were torn by internal conflict, Brazilians, for the most part, were ready to give their support to their enlightened and popular ruler. It was the final emancipation of the slaves in 1888 which brought an end to the institution of the monarchy, and the landed aristocracy on which the monarchy was based.

In 1894, after a few years of military government, there started a succession of civilian presidents. By this time the modern political alignments had made their appearance. São Paulo state was already the strongest economically, but Minas Gerais had the largest population, and the states of the Northeast, acting as a unit for political purposes, often held the balance of power. For many years the presidency went alternately to a candidate from São Paulo and then one from Minas Gerais. Some of the presidents turned out to be able and honest administrators, but there were also examples of corruption and confusion.

Always in the background of Brazilian politics were the sertões, with their scattered, isolated inhabitants. During the first civilian administration, 1894–1898, much money and effort was spent in putting down a revolt in the backlands of Bahia.[3] In the two years between 1925 and 1927 the communist leader, Luiz Carlos Prestes, led a column of rebellious soldiers through the backlands of Brazil, touching at every state, and covering a distance of more than two thousand miles. He sought to arouse the spirit of revolt among the people of the back country, and among the "serf-like" workers on the coffee plantations and the cattle ranches. He was not successful in gaining many followers; but he gained a mythical reputation as a kind of modern Robin Hood, who had entered the great Brazilian backlands and conquered them.

In 1930, with the collapse of the financial structure that had been erected to maintain the speculative profits in coffee planting, the federal

[3] Euclydes da Cunha, *Os Sertões*, translated by Samuel Putnam, *Rebellion in the Backlands*, Chicago, 1944.

government was attacked and overthrown by army units from Rio Grande do Sul, led by Getúlio Vargas. From 1930 to 1945 Vargas remained in control of Brazil, setting up in 1937 what he called the *Estado Novo,* modelled on fascist Italy. Although the Brazilian people tolerated their dictator, they would not be regimented on the fascist pattern. In 1945 the army removed Vargas and called for new elections and the end of the New State. Elections were actually held and honestly counted. In fact, after an interval Vargas himself was elected president in 1951, and he held office until his suicide in 1954.

In the period after World War II there were three main political groups. The conservatives were mostly represented by the *União Demo-crática Nacional;* those who wanted to find political expression for their dissatisfaction with administrative dishonesty and with social and economic inequality either gave their support to Vargas or to the communists under Prestes. In terms of actual numbers the communists reached the peak of their strength in the period between 1945 and 1947. Since then they have declined in number, but are stronger and more tightly disciplined. They have launched attacks on the United States, and have succeeded in blocking the entry of foreign capital in the development of Brazil's presumed oil resources. *"O petróleo é nosso"* is the slogan that proclaims "the oil is ours." Supporting the communists in this policy of restricting the investment of foreign capital in resource development are many noncommunist but strongly nationalistic groups, including the politically powerful officers of the army.

Forces for Union and Disunion

The political situation raises again the question regarding the potential coherence and unity of Brazil. Can this huge country develop the internal strength to continue to progress as a unit? Would communist guerrilla warfare result in a fatal split among the various parts of the country?

It is a principle of political geography that if the national territory of a country is divided into two sharply differentiated parts, each occupied by people of one political group antagonistic to the political group or groups in other parts of the country, the situation could lead to civil conflict. If, on the other hand, two strongly antagonistic political groups are widely scattered in all the parts of a country, the danger of civil conflict is lessened. In Brazil the communists are active in almost all parts of the country; the conservatives, too, are represented in all the states. On the other hand, whatever the political faith, loyalty to state is a very important matter in Brazil. A Paulista (a citizen of São Paulo) is conscious of being different from a Mineiro (a citizen of Minas Gerias), and is proud of the difference. The Mineiro, similarly, is loyal to his state first. The very unequal economic development of São Paulo as compared with the other states is certainly a force leading toward disunity.

The geographic position of São Paulo near the center of the economically developed part of the national territory is of critical importance. If São Paulo were located near the borders of Brazil the possibility of secession would be a very real one. But the center of a political unit could scarcely secede from the periphery. There are many Paulistas who resent paying taxes to provide economic support for the poorer parts of Brazil; but the geographic arrangement of these states is such that this resentment is not at all likely to be translated into any movement to break away from Brazil as a whole.

There are many forces leading toward more coherence and unity. Modern transportation, especially the airplane, has come to Brazil in time to permit rapid movement from place to place, and again to minimize the separatist tendencies of some states. The industrial and urban type of economy has come first to São Paulo and Rio de Janiero; but it has also gained a strong base in Porto Alegre, and in other parts of the country. The sense of unity is increased, also, by the use of the Portuguese language, which sets off the Brazilians from the other Latin Americans. Brazil has developed a common heritage and a common tradition which has gone a long way to establish a Brazilian state-idea to which people in all parts of the country remain loyal.

The New Capital

It is important to estimate the possible consequences of establishing the new capital in the backlands at Brasília. Unless the cost of the new capital wrecks the Brazilian economy before the work on it can be completed, it seems certain that the project will go forward. It may well be that even if the project is economically a failure, it may be a great political success, in that the material existence of a "dream-city" rising in the sertão will of itself focus and strengthen a characteristically Brazilian state-idea. People all over the country, conservatives and communists alike, will look at Brasília and exclaim, " It is good, and it is ours."

The selection of the site reflects the realities of Brazilian political geography. Two separate commissions, one staffed by professional geographers, examined the Brazilian backlands and prepared recommendations regarding the location. For the site it was necessary to have proper terrain and climate, adequate supplies of water, a forested area nearby where vegetables can be grown and dairy cattle pastured, and where charcoal can be produced, and a number of other needs such as building materials, good subsoil suitable for foundations, and attractive landscapes and recreation areas. The geographers selected a place in the Triangulo of Minas Gerais just north of São Paulo state. But the second commission, composed of representatives of each of the states, would not consider a location so close to São Paulo. A majority of the state representatives agreed on a location almost at the divide between the three major rivers, the Paraná, the São Francisco, and the Tocantins. The selection of this site reflects the fact that the Northeast has nine states, each with a vote, whereas the South and São Paulo have only four states and four votes, even when they work together.

An outside observer may agree that Brasília will quicken the pulse and command the loyalty of Brazilians to a far greater degree than would the large-scale economic development of the iron-ore bodies of Itabira, or the discovery of a vast oil field somewhere within Brazilian territory. The Brazilians, whether communist or not, are attracted by ideas of national self-sufficiency, and at least by the symbols of centralized authority. The outside observer will fear that the high costs of this project may seriously postpone the solution of many pressing problems of poverty, and he may doubt the economic justification for promoting a westward movement, at least in advance of a land survey. But for the Brazilians there are other programs more exciting than those of economic development; and meanwhile speculative gain is still possible, not only in the federal lottery, which is open to any one with a few cruzeiros, but also in the rising urban land values, even those around the new capital itself.

Brasília's Palace of the Dawn, designed by Brazilian architect, Oscar Niemeyer

The Antilles
and the Guianas

Workers cutting sugar cane

CHAPTER ELEVEN

The Antilles and the Guianas

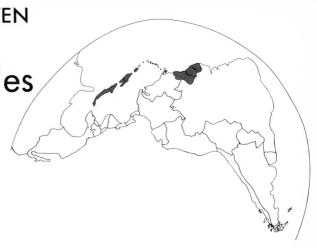

Great Britain, Spain, and Portugal were the three European nations that finally won out in the struggle to obtain control of the sources of wealth in the Americas. Other nations involved in the conflicts of the sixteenth to the nineteenth centuries were France, the Netherlands, Denmark, and even Russia (in northwestern North America). Germany and Italy entered the colonial field too late to obtain actual sovereignty over any part of the Americas, although in the modern period their emigrants and their commercial enterprises have played roles of great importance in all parts of the New World. The last of the great nineteenth-century imperialist nations to turn its attention toward Middle America was the United States. Near the end of the nineteenth century, having completed the conquest of a once thinly populated continent, the "colossus of the north" began to look southward. Territory in the Antilles was annexed and there was a considerable amount of intervention in the domestic affairs of Latin-American countries. Not until the era of the Good Neighbor Policy in the 1930's were imperialist aims officially renounced.

Among the islands today there are five independent countries, one self-governing commonwealth, and a variety of colonial possessions of the United States, Great Britain, France, and the Netherlands. The five independent states are Cuba and the Dominican Republic (former Spanish colonies), Haiti (a former French colony), and Jamaica and Trinidad (former British colonies). Puerto Rico (a former Spanish colony that became a possession of the United States in 1898) is now a self-governing commonwealth "freely associated with the United States." In addition there are possessions of Great Britain, the United States, France, the

Maps 1, 3, 5, 6, 8, 11, 12, 13, 14, 25, 27 are pertinent to this chapter.

POLITICAL CLASSIFICATION OF THE ANTILLEAN COUNTRIES AND COLONIES AND THE GUIANAS

Independent countries, former colonies of Spain
   Cuba, and Isla de Pinos
   The Dominican Republic

Independent country, former colony of France
   Haiti, Île de la Tortue, Île de la Gonave

Independent countries, former colonies of Great Britain
  Members of the Commonwealth of Nations
   Jamaica
   Trinidad and Tobago

Self-Governing commonwealth, voluntarily associated with the United States
   Puerto Rico and its dependency, Víeques

British Crown Colonies
   The Bahamas
   Caicos Islands and Turks Islands, Cayman Islands
   British Virgin Islands
     Tortola, Virgin Gorda, Anegada

   The Leeward Islands
     Antigua, Barbuda, Redonda
     St. Kitts-Nevis, Anguilla, Sombrero
     Montserrat

   The Windward Islands
     Dominica
     St. Lucia
     St. Vincent
     Grenada, The Grenadines

   Barbados
   British Guiana

Unincorporated territory of the United States
   American Virgin Islands
     St. Croix, St. Thomas, St. John

French Overseas Departments
   Guadeloupe (Basse-Terre, Grande-Terre)
     with its dependencies: Marie Galante, Désirade, Les Saintes, St. Barthélemy, St. Martin (in part)
   Martinique
   French Guiana

Integral Parts of the Kingdom of the Netherlands
   Netherlands Antilles
     Curaçao, with its dependencies: Bonaire and Aruba
     St. Martin (in part)
     Saba
     St. Eustatius
   Surinam

Part of Venezuela
   Margarita
   La Tortuga and outlying small islands

Netherlands, and Venezuela. In the Antilles there are more than fifty inhabited islands, and innumerable small rocks and reefs.[1] The list on page 274 presents a political classification of the Antilles and the Guianas.

The Physical Nature of the Islands

The Antilles differ in their physical character. There are some with connected ranges of mountains, geologically related to the mainland. These include Cuba, Jamaica, Hispaniola,[2] Puerto Rico, and the Virgin Islands—all of which are an eastward extension of mountain ranges of Central America. Similarly the mountainous islands close to the South American shore are related to the Andean structures—such as Curaçao, Bonaire, Aruba, Margarita, Trinidad, and Tobago. The Bahamas are all low-lying islands formed by a platform of coral limestone barely above sea level. Somewhat higher coral limestones form the greater part of Cuba, and also Florida and Yucatán. Among the Lesser Antilles some are volcanic and mountainous, others are limestone platforms—such as Barbados. Active volcanoes are still found on Guadeloupe and Martinique. In places like the Antilles one finds the truly "temperate" climates of the world. These islands are bathed by currents of warm ocean water and swept by the easterly trades of the open sea. The temperatures are moderately high, and vary little from season to season. In Habana, Cuba, for example, the average temperature is 76.9° with a range between warmest and coldest months of about 10°; San Juan in Puerto Rico has a range of less than 6°; and Bridgetown in Barbados has a range of only about 4°. From Habana to Bridgetown the average of the warmest month is about the same—between 80° and 82° (except Port-au-Prince, Haiti, which is in a lowland pocket protected from the moderating influence of the open sea). The winters, however, average a little lower in Cuba than in the islands farther east because of the exposure of that island to the cold air masses which emerge from North America during that season. In every month of the year the maximum temperatures are about the same; but the minimum temperatures of the winter are much lower than the minimum temperatures of summer, and this has the effect of lowering the monthly average. Excessively high temperatures, such as are experienced in the Middle West of the United States, never occur in the Antilles; but neither are the cold waves characteristic

[1] The name *Antilles* is applied to all the islands of the West Indies. The name is derived from Antilia, the mythical island that appeared on maps of the Atlantic Ocean before Columbus. The Antilles include: the Greater Antilles; the Lesser Antilles; and the Bahamas.

[2] The United States Geographic Board adopted the name Hispaniola to apply to the island occupied by Haiti and the Dominican Republic. There is some historical precedent for this, although the European writers are accustomed to refer to the whole island as Santo Domingo. There is no justification for the designation of the whole island as Haiti.

of mid-latitude winters experienced. The climate of the Antilles is truly temperate.

But the Antilles do not always remain undisturbed by climatic violence. This is one of the parts of the world in which tropical cyclones, or hurricanes, are frequent occurrences. The hurricane season begins in August and lasts through October. Of all the storms reported between 1887 and 1923, August had 16 percent, September had 33 percent, and October, 30 percent. These storms originate off the coast of Africa and sweep westward toward the Lesser Antilles, bending toward the north as they proceed. The island of Trinidad never experiences these violent storms, and the southern members of the Lesser Antilles rarely, but the northern Antilles are frequently traversed by them. The hurricanes follow two chief tracks. One crosses the Caribbean to the Yucatán Channel, and thence proceeds across the Gulf of Mexico, where the storms either ravage the Gulf Coast of the United States, rapidly losing violence as they proceed into the interior, or curve toward the east again across Florida. The other track follows the Lesser Antilles, passing east of Puerto Rico, across the Bahamas to the east coast of the United States, after which it curves again toward the east, following the Gulf Stream. Of course there are many storms which fail to proceed along the usual tracks, and which do unexpected damage to the eastern part of the United States—all the way from southwestern Texas to New England.

The Course of Settlement

It was to the Antilles that the Spaniards came on that momentous first voyage of Columbus in 1492. Land was first reached probably on Caicos Island in the Bahamas. To the everlasting confusion of succeeding generations, Columbus, believing that he had come upon the eastern coast of Asia, made use of the name, the "West Indies," and designated the native inhabitants as Indians.

The first permanent European settlement in America was made in 1496 at the site of the present Santo Domingo on the southern shore of Hispaniola. On this island the native people numbered perhaps a million, making this the most densely populated of the Antilles; and also on this island the Spaniards promptly discovered that the stream gravels contained gold. The result was a "gold rush." By 1513 there were seventeen towns on Hispaniola, and already the problem of the exploitation of the native peoples was worrying the authorities. Meanwhile, the first settlement had become a primary settlement center, for colonies were sent out from it not only into the interior of Hispaniola, but to other parts of the Antilles and even to Panamá. In 1509 a town was founded in Puerto Rico; later, because of unhealthful conditions at the first site, the colony was transferred to the present San Juan (1511). Also in 1509 a colony was established in Jamaica. The occupation of scantily populated Cuba began in 1511, and the city of Habana was founded in 1515. From Habana Cortés started out on his voyage of conquest to Mexico.

The Indians of the northern Antilles were, therefore, the first to feel the destructive effects of the Spanish conquest. At first friendly, they soon turned hostile, for in spite of the efforts of the authorities, the natives were set to hard labor in the placer mines, or on the plantations. The new European diseases introduced among these people had a devastating effect: in 1542, Las Casas reported that the Indians in Hispaniola, Puerto Rico, Jamaica, and Cuba were almost all gone. Only in some of the mountain valleys of the Lesser Antilles could small remnants of the Caribs and Arawaks, who once occupied the whole region, find a refuge sufficiently isolated to permit their survival.

The scramble for colonies in the Antilles and the Guianas did not begin for a century or more after the first Spanish conquest. By this time the main stream of the Spanish conquest had been directed to Mexico, and, by way of Panamá, to Peru. The Guianas were empty and densely forested. On the Antilles small Spanish settlements survived in the eastern part of Hispaniola, around San Juan in Puerto Rico, in Jamaica, and around Habana in Cuba. Otherwise the Antilles remained unsettled and unclaimed. It was to these lands not effectively colonized by either Spaniards or Portuguese that the other European countries turned their attention.

The scramble for colonies was started by the Dutch. The period between 1624 and 1654, when the Dutch occupied the Northeast of Brazil, was long enough for the invaders to learn the essentials of planting sugar cane and the handling of Negro slaves. The Dutch, pushed out of Brazil, promptly settled in Guiana and on the Antilles, where they started their own sugar cane plantations. From them the Spaniards, the British, and the French learned to grow sugar cane. Even the Danes were involved in the rush to secure tropical colonies. In 1667 the Dutch exchanged their colony on Manhattan Island and the Hudson Valley for sugar-producing land in Guiana (now Surinam).

At first the sugar-cane plantations were concentrated on the low-lying islands of the Lesser Antilles. Later three of the larger islands became the most productive cane lands: the French in the western part of Hispaniola; and the British in Jamaica and Barbados.

It was during the nineteenth century that the sugar colonies faced their first challenge. The industry had to face two difficulties. The first was the increasing competition with sugar beets grown in the Middle Latitudes and subsidized by the governments in Europe and North America. The second was the freeing of the slaves. Negroes were first given their freedom in the British colony of Antigua in 1834, and in the rest of the British possessions in 1836. The other parts of America followed this

A reservoir near Santa Clara

lead over a period of fifty years: French possessions in 1848; Dutch possessions and the United States in 1863; Puerto Rico in 1873; Danish
posessions in 1876; Cuba in 1880; and Brazil in 1888. During this period
sugar production was reorganized on the basis of wage workers, tenants,
or small independent planters selling to nearby mills. The latter part
of the century was a period of difficult readjustment for the cane planters.

About 1900, conditions were changed by the development of modern
technology, including the construction of improved machinery for extracting juice and producing sugar. The new machines were much more
efficient; but to derive the maximum of profit it was necessary to operate
on a large scale. This was the beginning of the rise of Cuba to world
leadership, chiefly with the aid of capital investment from the United
States. Since 1900 the proportion of the world's sugar produced from
sugar cane has again risen in relation to beet sugar. For large-scale
operations the island of Cuba, long a neglected Spanish colony, offered
unusual advantages. After the Spanish-American War (1898), which gave
Cuba its political independence, this part of the Antilles forged rapidly
ahead in sugar production, leaving the Lesser Antilles far behind.

CUBA

In many ways it was Cuba's misfortune to be the Latin-American country located closest to the United States. When people in the centers of American political and economic life looked southward, the first country that they saw was Cuba. For a long time they did not look to the south, but rather to the west where there was a continent to be occupied. In the 1870's a revolt against Spanish rule in Cuba went unnoticed in the United States. In 1898, on the other hand, the North American continent had been largely occupied, and attention had turned southward. The United States went to war with Spain to rescue the last of Spain's colonies in the Western Hemisphere.

In the years after 1899 it was American capital that built the Cuban sugar industry. It was American capital that developed the mines and that transformed Habana into a major tourist attraction. It was the American market that absorbed Cuban products and from the United States came most of Cuba's imports. Cuba, by the beginning of World War II, was essentially an economic dependency of the United States. By 1950 Cuba ranked fifth in Latin America in manufacturing industry, built largely with American capital. The Cuban economy had become almost as productive as that of Italy, and in Latin America was exceeded only by those of Venezuela, Argentina, and Chile. Americans pointed to Cuba as an example of the benefits to be derived from economic development. Americans came to Cuba to enjoy the carefree Latin atmosphere of Habana night life.

Americans knew almost nothing of what Cuba was really like, or what Cubans thought about the benefits of economic development. They were quite unprepared, therefore, for Castro's revolution and its aftermath. When Soviet missile bases were found only ninety miles from the United States there was shocked anger, and widespread bewilderment about how such things could have happened. They happened precisely because of the kind of economic development imposed on Cuba, and because of Cuba's strategic position so close to the major centers of the United States.

The Cuban People

When Cuba gained its independence from Spain the island was still not very densely populated. The chief area of concentrated settlement was around Habana, where sugar cane had long been cultivated, at first with Negro slave labor. But the sugar prosperity of the twentieth century brought many immigrants to Cuba. By 1957 the total population had grown to 6,410,000, giving an average density of about 145 people per square mile. The census of 1953 classes 73 percent of the people as of pure European descent, 12 percent as Negro, 14 percent as mestizo, and 1 percent as Oriental.

The desire for freedom from outside interference was as strong among the Cubans as it was in other parts of Latin America. When the other Latin countries were freeing themselves of Spanish rule, the Cubans were not numerous enough to stage a successful revolt against the strong Spanish garrison in Habana. Yet all during the nineteenth century there was constant unrest. The great Cuban liberal leader, José Martí (1853–1895), was one of the most eloquent spokesmen for liberty. His warning to Latin Americans was prophetic: be careful about too close an attachment to the economy of the United States, because economic domination could easily be followed by political domination. It was Martí who said *"nuestro vino es agrio, pero es nuestro vino,"* ("our wine is sour, but it is our wine"), which is a variant on the story recounted in the beginning of this book. It expresses a very basic Latin-American attitude—the undiminished desire to be free from outside domination. Yet Cuba's position close to the United States made it almost impossible for Cuba to escape from the predominant influence of so powerful a country. And this same position, for a people determined to escape from American domination, brought about the domination of the Soviet Union.

The Spread of Sugar-Cane Planting

The treaty of 1901 between the United States and Cuba gave Cuban sugar a reduction of 20 percent on the tariff imposed on imported sugar. It also reserved to the United States the right of intervention in Cuban domestic affairs, a right which was used repeatedly until the treaty was abrogated in 1934. Because Cuban sugar paid a lower duty than sugars imported from other foreign countries, and because security was gained by the right of the United States government to intervene in Cuba, North American capital amounting to more than a billion dollars poured into the newly created republic. Roads and railroads were built; Habana was modernized; and in the rural districts new sugar mills were built to equip the sugar producers with the very latest technical devices for grinding the cane and extracting the raw sugar. In technical equipment no part of the world could compete with Cuba. The cost of production per unit was reduced three or four times as a result of this new capital investment.

As a result Cuba became the world's largest producer of sugar, and sugar exports made up more than 70 percent of the value of all exports.

Other economic activities, such as tobacco growing, mining, manufacturing, or providing for the needs of American tourists, were secondary.

The planting of sugar cane in areas directly dependent upon rainfall involves certain problems that have yet to be solved. In Cuba the harvest season is from December to June, and during this period there were more jobs than there were people to work. It was customary to bring in temporary workers from Jamaica and Haiti, so great was the need for more workers. During this time every one was busy, and money was plentiful. But between June and November the great majority of the cane workers were unemployed. Many families actually suffered from hunger, even those that lived in the shadow of the luxury hotels patronized by American tourists. The contrast between the very wealthy Cubans —the political leaders, the large landowners, and others—and the very poor Cubans, was greater than ever before. The figures that showed Cuba's large income per capita did not make it clear that most Cubans did not share in the wealth from planting, harvesting, and grinding the cane. During the idle season from June to November Cuba was frequently disturbed by uprisings and revolts that had to be held in check by the police.

Matters were aggravated by another common problem in sugar-cane country. Cane is a crop that speedily reduces soil fertility. Even on such naturally productive soils as those of Cuba, the cane plantations had to be extended to new land as the older plantations began to decline in yields. Therefore the large planters owned much land into which they could expand the cane plantations. This land remained idle, or was used for the pasture of oxen. There was not room enough on the island to permit any large area to be used for the production of foods. Cuba was dependent on imports of such basic things as rice, wheat flour, maize, lard, vegetable oils, beans, peas, and salt codfish. For most of the cane workers these imported foods were priced so high that there were many hungry people during the idle months.

Castro's Revolution

Independence from Spain brought no real freedom to Cuba. When Cuba was recognized as independent in 1899, United States and Cuban leaders worked out a constitution for the new country. In accordance with the so-called "Platt amendment," accepted by Cuba as part of the constitution, Cuba agreed not to incur debts its revenue would not bear, to continue the sanitary measures started by the United States army, to lease a naval base to the United States at Guantánamo Bay, and to acknowledge the right of the United States to intervene if necessary in the domestic affairs of the island. During the first thirty years of Cuba's independence the United States did in fact intervene many times to maintain order and to protect the increasing capital investment in the Cuban economy. Subservience to the United States, however, proved even more irritating than rule by Spain. The Platt amendment was finally renounced by the United States in 1934.

This did not bring an end to the political conflicts, or to dishonesty and mismanagement by the persons who occupied positions of power. From 1933 to 1959 Batista had been the one focus of political direction in Cuba. He rose from the noncommissioned grade of sergeant to become the commander-in-chief of the military forces. His long control over Cuban affairs was based on his ability to command the complete loyalty of the army. He saw to it that all members of the armed forces, officers and men alike, were well paid, and his treasury was well supplied with funds. For several periods Batista permitted another general to become president; and each man who held this office made millions of dollars. There was no such thing as political liberty, honest elections, or equality before the law. And Batista's police were so ruthless and brutal in keeping order, especially among students and intellectuals, that the whole system was bitterly resented. Hatred of Batista and hatred of the United States for supporting him became more and more widespread among Cubans of all classes.

In December 1956, Fidel Castro and a force of eighty-two men landed on the rugged southeast coast of Cuba. Attacked by Batista's troops, most of the landing party were killed or captured, but Castro succeeded in escaping with twelve men to the rugged mountains that here border the coast. For the next three years he carried on a kind of guerrilla warfare, descending from the mountains to raid cane plantations and mines, then hiding out in the mountains again. Gradually, he increased his military force. In May 1958, when he launched his attack on Batista, Castro still had a force of less than 3,000 with which to confront Batista's army of 40,000. But many of Batista's units refused to fight the liberator. Many Cubans gave their support to Castro because he promised to free Cuba not only from the dictator, but also from the dominance of the United States. He also promised free elections. With the support of Cuba's middle class, he took control of Cuba on January 1, 1959.

Castro had dropped all pretense concerning the objectives of his revolution by the end of 1961. Step by step American-owned businesses were expropriated, and the Cuban middle class was liquidated. The fortunate ones escaped to Florida. Cuba today is even more completely a police state than it was under Batista, and the people in positions of power are the members of the ruling Communist Party. Cuba's economy was destroyed as the first step in the creation of a soviet state, and the Soviet Union has had to provide the necessary foods, fuels, and military assistance to keep Castro in power. But Cuba is costing the Soviet Union millions of dollars every day, and since the open missile sites had to be

A once-crowded street in Habana

abandoned Cuba is no longer of such direct military value. Cuba is a
training ground for undercover agents who can spread to such critical
places as Venezuela to spread terror and destruction. Fidel Castro, as the
leader who could successfully challenge the power of the United States,
gained a large popular following in Latin America: but Fidel Castro,
the leader who exchanged subservience to the United States for subservience to the Soviet Union, has lost much Latin-American support.

HAITI AND THE DOMINICAN REPUBLIC

The variety of lands and of peoples and the sharp contrasts in the economic life within small geographical areas which we have learned to look for as an outstanding characteristic of Latin America are illustrated in still another striking manner on the island of Hispaniola. Here two independent states are locked within the narrow confines of a single island. In the west is Haiti—Negro in race, Negro in the manner of living in spite of a superficial French tradition and in spite of the use of the French language; and in the east is the Dominican Republic—mostly mulatto, but essentially Spanish in the way of living. The western one-third of Hispaniola was occupied in 1962 by about 4,300,000 Haitians, with a density of 406 people per square mile; the eastern two-thirds was occupied in 1962 by about 3,217,000 Dominicans, with a density of about 161 people per square mile. On the Haitian side of the border the land is marked off in a patchwork of small farms, cultivated with the hoe and machete, used for the production of food crops for the people who work them; on the other side are large estates, with extensive thinly populated areas on which cattle graze, with the best lands devoted to crops raised for sale, with many tenant workers and few farm owners. On the one side the way of living is a strange mixture of African and French customs; on the other the economic, political, and social life proceeds in accordance with the Spanish tradition. The presence of two such contrasted peoples, politically separate, within so small an island area, creates the possibility of conflict.

HAITI

The first settlers to make use of the western side of the island of Hispaniola were English and French pirates. About 1625 the Île de la Tortue (Tortuga) became one of the chief pirate strongholds of the Antilles. Bands from this base would come over to Hispaniola to hunt the wild cattle and hogs which had escaped from the Spanish settlements in the east. Large fires were built, and over these the carcasses, laid on grills (boucans), were processed for tallow. Here in the hills of Haiti, the pirates came to be known as boucaniers, or buccaneers. In the course of time the French drove out the English, and, supported by the French colonies on other nearby islands, they established settlements on Haiti, especially along the northern coast. In spite of repeated attempts, the

Spaniards of eastern Hispaniola could not drive them out, and in 1697 Spain recognized France's claim to the western third of Hispaniola. The new French colony, now officially established, was known as *Saint Domingue*.

The French Period

The century of French ownership witnessed the rise of Saint Domingue to the status of one of the world's richest colonies—almost equal to Java as a producer of revenue for the home government. In those days, when the Antilles were producing sugar for Europe's growing markets, colonies were far from being a financial liability. The destructive exploitation of land, together with the use of slave labor, could be made, for a time at least, to yield enormous profits to the owners.

Meanwhile the political and social situation in Saint Domingue was becoming explosive. The Negroes greatly outnumbered the French, but this condition might not have led to disastrous revolts had it not been for the mulatto class. These were the sons and daughters of French planters and Negro women. The boys were usually sent to France for an education, where they were exposed to the explosive new ideas of liberty then being proclaimed. Returning to Haiti, however, the mulattoes were accepted neither by the whites nor by the Negroes. Under the leadership of the mulattoes the Haitians rose up and forced the French planters to flee or be killed. In 1804 Haiti declared its independence from France, the first of the Latin-American countries to achieve independence. The Haitians also invaded eastern Hispaniola and in 1822 brought the whole island under their rule. The Dominican Republic did not become independent until 1844.

Independence

The period of independence in Haiti resulted in a number of changes in the relation of the people to the land. The breakdown of the systems of irrigation because of the lack of strong central authority made most of the lowlands uninhabitable for an agricultural people. The result was a marked decrease in population in these areas, except in the wet Plaine du Nord and around the shores of the southern peninsula. Great numbers of the Haitians withdrew to the mountain regions, or to the southeastern part of the Plaine Centrale. The former slaves established themselves on small properties on which, with African agricultural techniques, they raised their own supplies of food. Production of sugar for export practically ceased, but the export of coffee was continued. The carefully cultivated plantations of the French were given no attention except at harvest time, and new coffee trees planted on the steep mountain slopes were allowed to grow as wild trees of the forest, entirely without care. Yet the coffee produced in this manner in Haiti proved to possess such an excellent aroma that it commanded a special place on the French market, and is to this day one of the highest priced coffees in the world. Haitian coffee, mixed with the coffees of Brazil, together with much chicory, gives distinctive flavor to the coffee served in France.

During most of the nineteenth century Haiti was a land of intrigue and disorder. About three hundred mulatto families fought with each other for control of the government, if it can be called that. Each group in turn, as it came to power, raided the public treasury, and political corruption brought the country to financial ruin. Insecurity in the rural districts was a result not only of banditry, but also of the system of recruiting for the army—for an army had to be maintained to keep a political faction in power after it had been successful in seizing that power, and other armies had to be recruited to carry on a successful revolt. The able-bodied men were "conscripted" wherever they could be found. As a result, the men feared to venture forth on the trails, and attendance at markets was largely restricted to women.

From 1915 to 1934 Haiti was occupied by the United States Marines. The chaotic conditions within Haiti were considered to threaten the security of the approaches to the Panama Canal during World War I. The occupation brought order, and a large number of material improvements, including the building of roads. A North American sugar company built a mill to extract the sugar from the cane, and the area around the mill, inland from Port-au-Prince, became an important cane-growing area. Other new commercial crops were introduced, including bananas, cotton, sisal, and cacao.

The Economic Situation

The people of Haiti remain very poor. The estimated gross national product per capita of $78 in 1962 was lower than any other Latin American country except Bolivia. The great majority of the people, however, are purely subsistence farmers, who remain outside of the economic system. This they are quite content to do, for only in places like Port-au-Prince do they have a chance to see the higher standards of material comfort to which some people aspire.

The Political Situation

The political situation in Haiti is chaotic. About 89 percent of the people cannot read or write and therefore are not reached directly by party political action. To be sure Haiti has an amazing system of communication, by means of drums which spread news rapidly to the most remote mountain hamlets. But there is no means for discussing issues of public policy, and no disposition on the part of the political leaders to permit such discussion. Political controversy is apt to be violent, even though limited to a small minority, mostly in Port-au-Prince.

Yet in a way there is more cohesion in Haiti, as a state, than is to be found in most other Latin-American countries. The Haitian has one strongly held state-idea—the idea that his government must keep Haiti free, and that the people of Haiti must be shielded from any authority. The fact that Haiti is the only French-speaking Negro republic in the Americas is a matter of national pride. Haitian delegates, who speak English or Spanish well enough, insist in Pan-American gatherings that the proceedings be translated into French. French and African traditions constitute an important part of the Haitian state-idea. Yet no government in Haiti would last long if it should attempt to use force in changing the way of living of the individual peasant.

The rural Haitian supports the idea of a Negro republic; but more than anything he supports his own personal independence. He owns a little piece of land—not large enough to give him a good living, but easily large enough to give him contentment. He is in no mood to join a revolution or a crusade. One party is about as bad as another in charge of the government. It doesn't much matter as long as the government attends to its business and leaves the individual alone. Here is truly a unique society in the American hemisphere, and one that adds one more element of diversity to the already diverse American scene.

THE DOMINICAN REPUBLIC

The eastern two-thirds of Hispaniola is included in the territory of the Dominican Republic. On the Haitian side of the boundary more than four hundred people per square mile work to make a living on all but the steeper and drier areas. On the Dominican side about one hundred and sixty people per square mile have land to spare. The Dominicans are clustered in certain areas of concentrated settlement, and there are large parts of the country which are almost unoccupied. Naturally the Haitians look covetously eastward across the border.

Conditions in the Dominican Republic during World War I were no less chaotic than conditions in Haiti. In 1916 the Marines took control of the eastern part of the island. Order and security were established, roads and railroads were built, and a considerable increase in the production of export commodities took place. When the Marines left the Dominican Republic in 1924 they left the maintenance of internal order to a Marine-trained police force under the command of General Rafael Leonidas Trujillo Molina.

In 1930, having gone through the formality of an election, General Trujillo assumed the complete authority of a dictator. With the aid of the armed forces and a secret police he ran the Dominican Republic as his private property. Those who challenged his authority were promptly jailed and executed or exiled. He permitted no free elections, no discussion of public issues, no protection of the individual from arrest without warrant, no such thing as equality before the law. General Trujillo saw to it that there were no divided loyalties among the army officers. He gave the rural people security. But he also gained the loyalty of many Dominicans by formulating a powerful state-idea—the idea of a white country, in contrast to Negro Haiti. Fear of Haitian aggression outweighed fear of the arbitrary acts of the dictator.

Trujillo set his stamp on the Dominican Republic in many ways. Among other acts he renamed the old city of Santo Domingo (which was largely destroyed by a hurricane in 1930) Ciudad Trujillo. He named the highest peak in Hispaniola, Pico Trujillo. He saw to it that his relatives occupied the highest posts in the government. But he also undertook many important programs of economic development. He secured a considerable amount of foreign capital to invest in commercial production and increased the export of sugar, coffee, cacao, tobacco, vegetables, and certain manufactured items, such as chocolate candy. The Dominican Republic became the chief supplier of fresh foods and milk to the semi-arid island of Curaçao, the part of the Netherlands Antilles where much of Venezuela's oil is refined. He also devoted attention to the domestic food supply by increasing the production of maize, rice, beans, bananas, manioc, peanuts, and other things. He opened a part of the northern coast to immigrants from Europe.

These economic benefits had to be matched against the complete elimination of democracy. Many people in the United States looked at the relative security and order in the Dominican Republic, and its many evidences of economic growth, and felt that this situation was better than the chaos and confusion of an inexperienced people struggling toward responsible democracy. But there were many others, especially in Latin America, who looked on the Dominican Republic as a dark spot in the Hemisphere. The same division of opinion still exists despite Trujillo's assassination on May 30, 1961.

The Economic Situation

The economic situation in the Dominican Republic since the death of Trujillo has been protected from the inevitable decline of production accompanying political changes by foreign aid, including aid from the

Alliance for Progress. The chief export products remain the same: in 1961 sugar made up 42 percent of the value of all exports; coffee, 10 percent; sorghum, 8 percent; tobacco, 7 percent; bauxite, 7 percent. The leading purchasers of these exports were the United States and Great Britain, followed by the Netherlands, Germany, and Japan. The imports came from the United States (53 percent) and a variety of other countries. The political leaders and the owners of plantations continued to gain the most from the economic system, while the great majority of the people remained poor.

The Political Situation

The Dominican Republic since Trujillo has gone through a typical cycle of confusion. Efforts were made to establish a free democratic system. The first result was the appearance of many political parties displaying all shades of political opinion from extreme left to extreme right. As usual compromise among these parties proved most difficult and the extremists from both sides attempted to impose their policies by force. Democracy, which calls for compromise and the use of persuasion rather than force, ran into the solid fact that the Dominicans were not accustomed to such procedures. A freely elected president took office in 1963, representing a prodemocratic left of center party which was strongly anticommunist. The new president attempted to start a program of land redistribution in accordance with the policies of the Alliance for Progress. But he had been in office only a few months when he was removed by the army. It was clear that those with political power were not ready to relinquish this power to such an uncertain element as majority opinion.

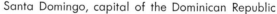

Santa Domingo, capital of the Dominican Republic

Ponce on the southern shore of Puerto Rico

PUERTO RICO

Something very important has happened in Puerto Rico. All over the world there are countries where a crowded population struggles hopelessly to make a bare living from antiquated agriculture. Each year the increase of people is greater than the increase of the gross national product, and each year the destruction of the resource base becomes more and more apparent. Enmeshed in a cycle of poverty, there seems no way out. Before 1940, Puerto Rico was such a country. When it became a possession of the United States as a result of the Spanish-American War it was already deep in the kind of rural poverty associated with the Spanish agrarian tradition. Then came the great sugar corporations, together with the medical services; with a high birth rate and a falling death rate, the net increase of population became alarming. In the 1930's Puerto Rico was described as "the greatest concentration of destitute people under the flag of the United States." But since 1940, Puerto Rico has provided the world with a demonstration of how such a situation can be changed, and how this can be done within the framework of the democratic system. Now thousands of visitors come to Puerto Rico from the underdeveloped countries of the world to see for themselves that a miracle has taken place.

The transformation of Puerto Rico, however, is no miracle. It is the result of inspired leadership and hard work. Here a Latin-American political leader, Luis Muñoz Marín, adopted a program of economic and social reform instead of seeking solutions in the traditional way through political change. Instead of demanding complete independence from the "Yankee imperialists," Muñoz laid before the Puerto Ricans an alternative. In 1952, with the approval of the Congress of the United States and with the support of more than 80 percent of the voters of Puerto Rico, this little island became the Commonwealth of Puerto Rico, voluntarily associated with the United States.[3] The more than two million Puerto Ricans maintain their citizenship in the United States, travel freely back and forth to the mainland, enjoy a position within the huge area of free commercial exchange, and at the same time are granted all the rights of self-government. A program of balanced economic development has not only improved the agricultural picture, but has also led to the rapid increase of manufacturing industry, until, in 1956, the value of manufactured products moved ahead of the value of agricultural products. The problems of poverty have not been solved, for Puerto Rico still has more than 670 people per square mile, almost 60 percent of them rural. But life for these people is no longer hopeless. They have an exciting new state-idea, a new reason for working hard.

The state-idea is made up of all the reasons why the Puerto Rican voters support their government. There is not just one simple reason, but a complex of ideas that make a people feel a love of country, or *patria*. As Muñoz Marín once said: "To the Puerto Rican, *patria* is the colors of the landscape, the change of the seasons, the smell of the earth wet with fresh rain, the voice of the streams, the crash of the ocean against the shore, the fruits, the songs, the habits of work and leisure, the typical dishes for special occasions and the meager ones for everyday, the flowers, the valleys, and the pathways. But even more than these things *patria* is the people: their way of life, spirit, folkways, customs, their ways of getting along with each other."[4] The Puerto Ricans can now look at the changes taking place in their land and say with feeling, *"Es bueno, y es nuestro"*—it is good, and it is ours.

The Course of Settlement

Puerto Rico was a paradise for the Indians, who took advantage of its productive lands to reap abundant harvests; and when the Spaniards saw a prosperous and contented Indian population, they thought they too had

[3] The relationship with the United States is expressed in Spanish: *Estado Libre Asociado.*

[4] Luis Muñoz Marin, "Development through Democracy," *The Annals of the American Academy of Political and Social Science,* Vol. 283, January 1953. pp. 1-8.

found a paradise. When the white men first settled on the island in 1508, there were probably between 80,000 and 100,000 native people living on it. But by 1515 the dreadful epidemics of imported diseases had reduced the Indians to not more than 4,000. As a result the plantations were abandoned and the search for precious metals given up. A few groups of colonists remained in San Juan and Ponce, and most of the mountainous interior of the island was used for the grazing of herds of cattle on larger estates.

In the eighteenth century, however, Puerto Rico, along with the other Spanish possessions in the Antilles, shared moderately in the sugar prosperity. Into Puerto Rico, as into Cuba and Santo Domingo, there was some importation of Negro slaves, and in certain localities the cultivation of sugar cane was commercially important. About 1790 the Spanish colonies produced roughly 14,000 metric tons of sugar, while the French colonies were producing over 90,000 tons and the English colonies nearly 80,000 tons.

In Puerto Rico the new sugar-cane plantations were mostly located on the lands of low relief near the coast, and in these areas the Negro population soon came to outnumber the whites. The poorer white people were forced out of the sugar districts, for free workers cannot compete in the same area with slaves. In the mountainous interior the "poor whites" settled as squatters on the vast, unfenced cattle range of the large landowners, and supported themselves with a shifting cultivation of maize and beans.

Between 1800 and 1825 the island colony received a considerable number of white immigrants to balance the increase of Negroes. Some of these came from Spain—from Gallegos, Asturia, and the Balearic Islands; no doubt they selected Puerto Rico because it was one of the few Spanish possessions in the New World in which the spirit of revolt from the mother country had not developed. A number of immigrants to Puerto Rico came from the other Spanish possessions in America from which they had been forced to flee because of their loyalty to the Spanish crown. Consequently, in spite of a continued increase of the Negroes through importation and high birth rate, the proportion of the Negroes and whites remained approximately the same: in 1802 the Negroes made up 52 percent of the population; in 1845 they made up 51 percent. In the latter year Puerto Rico counted 216,183 white people and 227,056 Negroes.

During the nineteenth century the colonies left to Spain in the Western Hemisphere suffered from neglect and poverty. The economic collapse resulting from the decline of sugar prosperity was of course greater in those islands where the prosperity had been greater; but places like Puerto Rico also felt the effects. The Spanish government, involved with difficulties of its own in Europe, could do little to help the remnants of its colonial empire. In the nearly four centuries of Spanish rule in Puerto Rico only 166 miles of road were built, and these mostly in the sugar-cane districts along the coast. The interior was all but inaccessible, and therefore was limited in its possibilities of commercial production to cattle that could be driven out to market over rough trails, or to some high-grade commodity that could command a price high enough to offset the costs of transportation by muleback. The large landowners introduced coffee, and made use of the poor-white settlers of the interior as tenants and sharecroppers. So fine was the aroma of the Puerto Rican coffee that it commanded a special place on the Spanish market, much as Haitian coffee commanded a special place on the French market. The transportation costs were so high, however, that even with the high prices the Puerto Rican coffee could bring, only a small net profit was left to the landowners, very little of which was passed on to the tenants.

Typical rural landscape of the tobacco district, showing tobacco sheds and denuded slopes

At the end of the nineteenth century Puerto Rico showed all the worst aspects of the Spanish colonial system. There was the usual concentration of land ownership and wealth in the hands of a very small group, who maintained positions of prestige and economic security by exploiting the much more numerous laboring population. In Puerto Rico these exploited rural workers were not Indians, and only in the sugar plantations along the coast were they Negro; in the interior the tenants were almost pure European. The majority of the people lived in isolation, illiterate and ignorant of the most elementary rules of hygiene, and producing barely enough food to maintain themselves. The political, social, and commercial life was centered in San Juan and involved the participation of only a small fraction of the total population. Such was the condition of Puerto Rico in 1898 when, largely as a result of forces and events elsewhere, this last remaining Spanish colony became a possession of the United States.

A Territorial Possession of the United States

The United States set to work right away to provide the new colony with all sorts of public works. By 1919 the mileage of all-weather roads had been increased from 166 to 739, and as a result the landowners even in the remote districts could bring products to market cheaply enough to make a substantial profit. Schools were established, and in some of them the newer techniques of agriculture and animal husbandry were taught. The proportion of people able to read and write was greatly increased, although even in 1950 it was still only 74 percent. Sanitary measures were undertaken, and certain diseases, such as yellow fever, were virtually stamped out. As a result, the death rate was rapidly reduced. With a high birth rate, the result was a steep upturn of the net rate of growth.

Little by little it became apparent that a purely agricultural economy could not provide support for such population densities, and that all efforts to increase the gross national product were being frustrated by the increase in the net rate of growth. In the period 1950 to 1955 the birth rate was 36, and the death rate had fallen to 8—lower than that of any other political unit in Latin America. The rising net rate of increase was largely the result of better hygiene and better diet for babies.

Meanwhile the economy of Puerto Rico had been built around the cultivation of sugar cane and the export of sugar. There were about 1,000,000 acres of land in Puerto Rico suitable for the cultivation of crops. Of these, 300,000 acres were held by four large sugar corporations, and although the total area of sugar cane in 1940 was only 76,000 acres, the remainder was held in reserve and used to pasture the oxen needed for transporting the cane. That meant that in 1940, when the population density was 544 people per square mile of total territory, there was less than half an acre per person for commercial crops other than cane and for the basic food crops. Furthermore, much of the remainder was former cane land that had been so badly eroded as to be almost worthless without expensive reconditioning. In spite of an increasing migration of people to New York City, the poverty of those remaining grew more and more serious.

Poverty in Puerto Rico was further complicated by the nature of the sugar-cane industry. As we have seen in other cane-producing countries such as Cuba, the need for laborers is spread very unevenly throughout the year. There is always a certain amount of work to be done in clearing new land, plowing, planting cane, weeding, and maintaining irrigation and drainage ditches; but this off-season work adds up to only a fraction of the labor demanded at the harvest season. For most of the people who were crowded around the sugar district there was no employment at all for several months each year, and then a period of employment and steady income during the harvest from January to June. When wages were paid they were higher in the cane plantations than elsewhere. As a result, in the period from 1900 to 1949 the coffee-growing district of the interior lost about 13 percent of its rural population; the cane areas in the same period increased 31 percent. It was estimated, about 1940, that the average annual income of a cane worker was approximately $250—all concentrated in a few months of the year.

Most of the people who worked part of the year for the sugar companies lived with their families in the poor districts of the cities, especially San Juan. They occupied shacks made from any available materials and crowded together without water, light, or streets. One of the densest slums in San Juan was *El Fanguito* (the mudhole) which covered two miles along the mud flats at the water's edge. The children of these workers from the United States were exposed to the movies and the advertisements. If on special occasions the daughters emerged from these districts dressed to imitate the Hollywood mode, with silk stockings and high heels, this was no indication that the family had enough to eat.

The Transformation of Puerto Rico

The transformation of Puerto Rico began in 1940. Since 1929, when the economy of the United States was shaken by the great depression, there had been little new capital investment in Puerto Rico, and production had been cut. Widespread destitution was causing considerable unrest. It was during the late 1930's that Muñoz Marín organized the Popular Democratic Party with the slogan "Bread, Land, and Liberty." The new party was successful in 1940, and has won every election since that date. In 1947 the Organic Act was changed to permit the Puerto Ricans

Housing development on outskirts of San Juan

to elect their own governor, and in 1948 Muñoz Marín was elected to this office.

The Improvement of Agriculture

When the Popular Democratic Party came into power in the Puerto Rican Congress in 1940, reforms of the system of land tenure were immediately started. An act passed by the Congress of the United States in 1917 provided that no corporation might possess more than 500 acres of land, but this act had never been enforced. In 1940, about a third of all the arable land was owned by four sugar corporations, and there were many privately-owned estates well over the legal limit. The Puerto Rico Land Act of 1941 gave the island government permission to acquire illegally-held land, and within the next ten years almost all of the holdings in excess of 500 acres were purchased from the corporations and from the private owners. On the land thus acquired, small cane farmers were established on what were called "Proportional Profit farms," where each worker was paid a share of the profits in proportion to the amount of work he had put in. There were also small owner-operated plantations, and a considerable increase of land where the tenants could raise food crops for their own use.

Land redistribution and the improvement of agriculture were not done blindly in Puerto Rico. The Puerto Rico Planning Board, of which the chairman was the geographer, Rafael Picó, undertook to provide guidance for more efficient use of the island's resources. A first step was an inventory and evaluation of the resource base and of the land use. This was the Puerto Rico Rural Land Classification Program under the direction of Clarence F. Jones and Rafael Picó.[5] Between September 1949 and August 1951 detailed maps (1:10,000) of land quality and use were made for the whole island. Supplied with this knowledge, various agencies of the government have started programs of rural improvement. The Division of Agricultural Economics, in cooperation with other government agencies, prepared a set of maps showing recommended land use; the Planning Board selected the best routes for road extension and for the location of residential and industrial sites. The maps are used for planning rural electrification programs and for developing a great variety of public utilities. The value of such a survey goes far beyond its cost, and is reflected in the increase of agricultural income and the decrease of the costs of moving farm products to market.

Manufacturing Industry

To be successful, programs of economic development must be applied to all aspects of a national economy. We have discussed numerous examples of industrial development not accompanied by a program of agricultural improvement. In each case the result was inflation. It is also easy to find examples of agricultural improvement without industrial development. But when antiquated and inefficient methods of agriculture are improved this inevitably means that fewer farmers are needed. A part of the explanation of the success of Puerto Rico in its efforts to do something about economic underdevelopment has been the program of industrialization.

The industrialization of Puerto Rico began with the construction by the government of a modern cement plant in 1939. This plant turns out building materials for the many new construction programs under way— for factories, highways, and low-cost housing. The government proceeded to build factories to be offered to manufacturing establishments as an inducement to move to Puerto Rico. Industries were also offered a ten-year exemption from the payment of taxes. The result was a rapid expansion of manufacturing as many companies on the mainland either

[5] Reported in Clarence F. Jones and others, *The Rural Land Classification Program of Puerto Rico*, Northwestern University Studies in Geography, No. 1, Evanston (Illinois), 1952; and Clarence F. Jones and Rafael Picó, *Symposium on the Geography of Puerto Rico*, Río Piedras (University of Puerto Rico Press), 1955.

moved to Puerto Rico or established branch plants there. Because the island contains no mineral resources (other than limestone, salt, and building stone) it was obviously inadvisable to insist first on the establishment of a steel industry. Instead the government planning agencies looked for a variety of light and medium industries that might either process the agricultural products of the island, or that might import raw materials and profit from the value added by manufacture. The great human resource of Puerto Rico—its dense population of willing workers, ready to be trained in special skills—was used as the basis for a sound industrial development.

The Economic Situation

The population, already greater in proportion to the arable area than in all but a very few countries of the world, is continuing to increase at an accelerating rate. Economic prosperity in a country with a high birth rate has the first effect of increasing the birth rate. The fact is that the Puerto Ricans like to have large families, and the happier they are with what is happening to their country the more children they want to produce to share in this happiness. So far the program of economic development has been racing against the rate of population increase, and not doing much better than staying even with it. The steady emigration of Puerto Ricans to New York helps to relieve the pressure somewhat, but is no permanent solution. Furthermore, the concentration of Puerto Ricans in New York City is beginning to set up a problem in social welfare. Eventually Puerto Rico must face the necessity of reducing the birth rate.

Meanwhile, however, the income per capita has increased enormously since 1940, and the rate of improvement has increased since 1952. Puerto Rico had a per capita income in 1962 of $511.

Almost all the things produced on the island are now sold, and almost all the items that are consumed are purchased. The old dominance of the subsistence economy has been ended, not just for the minority of wealthy people, but for everyone. The chief exports are raw and refined sugar, molasses, rum, leaf tobacco, needlework, and medicinal preparations. Some 90 percent of all exports go to the mainland, and from the mainland come most of the imports. Puerto Rico now benefits far more than it suffers from being included within the domestic economic system of the United States.

The Political Situation

Since the formation of the Popular Democratic Party by Muñoz Marín and its first victory at the polls in 1940, this new party has never lost an

Sabana Grande in southwestern Puerto Rico

election. The transformation of Puerto Rico has been accomplished by thoroughly democratic processes, with ample opportunity for the issues involved to be discussed publicly, and with the decision left to a plebiscite secretly recorded and honestly counted. Puerto Rico is a demonstration to the world that the problems of poverty and inequality, and of the denial of human dignity, which loom so large throughout Latin America, can be solved within the framework of democracy.

Muñoz Marín himself records the stages of his thinking about the political problem involved. At first it seemed that there were only two alternatives: to demand complete independence from the United States, or to accept inclusion within the United States as another State. Many people were inclined to think of independence as the only way to escape from the status of a dependent colony. But independence, even when granted with terms as favorable as those offered to the Philippines, meant eventual exclusion from the mainland market, and eventual restrictions on population migration. Clearly, Puerto Rico did not possess either the resources or the financial backing to support a purely domestic economic development. And in spite of the ill-effects of the period of administration by the United States between 1899 and 1948, the Puerto Ricans during this time had learned to place a higher value on economic development than do most of the other Latin Americans. To be incorporated as a State was not at all popular in Puerto Rico, and although there are some who think that this must eventually be done, this move would not yet receive the endorsement of anything like a majority of the people. The more they develop the feeling of loyalty to *patria,* the less they are likely to accept any plan of incorporation in the United States.

The third way, developed by Muñoz Marín, seems to permit the Puerto Ricans to both have their cake and eat it. The Commonwealth elects its own governor, (as it started doing in 1948); it remains essentially self-governing with regard to domestic matters; it has its own Constitution developed within the framework of the Constitution of the United States; the people enjoy all the rights of citizenship except that they may not vote for the president, and because they do not vote for president they pay no income tax on money earned in Puerto Rico; taxes collected in Puerto Rico remain in the Commonwealth treasury. Puerto Rico is a separate, self-governing country; yet it is an integral part of the United States. The present status of Puerto Rico was approved by the United States Congress and accepted by the people of Puerto Rico in 1952.

Puerto Rico is a better answer to the communists than all the rockets, satellites, or bombs that might be produced. That Puerto Rico has been successful in its transformation carries with it more meaning for the future of mankind than all the noisier events of the modern period on which the attention of the world's people is focused.

JAMAICA

In accordance with the policy of the British government the colonies throughout the world were prepared for independence as rapidly as circumstances permitted. A plan was developed to form the Federation of the West Indies, to include Jamaica, Trinidad, Barbados, the Windward Islands, the Leeward Islands, and the islands of Turks and Caicos. But so great were the differences among these widely scattered islands that no state-idea powerful enough to hold them together in a single political unit could be formulated. After a period of internal self-government, the Federation was abandoned in 1962 when Jamaica and Trinidad became independent.

Jamaica had the most productive economy of all the islands included in the Federation. Its population of 1,600,000 (estimated in 1962) is unevenly distributed. There are dense concentrations in the sugar-cane areas around Kingston near the southern coast; there are dense populations of small farmers raising bananas and other food crops in the basins of the interior. But much of the island is thinly populated. In addition to sugar, molasses, and rum, the traditional products of Jamaica, a large part of the income is now derived from the export of bauxite, and from the tourist business. In 1962 the gross national product per capita was $265, which was a little higher than that of the Dominican Republic.

The Jamaicans have certain distinctive characteristics that set them off from other Caribbean peoples. The population is more than 75 percent Negro, yet the Jamaica Negro is quite different from the Haitian Negro. Jamaicans have long been recognized for their willingness to work, and for their resourcefulness in solving their problems. Jamaica Negroes were used to plant bananas in Costa Rica, and to do the hard work of development in other Caribbean areas. They form a notably coherent state on the island of Jamaica.

TRINIDAD

Trinidad has been settled much more recently than Jamaica. For a long time the island was a possession of Spain, but since it was densely forested and contained few Indians and no gold, it was left almost unoccupied. In 1797 it was seized by the British, and remained a British colony until it was granted independence and membership in the Commonwealth in 1962.

Palm-studded Maracas Bay, a two-hour drive from Port of Spain

Workmen cutting crude asphalt from the pitch lake at La Brea

Trinidad has an important oil field, and also its famous Pitch Lake, from which natural asphalt has been taken for many years. The island is also a source of sugar, cacao, and coconuts. However, its gross national product per capita is only $185, which is much less than that of Jamaica. Unlike Jamaica, Trinidad does have a considerable area of unused land suitable for plantation crops.

The population of Trinidad is much more diverse than that of Jamaica. In 1962 the population was estimated at 900,000. Of these about 35 percent are Negro, 10 percent mulatto, 29 percent of unmixed European ancestry, and 26 percent East Indians (mostly Hindus from Calcutta). The East Indians were brought in after 1845 as contract laborers, and it was they who provided the workers to plant and produce sugar cane. After the contracts expired, some returned to India, but many elected to remain in Trinidad as small farmers cultivating their own properties.

In the years since World War II, Trinidad has had its own program of industrial development. The discovery of an important oil field led to the building of refineries. Now a petrochemical industry has been added. Other maufacturing industries include the processing of sugar and coconuts. Trinidad has followed the lead of Puerto Rico in granting a period free from taxes for companies that build factories on the island.

THE COLONIES OF THE ANTILLES

With some exceptions the colonies in the Antilles and the Guianas suffer from a lack of resources, insufficient development of existing resources, and dense populations. Most of the populations are Negro, descended from the Negro slaves who once worked on the sugar-cane plantations. On some islands sugar cane is still planted, but in order to reach an export market the sugar is made into a more valuable product, such as rum or molasses. The American Virgin Islands produce Bay Rum. The British Antilles produce, in addition to rum, such tropical specialties as limes, oranges, coconuts, bananas, nutmeg, arrowroot, and cacao. Perhaps a major hope for increasing the income of these islands is in the tourist business. The Bahamas are already a major resort area.

There are two exceptions to this rather gloomy picture of the Antillean Colonies. One is the Netherlands Antilles that lie off the Venezuelan coast. At Curaçao and Aruba there are large oil refineries, and Willemstadt, on Curaçao, derives a considerable income from the sale of tax-free goods to tourists.

The other exceptional island is Barbados. This small island was entirely unoccupied when the British first landed there in 1627, and it has never been anything but British. Its population is 95 percent Negro. The population density is about 1,400 people per square mile, which is among the densest concentrations of rural people anywhere in Latin America (Map 27, page 304).

The economy of Barbados has long been based on the planting of sugar cane, and for this use it is almost ideal. The island is an upraised portion of the South American continental shelf, capped with coral limestone. Except for a bit of hilly land in the middle of the northeast-facing part of the coast, where the underlying rocks appear from beneath the limestones, the surface consists of gently rolling land—none of it too steep for cane. The average annual rainfall is between 50 and 70 inches, but since the water drains off through underground caverns it must be brought to the surface by pumping. For a long time this was done by windmills, but now diesel motors generate electric power for this purpose. The highest elevation on the island is only 1,100 feet above sea level.

The land has become so valuable that now few people are wealthy enough to afford ownership. Formally all the land was divided into large private estates, and the minority of whites who were the owners were extraordinarily prosperous. In the modern period most of the land is owned by syndicates, for the inheritance taxes and the rising cost of labor have made individual ownership impossible. But the enormous contrast

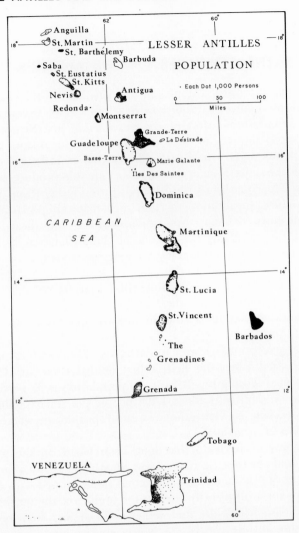

between the level of living of the well-to-do minority and the very poor workers remains as a dangerous social condition.

More than half of the workers on the island are employed by the cane plantations. During the harvest season, which lasts from four to six months, these workers receive a good wage; but for most of the year they remain unemployed. During this off-season the workers raise vegetables, and if they have a boat they engage in fishing. Some 1,500 workers are selected each year to go to the United States as temporary farm help, and these bring back with them much needed extra income.

The illiteracy rate is one of the lowest in the whole Western Hemisphere, and the Barbadoan schoolboys play cricket with such enthusiasm that this island contributes more than its share of major-league players.

The capital of Barbados is Bridgetown, located on the protected southwest side of the island. The whole metropolitan city, which extends beyond the political city limits, included a population of about 71,000 in 1955. The city workers are employed in the retail stores, banks, and hotels, and as civil servants. They make a poor living, but they enjoy a position of prestige not enjoyed by the rural workers. Increasing employment is offered in the expanding recreation business, for Barbados has earned an excellent reputation as a tourist area. Facilities for visitors include six expensive clubs, 12 luxury hotels, and a large number of less expensive hotels and guest houses. The hotel-owners are proud of the exceptional services they offer—it is a boast in Barbados that here, at least, the invasion of soft drinks has not diminished the popularity of rum punch.

THE GUIANA COLONIES

The first people to carry on a successful colonization of the Guiana Coast were the Dutch. The Spaniards had visited the area, searching always for El Dorado; but they found there no easy access to the interior, no large groups of friendly Indians with stores of accumulated treasure, and no known sources of gold. Only the forest stretched interminably back from the river banks covering a virtually uninhabited, and to the Spaniards uninhabitable, country. But the Dutch as early as 1596 established a post on the Essequibo as far inland as their ships could sail, and along the bank of the river around this post they attempted the planting of tobacco and sugar cane. Before long it was found that better conditions were offered along the immediate coast. Stabrock, today known as Georgetown, was settled early in the seventeenth century.

Meanwhile, the English had established a colony at Paramaribo, a short distance up the Surinam River, and in 1626 the French settled at Cayenne. These two groups of settlers, unlike the Dutch, were not familiar enough with the drainage of low coasts to undertake engineering works. The English sugar-cane plantations were restricted to the small spots of higher ground along the river; and the French took advantage of the one place along the coast where a low ridge borders the sea. In 1667 the Dutch, who thought they could develop the Surinam settlements as prosperous revenue-producing sugar lands, accepted this English colony in exchange for their foothold on Manhattan Island at the mouth of the Hudson River, which seemed to offer little possibility of quick financial returns. For various reasons none of the Guiana colonies prospered. Perhaps the chief of these reasons was the ease with which run-away slaves could find refuge in the forests of the interior. Compared with the islands in the Antilles, the coastal settlements of Guiana were decidedly unattractive. Nevertheless, they were valuable enough to cause the British to seize both the French and the Dutch colonies during the first decade of the nineteenth century. Finally the present division of the territory among the three European nations was agreed upon in a series of treaties between 1812 and 1817.

The Economic Situation

None of the Guiana colonies suffers from an excess of population. Quite the opposite. More workers are needed to clear the forests and create values out of land that still remains almost empty. Most of the settlements are strung along the immediate coast, where the usual tropical crops are grown—sugar cane, rice, and coconuts. But both British Guiana and Surinam are important as one of the world's major sources of bauxite. The ore is dug out with mechanical shovels, loaded on ships and exported to Europe, the United States, and Canada. The least amount of economic development is in French Guiana.

The Political Situation

British Guiana suffers from a difficult internal political conflict. The production of sugar cane there, as in Trinidad, was based on East Indian labor brought in under contract. Many elected to remain, so that today nearly half of the population is East Indian, practicing the Hindu religion. About a third of the population is Negro, and there are smaller numbers of Europeans, Chinese, and mixed races. Unfortunately the East Indians and the Negroes support different political parties. Unlike Trinidad, where ethnic differences are not expressed politically, in British Guiana bitterness and violence has broken out along racial and religious lines. Great Britain has been anxious to push this colony forward to independence as rapidly as possible, but has been unable to find a way to resolve the political differences.

The political conflict is complicated by the fact that the East Indian leader is an avowed communist. Although the establishment of a communist-controlled state in British Guiana would not be as serious as in Cuba—because of the isolation of Guiana from the other parts of the hemisphere—the British are reluctant to grant independence under the circumstances. If an autocratic state were established, and dominated by the East Indians, the position of the Negro minority would be unhappy indeed.

General Conclusion

Iliniza Mountain at dawn, Quito, Ecuador

CHAPTER TWELVE

Toward a
Latin-American
Policy

Latin America is not a new land. For more than four and a half centuries various European peoples have been at work ransacking the world that Columbus discovered, claiming and turning to a quick profit those resources stored over long periods of time by a bountiful nature—specifically the soils, the forests, and the minerals. El Dorado beckoned not only to the Spaniards and the Portuguese, but also to the British, the French, the Dutch, and more recently to the people of Germany, Italy, and the United States. All these groups have been at work in the lands of Latin America, each one guided by its own peculiar objectives, attitudes, and technical abilities. In the course of the centuries many of the now empty parts of Latin America have been searched, ransacked, and abandoned.

In this, the second half of the twentieth century, no part of the world is going through so rapid a process of change as is Latin America. Both of the great revolutions of human living—the Industrial Revolution, and the Democratic Revolution—are sweeping over Latin America, changing a preindustrial society into something quite new. The common man, long submerged economically and politically, accustomed to clinging to the hope of human dignity after death through the intercession of the Catholic Church, is now emerging into a new world. To him it is a world full of opportunities and hopes, yet also full of half-understood demons ready to frustrate his efforts. He has learned from bitter experience to trust no one: he wants the freedom to make his own society, in which his own concept of human dignity can be achieved on this earth. To him economic well-being is a matter of small consequence compared with the kind of social well-being that is built in accordance with his own fundamental concepts.'He can repeat with the deepest feeling the words of the Cuban revolutionary leader, José Martí, who said, *"Nuestro vino es agrio, pero es nuestro vino."* The outsider who does not comprehend this attitude, this passionate desire to drink one's own wine however bitter, does not comprehend the profound changes now going on in Latin America.

But Latin America is by no means all alike. Anyone who has followed, chapter by chapter, the contrasts and unique conditions described in this book, must appreciate the reality of the differences that distinguish one place from another. Latin America, in fact, is composed of many different kinds of land, with a great variety of resources, some of them superlative, and is occupied by an extraordinary variety of peoples, with varied traditions and languages. The population of Latin America is very un-evenly distributed in numerous isolated clusters, separated by large areas of only scantily occupied territory. Each of these clusters of people possesses its own peculiar individuality; each area of concentrated settle-ment differs from the others in the racial composition of the inhabitants, in the forms of economy, even in the attitudes toward life and in the objectives which the people set up as worth striving to reach. And in each of these areas the problems of living must be faced in the presence of a unique combination of the elements of the physical land. The general theme of diversity is illustrated again and again—not only by comparison between different countries, or between different areas of settlement, but also by the contrasts which separate the people occupying the land to-gether in specific areas. There are no short cuts, no simple generaliza-tions of wide application, which lead to a quick understanding of Latin America or of Latin Americans as a whole.

The Struggle to Establish Order

The struggle to establish order among diverse and discordant elements takes many different forms in Latin America. Such a struggle is not limited to the peoples of South and Middle America, for in any country, or any society, a continued effort is necessary to establish and main-tain coherence and order. A society which assumes that such effort is unnecessary lies in grave danger of disruption at the first signs of stress. The maintenance of order is one of the objectives of government, one of the objectives of education, one of the objectives of religion. But in many parts of Latin America the racial and cultural elements which have been combined are so fundamentally divergent that to gain some kind of coherence, some kind of common objective in which a substantial major-ity of the inhabitants can enjoy a real participation, seems all but im-possible. Yet in some countries, such as Mexico for example, the impossible is being accomplished.

Let us be quite clear about this concept of order and national co-herence. All the countries of Latin America started out with negative state-ideas, supported primarily by the minority of politically powerful people. The struggle to establish order is involved with the formulation of a positive state-idea—that is, a body of traditions and principles to which a majority of the citizens of the state give their allegiance. In any politically organized area there are forces of disintegration that tend to disrupt the state; but if the state is workable, or viable, the forces of integration must be stronger than those which lead to disruption. The forces of integration that bind a state together, that give it order and coherence, constitute the state-idea. The kind of order that is imposed by force may seem to the superficial observer to have achieved its purpose. The kind of order that existed in Venezuela under Gómez or Pérez Jiménez, or in Mexico under Díaz, or in Argentina under Perón, or in the Dominican Republic under Trujillo, or in Cuba under Batista or Castro, is not real order. The longer this kind of order is imposed by strong central authority the greater is the explosion when pent-up disunity is released. The kind of order that brings true national coherence is based on the true aspirations of the people.

The struggle to establish order is a process that takes different forms in the specific context of particular places. Each habitat, each physical land, provides a part of the context and guarantees diversity in the results of this struggle. The nature, size, and rate of growth of the population, and the social characteristics of the population, are another part of the context. And then there is the relationship existing between people and the land. In most parts of Latin America the population is still predominantly rural and the economy is agricultural: the nature of the agricultural base is a part of the context. And all over Latin America the old order, such as it was, is in process of change in the face of the impact of the two great revolutions: the Industrial Revolution, and the Democratic Revolution. We need to review the situation in Latin America with respect to these four aspects: population; the agricultural base; the technological changes brought by the Industrial Revolution; and the fundamental social changes brought by the Democratic Revolution. Finally, we should re-examine the meaning of all this with respect to the Inter-American system and consider what the situation in Latin America may mean to the United States.

Population Problems[1]

Latin America is still very thinly settled. On 15 percent of the world's inhabited areas there is less than 7 percent of the world's population. There are, to be sure, certain areas of great density, where population pressure is so great that programs of economic development are difficult

[1] See the symposium on population problems in the Western Hemisphere in Kingsley Davis (ed), "A Crowding Hemisphere: Population Change in the Americas," *The Annals of the American Academy of Political and Social Science,* Vol. 316, 1958, pp. 1-136.

to carry out. Such is the situation in most parts of the Antilles, and in countries such as El Salvador. On the other hand there are many places, such as the Amazon Basin, where programs of economic development are frustrated by lack of people. The pattern of population clusters, of areas of concentrated settlement each built around an urban core, and of empty country between the clusters, still prevails after more than four centuries of settlement. What is the significance of this peculiarity of Latin-American population geography?

The Increase of Population

In the period since 1920, the population of Latin America has been increasing faster than that of any other major region of the world. In fact the population of the whole American hemisphere has grown faster than the world average. Anglo-America (the United States and Canada) has grown faster than the average rate of growth for those regions of the world that are described as economically developed. Latin America has grown faster than any other region of the world. The table shows the relative positions of these two parts of the Western Hemisphere. The United Nations demographers forecast that these rates of increase will

RATE OF POPULATION INCREASE BY REGIONS*
1920–1960

Regions	Percentage Gain 1920–1960
Underdeveloped Regions	70.5
Latin America	126.3
Asia (excluding Japan)	68.4
Africa	67.6
Pacific Islands	63.6
Southern Europe	42.6
Developed Regions	41.1
Australia-New Zealand	92.4
Japan	71.7
Anglo-America	68.4
U.S.S.R.	36.1
Northwest and Central Europe	23.3

* *United Nations Demographic Yearbook*, quoted by Kingsley Davis, *op. cit.*

not decline in the decades immediately ahead, and that by the year 2000 the total population of Latin America will have increased from about 206 million in 1960 to about 593 million. In that same period the population of Anglo-America, according to this forecast, will have grown from 197 million in 1960 to 312 million. A very large part of this increase will be in the tropical parts of Latin America. The table presents this forecast broken down into subregions.

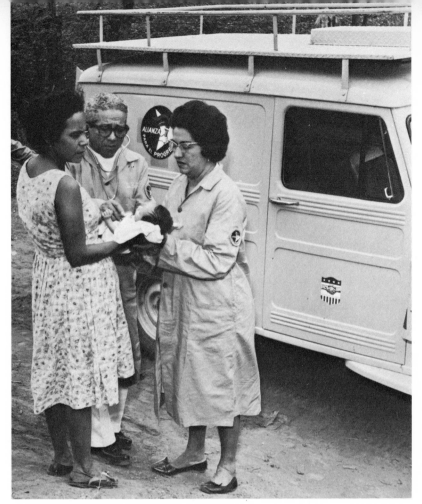

Saving babies has produced a population explosion—not yet matched by increased supply of food

MEDIUM ESTIMATES OF FUTURE POPULATION BY SUBREGIONS*

(Population in millions)

Regions	1960	1975	2000
Central America	46.3	72.3	150.0
The Antilles	19.6	27.1	48.0
Low-Latitude South America	107.0	163.0	339.0
Middle-Latitude South America	32.9	41.7	55.8
Latin America as a whole	205.8	304.1	592.8

* Population Branch, United Nations, quoted by Kingsley Davis, *op. cit.*

The demographers point out that the causes of this rapid rate of population increase are fundamentally different in Anglo-America and in Latin America. In Anglo-America changes in the rate of increase are due to changes in the fertility, or in the production of children. In Latin America, on the other hand, the fertility remains high, but the rapid jump in the rate of increase is due to an increasingly rapid lowering of the death rate. During the 1920's the death rate in eleven Latin-American countries for which adequate data exist was lowered by 6 percent; but during the period from 1945 to 1954 the death rate was lowered by 17.1 percent. With a continued high rate of reproduction the result is a "population explosion."

This decrease of the death rate has taken place in all parts of Latin America, and not only in the economically most advanced areas. This means that the drop in the death rate is not related to a rise in the level of living. The table compares death rates in the late 1930's with those in the mid-1950's in areas where data are considered to be comparable. In other parts of the world where the industrial society has developed, the rise in the economic well-being of the people, the better diet, better housing conditions, higher rate of literacy, all accompanied the decline in death rates. But in Latin America since World War II, the decline in the death rate has taken place in countries where the level of living is still low.

CRUDE DEATH RATES IN SELECTED AREAS*
Late 1930's and mid-1950's (Deaths per 1,000)

Area	Late 1930's	Mid-1950's
Mexico	23	13
Chile	24	12
Costa Rica	20	10
Jamaica	17	11
British Guiana	22	12
Trinidad and Tobago	17	10
Puerto Rico	19	7
Argentina	12	8
Venezuela	18	10
El Salvador	21	14
Guatemala	27	20
Barbados	21	12

* United Nations sources, quote in Kingsley Davis, *op. cit.*

The drop in the death rate has been the result of vigorous programs of health improvement, carried out in part with the assistance of such Inter-American agencies as the Pan American Sanitary Bureau. It is estimated, for example, that about 80 percent of the people of Latin America live in areas where malaria used to be prevalent. In the period since 1945 the widespread use of DDT and other insecticides, and the organization of mosquito-control programs has virtually eliminated malaria from large parts of tropical America. And the health programs have not been aimed at malaria alone: the smallpox cases in Latin America were cut down by half between the late 1940's and the 1950's; yellow fever is no longer a leading cause of death; there has been a significant decline in hookworm; and yaws, a crippling disease which formerly was present among a majority of the people of Haiti, has now been brought under control. The use of antibiotics has saved lives in cases that once would have been considered hopeless. In addition, the program of decreasing the rate of illiteracy now makes it possible to tell more people about the elementary rules of hygiene. It is true that in the 1960's gastro-intestinal diseases, due to bad hygiene, are the chief cause of death; but the continued programs of public education will eventually also decrease these maladies.

The result is that fertility remains very high—among the highest in the world—and deaths are in process of being enormously reduced. The net rate of increase, everywhere in Latin America, is rapidly rising.

Population Movement to Empty Areas

A detailed examination of population maps suggests that, with a few exceptions, the Latin-American countries still have large thinly populated areas within the national territories. There are two ways in which these empty areas might be settled. One is through the pioneer expansion of the frontiers of settlement around the margins of the clusters. The other is through the establishment of immigrant colonists.

Expanding Settlement.   We have seen that up to World War II there were only four regions in the mainland parts of Latin America in which there were frontiers of expanding settlement that were not hollow ones. These were not areas to which immigrants came in large numbers. They were areas where pioneers moved out from a nucleus of concentrated settlement without reducing the density of population in the center. These four areas include: (1) the highlands of Costa Rica; (2) the highlands of Antioquia in Colombia; (3) Middle Chile; and (4) the three southern states of Brazil. We can also find examples of the outward movement of a frontier of settlement around an area into which immigrants from overseas were pouring, as in the case of the Argentine Humid Pampa. And we can see examples of hollow frontiers, where a wave of pioneer expansion was succeeded, in the older settled area behind the frontier, by a decrease of the population. We can also find many clusters of people which have covered essentially the same areas since they were first established by Spaniards or Portuguese in the sixteenth century. In Brazil, new areas of concentrated settlement have been developed since the earliest ones, but the frontiers that have appeared around the margins have been hollow ones except in the southern states.

What characteristics do the four areas of expanding settlement have in common? First, it is clear that all of them have a high net rate of population increase in the original nuclei, and that this high net rate of growth existed long before the general rise in net growth rates which followed World War II. But there are other clusters of people with substantial growth rates that have not expanded in area. Second, in every case the system of land tenure is that of small owner-operators, not of large estates with tenant workers. But there are examples of small-farmer settlements that have stagnated, or even lost population. The third common characteristic is that the pioneer zone into which expansion of settlement has taken place is connected to a market by adequate means of transportation. When all three of these characteristics are combined, the result has been pioneer expansion.

Immigration. Since the end of the Spanish and Portuguese colonial periods, there has been some immigration of new European settlers into parts of Latin America. Richard Robbins estimates that since 1800 some 52 million Europeans have migrated to the Americas.[2] Of these, nearly 40 million came to the United States, and 12 million to Latin America. Of the 12 million immigrants to Latin America, about 4 million were of Spanish descent, over 4 million were Italian, and about 2 million were Portuguese. There were also smaller groups of Germans, Poles, and other Europeans. Among the other immigrants there have been Japanese, Chinese, and Syrians; and in certain areas East Indians and Javanese are of chief importance. There have also been large numbers of Negroes from Africa whose immigration to the Americas was forced. The resulting ethnic arrangements are shown on Maps 5 and 6.

As we have seen, the greater part of the immigration went to the Humid Pampa of Argentina and to the coffee region of São Paulo in Brazil. The southern states of Brazil were also occupied by European colonies—German, Italian, Polish, and others. In the period since World War II, more than two and a half million Europeans have moved to the Americas, but more than 60 percent of them have gone to Anglo-America. Of those who have gone to Latin America, the largest numbers have gone to Argentina, Brazil, and Venezuela. Especially in Brazil and Venezuela government policy with respect to the immigrants has been to direct them to the empty areas. The attempt has been made to stimulate an expansion of settlement into thinly peopled areas, such as the *campo cerrado* of interior Brazil, or the Orinoco Llanos, by first placing in these areas colonies of European farmers, many of them from Eastern Europe, whose homes and farms were lost during the disruption of World War II and the subsequent communist take-over. The results have not been encouraging. After the first feeling of security wears off, the immigrants yield to the lure of jobs and of a better living in the cities.

[2]In Kingsley Davis, *op cit.,* p. 103.

We need to ask a few simple questions. What makes a person willing to leave his homeland to settle permanently in another land? In only a few cases has the basic motive been to escape persecution or to build a new community free from the conflicts and restrictions of the old world. The Mormons built a community on such a basis in the United States. In Latin America, Mennonite colonists, as in the Paraguayan Chaco, have been motivated by the desire for freedom from outside interference. But the overwhelming majority of people who move from one place to another of their own free will do so for the purpose of economic gain—to make a better living, to take advantage of a larger number and variety of opportunities for employment. In the modern world where are the greatest opportunities for employment? Surely not in the thinly populated backlands of Latin America.

Population Movement to the Cities

The fact is that in Latin America the thinly peopled areas are becoming more thinly peopled, and the areas of concentrated settlement are becoming denser. It is in the cities, or in the densely populated areas around the cities, that one finds the greatest number and variety of economic opportunities. It is in the largest city, the primate city, that one finds the greatest variety of opportunities. It is to the city, and if possible to the largest city, that the countryman wants to go. And the more the rural farm worker earns the more he learns, the more he widens the horizons of his knowledge, the more he wants to move into the urban centers. This trend toward increased urbanization, taking people away from the empty areas toward the more densely crowded spots, is a basic fact. The table shows the population and the proportion of the total population of the country in the nine largest metropolitan areas or conurbations of Latin America at two dates.

GROWTH OF LARGE METROPOLITAN AREAS*

City	Year	Population	Proportion of national Population	Year	Population	Proportion of national population
Buenos Aires	1895	767,085	19.0	1955	5,617,300	29.4
Mexico City	1900	541,516	4.0	1955	4,005,000	13.0
Rio de Janeiro	1900	744,998	4.3	1955	3,625,000	6.2
São Paulo	1900	239,820	1.4	1955	3,325,000	5.7
Santiago	1907	332,724	10.3	1952	1,387,600	22.4
Habana	1899	308,067	19.6	1953	1,240,400	21.4
Lima	1876	155,486	5.8	1955	1,169,000	12.4
Caracas	1920	118,312	4.8	1955	967,200	16.5
Bogotá	1905	100,000	2.3	1955	903,200	7.1

* From Harley L. Browning, in Kingsley Davis, op. cit., p. 113.

A study of the population patterns of Latin America shows that there is an urban core in the midst of each separate cluster of people, and that in most cases there is only one such central city. Because the clusters have generally remained separate, the service areas of the central cities usually do not overlap with those of other cities. Usually, also, each country has a primate city which is many times larger than any other city in the country. Montevideo is seventeen times the size of Uruguay's second city. Buenos Aires is nearly nine times the size of the second city. In only two countries are there two cities of nearly equal size: in Brazil and Ecuador.

The concentration of people in cities is one of the distinguishing traits of the industrial society. The proportion of the people of a country employed in agriculture, and the proportion of people in large cities may be used as rough indices of the degree of economic development. In Latin America, however, there are certain peculiarities that need to be noted. In the urbanized societies of Western Europe, of Anglo-America, and of Australia and New Zealand, employment in manufacturing industry was the first reason for city growth. Capital was invested in factories and machines, and the new jobs that became available after the Industrial Revolution were in these factories. For each person employed in a "basic industry"—that is, an industry that sends its products outside of the community in which it is located—there are now at least two employed in service occupations—that is, as professional people, teachers, lawyers, police, and many others. The industries appeared first and then led to the multiplication of service employment. But in Latin-American cities the service occupations appeared first, before the rapid increase of jobs in manufacturing. The Economic Commission for Latin America, an agency of the United Nations, concludes that the "urban population appears overburdened with services, whose development is apparently out of proportion to existent manufacturing activities."[3] It is for this reason that many of the cities in Latin America seem to be less well served by lines of transportation than cities of comparable size in Western Europe or Anglo-America.

In this situation we may well ask whether the rapid net rate of population growth in Latin America will aid or retard the economic development.

Problems of Agricultural Development

Most of the people of Latin America still live in rural areas. The processes of urbanization and industrialization have only recently started to work, and only in a few of the countries have they gone on rapidly, thus increasing the contrasts among the countries. In only five countries is the proportion of the total working force employed in agriculture less

[3] Harley L. Browning, in Kingsley Davis, *op. cit.*, p. 117.

than 40 percent: these countries are Argentina, Chile, Puerto Rico, Trinidad, and Uruguay. In Argentina only 25 percent of the workers are in agriculture. In contrast over 80 percent of the Haitians are farmers, and there are many countries with more than 60 percent employed in agriculture. Before World War II, not only were more than 65 percent of the working people of Latin America employed in agriculture, but a very large proportion of these rural people consumed almost nothing that they did not themselves produce, and they produced almost nothing for sale to others. In other words a very large proportion of the people of Latin America were then, and still are, largely outside of the economic system of buying and selling. The agriculture is inadequate for the support of these people. The improvement in health that has been made results, as we have seen, from disease and insect control rather than from building strength to resist disease through proper diet. The undernourishment in Latin America is by no means so great as in the Oriental world; but it is still great enough so that we can report that a very large proportion of the people are suffering from hunger and sickness, and from the apathy produced by these conditions.

The Agrarian Tradition

Throughout the greater part of Latin America the agrarian tradition, although challenged, still persists. The large land property, except in certain areas, is still the chief form of land tenure. On the large property the owner makes use of the most accessible or the potentially most productive part of the land to raise something for sale. Perhaps it is coffee, perhaps sugar cane, or cacao, or cotton—whatever is customary and whatever is made possible by the nature of the soil and climate. But very often we find that the large landowner is chiefly interested in cattle, horses, or sheep. He makes use of the most productive land for pasture or for feed crops. In this system the land that is too remote or too poor to be developed by the owner is often made available for the subsistence farms of the tenants. The crop which occupies more area than all other crops combined in most of the countries is maize. Maize, rice, and beans are grown, not in the places best suited to them, but on land too poor for other uses. The result is that yields per acre are every low, and the rate of land destruction through erosion is appalling. Large areas of very thinly peopled land are severely damaged through the practice of shifting cultivation (land rotation), and the gradual destruction of the forest cover. When the forest is removed from steep slopes and watersheds the rain runs off rapidly, leaving a relatively small proportion of the total fall to sink into the ground. The soil is carried downhill into the streams, which turn brown. Then in the intervals between rains the land is parched and the streams dry up. The alternation of flood and drought is, in many places, a man-made phenomenon. Under tropical conditions, too, the removal of the forest has the effect of killing soil bacteria which normally perform the function of creating humus. Organic matter that falls on the surface dries up before it is worked into the soil. The progressive impoverishment of the soil over vast areas that look empty on the population map is one of the unexpected findings of direct field observation in many parts of Latin America.

The result is what we may call the cycle of poverty. The ordinary subsistence farmer, trying to make a bare living on land he does not own, is too poor, and probably also too ignorant, to make use of the modern technology in land use. Since he cannot increase his production of food, or even gain a small surplus for sale, he cannot escape from his condition of poverty. He is forced to accept additional employment for miserable wages on the property of the landowner; but his wages are in many cases not enough to pay off his debts. Even if he knows that he should not try to grow maize on steep slopes, there is nothing else he can do.

Modern Agricultural Technology

The technology exists to change all this. Ultimately the population of any area will continue to grow until it is limited by the amount of food that can be grown or shipped in. But within a given habitat (soil, slope, water, climate) the amount of food that can be produced is determined by the technology, or skill of the people. In the United States since World War II there has been an extraordinary increase in productivity per farmer. Whereas in the 1930's a farm worker could raise enough food to feed himself and ten other people, by 1960 the same worker could raise enough to feed himself and twenty-seven others. This increased productivity has resulted from the more efficient use of machinery, from better plants (such as hybrid corn), from animals bred to gain weight faster on less feed, or to yield more milk on less feed. It has come as a result of the new insecticides and soil conditioners, the new fertilizers, and the new methods of soil conservation. Now the farmers in the United States can raise 10,800 vegetable calories per day. Because of the dietary traditions of the people of the United States, most of the crops are fed to livestock. From domestic animals only about 10 percent of the calories are returned in the form of meat, milk, and eggs. If the people of the United States shifted from these foods to cereals, a vastly larger population might be supported.

But in Latin America how are these new techniques to be adopted? Only in a few cases, such as those reported in São Paulo, are the large landowners interested in an improved use of the land. And the tenant farmers, or owners of small farms, are either too ignorant or too poor, or both, to adopt these methods. Nelson Rockefeller has financed several organizations with the purpose of improving agriculture, and in a few places the results have been encouraging—as in São Paulo or in Venezuela. But tradition, ignorance, and poverty change but slowly.

The widespread adoption of modern agricultural technology in Latin America would have two important results. First the use of machinery would require the abandonment of the steeper slopes. Steep slopes could be used for tree crops, such as coffee; but not for maize, upland rice, tobacco, cotton, or sugar cane. The amount of land suitable for crop cultivation would be enormously reduced in countries like Brazil, where a very large proportion of the total area is hilly. It might be presumed that agriculture would concentrate in the best-suited and most accessible places, and that large areas would be reforested. Plans to encourage the pioneer settlement of remote areas are out-of-date in the twentieth century.

The second result would be an acceleration of the movement of rural people into the cities. For wherever in the world modern agriculture has been adopted, the result has been that the number of people employed in farming is decreased. One man with a tractor-drawn plow can do the work of hundreds of workers with hoes and machetes. As long as the men with hoes are not paid very much, they can do the work more cheaply than the tractor. But if they are paid a living wage, the tractor is cheaper.

And so two parts of the problem become clear. In the light of modern understandings it is quite inexcusable to undertake a health and medical program in an underdeveloped country without at the same time making plans to increase the available supply of food. And it is important to remember that in Mexico, using great energy and directing skill, the production of food over a twenty-year period was increased by 80 percent. The increase of population, resulting from health programs already started, has just about equalled the increase of food production. To start a health program irresponsibly, without thinking of the sources of food, is to invite disaster. And the second part of the problem is the resulting movement of surplus farmers away from the rural areas into the cities. Whoever plans a program of modern agriculture must also think of ways to increase the number of job opportunities in nonagricultural pursuits.

The Industrial Revolution

The Industrial Revolution is in process of sweeping over Latin America. If contrasts existed before between one part of a country and another, the contrasts developed by these basic changes in technology and in economic attitudes are vastly greater. There has always been a different quality to life in the cities and in the country; but in the new industrial cities the contrasts with the older order of things are more fundamental and more obvious.

The Industrial Revolution, which started in the eighteenth century around the shores of the North Sea, has developed as it spread from this place of origin. Fundamentally it means the change from the use of human or animal muscles, wind or falling water, to the use of controlled inanimate power. As one writer puts it, "man ceases to be a lifter and mover, and becomes, rather, a stopper and starter of complex machinery." Machines and automation enormously increase the production per worker; and increased production enormously increases the need for raw materials. But there are other changes associated with the changes in technology. The population, which could once be characterized as illiterate, rural, and agrarian now becomes literate, urban, and industrial. The growth of large conurbations, and the increase of the proportion of the total population concentrated in cities, are phenomena associated with the Industrial Revolution. And in Anglo-America the Industrial Revolution has meant the organization of industry for high-volume production, with high-volume sales and low profit per sale. This is in the strongest possible contrast with the preindustrial concept of low-volume production and sales, and large profit per sale. In Anglo-America the Industrial Revolution has meant the wide participation of the people in the increased productivity resulting from technological change.

Manufacturing Industries

Now the Industrial Revolution is sweeping over Latin America, creating greater contrasts between rich and poor, between industrial and preindustrial, than ever existed before. In all parts of the underdeveloped world the favorite prescription for rapid remedial action is industrialization. It is estimated that, to shift one worker from agriculture to industry, requires a capital investment of more than $10,000 (primarily for machinery which must be imported). Since Latin-American countries do not have sufficient capital, there is a clear need for foreign investment and foreign aid. As a result of foreign private and government investment, manufacturing industries have appeared in many parts of Latin America —notably in São Paulo and Rio de Janeiro, Buenos Aires, Mexico City, Santiago, Caracas, and Medellín. Traditionally, there have been only two classes: the wealthy landowners and the very poor workers. The hope is that where manufacturing industry becomes established a prosperous middle class will make its appearance, to fill the gap between these two traditional classes.

A major problem in Latin America today stems from the fact that the establishment of manufacturing industries does not automatically create a middle class. If the owners of the new industries subscribe to the principle of large-volume production, low profit per sale, they attempt to enlarge the number of sales by lowering the price of their product. According to Anglo-American economic theory each drop in the price brings in an increasing number of new purchasers. But in Latin America, where the middle-income groups have not yet been built up, a drop in the price fails to bring in more customers. As a result manufacturers attempt to pay the cost of their new machinery by increasing prices. Furthermore, in many industrial countries, not only in Latin America, manufacturers tend to think of wages as solely a production cost, and therefore that wages should be kept as low as possible. In countries where middle-income groups scarcely exist between the very wealthy and the very poor, this attitude toward wages has long-term disastrous effects. If manufacturers should think of wages as an investment in market expansion, the possibilities of rapid economic development would be much brighter. Long-term thinking of this sort is not at all common in countries where the returns on invested money sometimes run as high as 50 percent per year. This is an example of how preindustrial attitudes can frustrate or delay the spread of the Industrial Revolution.

As the economist Simon G. Hanson puts it, "We must pose the simple question whether in Latin America the primary motivation is more and cheaper goods or whether it is another attempt to create a privileged position for a small group rivalling that of the traditional landowning group."[4]

Capital and Resources

Whatever may be the motives, industrial development cannot take place without capital, raw materials, and labor. Potentially, at least, there is an abundance of labor—and experience throughout Latin America contradicts the old idea that Latin Americans cannot be trained for mechanical or industrial work. But Latin America is handicapped by lack of domestic capital and inadequacy of raw materials.

The formation of capital in Latin America, as in all underdeveloped countries, is slow. It is important to note that only recently have wealthy people in Latin America invested money in domestic industries. In the traditional agrarian society money was spent for luxuries, for travel and education, or for investment abroad. In fact, in many Latin-American countries the landowner who entered into business lost prestige. The Chilean landowners have for a long time been different in this respect, for they did not hesitate to become the owners of manufacturing plants or to enter into business careers. In Brazil, however, the chief industrial owners are not Portuguese-Brazilians, but rather people of Italian ancestry. In each of the countries this reluctance to invest money in industry is gradually decreasing.

Economic development, for the most part, has been dependent on foreign investments. And foreign investment has come from different sources and been applied to different parts of Latin America. The period

[4] Simon G. Hanson, *Economic Development in Latin America . . .* , Washington, D.C. (Inter-American Affairs Press), 1951.

from 1880 to 1914 saw the first important movement of new capital from outside. This was almost exclusively British capital, and a very large proportion of it was invested in Argentina. The British built railroads, packing plants, port facilities, sugar refineries, and a variety of manufacturing plants. By the beginning of World War I, Argentina had become by far the leading country of Latin America in its economic development. It had, by that time, about half of all the production of goods and services in all of Latin America. It was the one important trading country. Its economy was closely tied to that of Great Britain, for Britain absorbed Argentine exports of meat, wheat, maize, and linseed, and supplied the coal on which Argentina was dependent. Most of Argentina's supply of wheat flour was imported from Great Britain, as were also textiles and a variety of other manufactured products. This economic relationship formed almost the perfect example of nineteenth-century ideas of international trade. The industrial development was in Great Britain, and British merchants and manufacturers were the ones who profited most from the import of raw materials and the exports of manufactured goods. British coal provided cargoes for the British ships on the outward voyages, and as Argentina developed it became more and more dependent on the imports of coal. On the return voyage the ships carried wheat and meat. In Argentina the people who gained the most were the large landowners and the political leaders; but the immigrant tenants at that time were better off than they had ever been before. World War I rudely shattered this apparently perfect arrangement, and for the first time the Argentines appreciated the need for developing their own manufacturing industries.

Investments in Latin America from the United States were, at first, exclusively in the mining industries. Chilean copper and nitrate, Peruvian copper, Mexican copper—these were the first raw materials to interest the people of the United States. By the end of the nineteenth century, however, investment of United States capital in such tropical agricultural products as sugar and bananas had started. After World War I, the flow of United States capital into Latin-American economic development increased rapidly. Money was invested in mining, in tropical plantation crops in the Caribbean, in public utilities, and to a certain extent in manufacturing industries. But the largest volume of capital investment from the United States after 1920 went into the oil fields of Venezuela. Just as Argentina rose to preeminence in Latin America in the nineteenth century due to British investment, Venezuela achieved first place in income per capita in the middle of the twentieth century as a result of United States investments. Now, since 1950, United States investments in Mexico are producing a rapid economic development in that country—but under very different conditions from those prevailing in either Argentina or Venezuela.

At the beginning of 1957 the direct investments by private business in Latin America reached a total of $7,408,000,000. This represented 24.6 percent of all United States investments abroad (compared with 24.9 percent invested in Canada). Some 26 percent of all United States private investments in Latin America in 1957 were in the oil fields and refineries of Venezuela. The year 1957 was a peak year in new private investment, and the flow of new capital to Latin America declined after that.

In spite of this considerable flow of North American capital into Latin-American economic development up to 1957, it constituted only a fraction of what the Latin Americans needed. There were many undertakings that private business could not finance. In addition to the private investments, the United States government had loaned more than $2,000,000,-000 to Latin-American governments to support development projects. This was much less than the money sent to other parts of the world, and was the cause of some feeling of resentment among the Latin Americans.

The Alliance for Progress

In 1961 the pressures against the traditional economic, social, and political institutions in Latin America were at last given political expression. As more and more people gained the capacity to read and write, and especially as the proportion of sick people among the Latin-American populations was drastically reduced, the demand for a better living swelled to an irresistible tide. The better living meant more education, adequate food, clothing, and shelter, equal treatment before the law and an end to the inequities of special privilege. It meant the rising demand for popular participation in decisions of public policy. Adlai Stevenson called it "the revolution of rising expectations." Viewed from the perspective of historical geography it meant that Latin America in the 1960's was feeling the full impact of the Industrial Revolution and the Democratic Revolution.

The political expression of these pressures was incorporated in the Alliance for Progress—the *Alianza para Progreso*. In August, 1961, the representatives of nineteen of the American countries met at Punta del Este in Uruguay to work out the details of a program of mutual aid first named and outlined in the inaugural address of President John F. Kennedy. The program called for an effective attack on problems of poverty and inequity. The United States agreed to devote a considerable amount of financial support, but government support was to be supplemented by an increased flow of private capital. The major part of the effort was to be made by the Latin Americans themselves. One goal was to raise the gross national products per capita of the Latin-American countries by a minimum of 2.5 percent per year—which was then estimated to require the investment of some five or six billion dollars of new capital. Each country was to draw up its own plans for development. Each participating country was expected to take serious steps to adopt and enforce an equitable tax structure, and to carry out an effective program of land redistribution. Essentially the Alliance for Progress promotes revolutionary changes within the framework of a free society, to counteract the appeal of a communist revolution exported by violence from Cuba.

Of course, so revolutionary a program met resistance, and the first few years were disappointing to those who looked for immediate results. Many Latin Americans were critical because tangible results were few, and there was always the danger that, along with financial support, the United States would demand development in its own image. And there were many people in the United States who felt that the program was not bringing results comparable with the costs. Many business men could not see why they should be called on to finance Latin-American governments so that they could take over private business. By 1963 there was little real progress to report in the development of educational facilities: even in the cities only 56 percent of the children of school age actually went to any kind of school, and in the rural areas the proportion was much lower; half of those who started school dropped out before the end of the third grade. Among those of high school age only 15 percent were in school; only 3 percent of the young men and women went to college (compared with 35 percent in the United States). Yet there had been a drop in the rate of illiteracy in countries like Venezuela from 56 percent in 1959 to 18 percent in 1963.

But the program of the Alliance in some countries was so strongly resisted by the traditional political leaders that there were army coups overthrowing democratically elected governments. Such a reaction took place in the Dominican Republic, where Trujillo's regime had been overthrown and a government had been elected by ballot. Similar revolts took place in several other countries, where the armies took control of the governments that had been duly elected. In most of these cases it seemed that the programs of land redistribution and other fundamental changes were being pushed too rapidly.

In 1963 at a meeting in São Paulo, the representatives of the participating countries made certain revisions of the structure of the Alliance. Henceforth it was to be directed by an executive committee of eight, elected by the Inter-American Economic and Social Council of the Organization of American States. The United States was to have permanent representation on this committee but the Latin-American representatives would be rotated. The chairman was to be a Latin American. The new committee faced serious problems. The investment of private capital in Latin America had reached its peak in 1957 and since then had greatly decreased as more and more businesses were expropriated in Latin America. Furthermore, the well-to-do people in Latin America had so little confidence in their democratically controlled governments that there was a steady flow of capital out of Latin America and into the United States and Europe. It was proving difficult to explain that the alternative to a liberal revolution was a take-over by the Communist Party and a subsequent loss of the last vestiges of democracy. However, the communists were doing their best to make this clear to every one by the example of Cuba, and by a program of violence in Venezuela.

Commerce and the Common Markets

Before 1890, the United States carried on very little of its foreign commerce with Latin America. In that year, however, the first of the reciprocity treaties began to point the way to potential markets in the south. Shortly thereafter the results of the Spanish-American War and the opening of the Panama Canal placed the United States in a predominant position in the commerce of the Caribbean countries, and greatly increased North American interest in the more remote countries of South America. Yet, until the currents of world trade were disturbed by the international controls and subsidies of the 1930's and by World War II, the United States, a great industrial country, did most of its trading with the other great industrial countries of the world, notably those of Western Europe. If "other things" are anywhere near equal, the greatest volume of trade is between two highly industrialized countries. But "other things" have not been equal for a long time.

In the 1930's, only about 12 percent of the exports of the United States went to all of Latin America, as compared with 49 percent to Europe; and only about a quarter of the imports came from Latin America. During World War II the trade of the United States with Latin America was greatly increased—in part because the European countries could no longer supply the Latin-American countries with manufactured products. Many Latin Americans who were otherwise friendly with the United States, agreed with Martí that too great a dependence on the United States, either as a place to sell or to buy, was dangerous. Efforts were made, after World War II, to increase the sale of exports to Europe and Japan, and even to the Soviet Union. Imports remained chiefly from the United States in spite of the common desire to buy from other sources.

In the 1960's Latin America's share of the foreign trade of the United States declined. To be sure there were a few products from Latin America on which the United States was dependent: among the more important were bauxite, oil, iron ore, coffee and some tropical fruits. Yet coffee, a long-time Latin-American product, was coming in increasing quantity from Africa. Of the total value of the United States' foreign trade in 1961, Latin America's share was only 11 percent, compared with Europe's 30 percent.

The success of the European Economic Community in raising the level of living among the member countries after 1957, was reflected in similar international free trade agreements elsewhere in the world. By 1963 there were two such agreements among the countries of Latin America. The Central American Free Trade Area included Guatemala, El Salvador, Honduras, and Nicaragua, all of which agreed to a program of tariff reduction leading toward complete freedom of trade among themselves. The Latin-American Free Trade Association was started in 1960 by seven countries: Argentina, Paraguay, Uruguay, Brazil, Chile, Peru, and Mexico. By 1963 Colombia and Ecuador had joined and others had made application. The aim was to gradually reduce the tariffs among the member states, and thus greatly to enlarge the exchange of products among them. Both of these free trade associations will have an increasing effect on the long-established currents of trade, and will help to enlarge markets sufficiently to support continued development of manufacturing industries. The principle is still important: that the greatest volume of trade flows among economically developed countries, and contributes to their further development.

National Economic Development

In contrast to these efforts to establish greater freedom of trade among the Latin-American states, there was still an important body of opinion in Latin America opposed to any further growth of economic interdependence. Many Latin Americans who have watched their national economies suffer through two world wars and a depression are not at all convinced of the principle of economic interdependence. These are the people who have watched the Brazilians burn their surplus coffee during the 1930's, or who have seen the price of copper drop from 18 cents per pound to five cents so that in Chile the value of all exports in 1932 amounted to only 12 percent of the value of exports in 1929. These are people who have seen Cuban sugar drop from 22 cents a pound to less than one cent. These are people, too, who watch the collapse of their own national economies and the huge increase of unemployment because the United States, for its own domestic reasons, suddenly and unpredictably raises the tariff on an imported article. These are people whose cotton or wheat or tobacco is, without warning, deprived of a market because the United States has made a deal to dispose of some of its own stored surpluses, accumulated at government expense. These are the experiences that cause many intelligent Latin Americans to urge national economic self-sufficiency at whatever cost—because a country which is not dependent on foreign markets or foreign purchases may be poor but it is at least stable.

Since World War II there has been, throughout Latin America, a continuing demand for industrialization. With equipment and technical assistance from North America or from Europe steel plants have been built in Brazil, Argentina, Chile, Mexico, Venezuela, Colombia, and Peru. So far the leading producers are Brazil, Chile, and Mexico. The hope is that even if steel produced in these plants is more costly than that produced in North America or Europe, it can relieve the country of the need to use foreign exchange to import this basic material. In most countries the import of fuels is a necessity which no program of national self-sufficiency can evade. But, at a cost, steel can be produced locally—and in the course of time many steel-fabricating industries will be built near the steel plants.

Is industrialization the panacea that many Latin Americans think? Langdon White and Donald Alderson have summarized the problem.[5] They underline the need for examining each country as a separate problem, and the essential requirement that industrialization be made a part of a balanced program of economic development—in which the agricultural sector of the economy is not neglected. Puerto Rico provides the outstanding modern example of the kind of success that can be gained from such a balanced approach to the problem.

The long-term trend is quite clear. However the immediate programs of economic development are conceived, whatever may be the motives and practices of businessmen, foreign and domestic, as time goes on more and more of the isolated, self-sufficient, subsistence farmers will be brought into the economic system of sales and purchases. The volume of this increased market for goods and services is enormous. Perhaps the greatest El Dorado Latin America has ever offered lies in this vast population still outside of the commercial economy.

Industrialization that is accompanied by the growth of democracy would contribute to this process of change. The owners of capital need to consider the possibility that wages higher than those currently paid might be considered as an investment in market expansion. Only in this way can industrialization be accompanied by the development of a mass purchasing power which alone could absorb the larger volume of goods made possible by industrial expansion.

The Democratic Revolution

Associated with the Industrial Revolution, yet separate from it, is the second of the two great revolutions of our times. This one, like the

[5] C. Langdon White and Donald J. Alderson, "Industrialization: Panacea for Latin America?" *Journal of Geography,* Vol. 56, 1957, pp. 325-332.

changes in technology, originated in the countries around the shores of the North Sea, and spread irregularly from that source. Only now is the Democratic Revolution sweeping into Latin America—and not necessarily into those places where the Industrial Revolution is most advanced.

The word "democratic" is so frequently misused that we must review again the meaning we attach to it here. The political scientist, James L. Busey, describes democracy as "a political condition where the maximum possible numbers of people enjoy the maximum possible freedom of choice, political and social participation, and security of the rule of law." We have suggested previously that there are five basic aspects to the revolutionary changes that introduced democracy as a principle of political organization: (1) equality before the law; (2) the right to the protection from the arbitrary acts of those in authority; (3) the right of a people to select their own form of government and to be represented where laws are made or taxes are levied; (4) the right to select representatives or to express opinion on public policy in a secret ballot; and (5) the right to knowledge and the free use thereof. These concepts are widely accepted in the English-speaking world. In the United States, in spite of the publicity given to still-unsolved problems of race relations, these principles have in fact been accepted and applied to more people over a wider geographic area than ever before in the entire history of mankind. Although there have long been outstanding liberal leaders in Latin America, and al-

Students demanding resignation of a dictator

though liberal movements have gone a long way toward the establishment of these principles in some countries, they are still far from widely accepted, especially by the politically powerful groups.

Democracy is not something a country has, or does not have. No perfect democracy has ever existed, human behavior being what it is. But it is possible to establish a scale, running from the complete subservience of the individual to the state, on the one hand, to the complete acceptance within the state of the democratic principles enumerated above. There are five criteria for measuring the degree to which democratic principles are actually in operation: (1) do the people of a country enjoy complete freedom of expression? (2) are elections held with ballots that are really secret, and are the ballots honestly counted? (3) does the government accept the verdict of the voters and step down from office when the people so direct? (4) are political parties permitted to organize and to discuss public issues freely? and (5) are the courts truly independent?

Applying these measurements to the countries of Latin America, we must place among the more democratic states Puerto Rico, Costa Rica, and Uruguay; and among the least democratic states Cuba, Haiti and Paraguay. The others are at various stages in between. All except Cuba are in process of more or less rapid movement toward the democratic end of the scale. The rise of democracy, so defined, is one of the outstanding facts about Latin America in the second half of the twentieth century; and any failure to appreciate just what this means could be a most fundamental error of judgment on the part of countries outside of Latin America.

Attitudes toward Economic Development

As long as the great majority of the people have nothing to say about public policy it makes little or no difference what they think about economic development. Traditionally in Latin America, economic development has been for the benefit of a privileged minority—the landowners, the officers of the army, the Church, the political leaders. The concept of a mass market, and of an economy based on high volume-low profit per sale, was something people read about but scarcely understood. Especially in Brazil the idea was to get quick returns on invested funds: the idea of long-term investments made little sense in the midst of a rapidly shifting speculative economy. In Argentina the people who gained most from the British investments were the landowners. In most countries the man who made the largest income was the president.

In modern Latin America this situation is changing rapidly. The change began with the health programs and with the effort to reduce the proportion of illiterates. As more and more people learned how to read and write, the ideas of democracy began to spread. But the centers of change, and the groups most insistent on attacking the traditional system of power and privilege, were the universities and the students. Students have always taken a more active interest in political questions in Latin America than they do in Anglo-America; and students have been accustomed to seek radical solutions, even to the extent of attacking the established order with violence. There was a time when a majority of the people, in a country like Peru, would watch in wonder the student uprisings and strikes; but now, as more people find out what is going on, more people are ready to join in the demands for change.

And what do people want to change? Primarily they resent any system in which certain individuals enjoy special treatment before the law, or enjoy privileges because of status. Especially do they resent it when foreigners enjoy such privileges. The struggle for independence from Spain derived its support chiefly from people who resented Spanish administrators appointed by the King and sent to govern the colonies. In more recent times, there has been a mounting resentment against foreigners who enjoy a higher standard of living than the Latin Americans, receive more pay for the same kind of work, live in exclusive colonies, and patronize exclusive clubs in Latin-American cities. The resentment against the British has been especially strong where the British businessmen were most active—in Argentina. The resentment against North Americans is greatest where there are the most North Americans—in Venezuela. As more people find themselves able to express resentment, they cry out as if with one voice against economic colonialism, of the kind developed by the British in Argentina, or by the North Americans in Puerto Rico, Cuba, and Mexico. They are opposed to economic development which involves the production of raw materials by workers who are paid low wages, and which involves the export of raw materials and the import of manufactured articles. Especially are they opposed to systems that reduce the price received for raw materials at the same time that prices of manufactured articles are rising. They want and need investments of foreign capital, but they do not want foreign capital in speculative undertakings. And because public utilities, such as electric power, urban transportation, gas, and water, are so important in the daily affairs of the people, there is an insistent demand that these businesses should be owned by the government, not by private foreign corporations. The strength of this demand bears little relation to the quality of the services rendered. And all over Latin America the newly literate people learn of the improved level of living in Venezuela resulting from the profits from oil, and they resent the idea that even half of these profits should be carried away by a foreign-owned corporation. None of the Latin-American countries possesses either the capital or the know-how to explore for oil themselves, yet they are all reluctant to permit exploration and development by the big corporations. In Brazil one of the most popular slogans is *"O petróleo é nosso"*—the oil belongs to us. This expresses the idea that the Brazilians would prefer

to go without oil rather than permit the large oil corporations to develop it.

José Figueres, ex-president of Costa Rica, expressed all this in a commencement address at a North American college.[6]

All this tendency to pay low prices for the work of other countries and then
devise means of rendering economic help for their development, we consider
undesirable. The healthiest source of income for any nation, as for any man,
is the fair compensation for his own efforts.

This fair compensation for the work of our people, represented in our exports,
would probably have been obtained long ago if it were not for the short-sighted-
ness of our ruling class, who are often satisfied to make a personal profit in
business, basing their calculations on a miserable wage scale. When a sub-human
standard of living for the masses is taken for granted by the Latin American
employers, it is little wonder that low prices are considered acceptable for our
exports, and that no consistent efforts are made to improve such prices.

Since the wealthy class customarily controls our governments, the representatives of our countries to the international organizations care little for the living
conditions of the majority of our people, and act as spokesmen of that tiny
minority who always live well, whether the national income is low or high.
Hence the comparative disregard for the prices of our export products, which
constitute an important share of our national income, and the best possible
source of savings and development.

The Development of State-Ideas

The spread of democratic ideas has brought fundamental changes in
the nature of the state-ideas and in the struggle each country is waging to
bring order and coherence into the national life. Those countries which
are furthest from the democratic end of the scale have no well-developed
state-ideas to which a majority of the people subscribe. Order is maintained by the force of a secret police and a well-equipped army. At the
other end of the scale, however, are the countries operated along democratic lines, in which order must be maintained on the basis of the con-
sent and support of the people. Such countries must have state-ideas
strong enough to counteract the disruptive forces that are present in any
state. There are always forces of disintegration tending to break a state
apart—and these become especially disruptive if they are concentrated
in separate geographic areas located near the periphery of the national
territory. The forces of integration must be stronger than those of disintegration if a politically organized area is to remain strong or viable.
The analysis of these two opposed forces is an important aspect of
political geography.

Communism

The part played by the communists in Latin America needs to be carefully examined. The communists have had their greatest success in pre-

[6] From a commencement address at Grinnell College, Grinnell, Iowa.

industrial countries where there is a small land-owning aristocracy and a large majority of peasants. The communists have had much experience in the treatment of problems of land redistribution, and much sympathy for the landless peasant. In Latin America the communists join forces with other groups demanding reform. Wherever there are frustrations and conflicts the communists are on hand to provide expert leadership. Many intelligent Latin Americans, impatient with the compromises and delays inherent in the democratic processes, support communism as the best way to attack a situation which they consider to be hopeless. The communist movements are strongest in those countries where liberal reform movements are weakest. On the other hand, where successful liberal movements exist, communism holds little appeal.

In dealing with the problem of communism, two points need to be clearly appreciated. First, it is all too common to label all one's political enemies as communists. The expression of anti-United States feelings is often attributed to communist intrigue. Actually, however, the expression of such feeling is always found to have arisen from purely domestic causes, and the communists have moved in to take advantage of the situation. It is of the utmost importance that we learn to distinguish between communists and liberals. And second, Latin Americans need to understand that the Communist Party is in reality a group of devoted people, strictly disciplined and totally subservient to the authority of a foreign state. That these groups actually represent an intervention in domestic affairs is not adequately appreciated. When communism comes to power, it does move rapidly to wipe out the privileged classes; but it then establishes a new privileged class. Communism, all over the world, represents a reaction *against* the Democratic Revolution.

Problems of Inter-American Relations

Our examination of Latin America makes possible certain general conclusions regarding the inter-American relations of the United States. Certainly no nation, however strong, can neglect its relations with other countries; and in a world split by the antagonism of two world powers— the Soviet Union and the United States—no remote corner of the earth can be considered unimportant. The questions are: How do we stand in our relation with Latin America? And what should be the objectives of our foreign policies?

How Do We Stand?

We do not stand very well. First of all we have to live down the historical record of military invasion and conquest which started with Texas and only ended with the withdrawal of the Marines from the Antilles and the abrogation of the Platt amendment. Only since 1948 have we been committed to cooperative action on a basis of equality with other countries of the Hemisphere. In many countries there is genuine fear that the United States might return to its policies of expansion and of the use of force in international dealings.

Second, for the reasons presented in the preceding parts of this chapter, North American business enterprise in Latin America has not always accepted the kind of social responsibility that today seems to be "good business." There are still some North American business concerns whose dealings with Latin Americans are strictly for the purpose of quick profits. The fact that most businessmen today realize the need for bringing long-term benefits to their customers and are ready to accept responsibility for social problems in the communities they serve is not widely believed in Latin America.

Third, the prevailing ignorance regarding conditions in Latin America is a constant source of irritation. All too often our schools, our popular books, and especially our tourists have adopted what may be described as "the little brown cousin" attitude. The Latin American is portrayed as an amusing character, probably asleep under a cactus, or strumming a guitar under the balcony of some damsel. Latin Americans are not like this, and they have not been for many generations.

And fourth, the Latin Americans are very poorly informed about the United States. Most of their impressions of life in North America are derived from the movies—and usually the more lurid ones. That North Americans appreciate music, literature, art, or that they might have high ideals of fair-play and service in their dealings with other people, comes as a surprise to many of our neighbors. Newspapers give big headlines to race conflicts, to strikes, to the trials of dishonest labor leaders; but the positive accomplishments, in which the people of the United States ought to take pride, are not adequately presented.

The average Latin American looks at the United States with a mixture of envy and dislike. He is envious because of the material comforts we possess, the efficiency with which our engineers and our workers carry out complicated programs of construction, even because of the prestige of the United States as a nation. But he is disgusted by these same things: he regards other things as more desirable than material comfort and efficiency, and he resents the implication that his own country is not equal in dignity and worth to any other country in the world. But when the Latin American thinks of equality what he means is the equal right to be distinctive, to develop his own way of living, his own system of values. He resents the idea that to make progress he must adopt anyone else's standards. Equality means to him the right to be different.

Policy Objectives

What, then, do the people of the United States desire to obtain from their relations with the countries of the "good neighborhood"? It would seem that there should be at least three major objectives. First, in a world of conflict between nation-states, from which the United States cannot stand aloof, we need security from attack. A study of the geography of our international position as seen on a globe shows that all the major actual or potential centers of economic or military power in the world are to the north of the United States. Latin America constitutes the rear of our international position. Security from attack suggests the building of friendly cooperative arrangements for purposes that are openly and mutually agreed upon. The need for security is most pressing in the countries and colonies of Middle America, and in Brazil where the great bulge of the continent in the Northeast provides an easy route of approach to the Western Hemisphere from Africa. The need is less pressing in the more remote parts of South America.

In the second place, the United States needs continued access to certain raw materials of strategic importance. As long as there is a threat of war, it is a matter of protection to build up Western Hemisphere sources of essential raw materials even when these sources are more costly than are those of southeast Asia—for example, the tin of Bolivia. This should be done, however, as a defense measure, not as an attempt at permanent and complete self-sufficiency.

In the third place, the United States must recognize that in the long run, however the conflicts of the present period may be resolved, the maintenance of a high standard of living in any one part of an interdependent world becomes difficult or impossible if there are large numbers of very poor people elsewhere. It should be a matter of national policy to do all in our power to raise the material well-being of the Latin-American people. But such a program is by no means so simple as it can be made to sound.

Our study of the Latin-American countries suggests that no policy of this sort can be applied everywhere by the same methods. The greatest care and understanding must be used to adjust the methods to the conditions and needs of each country. Investments that are not excessively speculative and which do not result in the destructive exploitation of resources are welcomed; and technological instruction where North American technology is superior to that in use in Latin America (which is not everywhere the case) would have the effect of raising living standards. But technological assistance must be given intelligently. To establish a modern medical service in Latin-American countries with high birth rates without also making equal efforts to increase the production of basic foods is

the kind of unintelligent application of technology which went
before 1940 to impoverish the people of Puerto Rico. Before
apply North American technologies to Latin-American conditions w
to study all the conditions of life in the communities to be benefite
need to recognize that when one part of life in a community is cha
this change brings far-reaching readjustments that go far beyond the
understanding of the technologists themselves. We need programs of
"area study" in which the whole way of living, the whole relationship of
the people of a community to the land, are described as a basis for planning the proposed changes and forecasting the consequences of remedial
policies. If we attempt to export North American technologies blindly
and piecemeal, the results could be disastrous.

We need, also, to plan our intergovernmental relations with great care.
In the atmosphere of the second half of the twentieth century the use of
armed force to intervene in the affairs of another country is no longer
possible for democratic countries. Yet almost every act of the "colossus of
the North," even the act of refraining from acting, constitutes a form of
intervention. We should not lose sight of the principle that we in the
United States are the custodians of some of the most revolutionary new
ideas of human relations the world has seen for thousands of years. We,
not the communists, are the revolutionaries of our time. We should not
permit our desire to refrain from interfering in the domestic affairs of
another country to lead us to bestow medals of honor on dictators, however friendly they may be toward the United States. No better way could
be designed to insure a widespread hatred of the United States which
would break loose as soon as the inevitable trend toward democracy had
deposed the dictators. We should make it clear that a dictatorship based
on force is abhorrent to the United States, and that we look with favor
on the rise of liberal governments.

The arrangement of the peoples of Latin America and the differences
from place to place among the lands they occupy are fundamental to an
understanding of these problems. We have estimated that over two-thirds
of the people are only indirectly touched by problems of international
conflict, or of commercial exchange. These many people, engaged in producing from the land the bare necessities of food, clothing, and shelter,
are not affected by such things as surpluses and raw-material deficiencies,
nor do many of them share the sentiments of nationality which motivate
the other third. While the intellectual, professional, and governing classes
in Latin America are widely educated and thoroughly in touch with
modern problems, the majority of the inhabitants of the countries in
Middle and South America are illiterate and have only the vaguest concepts regarding the lands and problems which lie over the immediate
horizon. Between these dwellers in the rural districts, smaller towns, and

villages and the people who live in the modern metropolises the contrasts are so profound that the development of a coherent society seems all but impossible.

The map of population does not distinguish between all these different kinds of people, nor does it suggest the variety of kinds of communities which are actually to be found in Latin America. The long search for new sources of wealth, for the sacred lake of El Dorado, has brought groups of settlers into many diverse regions, forming new zones of concentrated settlement, only to leave the majority of the people behind as the search is directed elsewhere. From these regions of decadence the most energetic and successful of the inhabitants have moved away, leaving the stranded remnants poverty-stricken, isolated, hopeless, and dependent on the local resources for a mere subsistence. All over Latin America such groups are to be found: on the banana lands of eastern Costa Rica; in the dead mining communities of Mexico and Peru; along the banks of the Amazon where, more than fifty years ago, there was a frenzy of activity in the production of rubber; in the decadent coffee and sugar zones of Minas Gerais, and in the vast sertões beyond; in the inactive nitrate ports of Northern Chile; and on the remote sheep ranches of southern Patagonia where the decline of wool prices left the sheep men with a product which could be sold only at a loss.

The map of population also includes other clusters of people, other zones of concentrated settlement, which have survived the passage of the centuries almost without change. These are the places where the highland Indians remain almost unmixed with the Europeans: the out-of-the-world villages of Atacama; the agrarian communities of Bolivia; the villages of Indian shepherds in the Andes of southern Peru.

Against this background of varied lands and varied peoples there now appears the most modern form of community—the industrial city. Around the new urban centers more and more of the rural people are attached, first economically and then in other ways, to the life of the city. The new way of living is so fundamentally different from the way of living of a feudal society that the contrasts and cleavages have, for the moment, been made greater than ever before. But the Industrial Society, welcomed or not, will bring certain changes to Latin America, and these changes cannot long be resisted. There will be a greater productive capacity for each person, and supposedly, therefore, a wider opportunity for the fuller enjoyment of life. There will be an attack on the problems of illiteracy, hygiene, and diet. Step by step the people now engaged in subsistence living will be reclaimed as a part of the new society. Suddenly someone will realize that here in this great reservoir of population, now living unproductively, lies the real wealth of El Dorado for the man or the government that can bring order and coherence out of all these diverse elements.

Appendices

Climatic Data for Selected Stations

MEXICO

$T.$ = Temperature in Degrees Fahrenheit; $Rf.$ = Rainfall in Inches

Station	Altitude (in feet)	Time of Record (temperature)	Time of Record (rainfall)		Jan.	Feb.	Mar.	Apr.	May	June	July	Aug.	Sept.	Oct.	Nov.	Dec.	Year
Tampico	26.3–59.1	1889–1927	1889–1927	$T.$	66.0	68.2	71.8	76.5	80.2	82.0	81.9	82.4	80.8	77.2	72.3	66.9	75.5
				$Rf.$	1.5	1.2	1.0	1.5	1.9	8.7	4.9	4.8	10.8	5.0	2.0	1.6	44.9
Jalapa	4590.4	1894–1927	1894–1927	$T.$	57.6	60.1	63.5	66.6	67.6	66.6	66.2	66.4	65.5	63.5	61.0	58.8	63.6
				$Rf.$	1.9	2.3	2.4	2.9	4.4	12.4	6.8	6.5	10.8	5.7	3.0	2.4	61.5
Veracruz	23–52.5	1878–1927	1878–1927	$T.$	70.0	71.2	74.1	77.9	80.6	81.3	80.6	81.1	80.1	78.4	74.7	71.2	76.8
				$Rf.$	1.0	0.6	0.5	0.6	1.1	11.4	13.0	10.7	12.0	5.7	3.1	1.0	60.3
Mérida	72.2	1894–1927	1894–1927	$T.$	72.7	73.6	77.9	80.6	83.3	81.7	81.5	81.1	80.6	78.4	75.4	73.2	78.3
				$Rf.$	1.1	0.7	1.0	0.9	2.6	7.0	4.5	5.4	5.3	3.3	1.6	1.1	34.6
Saltillo	5278.8–5344.4	1886–1927	1886–1927	$T.$	53.1	55.2	60.8	66.2	71.2	73.0	72.3	71.8	66.9	62.6	56.8	52.5	63.5
				$Rf.$	0.7	0.6	0.4	0.7	1.0	2.2	2.9	2.9	2.9	1.5	1.2	0.6	17.6
Monterrey	1624.0	1886–1927	1896–1927	$T.$	57.7	62.6	68.0	73.8	78.4	81.5	81.7	82.4	77.9	71.6	63.5	57.6	71.3
				$Rf.$	0.6	0.7	0.8	1.3	1.3	3.0	2.3	2.4	5.2	3.0	1.5	0.8	22.9
Galeana	5426.5	1905–1927	1905–1927	$T.$	54.5	57.2	61.3	66.7	70.2	69.8	70.0	68.7	68.2	64.6	60.3	56.8	64.0
				$Rf.$	0.7	0.7	0.5	1.3	1.5	2.7	2.2	2.6	3.2	1.1	1.0	0.8	18.9
San Luis Potosí	6158.1–6223.7	1878–1927	1878–1927	$T.$	54.7	58.1	62.6	68.2	70.9	69.6	67.6	67.6	65.3	62.8	58.1	54.9	63.4
				$Rf.$	0.3	0.6	0.5	0.5	1.1	2.8	1.9	2.0	2.0	1.1	0.6	0.5	13.9
León	5902.2–5935.0	1878–1927	1878–1927	$T.$	57.2	60.4	65.5	70.5	73.8	71.6	69.3	69.0	67.8	64.8	61.0	57.6	65.7
				$Rf.$	0.3	0.3	0.4	0.4	1.1	4.9	6.1	5.1	4.7	1.3	0.5	0.5	25.4
Pachuca	7959.3–7992.1	1893–1927	1893–1927	$T.$	53.2	55.4	58.6	61.3	62.8	61.3	59.2	60.4	58.8	57.0	55.2	53.8	58.1
				$Rf.$	0.1	0.3	0.5	1.0	1.4	2.7	2.1	2.3	1.9	1.3	0.6	0.2	14.4
Mexico City	7486.9	1878–1927	1878–1927	$T.$	54.3	57.4	61.2	63.3	65.1	63.9	62.1	62.2	61.3	59.2	57.0	54.7	60.1
				$Rf.$	0.2	0.3	0.5	0.7	1.9	4.1	4.5	4.3	4.1	1.6	0.5	0.3	23.0
Puebla	7053.8–7175.2	1887–1927	1878–1927	$T.$	54.3	57.0	61.2	64.6	67.6	64.0	63.0	63.3	62.1	60.4	57.9	54.7	60.8
				$Rf.$	0.3	0.4	0.4	1.0	3.3	6.8	7.0	5.6	6.1	2.5	1.0	0.4	34.8
Chihuahua	4668.6	1900–1927	1900–1927	$T.$	50.0	53.4	60.1	66.4	73.4	78.8	76.6	75.2	71.4	64.8	55.4	49.3	64.6
				$Rf.$	0.2	0.4	0.3	0.2	0.2	1.7	3.6	3.7	3.3	0.9	0.5	0.4	15.4
Durango	6187.7–6243.4	1878–1903	1878–1927	$T.$	54.1	56.3	62.2	65.7	71.4	71.1	69.1	69.1	66.2	63.0	57.9	53.8	63.3
				$Rf.$	0.3	0.3	0.2	0.2	0.2	2.6	4.1	3.2	4.1	1.1	0.6	1.1	18.0

Source: W. Köppen and R. Geiger, *Handbuch der Klimatologie*, Vol. 2, Parts G, H, I, and J. Berlin.

MEXICO — Continued

T. = Temperature in Degrees Fahrenheit; Rf. = Rainfall in Inches

Station	Altitude (in feet)	Time of Record (temperature)	Time of Record (rainfall)		Jan.	Feb.	Mar.	Apr.	May	June	July	Aug.	Sept.	Oct.	Nov.	Dec.	Year
Zacatecas	8569.6	1878–1927	1878–1927	T.	50.7	52.7	55.6	61.3	65.1	64.2	60.8	61.2	59.4	57.6	54.9	51.1	57.9
				Rf.	0.5	0.3	0.4	0.2	0.9	4.1	4.1	3.4	3.5	1.6	0.6	0.6	20.2
Ensenada	19.7	1925–1927	1895–1927	T.	55.0	57.2	57.7	59.5	62.1	63.3	69.6	69.6	66.0	63.0	60.6	56.8	61.7
				Rf.	2.6	1.9	1.5	0.9	0.2	0.1	0.1	0.1	0.0	0.6	1.1	1.7	10.8
La Paz	32.8–39.4	1906–1927	1907–1927	T.	63.0	65.1	68.4	70.5	74.1	77.9	82.4	83.5	82.2	78.8	72.3	65.7	73.6
				Rf.	0.2	0.1	0.0	0.0	0.0	0.0	0.4	1.2	1.4	0.6	0.5	1.1	5.7
Ahome	111.6–278.9	1921–1927	1921–1927	T.	63.1	64.4	67.8	71.8	77.0	82.2	86.7	86.0	85.1	79.7	71.4	64.0	75.0
				Rf.	0.0	0.1	0.2	0.0	0.0	0.4	1.6	3.2	3.2	0.3	0.5	2.6	12.1
Mazatlán	13.1–255.9	1880–1927	1880–1927	T.	68.4	67.8	69.4	71.8	76.1	81.1	82.6	82.8	82.4	80.4	75.2	70.2	75.7
				Rf.	0.8	0.5	0.2	0.1	0.1	1.5	5.9	8.3	8.0	2.6	0.9	1.3	30.2
Guadalajara	5104.9–5193.5	1878–1927	1878–1927	T.	59.9	62.4	66.0	70.5	73.9	72.1	69.4	69.3	68.4	67.1	63.9	59.9	66.9
				Rf.	0.4	0.2	0.2	0.2	1.1	8.8	9.4	8.5	7.2	2.2	0.7	0.7	39.6
Manzanillo	9.8–23	1908–1927	1910–1927	T.	74.7	73.6	74.1	75.2	78.1	81.5	81.7	82.0	81.1	81.9	77.9	75.7	78.2
				Rf.	0.0	0.0	0.0	0.0	0.0	4.0	5.1	5.7	13.1	4.5	0.5	3.0	36.1
Acapulco	9.8	1920–1927	1920–1927	T.	77.9	77.7	78.8	80.4	82.6	82.8	82.6	80.8	81.1	82.9	80.2	78.6	80.5
				Rf.	0.6	0.0	0.0	0.0	1.7	16.5	6.0	6.3	14.7	5.9	1.9	0.7	54.3
Cuicatlán	1952.1	1906–1925	1906–1925	T.	71.4	73.0	75.7	80.1	81.5	79.2	77.7	79.0	77.5	76.1	72.5	70.9	76.2
				Rf.	0.0	0.2	0.2	0.5	0.8	4.1	3.0	2.5	2.5	1.3	0.1	0.2	15.4
Oaxaca	5036.1–5164	1878–1927	1878–1927	T.	62.8	65.8	69.4	72.5	72.9	70.7	69.4	69.8	67.1	65.3	68.5	63.0	68.1
				Rf.	0.1	0.1	0.6	1.5	3.2	6.7	3.5	4.1	4.9	2.0	0.4	0.2	27.4
Salina Cruz	49.2–183.7	1903–1907	1903–1927	T.	76.3	77.2	79.3	81.3	82.8	81.1	81.9	82.0	80.8	80.2	79.0	77.2	79.9
				Rf.	0.0	0.4	0.6	0.5	3.3	11.9	4.5	5.5	7.0	4.0	0.9	0.1	38.7
Comitán	5364.2	1912–1927	1912–1927	T.	59.9	62.2	64.8	66.9	67.5	66.0	64.9	65.3	65.5	63.9	61.3	61.7	64.2
				Rf.	0.5	0.5	0.3	1.7	4.7	9.1	4.6	4.2	5.9	4.7	1.0	0.4	37.6

CENTRAL AMERICA

Station	Altitude (in feet)	Time of Record (temperature)	Time of Record (rainfall)		Jan.	Feb.	Mar.	Apr.	May	June	July	Aug.	Sept.	Oct.	Nov.	Dec.	Year
Belize	Coast Level	1888–1895	1888–1895	T.	74.8	76.8	79.2	79.9	81.9	82.4	82.6	82.6	82.0	79.3	76.1	73.6	79.3
				Rf.	5.1	2.6	1.6	1.5	4.1	9.1	9.6	8.5	9.4	11.0	10.2	6.3	79.0
Guatemala City	4888.4	1898–1902	1857–1902	T.	61.7	63.2	65.8	66.2	69.4	67.5	66.7	66.7	66.7	65.1	63.5	61.3	65.4
				Rf.	0.3	0.2	0.5	1.3	5.5	11.7	7.8	7.8	9.3	6.6	0.9	0.2	52.1
San Salvador	2155.5	1889–1902	1889–1902	T.	71.8	72.9	74.5	76.3	75.6	74.3	74.1	74.1	73.2	72.7	72.3	71.4	73.6
				Rf.	0.7	0.2	0.6	1.6	6.6	11.0	12.3	11.5	11.7	10.3	1.9	0.4	68.2
San Ubaldo	108.3	1900	1900	T.	79.5	80.8	82.9	86.4	85.8	82.9	81.3	82.9	83.1	80.6	80.2	81.1	82.3
				Rf.	1.2	0.2	0.3	0.0	7.4	9.8	24.9	5.3	14.1	8.9	1.4	0.6	74.1
Greytown	Coast Level	1898–1900	1890–1900	T.	77.5	77.7	78.8	80.8	80.8	80.1	79.2	79.3	80.4	80.2	78.4	77.5	79.2
				Rf.	23.3	11.3	6.5	11.4	20.4	23.2	34.4	27.3	17.4	20.0	36.5	27.8	259.4
San José	3723.7	1889–1900	1888–1895	T.	66.0	66.7	67.8	68.7	68.9	68.2	67.6	67.5	67.6	67.3	68.7	65.9	67.6
				Rf.	0.2	0.2	0.5	1.1	10.0	11.0	8.3	10.6	14.2	13.3	4.9	1.7	76.0
Colón	Coast Level	1907–1926	1907–1926	T.	79.9	79.7	80.2	80.8	80.4	79.9	79.9	80.8	80.4	79.0	78.6	79.9	79.9
				Rf.	3.5	1.7	1.5	4.5	12.2	13.9	15.5	14.8	12.6	15.2	21.7	10.8	127.9
Balboa Heights	98.4	1907–1926	1906–1930	T.	78.3	78.4	79.5	80.1	79.2	78.6	78.6	78.4	78.4	77.7	77.4	78.3	78.6
				Rf.	0.9	0.9	0.6	2.8	7.8	8.2	7.2	7.8	7.9	10.1	10.1	4.2	68.6

T. = Temperature in Degrees Fahrenheit; Rf. = Rainfall in Inches

343

SOUTH AMERICA

T. = Temperature in Degrees Fahrenheit; Rf. = Rainfall in Inches

Station	Altitude (in feet)	Time of Record (temperature)	Time of Record (rainfall)		Jan.	Feb.	Mar.	Apr.	May	June	July	Aug.	Sept.	Oct.	Nov.	Dec.	Year
Maracaibo	26.3	1918–1925	1920–1925	T.	80.6	81.0	81.1	82.6	83.1	83.5	84.2	84.4	83.5	82.0	81.3	81.0	82.4
				Rf.	0.0	0.0	0.3	0.5	2.4	1.6	1.4	1.3	3.3	4.3	2.5	0.4	18.0
La Guaira	Coast Level	3 years	1920–1925	T.	78.4	78.4	79.3	80.2	81.1	81.7	81.1	82.6	82.9	82.6	81.5	78.8	80.7
				Rf.	0.5	0.2	0.8	0.2	0.6	0.9	1.0	1.1	1.1	1.2	1.6	1.5	10.7
Caracas	3415.4	1895–1925	1891–1925	T.	64.4	64.9	65.8	68.2	69.4	68.7	68.0	68.4	68.5	68.4	67.3	65.3	67.3
				Rf.	0.9	0.4	0.6	1.6	2.8	4.3	4.1	4.3	4.0	3.9	3.4	1.7	32.0
Mérida	5380.6	1918–1925	1918–1925	T.	64.0	65.1	65.5	66.6	66.6	66.0	66.0	66.7	66.4	66.0	65.1	64.2	65.7
				Rf.	2.6	1.5	3.8	6.7	11.2	6.9	4.0	5.7	6.3	9.9	8.0	3.3	69.9
Ciudad Bolivar	124.7	1919–1924	1917–1925	T.	78.8	79.9	81.0	82.2	82.4	80.1	79.7	80.8	81.7	81.7	81.0	78.8	80.7
				Rf.	0.5	0.2	0.2	0.9	2.6	5.6	6.2	6.3	3.1	3.4	3.4	1.9	34.3
Medellin	4950.73	1875–1879	15 years	T.	70.9	71.6	70.9	70.7	70.9	70.7	70.5	70.7	70.5	69.4	69.1	69.8	70.5
				Rf.	2.7	3.5	3.3	6.6	7.7	5.5	4.1	4.6	6.2	6.9	5.2	2.5	58.8
Bogotá	8727	6½ years	{ 1866–1885 1894–1922 }	T.	57.9	58.3	59.0	58.8	58.6	58.3	57.2	57.2	57.4	57.9	58.3	57.9	58.1
				Rf.	2.3	2.6	4.0	5.7	4.4	2.4	2.0	2.2	2.4	6.3	4.7	2.6	41.6
Pasto	8510.5	1924–1925	1924–1925	T.	55.9	56.7	57.2	57.7	59.0	57.6	57.7	57.9	57.2	57.7	57.0	57.4	57.4
				Rf.	1.3	1.7	3.4	3.1	0.9	2.6	1.0	0.3	4.6	2.4	7.6	3.4	32.3
Quito	9350.4	1895–1907	16 years	T.	54.7	54.5	54.5	54.5	54.7	54.7	54.5	54.7	54.9	54.7	54.5	54.7	54.6
				Rf.	4.2	4.3	5.2	7.4	5.0	1.5	0.9	1.5	3.0	3.7	3.8	3.8	44.3
Guayaquil	39.4	3 years	3 years	T.	79.3	79.3	79.7	80.4	78.8	77.4	75.4	76.1	77.2	76.6	78.4	80.2	78.2
				Rf.	9.7	10.5	7.4	5.3	2.1	0.7	0.4	0.0	0.1	0.4	0.3	1.9	38.8
Iquitos	347.8	1 year	1 year	T.	77.5	78.3	76.3	77.0	75.6	74.3	74.1	76.3	76.3	77.2	78.4	77.9	76.6
				Rf.	10.0	10.6	12.0	6.6	9.8	7.3	6.5	4.5	8.8	7.1	8.5	11.3	103.0
Chiclayo	Coast Level	1909–1912	3–4 years	T.	76.1	78.3	77.4	73.2	68.9	63.5	64.0	64.6	65.0	65.6	68.0	72.9	69.8
				Rf.	0.0	0.1	0.5	0.0	0.0	—	0.0	0.0	0.1	0.0	0.0	0.0	0.7
Trujillo	196.9	1896–1915	2–4 years	T.	77.2	77.0	74.3	72.0	68.0	63.0	64.0	64.2	63.7	67.5	68.7	72.0	69.3
				Rf.	0.2	0.5	0.3	0.0	0.0	0.0	0.1	0.0	0.0	0.0	0.1	0.0	1.2
Cerro de Pasco	14,271.6	1909–1912	3–5 years	T.	44.1	43.2	44.1	44.1	42.6	41.0	40.5	40.8	41.0	41.7	42.3	42.4	42.3
				Rf.	4.6	4.5	3.6	3.4	2.3	0.9	1.1	1.2	2.8	3.3	3.4	3.7	34.8

Lima	518.4	1893–1897 / 1910–1919	18 years	T. Rf.	72.6 0.0	74.3 0.0	73.6 0.0	70.2 0.0	66.0 0.0	62.6 0.1	61.2 0.2	61.0 0.4	61.3 0.4	63.0 0.4	65.7 0.2	69.6 0.1	66.8 1.8
Santa Ana	3412.1	1894–1895	1894–1895	T. Rf.	71.6 9.8	71.1 6.6	71.4 8.1	72.1 3.5	71.8 2.8	71.1 1.2	70.2 0.3	70.7 1.1	72.3 5.6	73.9 4.0	74.1 1.5	73.2 7.3	72.0 51.8
Cuzco	11,089.2	1894–1898	12 years	T. Rf.	52.5 6.4	52.2 5.9	52.0 4.3	51.4 2.0	50.5 0.6	48.4 0.2	46.9 0.2	49.8 0.4	51.6 1.0	52.9 2.6	53.8 3.0	52.2 5.4	51.2 32.0
Vincocaya	14,370	1896–1900	1 year	T. Rf.	38.3 3.0	38.7 4.1	38.1 2.6	36.3 0.0	32.5 0.0	29.3 0.0	27.9 0.0	31.5 0.0	34.5 0.2	38.7 0.0	40.6 0.3	38.5 0.5	35.4 10.7
Arequipa	8041.3	1888–1920	1888–1924	T. Rf.	57.0 1.2	57.0 1.8	56.3 0.6	57.4 0.2	56.8 0.0	55.8 0.0	55.6 0.0	56.8 0.0	57.9 0.0	56.5 0.0	57.0 0.0	57.4 0.4	56.8 4.2
Mollendo	78.7	1889–1895	1888–1900	T. Rf.	70.2 0.0	70.7 0.1	69.6 0.0	67.3 0.0	65.3 0.1	61.7 0.0	59.5 0.2	59.4 0.2	59.9 0.2	62.1 0.1	65.8 0.1	68.4 0.0	64.4 0.8
La Paz	12,001.3	1918–1925	1898–1902	T. Rf.	50.4 3.8	50.4 4.9	50.0 2.6	48.4 1.5	47.7 0.5	44.8 0.1	43.5 0.2	46.2 1.1	49.3 0.8	50.0 1.3	51.8 1.6	51.4 4.2	48.7 22.6
Cochabamba	8448.2	3 years	1903–1918	T. Rf.	65.8 4.1	65.3 3.8	63.1 2.4	62.4 0.4	60.1 0.4	57.2 0.3	59.5 0.2	61.3 0.2	63.9 0.7	67.5 0.6	68.0 1.3	66.2 3.9	63.2 18.3
Arica	16.4	1911–1921	1903–1918	T. Rf.	72.3 0.4	73.0 0.0	71.6 0.0	68.4 0.0	65.7 0.0	53.1 0.0	61.3 0.0	61.2 0.0	62.4 0.0	64.0 0.0	66.9 0.0	70.0 0.0	66.7 0.4
Iquique	29.5	1911–1924	1886–1925	T. Rf.	69.8 0.0	69.6 0.0	67.6 0.0	65.1 0.0	63.1 0.0	61.3 0.0	60.1 0.0	60.3 0.0	61.2 0.0	63.0 0.0	65.7 0.0	68.2 0.0	64.6 0.0
Calama	7414.7	1913–1914	1913–1914	T. Rf.	62.4 0.0	59.7 0.0	58.1 0.0	54.7 0.0	51.8 0.0	47.5 0.0	46.4 0.0	55.8 0.0	54.3 0.0	58.3 0.0	60.3 0.0	61.9 0.0	55.9 0.0
Coquimbo	88.6	1911–1924	1900–1925	T. Rf.	64.0 0.0	63.7 0.0	62.1 0.0	58.8 0.0	56.8 1.1	54.3 1.5	53.6 1.1	54.0 0.5	55.0 0.2	57.0 0.0	59.4 0.0	61.7 0.0	58.4 4.4
Los Andes	2677.2	1911–1924	1905–1925	T. Rf.	71.2 0.3	70.2 0.0	65.7 0.1	59.5 0.4	53.1 2.2	47.5 2.5	48.7 1.3	51.4 0.9	54.3 1.0	59.9 0.2	65.1 0.1	69.3 0.1	59.7 8.8
Valparaiso	134.5	1911–1924	1869–1925	T. Rf.	63.7 0.0	63.1 0.0	61.3 0.4	58.1 0.6	55.6 3.8	52.3 5.7	52.3 4.0	53.1 2.6	54.1 1.3	56.7 0.4	60.1 0.3	62.4 0.2	57.7 19.3
Santiago	1706	1911–1924	1867–1925	T. Rf.	68.7 0.0	67.1 0.1	62.4 0.2	56.7 0.6	51.1 2.4	45.7 3.3	46.2 2.8	48.6 2.1	51.8 1.3	56.8 0.5	62.2 0.2	66.6 0.2	57.0 13.7
San Fernando	1099	1911–1924	1911–1925	T. Rf.	67.8 0.1	66.0 0.0	61.5 0.4	55.2 1.2	50.0 6.1	44.4 8.2	45.1 4.6	47.1 3.2	50.4 2.8	55.8 0.9	60.8 1.0	65.5 0.3	55.8 28.8
Contulmo	124.7	1911–1924	1911–1925	T. Rf.	62.2 1.3	61.0 1.4	58.5 3.3	54.9 6.6	51.8 12.5	48.2 10.9	48.4 11.6	48.2 8.8	49.8 6.5	53.6 2.6	56.1 4.2	59.7 2.3	54.4 72.0

SOUTH AMERICA—Continued

Station	Altitude (in feet)	Time of Record (temperature)	Time of Record (rainfall)		Jan.	Feb.	Mar.	Apr.	May	June	July	Aug.	Sept.	Oct.	Nov.	Dec.	Year
									T. = Temperature in Degrees Fahrenheit; Rf. = Rainfall in Inches								
Valdivia	19.7	1911–1921	1852–1925	T.	61.9	60.4	57.9	53.1	49.6	45.5	45.7	46.4	48.0	52.0	55.0	59.0	52.9
				Rf.	2.4	3.0	5.6	9.4	11.3	17.0	16.1	13.2	8.7	5.2	5.0	4.1	101.0
Puerto Montt	32.8	1911–1921	1862–1915	T.	59.5	58.1	55.9	52.3	49.6	45.9	45.9	46.0	47.3	51.1	53.6	57.0	51.8
				Rf.	4.6	4.4	5.9	7.4	10.6	10.0	10.8	9.3	6.3	5.5	5.5	5.4	85.7
Evangelistas	180.5	1911–1924	1899–1925	T.	47.5	47.5	47.1	44.4	42.1	40.3	39.6	39.4	40.6	42.3	43.2	45.5	43.3
				Rf.	11.5	10.4	11.2	11.6	9.6	9.4	9.2	8.5	9.0	8.7	9.9	10.1	119.1
Punta Arenas	91.9	1911–1924	1888–1925	T.	52.5	51.3	48.7	43.7	39.0	36.5	35.8	36.7	40.6	45.3	47.3	50.9	44.0
				Rf.	1.1	1.3	1.5	2.1	2.0	2.2	1.7	2.1	1.7	1.1	1.3	1.3	19.4
La Quiaca	11,358.2	1901–1920	1901–1920	T.	54.5	54.3	53.4	51.4	42.8	37.4	37.4	42.1	48.0	51.4	54.0	54.7	48.5
				Rf.	3.2	2.6	2.0	0.3	0.0	0.0	0.0	0.0	0.0	0.2	1.1	2.1	11.5
Jujuy	4166.7	1901–1920	1901–1920	T.	70.5	68.9	66.2	62.2	57.0	52.2	52.2	54.9	61.5	65.3	69.1	70.2	62.5
				Rf.	6.5	5.5	5.4	1.3	0.5	0.2	0.2	0.1	0.4	1.5	2.6	5.2	29.4
Salta	3894.9	1901–1920	1901–1920	T.	72.0	70.9	67.6	63.9	58.3	53.1	53.6	56.1	63.3	67.8	70.3	71.2	64.0
				Rf.	6.7	6.2	3.9	1.2	0.3	0.1	0.0	0.2	0.4	1.2	2.3	5.4	28.0
Tucumán	1476.4	1901–1920	1901–1920	T.	76.8	74.7	71.6	66.4	59.9	53.6	53.6	56.8	64.2	68.9	72.7	75.0	66.2
				Rf.	6.3	7.5	5.5	3.1	1.2	0.6	0.3	0.5	0.6	2.3	4.2	5.9	38.0
Santiago del Estero	623.4	1901–1920	1901–1920	T.	83.1	80.6	76.6	70.3	62.8	55.9	56.7	60.6	67.5	72.3	77.5	80.6	70.4
				Rf.	3.3	3.0	3.0	1.3	0.6	0.3	0.2	0.2	0.5	1.4	2.5	4.1	20.4
La Rioja	1673.2	1901–1920	1901–1920	T.	81.5	78.1	74.5	68.4	60.1	51.8	53.1	57.7	63.3	70.5	75.9	79.3	67.9
				Rf.	2.6	2.7	2.2	0.8	0.5	0.2	0.1	0.2	0.2	0.8	1.4	1.8	13.5
Córdoba	1387.8	1901–1920	1901–1920	T.	73.9	72.3	68.5	62.1	55.8	49.6	50.5	53.4	58.6	63.3	68.4	72.1	62.4
				Rf.	3.7	5.0	3.2	2.1	1.1	0.2	0.5	0.6	0.9	2.2	4.0	4.6	28.2
San Juan	2178.3	1901–1920	1901–1920	T.	77.0	74.7	69.8	61.2	53.2	47.1	46.9	51.6	58.6	65.3	70.3	75.0	62.6
				Rf.	0.8	0.7	0.4	0.1	0.0	0.0	0.3	0.1	0.1	0.2	0.2	0.4	3.3
San Luis	2322.9	1901–1920	1901–1920	T.	75.2	72.5	68.5	61.5	54.3	48.0	48.6	51.6	56.1	63.7	69.1	73.4	61.9
				Rf.	4.2	4.1	2.3	1.5	0.7	0.2	0.4	0.4	0.7	1.3	2.8	3.6	22.2
Buenos Aires	82.0	1856–1924	1901–1920	T.	73.6	72.5	68.7	61.3	55.0	49.6	48.9	51.1	55.0	59.9	65.8	70.9	61.0
				Rf.	3.1	2.8	3.9	4.8	2.8	2.0	2.1	2.2	2.9	3.3	4.0	4.0	37.9
Mendoza	2477	1901–1920	1901–1920	T.	74.5	71.6	67.5	59.4	52.0	45.5	46.4	50.0	56.1	61.9	68.0	71.6	60.4
				Rf.	0.9	1.3	1.1	0.5	0.4	0.4	0.2	0.3	0.5	0.7	0.7	0.7	7.7
Mar del Plata	82.0	1901–1920	1901–1920	T.	66.9	66.4	63.9	59.4	52.7	47.3	46.2	46.8	49.6	53.2	58.8	63.7	56.2
				Rf.	2.1	3.1	3.1	3.1	1.9	2.4	2.1	1.8	2.6	2.4	2.6	2.7	29.9

Estación	Alt.	Período (T.)	Período (Rf.)		I	II	III	IV	V	VI	VII	VIII	IX	X	XI	XII	Año
Bahía Blanca	82.0	1901–1920	1901–1920	T.	74.5	71.6	67.5	60.1	53.1	47.1	46.4	48.9	53.6	59.2	66.4	71.8	60.0
				Rf.	2.2	2.4	2.2	3.5	1.1	0.6	0.9	0.7	0.7	3.4	1.9	2.0	21.6
Choele Choel	456.0	1901–1920	1901–1920	T.	75.4	72.5	67.3	58.5	51.3	44.8	45.1	47.7	53.1	59.9	66.7	72.1	59.5
				Rf.	0.7	0.7	1.0	0.9	1.1	0.6	0.5	0.3	0.8	0.9	0.5	0.6	8.6
Col. 16 de Octubre	1837.3	1901–1920	1901–1920	T.	60.6	58.8	54.9	47.7	42.3	37.0	36.7	38.7	42.8	48.4	51.8	55.9	48.0
				Rf.	0.5	0.5	0.8	2.2	3.2	2.8	1.5	1.5	1.5	0.4	0.5	0.6	15.8
Santa Cruz	39.4	1901–1920	1901–1920	T.	58.6	57.6	54.7	47.7	40.8	35.2	35.2	38.3	43.5	48.7	52.9	56.3	47.5
				Rf.	0.6	0.3	0.4	0.6	0.4	0.5	0.4	0.6	0.3	0.3	0.4	0.6	5.5
Ushuaia	26.3	1901–1920	1901–1920	T.	49.6	49.1	46.8	40.5	36.7	33.3	33.6	35.2	39.2	43.0	44.4	49.1	41.7
				Rf.	1.7	2.1	1.7	1.9	1.5	1.6	1.2	0.9	1.2	1.5	1.9	1.8	19.0
Asunción	344.5	1893–1924	1893–1923	T.	80.4	79.9	77.9	72.1	66.6	62.6	64.0	66.0	69.6	72.5	76.1	79.9	72.3
				Rf.	5.4	5.5	4.2	5.3	4.5	2.8	2.2	1.5	3.1	5.4	6.0	6.1	52.0
Montevideo	82.0	1901–1924	1901–1924	T.	72.0	71.8	68.5	63.0	56.7	51.3	50.5	51.3	54.9	58.1	64.6	69.4	61.0
				Rf.	2.6	3.1	3.2	4.6	3.4	3.2	2.4	3.5	3.4	2.5	3.2	3.5	38.6
Belém	32.8	1893–1910	1912–1924	T.	78.1	77.4	77.7	78.1	78.8	78.8	78.6	78.8	78.8	79.5	79.9	79.3	78.7
				Rf.	7.6	13.3	17.0	17.8	11.8	9.1	2.3	2.8	0.6	0.5	0.6	2.6	86.0
São Luiz	65.6	1912–1921	1912–1919	T.	79.7	79.2	79.2	79.0	79.2	79.2	78.8	79.2	79.9	80.4	80.1	80.2	79.5
				Rf.	7.4	10.4	18.5	16.6	12.4	5.8	4.1	1.1	0.5	0.4	0.7	6.5	84.4
Quixeramobim	679.1	1896–1921	1910–1924	T.	82.9	81.9	80.8	80.4	79.5	79.2	79.5	78.8	82.0	82.9	83.3	83.5	81.4
				Rf.	3.7	4.3	7.0	7.0	5.2	2.5	1.3	4.1	0.1	0.1	0.4	1.4	33.6
Natal	9.8	1904–1921	1912–1920	T.	81.0	80.8	81.0	80.1	79.2	77.2	75.9	76.3	78.1	78.3	80.4	80.8	79.1
				Rf.	2.8	5.2	5.9	8.9	7.8	12.3	6.7	3.5	2.4	1.1	0.3	0.7	57.6
Recife	98 4	1911–1921	1875–1922	T.	82.0	82.0	82.2	81.7	79.9	77.0	77.4	77.4	79.0	80.6	81.3	82.0	80.3
				Rf.	2.0	3.5	6.3	8.6	10.8	12.3	10.3	6.3	2.7	1.0	1.1	1.1	64.9
Ondina	154.2	1909–1921	1910–1924	T.	78.3	78.8	78.8	78.1	76.6	75.0	74.1	73.8	74.5	76.1	77.2	78.1	76.6
				Rf.	2.8	5.7	5.9	11.7	10.2	9.5	7.5	4.8	3.8	4.4	4.7	5.9	76.9
Belo Horizonte	2811.7	1910–1912	1910–1919	T.	71.4	72.1	71.1	68.7	65.5	62.6	62.2	64.4	68.4	70.3	70.3	70.2	68.1
				Rf.	12.8	9.5	6.3	2.9	0.6	0.5	0.4	0.9	1.5	4.9	8.3	10.7	59.3
Rezende	1312.3	1913–1921	1912–1924	T.	73.8	74.1	73.2	70.2	66.0	62.6	62.2	63.9	67.5	69.4	71.4	72.5	68.9
				Rf.	10.8	11.2	7.6	4.2	1.4	1.1	0.9	1.0	2.1	4.6	8.0	9.2	62.1
Rio de Janeiro	196.9	1851–1920	1851–1925	T.	78.6	79.0	77.7	75.2	72.0	69.6	68.7	69.6	70.3	71.8	73.9	76.6	73.6
				Rf.	4.9	4.8	5.2	4.3	3.1	2.3	1.7	1.7	2.6	3.2	4.1	5.4	43.3
Ribeirão Preto	1824.2	1901–1917	1910–1922	T.	74.1	75.0	73.9	70.9	65.3	63.3	63.3	62.6	70.5	72.5	74.1	74.3	70.0
				Rf.	11.0	7.9	6.1	3.1	1.4	2.0	0.6	1.2	2.2	4.4	6.8	8.5	55.2
São Paulo	2690.3	1902–1917	1902–1917	T.	68.9	69.1	68.0	64.6	60.4	58.6	57.9	59.0	61.5	63.0	65.5	68.0	63.7
				Rf.	7.7	8.7	5.6	2.2	2.5	2.2	1.7	2.0	3.2	4.7	7.2	8.5	56.2

SOUTH AMERICA—Continued

Station	Altitude (in feet)	Time of Record (temperature)	Time of Record (rainfall)		Jan.	Feb.	Mar.	Apr.	May	June	July	Aug.	Sept.	Oct.	Nov.	Dec.	Year
					\textit{T. = Temperature in Degrees Fahrenheit; Rf. = Rainfall in Inches}												
Santos	9.8	1895–1917	1895–1917	T.	76.3	77.9	75.9	72.7	68.9	66.2	66.4	66.0	66.9	68.9	73.0	75.6	71.2
				Rf.	10.4	9.2	8.1	6.8	6.1	2.4	4.4	4.6	5.6	6.1	7.8	7.0	78.5
Curitiba	2979	1884–1910	1885–1925	T.	68.7	70.0	66.7	62.2	56.7	54.0	54.5	56.3	58.3	61.0	64.4	67.3	61.7
				Rf.	6.6	6.3	4.4	3.1	4.0	4.0	2.5	3.2	4.9	5.5	5.0	5.5	55.0
Paranaguá	13.1	1910–1919	1910–1919	T.	73.6	71.2	69.6	64.9	60.8	59.5	60.1	62.2	64.8	69.1	70.9	73.4	66.7
				Rf.	10.4	10.9	4.8	3.6	3.8	2.3	3.0	5.4	6.3	5.5	8.3	8.9	73.2
Blumenau	49.2	1915–1921	1915–1919	T.	75.9	75.6	72.5	70.5	64.9	59.2	58.3	60.6	63.9	67.3	70.5	73.6	67.7
				Rf.	7.9	11.1	6.5	3.9	3.4	4.1	2.0	3.9	4.7	3.9	3.0	4.8	59.2
Porto Alegre	49.2	1909–1922	1909–1922	T.	76.1	76.5	72.9	68.9	63.0	56.3	56.5	58.3	61.7	65.1	70.2	73.8	66.6
				Rf.	4.3	3.7	3.6	4.8	4.1	5.0	4.3	5.1	4.6	3.1	3.3	4.1	50.0
Manaus	147.6	1911–1921	1902–1926	T.	79.9	80.1	79.7	79.9	80.1	80.1	80.6	81.7	82.8	82.8	82.2	80.6	81.0
				Rf.	9.2	9.0	9.6	8.5	7.0	3.6	2.2	1.4	2.0	4.1	5.5	7.7	69.8
Santarém	65.6	1914–1919	1914–1920	T.	77.5	76.6	77.2	77.2	77.0	76.5	77.0	78.3	79.7	80.4	80.4	78.8	78.1
				Rf.	6.2	12.0	10.6	10.9	10.3	6.2	3.0	1.9	1.5	1.1	1.5	5.0	70.2
Corumbá	380.6	1912–1920	1912–1919	T.	80.2	79.5	80.1	78.6	73.9	69.4	70.5	72.7	76.6	78.4	79.9	80.1	76.7
				Rf.	6.4	6.7	4.8	5.0	3.3	1.9	0.3	1.3	2.3	3.9	6.0	7.4	49.2
Tres Lagôas	1148.3	1913–1919	1913–1919	T.	81.0	79.5	79.3	77.7	73.2	69.6	68.4	71.4	75.4	77.9	79.2	79.5	76.0
				Rf.	5.4	4.0	3.0	4.8	4.4	3.2	1.0	1.8	3.9	3.1	5.4	5.0	44.0
Goiás	1706.0	1912–1921	1912–1919	T.	74.3	74.8	75.4	75.4	74.7	72.3	72.3	75.2	78.1	77.7	76.1	74.7	75.1
				Rf.	11.9	11.7	11.4	5.0	0.4	0.5	0.0	0.4	1.8	4.8	8.7	10.2	66.8
Caxambú	2919.9	1914–1922	1912–1924	T.	68.9	69.3	67.6	64.8	59.7	57.4	56.8	59.5	63.9	66.0	67.3	68.0	64.1
				Rf.	12.4	9.8	7.3	2.9	1.0	1.3	0.6	0.9	2.5	5.0	8.1	9.3	71.1
Georgetown	6.6	1887–1924	1846–1922	T.	79.3	79.3	79.9	80.6	80.6	80.2	80.6	81.3	82.2	82.0	81.5	79.9	80.6
				Rf.	7.3	5.9	6.1	6.7	11.1	12.1	9.6	6.4	2.8	2.3	5.8	11.3	87.4
Port of Spain	131.2	1862–1900	1862–1926	T.	75.0	72.2	76.3	77.7	79.0	77.9	77.5	77.5	78.1	77.9	77.2	77.2	77.0
				Rf.	2.6	1.6	1.8	1.9	3.4	7.9	8.6	9.4	7.5	6.6	7.2	4.7	63.2

THE ANTILLES

Station	Altitude (in feet)	Time of Record (temperature)	Time of Record (rainfall)	T. = Temperature in Degrees Fahrenheit; Rf. = Rainfall in Inches	Jan.	Feb.	Mar.	Apr.	May	June	July	Aug.	Sept.	Oct.	Nov.	Dec.	Year
Habana	78.7	1899–1927	1899–1927	T. Rf.	71.4 3.0	71.8 1.5	73.7 1.7	76.3 1.7	78.6 5.1	80.4 5.6	81.7 4.3	81.7 4.3	80.8 5.0	79.0 7.1	75.0 3.2	72.7 2.4	76.9 44.9
Santiago de Cuba	114.8	1899–1920	1899–1921	T. Rf.	75.4 1.4	75.0 0.9	76.6 1.7	78.3 3.3	79.7 6.3	80.8 5.5	81.9 2.2	82.2 3.5	81.0 6.7	80.1 7.3	77.7 3.7	76.3 1.1	78.8 43.6
Kingston	23.0	1908–1927	1899–1927	T. Rf.	76.6 0.7	76.5 0.5	77.4 0.8	78.6 1.3	80.1 3.1	81.3 3.6	81.7 1.2	81.9 2.7	81.3 4.0	80.4 6.3	79.0 3.5	77.5 1.1	79.3 28.8
Port-au-Prince	121.4	1906–1927	1899–1927	T. Rf.	78.1 1.2	78.4 2.7	79.2 4.1	80.2 6.7	81.1 8.0	82.8 4.0	84.0 2.7	83.5 4.8	82.2 7.7	80.8 7.4	79.5 4.2	78.4 0.9	80.7 54.4
Ciudad Trujillo	59.1	1910–1927	1899–1927	T. Rf.	75.7 2.5	75.6 1.3	75.9 2.4	77.4 3.7	79.0 5.8	79.7 5.9	80.2 7.1	81.0 6.9	81.0 7.1	80.4 7.0	79.2 5.1	77.2 2.0	78.5 56.8
Ponce	78.7	1899–1927	1901–1927	T. Rf.	75.4 1.1	75.4 1.1	76.0 1.4	77.5 2.2	79.5 3.0	80.6 3.6	81.0 3.0	81.5 4.1	81.3 4.9	80.4 6.4	79.0 4.0	76.8 1.1	78.7 35.9
San Juan	98.4	1899–1927	1899–1927	T. Rf.	74.8 4.1	74.8 3.0	75.2 3.0	76.6 4.1	78.6 5.2	79.5 5.4	80.0 5.8	80.4 5.9	80.4 6.0	80.0 5.7	78.3 7.0	76.3 5.4	77.9 60.6
Christiansted	82.0	1899–1927	1899–1927	T. Rf.	76.6 2.0	76.3 2.1	76.8 1.4	78.4 3.0	80.2 3.4	81.1 3.5	81.9 3.2	82.0 3.7	81.9 5.4	80.8 5.6	79.5 5.1	77.7 3.2	79.4 41.6
St. John's	78.7	1890–1926	1866–1927	T. Rf.	76.1 3.1	76.1 2.4	76.6 2.2	76.0 3.2	79.2 4.1	80.1 3.9	80.4 4.7	81.0 4.8	81.0 5.8	81.7 5.7	78.8 5.5	77.5 3.7	78.7 49.1
St. George's	508.5	1891–1927*	1899–1927	T. Rf.	76.8 4.4	77.2 3.1	77.7 2.5	78.8 1.8	79.7 3.7	79.0 8.0	79.1 9.4	79.9 9.1	80.2 7.3	80.1 8.1	79.3 8.0	78.1 6.9	78.8 72.3
Bridgetown	180.5	10 years	1899–1927	T. Rf.	76.3 2.1	76.5 1.7	77.0 1.5	78.4 1.8	80.1 1.7	80.2 4.5	80.1 4.7	80.1 6.0	79.9 6.4	79.3 6.5	78.6 5.0	77.2 3.5	78.6 45.4

References

The following selected list of references provides additional material on Latin-American geography. To keep the bibliographies up-to-date, and to provide for additional references, there are several bibliographical sources of importance to students of Latin America. Of major importance is the *Handbook of Latin American Studies,* published annually since 1935, edited at The Hispanic Foundation, Library of Congress. This handbook contains a selected and annotated list of publications concerning all aspects of Latin-American studies, not geography only. For geographical writings, the student is referred to the annual *Bibliographie géographique international,* published since 1923 by Armand Colin, Paris. The American Geographical Society of New York publishes its *Current Geographical Publications,* which is the accession list of the Society's library. Among the more important country bibliographies attention is called also to Rubens Borba de Moraes and William Berrien, *Manual Bibliográfico de Estudos Brasileiros,* Rio de Janeiro, 1949. For additional references to bibliographic sources see John Kirtland Wright and Elizabeth T. Platt, *Aids to Geographical Research,* American Geographical Society, (Research Series No. 22) New York, 1947.

For data concerning heights of mountains, elevations, and positions of cities see *The Columbia Lippincott Gazetteer of the World,* New York, 1952. For the most recent statistical data regarding population, production, trade, etc., see the latest Britannica Book of the Year, and the Encyclopedia Britannica World Atlas. For a summary of statistical data see Committee on Latin American Studies, University of California at Los Angeles, *Statistical Abstract of Latin America,* published annually since 1955. For concise geographic summaries of selected countries and problem areas see the series of pamphlets—*Focus*—published monthly (except July and August) by the American Geographical Society of New York. For monthly summaries of economic, social, and political developments in the countries of Latin America see the *Hispanic American Reports,* published by the Institute of Hispanic American and Luso-Brazilian Studies at Stanford University (Ronald Hilton, director).

Attention is also called to the Hispanic Foundation and the Map Division of the Library of Congress, Washington, D.C.

The following selected list of references dealing with various aspects of Latin America is arranged in order of the dates of publication.

Bryce, J. *South America, Observations and Impressions,* New York, 1912.

Ireland, G. *Boundaries, Possessions and Conflicts in South America,* Cambridge, Mass., 1938.

Ireland, G. *Boundaries, Possessions and Conflicts in Central and North America and the Caribbean,* Cambridge, Mass., 1941.

Pierson, W. W. (ed.). "Pathology of Democracy in Latin America: A Symposium," *The American Political Science Review,* Vol. 44, 1950: 100-149.

Whitaker, A. P. *The Western Hemisphere Idea: Its Rise and Decline,* Ithaca, N. Y., 1954.

Schurz, W. L. *This New World: The Civilization of Latin America,* New York, 1954.

Figueres, J. "Problems of Democracy in Latin America," *Journal of International Affairs,* Vol. 9, 1955: 11-23.

Gillin, J. "Ethos Components in Modern Latin American Culture," *American Anthropologist,* Vol. 57, 1955: 488-500.

Del Río, A. (ed.). *Responsible Freedom in the Americas,* New York, 1955.

East, W. G., and Moodie, A. E. *The Changing World—Studies in Political Geography* (Chapters 36, 37, 38, and 39), New York, 1956.

Alexander, R. J. *Communism in Latin America,* New Brunswick, N. J., 1957.

Palmer, Thomas W., Jr. *Search for a Latin American Policy,* Gainesville (Florida), 1957.

Davis, K. (ed.). "A Crowding Hemisphere: Population Change in the Americas," *The Annals of the American Academy of Political and Social Science,* Vol. 316, 1958: 1-136.

United States Department of Agriculture, Foreign Agricultural Service, *Agricultural Geography of Latin America,* Miscellaneous Publication No. 743, Washington, D.C., 1958.

Johnson, J. J. *Political Change in Latin America—The Emergence of the Middle Sectors,* Stanford, Calif., 1958.

Steward, J. H. and Faron, L. C. *Native Peoples of South America,* New York, 1959.

Lieuwen, E. *Arms and Politics in Latin America,* New York, 1960.

Porter, C. O. and Alexander, R. J. *The Struggle for Democracy in Latin America,* New York, 1961.

Schurz, W. L. *Brazil, the infinite Country,* New York, 1961.

Dulles, J. W. F. *Yesterday in Mexico: A Chronicle of the Revolution 1919–1936,* Austin, Tex., 1961.

Draper, T. *Castro's Revolution, Myths and Realities,* New York, 1962.

Berle, A. A. *Latin America, Diplomacy and Reality,* New York, 1962.

Matthews, H. H. (ed.). *The United States and Latin America,* (2nd. ed.), New York, 1963.

Bermúdez, A. J. *The Mexican Petroleum Industry, A Case Study in Nationalization*, Stanford, Calif., 1963.

Pike, F. B. *The Conflict Between Church and State in Latin America*, New York, 1964.

Smith, T. L. *Brazil, People and Institutions*, (3rd. ed.), Baton Rouge, La., 1964.

For additional references see James, P. E. *Latin America*, (3rd. ed.), New York, 1959.

Guide to Pronunciation—Spanish

Syllabication. A word has as many syllables as it has single vowels (Bu-ca-ra-man'-ga) or vowels and diphthongs, such as *ue* or *ai*, (Bue'-nos Ai'-res). A single consonant between vowels forms a syllable with the following vowel (Li'-ma). Two consonants between vowels are separated (San-tia'-go), except when the second consonant is *l* or *r*, in which case both consonants form a syllable with the following vowel (Chi-cla'-yo, Su'-cre). **ch, ll,** and **rr** are considered single letters in Spanish and cannot be separated.

Accent or stress. In general, words ending in a consonant, except *n* or *s*, are stressed on the last syllable (La Li-ber-tad'). Words ending in a vowel, or in *n* or *s*, are stressed on the next to the last syllable (Gra-na'-da, Ma-ni-za'-les). Exceptions to this rule are shown by a written accent on the vowel of the stressed syllable (Que-ré-ta-ro, Tu-cu-mán, Bo-lí-var).

Vowels. a is pronounced as in f*a*ther (Ha-ba'-na). **e** is pronounced as *a* in f*a*te (San Jo-sé). **i** is pronounced as in mach*i*ne (Ni-ca-ra'-gua). **o** is pronounced as in n*o*te (Co-lón). **u** is pronounced as in fl*u*te (Pe-rú). **u** is silent after q (*Que*-ré-ta-ro); it is also silent in the combinations **gue** and **gui**, in which case it makes the *g* hard, as in g*o* (San Mi-g*ue*l'). A diphthong is formed if the *u* in g*ue* bears a diaeresis (Ca-ma-g*üe*y', pronounced Ca-ma-gwäï). **y** is a vowel when standing alone or at the end of a word, and is merely a graphical substitute for *i*. **y** is also a consonant (see under consonants).

Diphthongs consist of a strong vowel (*a, e,* or *o*) and a weak vowel (*i* [*y*] or *u*), or of the two weak vowels, and are stressed on the strong vowel. Common diphthongs are: **ua** and **ue**, the *u* approximating the sound of *u* in q*ua*lity (G*ua*n-to, pronounced Gw*a*n'-to; B*ue*-na-ven-tu'-ra, pronounced Bw*ä*-na-ven-tu'-ra); **ai** (or **ay**) pronounced like *ai* in *ai*sle (Bue'-nos A*i*'-res); **ei** (or **ey**) pronounced like *ey* in th*ey* (N*ei*'-va); **oi** (or **oy**) pronounced like *oy* in b*oy* (To-ron-t*oy*'); and **ia** in which the two syllables are slightly slurred in pronouncing them (San-t*ia*-go). Two strong vowels do not form a diphthong (Ca-ll*a*'-o).

Consonants. d, f, l, m, n, p, and **t** are pronounced as in English. **b** and **v** are similar to a combination of *b* and *v* in English. **c** before *e* or *i* is pronounced as *s* in s*i*milar (Va-len'-*ci*a); otherwise as in *ca*ctus (Ca-ra'-*ca*s). **ch** is pronounced as in *ch*urch (*Chia*'-pas). **g** is pronounced as in g*o* (Bo-go-tá), but **g,** before *e* or *i*, and **j** are similar to the German *ch* (like English *h* forcibly hissed), as in Car-ta-*ge*'-na, Ja-lis'-co. (See also the explanation of **gu** under vowels and diphthongs.) **h** is always silent (Hon-du-ras, pronounced Ōn-du'-ras, and Hua-nu-co, pronounced Wa-nu'-co). **k** is not a Spanish letter; it is found only in foreign words, in which it has the same sound as in English. **ll** in Central America and in parts of Mexico is pronounced as *y* in y*e*s (Ciu-dad Tru-ji-*llo*, pronounced Sēudad Truhē'yo); in Spain and in some parts of Spanish America it has the sound of *lli* in mi*lli*on (Vi-*ll*a-ri-ca [Paraguay], pronounced Vēlyarē'ca); in southern South America and parts of Mexico it has the sound of *zh* in azure (A-ve-*ll*a-ne-da, pronounced Av*ä*z*h*an*ä*'da). **ñ** is pronounced like *ny* in ca*ny*on (Na-ri-ño, pronounced Narē'-nyo). **q** is always followed by *u* and is pronounced as in li*qu*or (*Que*-ré-ta-ro). **r** is slightly trilled on the tip of the tongue; initial **r** is pronounced with more vibration, and **rr** is pronounced like initial *r*. **s** is pronounced as in s*i*milar. **x**, in Mexico, when between vowels, is pronounced like Spanish *j* (O-a-*x*a'-ca); otherwise like *s* in s*i*milar (Ta*x*-co, pronounced Ta*s*'-co); in other parts of Spanish America it is generally pronounced as in ta*x*. **y** as a consonant is pronounced as in y*e*t, but with more force (Ÿu-ca-tán). **z** is always pronounced as *s* in s*i*milar.

Guide to Pronunciation—Portuguese

Syllabication. A word has as many syllables as it has single vowels (Pa-ra-ná) or vowels and diphthongs (São Pau'-lo). A single consonant between vowels forms a syllable with the following vowel (A-ma-zo'-nas). Two consonants between vowels are separated (San'-tos).

Vowels. a is pronounced as in f*a*ther (P*a*-rá). **e** is pronounced either as in b*e*t (Per-nam-bu'-co) or as *a* in f*a*te (C*e*-a-rá). **i** varies from m*i*lk (Es-p*i*-ri-to San'-to) to mach*i*ne (San'-ta Ca-ta-r*i*'na). **o** varies from m*o*ral to c*o*ld, and, when final, is pronounced like *u* in fl*u*te (Cam-p*o* F*o*r-m*o*-s*o*, pronounced Cam'pu Fŏrmŏ'su). **u** is pronounced as in fl*u*te (Per-nam-b*u*'-co). It is silent in the combination **gue** and **gui**, in which case it makes the **g** hard as in g*o*; the combination **gua** forms a diphthong as in Spanish (*Gua*-ra-tin-gue-tá, pronounced Gw*a*ratingāta'). For the pronunciation of **u** after **q**, see **q** below.

Diphthongs consist of a strong vowel (*a, e,* or *o*) and a weak vowel (*i* or *u*), as in Mi'-nas Ge-r*ai*s', or of the two weak vowels, as in J*ui*z' de Fo'-ra. Exceptions to this rule are shown by a written accent (Pa-ra-*i*-ba). Two strong vowels do not form a diphthong (A-la-g*ó'-a*s).

Nasalization. The tilde always nasalizes the vowel it covers, silencing the following vowel and resulting in a sound approximating awng (São Pau-lo, pronounced, approximately, Sawng Pow'-lo). Final *m* nasalizes the preceding vowel (Be-lém [Bāleng']; Jar-dim [Zharding']), as does final *ns* (To-can-tins [Tocantings']).

Consonants. b, d, f, k, l, p, t, and **v** are pronounced as in English. **c,** before the vowels *a* or *o* and before all consonants, is pronounced as in *c*actus (Cam'-pos); **c,** before the vowels *e* or *i*, and **ç** are pronounced as in *c*ement (Ce-a-rá, Al-co-ba'-ça). **ch** is pronounced as *sh* in *sh*awl (C*h*a-pa'-da). **g,** before *e* or *i*, is pronounced as *zh* in azure (Mi'-nas Ge-rais'); otherwise it is pronounced as in g*o* (Por'-to A-le'-gre). **h,** following *l*, is pronounced as *lli* in mi*lli*on (Il-*h*e-os, pronounced Ilyã'ozh); following *n*, it is pronounced as *ny* in can*y*on (U-be-ra-bin-*h*a, pronounced Uberabin'ya); otherwise it is silent. **j** is pronounced as *zh* in azure (São João, pronounced Sawng Z*h*õawng'). **m** is pronounced as in *m*other (Re-*m*e'-dios), except when it ends a word, in which case it loses its identity, combining with the preceding vowel to form a nasal (Be-lé*m*). **n,** before hard *g*, is pronounced as in si*n*g (Guaratinguetá); **n,** before final *s*, nasalizes the preceding vowel (Tocanti*n*s); otherwise it is pronounced as in *n*ame (Dia-man-ti'-*n*a). **q** is always followed by *u; qu* before *e* or *i* is pronounced as in li*qu*or (Pe-*qu*e'-no); before *a* or *o* it forms a diphthong and is pronounced *kw* (Puer-ta Je-ri-co-a-*qu*a-ra, pronounced Pwer'ta Zhericõakwara). **r** is pronounced in the throat and slightly trilled. **s,** between vowels, is pronounced as in ro*s*e (Cam'po Formo'*s*o). When final, or when preceding *b, v, d, g, l, m, n,* or *r*, it is pronounced, in Portugal and in Rio de Janeiro, as *zh* in azure (Mi-na*s* Ge-rais [Mē'naz*h* Zhārīz*h*']); in the outlying districts of Brazil it is pronounced as *s* in *s*imilar in these instances. In all other cases it is pronounced as *s* in *s*imilar. **x,** between vowels, is pronounced as z in E*z*ekiel (Fa-*x*i'-ma [Fa*z*ēma]); otherwise, in Portugal and Rio de Janeiro, it is pronounced as *sh* in *sh*awl (*X*in-gú [*Sh*ingu']), and in the outlying districts of Brazil as *s* in *s*imilar (*X*ingú [*S*ingu']). Recent regulations have excluded the use of the letter **y. z,** before a vowel, is pronounced as in E*z*ekiel (San'-ta Lu-*z*i'-a); otherwise, in Portugal and Rio de Janeiro, it is pronounced as *sh* in *sh*awl or *zh* in azure (Santa Cru*z* [San'ta Cru*sh*']), and in the outlying districts of Brazil it is pronounced as *s* in *s*imilar (Santa Cru*z* [San'ta Cru*s*']).

Index

Numbers in bold face refer to maps